lonely

ITALY'S
BEST TRIPS

40 AMAZING ROAD TRIPS

Duncan Garwood,
Brett Atkinson, Alexis Averbuck, Cristian Bonetto,
Gregor Clark, Peter Dragicevich, Paula Hardy, Virginia
Maxwell, Stephanie Ong, Kevin Raub, Brendan
Sainsbury, Regis St Louis, Nicola Williams

SYMBOLS IN THIS BOOK

✓ Top Tips	📖 History & Culture	📷 Essential Photo	
⑤ Link Your Trips	👪 Family	🏃 Walking Tour	
◐ Tips from Locals	🍷 Food & Drink	🍴 Eating	
↪ Trip Detour	🌳 Outdoors	🛏 Sleeping	

♪ Telephone Number	@ Internet Access
⊘ Opening Hours	📶 Wi-Fi Access
P Parking	✎ Vegetarian Selection
⊖ Nonsmoking	🏊 Swimming Pool
❄ Air-Conditioning	
🔲 English-Language Menu	
👶 Family-Friendly	
🐾 Pet-Friendly	

MAP LEGEND

Routes
- Trip Route
- Trip Detour
- Linked Trip
- Walk Route
- Tollway
- Freeway
- Primary
- Secondary
- Tertiary
- Lane
- Unsealed Road
- Plaza/Mall
- Steps
- Tunnel
- Pedestrian Overpass
- Walk Track/Path

Boundaries
- International
- State/Province
- Cliff
- Wall

Population
- ✪ Capital (National)
- ◉ Capital (State/Province)
- ● City/Large Town
- ○ Town/Village

Transport
- ✈ Airport
- Cable Car/Funicular
- Ⓟ Parking
- Train/Railway
- Tram
- Ⓜ Underground Train Station

Trips
- 1 Trip Numbers
- 9 Trip Stop
- Walking tour
- Trip Detour

Route Markers
- E44 E-road network
- M100 National network

Hydrography
- River/Creek
- Intermittent River
- Swamp/Mangrove
- Canal
- Water
- Dry/Salt/Intermittent Lake
- Glacier

Areas
- Beach
- Cemetery (Christian)
- Cemetery (Other)
- Park
- Forest
- Urban Area
- Sportsground

PLAN YOUR TRIP

ON THE ROAD

TOC for On the Road

CONTENTS

Northern Italy
p63

Central Italy
p205

Southern Italy
p289

Contents cont.

- - - - - - - - -

ROAD TRIP ESSENTIALS

- - - - - - - - -

Top: *Parmigiana di melanzane* (eggplant parmigiana)

Bottom: Scoglio di Pizzomunno, Vieste

WELCOME TO
ITALY

Few countries can rival Italy's wealth of riches. Its historic cities have iconic monuments and masterpieces at every turn, its food is imitated the world over and its landscape is a majestic patchwork of snow-capped peaks, plunging coastlines, lakes and remote valleys. And with many thrilling roads to explore, it offers plenty of epic driving.

The 40 trips outlined in this book run the length of the country, leading from Alpine summits to southern volcanoes, from hilltop towns in Tuscany to fishing villages on the Amalfi Coast, from Venetian canals to Pompeii's ghostly ruins. They take in heavyweight cities and little-known gems, and cover a wide range of experiences.

So whether you want to tour gourmet towns and historic vineyards, idyllic coastlines or pristine national parks, we have a route for you. And if you've only got time for one trip, make it one of our eight Classic Trips, which take you to the very best of Italy. Turn the page for more.

Rome Trevi Fountain
LEOKS/SHUTTERSTOCK ©

ITALY HIGHLIGHTS

Classic Trip 9
The Graceful Italian Lakes
Destination of choice for Goethe, Hemingway and George Clooney. 5–7 DAYS

Classic Trip 13
Grande Strada delle Dolomiti
Tour the piercing rock peaks of the Dolomites. 7–10 DAYS

Classic Trip 14
A Venetian Sojourn
Glide along the Brenta Canal to splendid frescoed villas. 5–6 DAYS

Classic Trip 2
World Heritage Wonders
Discover the Unesco-listed treasures of Italy's art cities. 14 DAYS

Classic Trip 24
Tuscan Wine Tour
Red wine fuels this jaunt around Chianti vineyards and Tuscan cellars. 4 DAYS

GERMANY
SWITZERLAND
AUSTRIA
SLOVENIA
LJUBLJANA
CROATIA
Rijeka
FRANCE
MONACO
Nice

Monte Bianco (4810m)
Parco Nazionale del Gran Paradiso
VALLE D'AOSTA
Aosta
Monte Viso (3841m)
Cuneo
Ventimiglia
Imperia
Savona
LIGURIA
Turin
Biella
Vercelli
Asti
Alessandria
PIEDMONT
Genoa
Golfo di Genova
La Spezia
Ligurian Sea

Locarno
Verbania
Lago Maggiore
Como
Lago di Como
Lecco
Sondrio
Parco Nazionale dello Stelvio
Ortles (3905m)
Valtellines
Parco Regionale degli Orobie Valtellinesi
Bergamo
Milan
Brescia
LOMBARDY
Cremona
Piacenza
Parma
Modena
EMILIA-ROMAGNA
Bologna
Ferrara
Po

Bressanone
Bolzano
ALTO ADIGE
TRENTINO
Trento
Lago di Garda
Cortina d'Ampezzo
Marmolada (3343m)
Tarvisio
FRIULI VENEZIA GIULIA
Udine
Trieste
Golfo di Trieste
Vittorio Veneto
VENETO
Treviso
Vicenza
Padua
Verona
Mantua
Venice

Po Delta
Valle di Comacchio
Ravenna
Forlì
Rimini
Pesaro
Ancona
SAN MARINO
Adriatic

Apuane
Parco Regionale delle Alpi Apuane
Massa
Lucca
Pistoia
Pisa
Livorno
Arno
Monte Cusna (1314m)
Florence
Arezzo
Siena
TUSCANY
Elba
Grosseto
Riserva Naturale Alto Merse
Monte Amiata (1736m)
Lago di Bolsena

LE MARCHE
Macerata
Ascoli Piceno
Parco Nazionale del Gran Sasso e Monti della Laga
Corno Grande
Perugia
Parco Nazionale dei Monti Sibillini
UMBRIA
Montepulciano
Orvieto
Lago Trasimeno
Terni

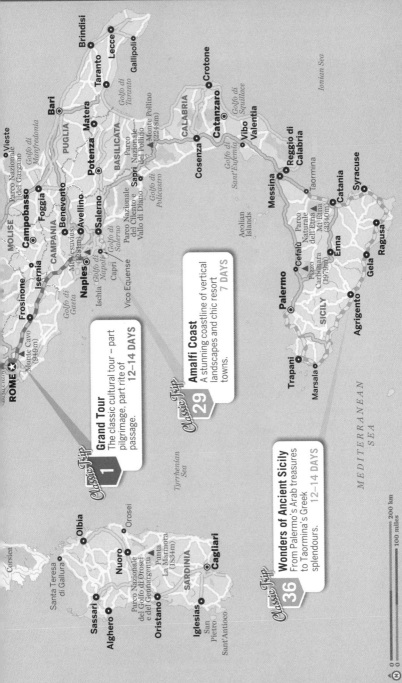

Classic Trip
1
Grand Tour
The classic cultural tour – part pilgrimage, part rite of passage. **12–14 DAYS**

Classic Trip
29
Amalfi Coast
A stunning coastline of vertical landscapes and chic resort towns. **7 DAYS**

Classic Trip
36
Wonders of Ancient Sicily
From Palermo's Arab treasures to Taormina's Greek splendours. **12–14 DAYS**

ROME

MOLISE

Frosinone
Isernia
Campobasso
Foggia

Monte Cavo
(949m)

Parco Nazionale
del Gargano

Vieste

Golfo di
Manfredonia

Bari

Brindisi

Lecce

Taranto

Gallipoli

PUGLIA

Matera

Benevento
Avellino
Salerno

Potenza

BASILICATA

CAMPANIA

Naples

Mt Vesuvius
(1281m)

Golfo di
Napoli

Capri

Ischia

Vico Equense

Golfo di
Gaeta

Golfo di
Salerno

Sapri

Parco Nazionale
del Cilento e
Vallo di Diano

Golfo di
Policastro

Parco Nazionale
del Pollino

Monte Pollino
(2248m)

Golfo di
Taranto

Crotone

Catanzaro

Golfo di
Squillace

Ionian Sea

CALABRIA

Cosenza

Golfo di
Sant'Eufemia

Vibo
Valentia

Reggio di
Calabria

Messina

Aeolian
Islands

Taormina

Catania

Syracuse

Parco
Naturale
dell'Etna

Mt Etna
(3340m)

Enna

Ragusa

Gela

Agrigento

SICILY

Palermo

Cefalù

Pizzo
Carbonara
(1979m)

Trapani

Marsala

MEDITERRANEAN
SEA

Tyrrhenian
Sea

Corsica

Santa Teresa
di Gallura

Olbia

Oroseï

Sassari

Alghero

Nuoro

Parco Nazionale
del Golfo di Orosei
e del Gennargentu

Punta
La Marmora
(1834m)

SARDINIA

Oristano

Iglesias

San
Pietro

Sant'Antioco

Cagliari

0   100 miles
0 100 200 km

Italy's best sights and experiences, and the road trips that will take you there.

ITALY
HIGHLIGHTS

Rome

All roads lead to Rome (Roma) and **Trip 1: Grand Tour** is one such, stopping off at the Eternal City en route from Turin (Torino) to Naples (Napoli). The one-time *caput mundi* (capital of the world) is a mesmerising city, home to celebrated icons – the Colosseum, Pantheon, Trevi Fountain, Michelangelo's Sistine Chapel – and spectacular works of art. Even strolling its romantic lanes and operatic piazzas is a thrill to remember.

Trips

Rome Roman Forum

Dolomites Gruppo di Odle

Venice

Drive **Trip 2: World Heritage Wonders** and the road runs out in Venice (Venezia), where highways give way to waterways. It's a soul-lifting experience to explore its backstreets and piazzas, revelling in East-meets-West architecture. Art treasures abound, but for 'wow' factor little can rival the Basilica di San Marco and its golden mosaics.

Trips

The Dolomites

One of the inspiring sights of northern Italy, the Dolomites are the stars of **Trip 13: Grande Strada delle Dolomiti**. Their pink-hued granite summits form the majestic backdrop for this drive along Italy's most famous mountain road between Bolzano and Cortina d'Ampezzo. Stop off en route to admire sweeping panoramas and explore the Alta Badia and Alpe di Siusi.

Trip

Tuscan Landscapes

Picture the ideal Italian landscape – golden fields, haughty cypress trees, hills capped by medieval towns. You're imagining Tuscany, a region whose fabled panoramas have inspired everybody from Renaissance artists to overwrought poets. Drive **Trip 24: Tuscan Wine Tour** or **Trip 25: Tuscan Landscapes** and give yourself up to its soothing beauty and delicious *vino*.

Trips

Amalfi Coast Positano

BEST DRIVING ROADS

Grande Strada delle Dolomiti Epic road through exhilarating Alpine scenery. **Trip** 13

SS17bis Traverses Abruzzo's awe-inspiring Campo Imperatore in the shadow of the Gran Sasso. **Trip** 19

SP146 Snakes through the classic landscapes of Tuscany's Val d'Orcia. **Trips** 24 25

SS163 Also known as the Nastro Azzurro, this road weaves along the precipitous Amalfi Coast. **Trip** 29

Amalfi Coast

The Amalfi Coast is Italy's most dazzling seafront stretch. Its single road – detailed in **Trip 29: Amalfi Coast** – curves sinuously along the coast, linking the area's steeply stacked towns and rocky inlets. All around, cliffs sheer down into sparkling blue waters, lemons grow on hillside terraces, and towering *fichi d'India* (prickly pears) guard silent mountain paths.

Trip 29

Italian Lakes Lago di Como

Lago di Como

The most picturesque and least visited of Italy's main northern lakes, Lago di Como (Lake Como) is a highlight of **Trip 9: The Graceful Italian Lakes**, a scenic jaunt around Lakes Maggiore, Orta and Como. Set in the shadow of the Rhaetian Alps, Lago di Como's banks are speckled with Liberty-style villas and fabulous landscaped gardens that burst into blushing colour in April and May.

Trip 9

BEST MUSEUMS & GALLERIES

Vatican Museums
Michelangelo's Sistine Chapel, Raphael frescoes and much, much more. **Trip 1**

- -

Galleria degli Uffizi Florence gallery housing Italy's finest collection of Renaissance art.
Trips 1 2 23

- -

Peggy Guggenheim Collection Striking modern art in a canal-side Venetian villa.
Trip 14

- -

Museo Archeologico Nazionale Naples' premier museum with breathtaking classical sculpture and mosaics from Pompeii. **Trips 1 27**

15

Florence Michelangelo's *David*

Pompeii Roman ruins

Florence

From Brunelleschi's red-capped Duomo to Michelangelo's *David*, Florence (Firenze) has priceless masterpieces and a historic centre that looks little changed since Renaissance times. Art aside, the city sets the perfect scene for al fresco dining. Lap it all up on **Trip 2: World Heritage Wonders** and **Trip 23: Piero della Francesca Trail**.

Trips   23 24

Pompeii

A once-thriving Roman port frozen in its 2000-year-old death throes, Pompeii is an electrifying spectacle. Head down on **Trip 27: Shadow of Vesuvius** and wander its fantastically preserved streets, exploring the forum, the city brothel, the 5000-seat theatre and the frescoed Villa dei Misteri. Body casts of victims add a sense of menace as Vesuvius looms darkly on the horizon.

Trips 27

Valle d'Aosta

Italy's smallest and least populous region is also one of its most beautiful. Follow **Trip 12: Valle d'Aosta** as it inches up a narrow mountain valley ringed by the icy peaks of Europe's highest mountains, including Mont Blanc (Monte Bianco), the Matterhorn (Monte Cervino), Monte Rosa and Gran Paradiso. Leave your car and take to the slopes for exhilarating hiking and hair-raising skiing.

Trip 12

17

Syracuse

An ancient metropolis turned model baroque town, Syracuse (Siracusa) is one of Sicily's most enchanting cities. Its wonderfully intact 5th-century BC amphitheatre is one of the many memorable Greek ruins on **Trip 36: Wonders of Ancient Sicily,** while its baroque centre is a vision of 17th-century urban design. At its heart, Piazza del Duomo is a glorious spot for an evening *aperitivo*.

Trips 36 37

Emilia-Romagna

Italy's culinary capital, Bologna, is just one of the gastro towns that feature on **Trip 26: Foodie Emilia-Romagna**. Feast on Bologna's trademark specialities such as mortadella and *tagliatelle al ragù* in between tastings of prosciutto and *parmigiano reggiano* cheese in Parma and aged balsamic vinegar in Modena. Further to the east, Ravenna provides food for the soul with its brilliant mosaics.

Trip 26

(left) **Syracuse** Teatro Greco
(below) **Sardinia** Emerald Coast

TRAVEL WILD/SHUTTERSTOCK ©

DUCHY/SHUTTERSTOCK ©

Sardinia

From idyllic coves framed by weird, wind-whipped boulders to open stretches of silky soft sand, Sardinia's beaches are legendary. To discover them for yourself **Trip 39: Emerald Coast** takes in the island's glorious north coast, while **Trip 38: Sardinia's South Coast** inches around the island's southwest corner, via capital Cagliari and the laid-back Isola di San Pietro.

Trips

BEST HILLTOP TOWNS

Matera Basilicata town famous for its primitive *sassi* (cave houses). **Trip** 34

Urbino A Renaissance gem in off-the-radar Le Marche. **Trip** 23

Orvieto Proud clifftop home of a stunning Gothic cathedral. **Trip** 25

Montalcino Tuscan producer of Brunello di Montalcino, one of Italy's top red wines. **Trip** 24

19

Piedmont Cheese for sale in Alba

IF YOU LIKE...

Art & Architecture

With an unparalleled artistic and architectural legacy, Italy is home to some of the Western world's most celebrated masterpieces. Works by Renaissance heroes and baroque maestros grace the country's churches, museums and galleries.

1 Grand Tour Take in the Scrovegni Chapel, *The Last Supper*, Michelangelo's *David* et al.

8 Northern Cities Admire Giotto frescoes, medieval cityscapes and Venice's labyrinthine canals.

23 Piero della Francesca Trail From Urbino to Florence, follow the trail of frescoes left by the Renaissance master.

37 Sicilian Baroque Swoon over extravagant baroque architecture in southeastern Sicily.

Ancient Relics

Everywhere you go in Italy you're reminded of the country's tumultuous past. Etruscan tombs and Greek temples stand testament to pre-Roman civilisations, while amphitheatres, aqueducts, even whole towns, recall the ambition and reach of ancient Rome.

2 World Heritage Wonders Rome's Colosseum and Verona's Arena headline on this classic cross-country drive.

20 Etruscan Tuscany & Lazio Duck into tombs decorated with ancient frescoes.

27 Shadow of Vesuvius Wander around Pompeii and Herculaneum, celebrated victims of Vesuvius' volcanic fury.

36 Wonders of Ancient Sicily Sicily's ancient Greek temples are the best you'll see outside of Greece.

Food & Wine

With its superb produce, culinary traditions and world-beating wine, Italy is a food- and wine-lover's dream destination. Whether it's tasting white truffles in Alba, dining al fresco on a medieval piazza, or tasting Chianti at a Tuscan vineyard, great foodie experiences await at every turn.

4 Gourmet Piedmont Feast on chocolate, cheese and truffles in Italy's Slow Food heartland.

15 Valpolicella Wine Country Sample bold wines at historic wineries in the vine-clad hills west of Verona.

24 Tuscan Wine Tour Savour Tuscany's great reds in Chianti vineyards.

26 Foodie Emilia-Romagna Discover the towns that put the Parma into ham and the Bolognese into spag bol.

Cinque Terre Vernazza

Coastal Scenery

From the cliffs of the Amalfi Coast to the villages of the Cinque Terre, from Sicily's volcanic seascapes to Sardinia's dreamy beaches, Italy's 7600km-long coastline is as varied as it is enticing. Add crystal-clear waters and you've got the perfect summer recipe.

7 Cinematic Cinque Terre Cruise one of Italy's most picture-perfect coastal stretches.

29 Amalfi Coast Italy's most celebrated coastline is a classic Mediterranean pin-up.

33 Salento Surprises Join Italian beach-goers in Puglia's summer hotspot.

39 Emerald Coast Sardinia's northern coast has dazzling beaches and heavenly waters.

Mountains

For a taste of the high life take to Italy's mountains. From the Alps to the Apennines, stunning roads snake past snow-capped peaks, over hair-raising passes and through silent valleys swathed in ancient forests. Outdoor enthusiasts will find superb skiing, hiking, climbing and cycling.

11 Roof of Italy Drive the fabled Stelvio Pass as you explore northern Italy's high-altitude borderlands.

13 Grande Strada delle Dolomiti Revel in the extraordinary beauty of the rocky Dolomites.

19 Abruzzo's Wild Landscapes Look out for wolves and bears in Abruzzo's remote national parks.

34 Across the Lucanian Apennines Go off-piste in the mountain country of southern Basilicata.

Villas & Palaces

Ever since ancient times, Italy's rulers have employed the top artists and architects of their day to design their homes. The results are imperial palaces, royal retreats, Renaissance mansions and aristocratic villas.

2 World Heritage Wonders Explore imperial palaces and art-filled *palazzi* (mansions) in Rome, Siena, Florence and Venice.

3 Savoy Palace Circuit Tour the Savoy family's royal palaces in Turin and the Piedmont countryside.

9 The Graceful Italian Lakes For grace and style, head to the villas and gardens of Italy's northern lakes.

14 A Venetian Sojourn Stop at Unesco-protected Palladian villas as you drive through Veneto's wine country.

NEED <u>TO</u> KNOW

CURRENCY
euro (€)

LANGUAGE
Italian

VISAS
Generally not required for stays of up to 90 days (or at all by EU nationals). Some nationalities will need a Schengen visa.

FUEL
Filling stations are widespread. Expect to pay around €1.46 per litre of unleaded petrol (*benzina senza piombo*), €1.29 for diesel (*gasolio*).

RENTAL CARS
Avis (www.avisautono leggio.it)

Europcar (www.europcar.it)

Hertz (www.hertz.it)

Maggiore (www.maggiore.it)

IMPORTANT NUMBERS
Emergencies (Police 📞 112, 113; Ambulance 📞 115)

Roadside Assistance (📞 80 31 16 from an Italian landline or mobile phone; 📞 800 116800 from a foreign mobile phone)

Climate

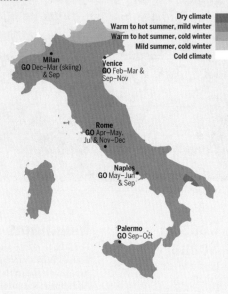

Dry climate
Warm to hot summer, mild winter
Warm to hot summer, cold winter
Mild summer, cold winter
Cold climate

Milan
GO Dec–Mar (skiing) & Sep

Venice
GO Feb–Mar & Sep–Nov

Rome
GO Apr–May, Jul & Nov–Dec

Naples
GO May–Jun & Sep

Palermo
GO Sep–Oct

When to Go

High Season (Jul–Aug)
» Queues at big sights, and congested roads, especially in August.

» Prices also rocket for Christmas, New Year and Easter.

» Late December to March is high season in the Alps and Dolomites.

Shoulder (Apr–Jun & Sep–Oct)
» Good deals on accommodation, especially in the south.

» Spring is best for festivals, flowers and local produce.

» Autumn provides warm weather and the grape harvest.

Low Season (Nov–Mar)
» Prices up to 30% lower than in high season.

» Many sights and hotels closed in coastal and mountainous areas.

» A good period for cultural events in large cities.

Your Daily Budget

Budget: Less than €100

» Dorm bed: €20–35

» Double room in a budget hotel: €60–110

» Pizza or pasta: €6–15

Midrange: €100–250

» Double room in a hotel: €110–200

» Local restaurant dinner: €25–45

» Admission to museum: €4–18

Top end: More than €250

» Double room in a four- or five-star hotel: €200 plus

» Top restaurant dinner: €45–150

» Opera ticket: €40–210

Eating

Trattoria Informal, family-run restaurant cooking up traditional regional dishes.

Ristorante Formal dining, often with comprehensive wine lists and more sophisticated local or national fare.

Vegetarians Most places offer good vegetable starters and side dishes.

Price indicators for a two-course meal with a glass of house wine and *coperto* (cover charge).

€ less than €25

€€ €25-45

€€€ more than €45

Sleeping

Hotels From luxury boutique palaces to modest family-run *pensioni* (small hotels).

B&Bs Rooms in restored farmhouses, city townhouses or seaside bungalows.

Agriturismi Farm stays range from working farms to luxury rural retreats.

Room Tax A nightly occupancy tax is charged on top of room rates.

Price indicators for a double room with private bathroom (breakfast included) in high season.

€ less than €110

€€ €110–€200

€€€ more than €200

Arriving in Italy

Rome Fiumicino

Rental cars Agencies are located near the multilevel car park.

Trains Run frequently from 6.08am to 11.23pm; €14.

Buses Take an hour and operate between 6.05am and 12.40am. Limited night bus services; €6-7.

Taxi Set fare to centre €48; 45 to 60 minutes.

Milan Malpensa

Rental cars Agencies in the Arrivals halls.

Trains Run half-hourly from 5.37am to 12.20am; €13.

Buses Run every 30 minutes from 3.45am to 12.15am; €10.

Taxis Set fare €95; 50 minutes.

Naples Capodichino

Rental cars Contact agencies from the Arrivals hall.

Buses Run frequently between 6am and 11.20pm; €5.

Taxis Set fares €18 to €27; 20 to 35 minutes.

Mobile Phones

Local SIM cards can be used in European, Australian and some unlocked US phones. Other phones must be set to roaming.

Internet Access

Free wi-fi is available in most hotels, hostels, B&Bs and *agriturismi* (farm stays), and in many bars and cafes.

Money

ATMs are widespread in Italy. Major credit cards are widely accepted, but some smaller shops, trattorias and hotels might not take them.

Tipping

Not obligatory but round up the bill or leave a euro or two in pizzerias and trattorias; 5% to 10% in smart restaurants.

Useful Websites

Lonely Planet (www.lonelyplanet.com/italy) Destination information, hotel bookings, traveller forum and more.

ENIT (www.italia.it) Official Italian-government tourism website.

For more, see Italy Driving Guide (p417).

CITY GUIDE

ROME

Even in a country of exquisite cities, Rome (Roma) is special. Epic, hot-blooded and utterly disarming, it's a heady mix of ancient ruins, awe-inspiring art, iconic monuments and vibrant street life. If your road leads to Rome, give yourself a couple of days to explore its headline sights.

Rome The Pantheon

Getting Around

Driving is not the best way to get around Rome. Traffic can be chaotic and much of the historic centre is closed to non-authorised traffic on weekdays and weekend evenings. Better to park and use public transport; a 24-hour pass is €7.

Parking

Blue lines denote on-street parking, which is expensive and scarce. There are a few car parks in the centre, which charge about €20 per day.

Where to Eat

For authentic nose-to-tail Roman cooking check out the trattorias in Testaccio, and for traditional Roman-Jewish cuisine head to the atmospheric Jewish Ghetto.

Where to Stay

The most atmospheric place to stay is the *centro storico*, where you'll have everything on your doorstep. Night owls will enjoy Trastevere, while Tridente offers refined accommodation. The Vatican is also popular.

Useful Websites

060608 (www.060608.it) Rome's tourist website.

Coopculture (www.coopculture.it) Information and ticket booking for Rome's monuments.

Vatican Museums (www.museivaticani.va) Book tickets and avoid the queues.

Lonely Planet (www.lonelyplanet.com/rome) Destination lowdown, hotel bookings and traveller forum.

Trips Through Rome 1 2

For more, check out our city and country guides.
www.lonelyplanet.com

TOP EXPERIENCES

➤ Get to the Heart of the Ancient City
Thrill to the sight of the Colosseum, Roman Forum and Palatino, where Rome was supposedly founded in 753 BC.

➤ Gaze Heavenwards in the Sistine Chapel
File past miles of priceless art at the Vatican Museums to arrive at the Sistine Chapel and Michelangelo's frescoes. (www.museivaticani.va)

➤ Villa Borghese's Baroque Treasures
Head to the Museo e Galleria Borghese to marvel at exhilarating baroque sculptures by Gian Lorenzo Bernini. (www.galleriaborghese.it)

➤ Admire the Pantheon's Dome
The Pantheon is the best preserved of Rome's ancient monuments, but it's only when you get inside that you get the full measure of the place as its dome soars above you.

➤ Pay Homage at St Peter's Basilica
Capped by Michelangelo's landmark dome, the Vatican's showpiece church is a masterpiece of Renaissance architecture and baroque decor.

➤ Live the Trastevere Dolce Vita
Join the evening crowds in Trastevere to eat earthy Roman food, drink in the many bars and pubs, and parade up and down the streets.

➤ Hang Out on the Piazzas
Hanging out on Rome's piazzas is part and parcel of Roman life – having a gelato on Piazza Navona, people-watching on Piazza del Popolo and posing on Piazza di Spagna.

Florence View over rooftops to the Duomo

FLORENCE

An essential stop on every Italian itinerary, Florence (Firenze) is one of the world's great art cities, with Renaissance icons and a wonderfully intact medieval centre. Beyond the Michelangelo masterpieces and Medici *palazzi* (mansions), there's a buzzing bar scene and great shopping in artisanal workshops and designer boutiques.

Getting Around

Nonresident traffic is banned from much of central Florence, and if you enter the Limited Traffic Zone (ZTL) you risk a fine of up to €200. Rather than drive, walk or use the city buses; tickets cost €1.50 or €2.50 on board.

Parking

There is free street parking around Piazzale Michelangelo and car parks (about €3.80 per hour) at Fortezza da Basso and Piazzale di Porta Romana. Otherwise, ask if your hotel can arrange parking.

Where to Eat

Florence teems with restaurants, trattorias, *osterie* (casual taverns) and wine bars catering to all budgets. Top neighbourhoods include hip Santa Croce, home to some of the city's best restaurants, and the increasingly gentrified Oltrarno.

Where to Stay

To stay right in the heart of the action, the Duomo and Piazza della Signoria areas are a good bet with some excellent budget options. Near the train station, Santa Maria Novella has some good midrange boutique/design hotels.

Useful Websites

Firenze Turismo (www. firenzeturismo.it) The official tourist site is comprehensive and up-to-date.

Visit Florence (www. visitflorence.com) Practical advice and info on accommodation, sights and tours.

Firenze Musei (www. firenzemusei.it) Book tickets for the Uffizi and Accademia.

Trips Through Florence 1 2 23 24

Naples Wood-fired pizza

NAPLES

Naples (Napoli) is an exhilarating sprawl of bombastic baroque churches, Dickensian alleyways and electrifying street life. Its in-your-face vitality can be overwhelming, but once you've found your feet you'll discover a city of regal palaces, world-renowned museums, superb pizzerias and sweeping seascapes.

Getting Around

Driving is not the best way of getting around Naples – the roads are anarchic and much of the city centre is off-limits to nonresident traffic. You'll be better off leaving your car as soon as you can and using public transport (bus, metro and funicular); a day pass costs €3.50.

Parking

Street parking is not a good idea – car theft is a problem – and few hotels offer it. There's a 24-hour car park east of the city centre at Via Brin; otherwise ask your hotel for advice.

Where to Eat

To taste authentic wood-fired pizza, head to the *centro storico* where you'll find a number of hard-core pizzerias serving the genuine article. For a more refined meal, make for seafront Santa Lucia and the cobbled lanes of Chiaia.

Where to Stay

For maximum atmosphere, consider staying in the *centro storico* where you'll have many sights on your doorstep. Seaside Santa Lucia is home to some of the city's most prestigious hotels, and Chiaia is cool and chic.

Useful Websites

I Naples (www.inaples.it) The city's official tourist-board site.

Comune di Napoli (www.comune.napoli.it) Official city website with Italian-language tourist information.

Napoli da Vivere (www.napolidavivere.it) Italian-language website listing upcoming festivals, special events and recent openings.

Campania Artecard (www.campaniartecard.it) Details discount cards covering museum admission and transport.

Trips Through Naples

VENICE

A magnificent, unforgettable spectacle, Venice (Venezia) is a hauntingly beautiful
city. For 1000 years it was one of Europe's great sea powers and its unique cityscape
reflects this, with golden Byzantine domes and great Gothic churches, noble *palazzi*
and busy waterways.

Getting Around

Venice is off-limits to cars, leaving you
to walk or take a boat. You'll inevitably
get lost at some point but directions
to Piazza San Marco, the Rialto and
Accademia are posted on yellow signs.
Vaporetti (small ferries) ply the city's
waterways; a one-way ticket costs €7.50.

Parking

Once you've crossed the Ponte della
Libertà bridge from Mestre, you'll have to
park at Piazzale Roma or Tronchetto car
parks; bank on €21 to €29 for 24 hours.

TOP EXPERIENCES

➡ **Cruise the Grand Canal**
Take a *vaporetto* (small ferry) down the Grand Canal for an uplifting introduction to the city's extraordinary sights.

➡ **Marvel at Mosaics at the Basilica di San Marco**
Step inside Venice's signature basilica to gape at golden dome mosaics. (www.basilicasanmarco.it)

➡ **Compare Titian and Tintoretto**
Soaring I Frari is home to Titian's masterpiece, *Assunta*. Nearby, the Scuola Grande di San Rocco has stunning frescoes by Tintoretto. (www.scuolagrandesanrocco.it)

➡ **Enjoy Modern Art at the Guggenheim**
Step inside the canal-side home of Peggy Guggenheim to peruse canvases by the giants of modern art. (www.guggenheim-venice.it)

Venice Gondolas on the lagoon

Where to Eat

Venice's version of tapas, bar snacks called *cicheti* are served in *osterie* across town at lunch and between 6pm and 8pm. Wash them down with a glass of local prosecco. Try the area around the Rialto Market and along Calle Lunga San Barnaba in the Dorsoduro district.

Where to Stay

Many Venetians open their historical homes as B&Bs. Dorsoduro and San Polo are charming areas, near major museums and with plenty of bar action. Cannaregio is another good option, relatively untouristy and in parts picturesque.

Useful Websites

VeneziaUnica (www.veneziaunica.it) News, events and city passes for public transport, museums, churches and special events.

Venezia da Vivere (www.veneziadavivere.com) Music performances, art openings, nightlife and child-friendly events.

Venice Comune (www.comune.venezia.it) City of Venice official site with essential info, including high-water alerts.

Trips Through Venice 1 2 8 14

ITALY
BY REGION

Driving in Italy is a thrilling way to experience the country in all its varied beauty. To help you on your way, we've divided the country into three areas and outlined what each has to offer.

Central Italy (p205)

Tour heavyweight destinations such as Rome, Florence and Assisi before exploring Etruscan tombs, remote Tuscan monasteries and medieval hill towns in Abruzzo, Umbria and Le Marche. Foodies can indulge their passions in Emilia-Romagna and Tuscany's historic vineyards.

Discover Etruscan treasures on Trip 20
Taste wine on Trip 24

Northern Italy (p63)

Revel in spectacular scenery as you drive epic Alpine roads, stunning coastlines and gorgeous lakesides. Our trips lead from the wine-rich hills of Piedmont to the pink-hued Dolomites, from Milan's designer streets to Venice's haunting canals.

Tour art-rich cities on
Trip 8

Scale the Dolomites on
Trip 13

Southern Italy (p289)

Take to the wilds of Calabria and Basilicata and enjoy stunning seascapes in Puglia, Sardinia and on the Amalfi Coast. Sicily has baroque treasures and ancient ruins, while Mt Vesuvius broods darkly over Naples and nearby Pompeii.

Discover the Amalfi Coast on
Trip 29

Explore Greek ruins on
Trip 36

ITALY
Classic Trips

What is a Classic Trip?

All the trips in our book show you the best of Italy, but we've chosen the eight below as our all-time favourites. These are our Classic Trips – the ones that lead you to the best of the iconic sights, the top activities and the unique Italian experiences.

Above: St Peter's Basilica, Rome
Left: Boathouse at Lago di Braies, Dolomites

1

Grand Tour

Taking in Italy's greatest hits, the Grand Tour was the gap-year trip of its day, a liberating search for art and enlightenment, adventure and debauchery.

TRIP HIGHLIGHTS

555 km

Venice
Marvel at marble palaces and gold mosaics

START
rin

● Genoa

710 km

Florence
Enjoy the world's greatest Renaissance hits

● Viterbo

9 FINISH

Rome
Catch up on 2000 years of Western history

Naples
Ponder the fallen in Pompeii and the treasures they left behind

070 km

1390 km

**12–14 DAYS
1390KM / 864 MILES**

GREAT FOR...

BEST TIME TO GO

Spring (March to May) is perfect for urban sightseeing.

 ESSENTIAL PHOTO

Florence's multicoloured, marble duomo (cathedral).

✓ **BEST FOR HISTORY**

Rome, the repository of over 2000 years of European history.

Classic Trip

1 Grand Tour

From the Savoy palaces of Turin and Leonardo's *The Last Supper* to the disreputable drinking dens of Genoa and pleasure palaces of Rome, the Grand Tour is part scholar's pilgrimage and part rite of passage. Offering a chance to view some of the world's greatest masterpieces and hear Vivaldi played on 18th-century cellos, it's a rollicking trip filled with the sights, sounds and tastes that have shaped European society for centuries.

1 Turin

In his travel guide, *Voyage through Italy* (1670), travel writer and tutor Richard Lassels advocated a grand cultural tour of Europe, and in particular Italy, for young English aristocrats, during which the study of classical antiquity and the High Renaissance would ready them for future influential roles shaping the political, economic and social realities of the day.

First they travelled through France before crossing the Alps at Mt Cenis and heading to Turin (Torino), where letters of introduction admitted them to the city's agreeable Parisian-style social whirl. Today Turin's tree-lined boulevards retain their elegant, French feel and many gilded cafes, such as **Caffè Al Bicerin** (www.bicerin.it; Piazza della Consolata 5; ⏱8.30am-7.30pm Thu-Tue, closed Aug), still serve its signature coffee and chocolate drink – as it has since the 1760s.

Like the Medicis in Florence (Firenze) and the Borghese in Rome (Roma), Turin's Savoy princes had a penchant for extravagant architecture and interior decor. You suspect they also pined for their hunting lodges in Chambéry, France, from where they originated, as they invited André le Nôtre, Versailles landscaper,

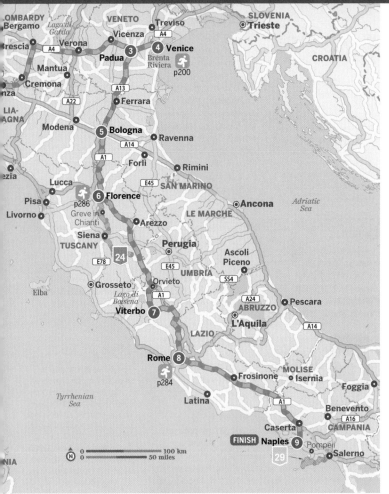

to design the gardens of **Palazzo Reale** (www.museireali.beniculturali.it; Piazza Castello; adult/reduced €12/2, 1st Sun of month Oct-Mar free; ⏱9am-7pm Tue-Sun) in 1697.

✕ 🛏 p46, p73, p81, p89

The Drive » The two-hour (170km) drive to Genoa is all on autostrada, the final stretch twisting through the mountains.

LINK YOUR TRIP

24 Tuscan Wine Tour

Linger in the bucolic hills around Florence and enjoy fine gourmet dining and world-renowned wine-tasting.

29 Amalfi Coast

Play truant from high-minded museums and head south from Naples for the Blue Ribbon drive on the Amalfi Coast.

Leave Turin following signs for the A55 (towards Alessandria), which quickly merges with the A21 passing through the pretty Piedmontese countryside. Just before Alessandria turn south onto the A26 for Genoa/Livorno. Expect heavier traffic in Genoa as cars are diverted around the collapsed Morandi Bridge.

- - - - - - - - - - - - - - - -

❷ Genoa

Some travellers, shy of crossing the Alps, might arrive by boat in Genoa (Genova). Despite its superb location, mild microclimate and lush flora, the city had a dubious reputation. Its historic centre was a warren of dark, insalubrious *caruggi* (alleys), stalked by prostitutes and beggars, while the excessive shrewdness of the Genovese banking families earned them a reputation, according to author Thomas Nugent, as 'a treacherous and over-reaching set of people'.

And yet with tourists and businessmen arriving from around the world, Genoa was, and still is, a cosmopolitan place. The **Rolli Palaces**, a collection of grand mansions originally meant to host visiting popes, dignitaries and royalty, made Via Balbi and Strada Nuova (now Via Giuseppe Garibaldi) two of the most famous streets in Europe. Visit the finest of them, the **Palazzo Spinola** (www.palazzospinola.beniculturali.it; Piazza Superiore di Pellicceria 1; adult/reduced €6/2; 🕒8.30am-7.30pm Tue-Sat) and the **Palazzo Reale** (📞010 271 02 36; www.palazzorealegenova.beniculturali.it; Via Balbi 10; adult/reduced €6/2; 🕒9am-2pm Tue & Fri, 9am-7pm Wed & Thu, 1.30-7pm Sat & Sun). Afterwards stop for sweets at **Pietro Romanengo fu Stefano** (www.romanengo.com; Via Soziglia 74r; 🕒9am-7.15pm Mon-Sat).

🍴 🛏 p46, p97

The Drive » This 365km drive takes most of the day, so stop for lunch in Cremona (p46, 116). Although the drive is on autostrada, endless fields of corn line the route. Take the A7 north out of Genoa and at Tortona exit onto the A21 around industrial Piacenza to Brescia. At Brescia, change again onto the A4 direct to Padua.

- - - - - - - - - - - - - - - -

❸ Padua

Bound for Venice (Venezia), Grand Tourists could hardly avoid visiting Padua (Padova), although by the 18th century international students no longer flocked to **Palazzo Bo** (📞049 827 39 39; www.unipd.it/en/guidedtours; Via VIII Febbraio 2; adult/reduced

DETOUR: MILAN

Start: ❶ Turin

No Grand Tour would be complete without a detour up the A4 to Milan (Milano) to eyeball Leonardo da Vinci's iconic mural **The Last Supper** (Il Cenacolo; 📞02 9280 0360; www.cenacolovinciano.net; Piazza Santa Maria delle Grazie 2; adult/reduced €10/5, plus booking fee €2; 🕒8.15am-7pm Tue-Sun; MCadorna). Advance booking is essential (booking fee €2).

From his *Portrait of a Young Man* (c 1486) to portraits of Duke Ludovico Sforza's beautiful mistresses, *The Lady with the Ermine* (c 1489) and *La Belle Ferronière* (c 1490), Leonardo transformed the rigid conventions of portraiture to depict highly individual images imbued with naturalism. Then he evolved concepts of idealised proportions and the depiction of internal emotional states through physical dynamism *(St Jerome)*, all of which cohere in the masterly *Il Cenacolo*.

While you're here, take some time to walk around other parts of the city, too (p202).

Florence Interior, Duomo

€7/4; ⏰ see website for tour times), the Venetian Republic's radical university where Copernicus and Galileo taught class.

You can visit the university's claustrophobic, wooden **anatomy theatre** (the first in the world), although it's no longer de rigueur to witness dissections on the average tourist itinerary. Afterwards don't forget to pay your respects to the skulls of noble professors who donated themselves for dissection because of the difficulty involved in acquiring fresh corpses. Their skulls are lined up in the graduation hall.

Beyond the university the melancholy air of the city did little to detain foreign visitors. Even Giotto's spectacular frescoes in the **Cappella degli Scrovegni** (Scrovegni Chapel; ☎049 201 00 20; www.cappelladegli scrovegni.it; Piazza Eremitani 8; adult/reduced €13/8, night ticket €8/6; ⏰9am-7pm, night ticket 7-10pm), where advance reservations are essential, were of limited interest given medieval art was out of fashion, and only devout Catholics ventured to revere the strange relics of St Anthony in the **Basilica di Sant'Antonio** (Il Santo; ☎049 822 56 52; www. basilicadelsanto.org; Piazza del Santo; ⏰6.20am-6.45pm Mon-Sat, to 7.45pm Sun).

The Drive » Barely 40km from Venice, the drive from Padua is through featureless areas of light industry along the A4 and then the A57.

TRIP HIGHLIGHT

④ Venice

Top of the itinerary, Venice at last! Then, as now, La Serenissima's watery landscape captured the imagination of travellers.

At Carnevale (www. carnevale.venezia.it) in February numbers swelled to 30,000; now they number in the hundreds of thousands. You cannot take your car onto the lagoon islands so leave it in a secure garage in Mestre, such as **Garage Europa Mestre** (☎041 95 92 02; www.garage europamestre.com; Corso del Popolo 55; per day €15; ⏰8am-10pm), and hop on the train to Venice Santa Lucia where water taxis connect to all the islands.

Aside from the mind-improving art in the **Gallerie dell'Accademia** (☎041 522 22 47; www. gallerieaccademia.it; Campo de la Carità 1050; adult/reduced €12/2; ⏰8.15am-2pm Mon, to 7.15pm Tue-Sun; ♿Accademia) and extraordinary architectural masterpieces such as the **Palazzo Ducale**, the **Campanile**, Longhena's

Classic Trip

WHY THIS IS A CLASSIC TRIP
DUNCAN GARWOOD, WRITER

Inspired by the 18th-century Grand Tour, this timeless route retraces the footsteps of the trailblazing tourists who set off for Italy in search of sun, culture and perhaps a little illicit adventure. Covering the country's show-stopping cities, it offers travellers a view of Italy's very best art, architecture and antiquities, while transporting them from snow-capped Alpine peaks to sun-kissed southern shores.

Above: Palazzo Ducale, Venice
Left: Chocolate tin in shopfront, Turin
Right: Basilica di Sant'Antonio doors, Padua

JULIET COOMBE/LONELY PLANET ©

Chiesa di Santa Maria della Salute and the glittering domes of the **Basilica di San Marco** (St Mark's Basilica; ☎041 270 83 11; www.basilicasanmarco.it; Piazza San Marco; ⏱9.30am-5pm Mon-Sat, 2-5pm Sun summer, to 4.30pm Sun winter; 🚤San Marco), Venice was considered an exciting den of debauchery. Venetian wives were notorious for keeping handsome escorts (*cicisbeo*), and whole areas of town were given over to venality. One of Venice's best restaurants, **Antiche Carampane** (☎041 524 01 65; www.antichecarampane. com; Rio Terà de le Carampane 1911; meals €55-63; ⏱12.45-2.30pm & 7.30-10.30pm Tue-Sat; 🚤San Stae), is located in what was once a den of vice, so called because of the notorious brothel at Palazzo Ca'Rampani.

Eighteenth-century tourists would inevitably have stopped for coffee at the newly opened **Caffè Florian** (☎041 520 56 41; www.caffeflorian.com; Piazza San Marco 57; ⏱9am-11pm; 🚤San Marco) and paid a visit to the opera house, **Teatro La Fenice** (☎041 78 66 54; www.teatrolafenice. it; Campo San Fantin 1977; tickets €25-250; 🚤Giglio), to hear ground-breaking concerts now being revived by the **Venice Music Project** (☎345 791 1948; www.venicemusicproject. it; St George's Anglican Church, Campo San Vio; adult/reduced €30/25; ⏱Mar-Jun & Sep-Nov; 🚤Accademia).

For more earthly pleasures take a tour of Venice's centuries-old markets with a gourmet food walk (p200).

 p46, p61, p117, p173

The Drive » Retrace your steps to Padua on the A57 and A4 and navigate around the ring road in the direction of Bologna to pick up the A13 southwest for this short two-hour drive. After Padua the autostrada dashes through wide-open farmland and crosses the Po river, which forms the southern border of the Veneto.

---

⑤ Bologna

Home to Europe's oldest university (established in 1088) and once the stomping ground of Dante, Boccaccio and Petrarch, Bologna had an enviable reputation for courtesy and culture. Its historic centre, complete with 20 soaring towers, is one of the best-preserved medieval cities in the world.

In the **Basilica di San Petronio** (☎051 648 06 11; www.basilicadisanpetronio.org; Piazza Maggiore; photo pass €2; ⏱7.45am-1.30pm & 3-6.30pm Mon-Fri, 7.45am-6.30pm Sat & Sun), originally intended to dwarf St Peter's in Rome, Giovanni Cassini's sundial (1655) proved the problems with the Julian calendar giving us the leap year, while Bolognesi students advanced human knowledge in obstetrics, natural science, zoology and anthropology. You can peer at their strange model waxworks and studiously labelled collections in the **Palazzo Poggi** (www.sma.unibo.it/it/il-sistema-museale/museo-di-palazzo-poggi; Via Zamboni 33; adult/reduced €5/3; ⏱10am-4pm Tue-Fri, 10.30am-6pm Sat & Sun).

In art as in science, the School of Bologna gave birth to the Carracci brothers Annibale and Agostino and their cousin Ludovico, who were among the founding fathers of Italian baroque and were deeply influenced by the Counter-Reformation.

See their emotionally charged blockbusters in the **Pinacoteca Nazionale** (www.pinacotecabologna. beniculturali.it; Via delle Belle Arti 56; adult/reduced €6/3; ⏱8.30am-7.30pm Tue-Sun Sep-Jun, 8.30am-2pm Tue-Wed & 1.45-7.30pm Thu-Sun Jul & Aug).

 p47, 283

The Drive » Bologna sits at the intersection of the A1, A13 and A14. From the centre navigate west out of the city, across the river Reno, onto the A1. From here it's a straight shot into Florence for 100km, leaving the Po plains behind you and entering the low hills of Emilia-Romagna and the forested valleys of Tuscany.

TRIP HIGHLIGHT

⑥ Florence

From Filippo Brunelleschi's red-tiled dome atop Florence's **Duomo** (Cattedrale di Santa Maria del Fiore; ☎055 230 28 85; www. museumflorence.com; Piazza del Duomo; ⏱10am-5pm Mon-Wed & Fri, to 4.30pm Thu & Sat, 1.30-4.45pm Sun) to Michelangelo's and Botticelli's greatest hits, *David* and *The Birth of Venus,* in the **Galleria dell'Accademia** (☎055 238 86 09; www.galleriaac cademiafirenze.beniculturali.it; Via Ricasoli 60; adult/reduced €12/6; ⏱8.15am-6.50pm Tue-Sun) and the **Galleria degli Uffizi** (Uffizi Gallery; ☎055 29 48 83; www.uffizi. it; Piazzale degli Uffizi 6; adult/ reduced Mar-Oct €20/10,

---

✓ **TOP TIP: JUMP THE QUEUE IN FLORENCE**

In July, August and other busy periods such as Easter, long queues are a fact of life at Florence's key museums. For a fee of €4 each, tickets to the Uffizi and Galleria dell'Accademia (where *David* lives) can be booked in advance. Book at www.firenzemusei.it.

Nov-Feb €12/6; 🕐8.15am-6.50pm Tue-Sun), Florence, according to Unesco, contains the highest number of artistic masterpieces in the world.

Whereas Rome and Milan have torn themselves down and been rebuilt many times, incorporating a multitude of architectural whims, central Florence looks much as it did in 1550, with stone towers and cypress-lined gardens.

🍴🛏 p47, p60, p257, p267

The Drive » The next 210km, continuing south along the A1, travels through some of Italy's most lovely scenery. Just southwest of Florence the vineyards of Greve in Chianti harbour some great farm stays, while Arezzo is to the east. Exit at Orvieto and follow on the SR71 and SR2 for the final 45km into Viterbo.

- - - - - - - - - - - - - - - - -

⑦ Viterbo

From Florence the road to Rome crossed the dreaded and pestilential *campagna* (countryside), a swampy, mosquito-infested low-lying area. Unlike now, inns en route were uncomfortable and hazardous, so travellers hurried through Siena, stocking up on wine for the rough road ahead. They also stopped briefly in medieval Viterbo for a quick douse in the thermal springs at the **Terme dei Papi** (📞0761 35 01; www.termedeipapi.it; Strada

TOP TIP: ROME INFORMATION LINE

The Comune di Roma (Rome city council) runs a **phone line** (📞06 06 08; www.060608.it; 🕐9am-7pm) providing info on sights, events, transport and accommodation. You can also book theatre, concert, exhibition and museum tickets. Staff speak English, as well as French, Spanish, German and Japanese. Its website is also a good source of up-to-date information.

Bagni 12; pool weekday/Sat & Sun/Sat night €12/18/20; 🕐pool 9am-8pm Wed-Mon summer, to 7pm winter, 9pm-1am Sat year-round), and a tour of the High Renaissance gardens at **Villa Lante** (📞0761 28 80 08; Via Barozzi 71, Bagnaia; adult/reduced €5/2; 🕐8.30am-1hr before sunset Tue-Sun).

The Drive » Rejoin the A1 after a 28km drive along the rural SS675. For the next 40km the A1 descends through Lazio, criss-crossing the Tevere river and keeping the ridge of the Apennines to the left as it darts through tunnels. At Fiano Romano exit for Roma Nord and follow the A1dir and SS4 (Via Salaria) for the final 20km push into the capital.

- - - - - - - - - - - - - - - - -

TRIP HIGHLIGHT

⑧ Rome

In the 18th century Rome, even in ruins, was still thought of as the august capital of the world. Here more than anywhere the Grand Tourist was awakened to an interest in art and architecture, although the **Colosseum** (Colosseo; 📞06

3996 7700; www.parcocolosseo.it; Piazza del Colosseo; adult/reduced incl Roman Forum & Palatino €12/7.50, SUPER ticket €18/13.50; 🕐8.30am-1hr before sunset; Ⓜ Colosseo) was still filled with debris and the **Palatine Hill** (Palatino; 📞06 3996 7700; www.parcocolosseo.it; Via di San Gregorio 30, Piazza di Santa Maria Nova; adult/reduced incl Colosseum & Roman Forum €12/7.50, SUPER ticket €18/13.50; 🕐8.30am-1hr before sunset; some SUPER ticket sites Mon, Wed, Fri & morning Sun only; Ⓜ Colosseo) was covered in gardens, its excavated treasures slowly accumulating in the world's oldest national museum, the **Capitoline Museums** (Musei Capitolini; 📞06 06 08; www.museicapitolini.org; Piazza del Campidoglio 1; adult/reduced €11.50/9.50; 🕐9.30am-7.30pm, last admission 6.30pm; 🚌Piazza Venezia).

Arriving through the Porta del Popolo, visitors first espied the dome of **St Peter's** (Basilica di San Pietro; 📞06 6988 3731;

SO.GOOD_PATRICK/SHUTTERSTOCK ©

www.vatican.va; St Peter's Sq; ☻7am-7pm Apr-Sep, to 6pm Oct-Mar; 🚍Piazza del Risorgimento, Ⓜ️Ottaviano-San Pietro) before clattering along the *corso* to the customs house. Once done, they headed to the **Piazza di Spagna** – the city's principal meeting place where Keats penned his love poems and died of consumption – and nearby **Trevi Fountain**.

Although the **Pantheon** (www.pantheonroma.com; Piazza della Rotonda; ☻8.30am-7.30pm Mon-Sat, 9am-6pm Sun; 🚍Largo di Torre Argentina) and **Vatican Museums** (Musei Vaticani; 📞06 6988 4676; www.museivaticani.va; Viale Vaticano; adult/reduced €17/8; ☻9am-6pm Mon-Sat, to 2pm last Sun of month, last entry 2hr before close; 🚍Piazza del Risorgimento, Ⓜ️Ottaviano-San Pietro) were a must, most travellers preferred to socialise in the grounds of the **Borghese Palace** (📞06 3 28 10; http://galleriaborghese.beniculturali.it; Piazzale del Museo Borghese 5; adult/child €15/8.50; ☻9am-7pm Tue-Sun; 🚍Via Pinciana).

Follow their example and mix the choicest sights with more venal pleasures such as fine dining at **Aroma** (📞06

9761 5109; www.aromarestaurant.it; Via Labicana 125; meals €120-180; ☻12.30-3pm & 7.30-11.30pm; 🚍Via Labicana) and souvenir shopping at antique perfumery **Officina Profumo Farmaceutica di Santa Maria Novella** (📞06 687 96 08; www.smnovella.com; Corso del Rinascimento 47; ☻10am-7.30pm Mon-Sat; 🚍Corso del Rinascimento).

🍴 🛏 p47, p60

The Drive ≫ Past Rome the landscape is hotter and drier, trees give way to Mediterranean shrubbery and the grass starts to yellow. Beyond the vineyards of Frascati, just 20km south of Rome, the A1 runs 225km to Naples (Napoli), a two-hour drive that can take longer if there's heavy traffic.

- - - - - - - - - - - - - - - - - - - -

TRIP HIGHLIGHT

⑨ Naples

Only the more adventurous Grand Tourists continued south to the salacious southern city of Naples. At the time Mt Vesuvius glowed menacingly on the bay, erupting no less than six times during the 18th century and eight times in the 19th century. But Naples was the home of opera and *commedia dell'arte* (improvised comedic drama satirising stock social stereotypes), and singing lessons and seats at **Teatro San Carlo** (📞box office 081 797 23 31; www.teatrosancarlo.it; Via San Carlo 98; ☻box office 10am-9pm

Mon-Sat, to 6pm Sun; 🚍R2 to Via San Carlo, Ⓜ️Municipio) were obligatory.

Then there were the myths of Virgil and Dante to explore at Lago d'Averno and **Campi Flegrei** (the Phlegrean Fields). And, after the discovery of **Pompeii**

Naples Interior, Teatro San Carlo

(📞081 857 53 47; www.
pompeiisites.org; entrances
at Porta Marina & Piazza Anfiteatro; adult/reduced €15/2;
🕙9am-7.30pm Mon-Fri, from
8.30am Sat & Sun, last entry
6pm Apr-Oct, 9am-5.30pm
Mon-Fri, from 8.30am Sat &
Sun, last entry 3.30pm Nov-
Mar; 🚋Circumvesuviana to
Pompei Scavi–Villa dei Misteri)
in 1748, the unfolding
drama of a Roman town
in its death throes drew
throngs of mawkish
voyeurs. Then, as now,
it was one of the most
popular tourist sights
in Italy and its priceless
mosaics, frescoes and
colossal sculptures filled
the **Museo Archeologico
Nazionale** (📞848 800288;
www.museoarcheologiconapoli.
it; Piazza Museo Nazionale 19;
adult/reduced €15/2; 🕙9am-
7.30pm Wed-Mon; Ⓜ️Museo,
Piazza Cavour).

🛏 p47, p301

Classic Trip

Eating & Sleeping

Turin ❶

✗ Fiorio   Cafe

(www.caffefiorio.it; Via Po 8; ☺8am-1am) Garner literary inspiration in Mark Twain's old window seat as you contemplate the gilded interior of a cafe where 19th-century students once plotted revolutions and the Count of Cavour deftly played whist. The bittersweet hot chocolate remains inspirational.

Genoa ❷

✗ Trattoria Rosmarino   Trattoria €€

(☎010 251 04 75; www.trattoriarosmarino.it; Salita del Fondaco 30; meals €28-34; ☺12.30-2.30pm & 7.30-10.30pm Mon-Sat) Rosmarino cooks up the standard local specialities, yes, but the straightforwardly priced menu has an elegance and vibrancy that sets it apart. With two nightly sittings, there's always a nice buzz (though there are also enough nooks and crannies that a romantic night for two isn't out of the question). Call ahead for an evening table.

Cremona ❷

✗ Hosteria 700   Lombard €€

(☎0372 3 61 75; www.hosteria700.com; Piazza Gallina 1; meals €33-40; ☺noon-2.45pm Wed-Mon, 7-11pm Wed-Sun) Behind the dilapidated facade lurks a diamond in the rough. Some of the vaulted rooms come with ceiling frescoes, dark timber tables come with ancient wooden chairs, and the hearty Lombard cuisine comes at a refreshingly competitive cost.

Venice ❹

✗ Grancaffè Quadri   Cafe

(☎041 522 21 05; www.alajmo.it; Piazza San Marco 121; ☺9am-midnight; ☻San Marco) Powdered wigs seem appropriate inside this baroque bar-cafe that's been serving happy hours since 1638. During Carnevale, costumed Quadri revellers party like it's 1699 – despite prices shooting up to €15 for a *spritz*. Grab a seat on the piazza to watch the best show in town: the basilica's golden mosaics ablaze in the sunset .

✗ CoVino   Venetian €€

(☎041 241 27 05; www.covinovenezia.com; Calle del Pestrin 3829; fixed-price menu lunch €27-36, dinner €40; ☺12.45-2.30pm & 7pm-midnight Thu-Mon; ☺; ☻Arsenale) Tiny CoVino has only 14 seats but demonstrates bags of ambition with its inventive, seasonal menu inspired by the Venetian terroir. Speciality products are selected from Slow Food Foundation producers, and the charming waiters make enthusiastic recommendations from the wine list. Only a three-course set menu is available at dinner; however, you can choose from two fixed-price options at lunch.

⌂ Locanda Fiorita   Boutique Hotel €€

(☎041 523 47 54; www.locandafiorita.com; Campiello Novo 3457a; d €80-180; ✳☺; ☻San Samuele) Few budget digs can match this smart 10-room hotel with flower-draped terraces and dreamy views of Chiesa di Santo Stefano from its rooms. Petite bedrooms offer a chic, updated take on Venetian style, with Rubelli-style fabrics and period furnishings. Room 10 has a private terrace. Head out for *aperitivo* on the roof terrace of adjoining B&B Bloom (same management) and breakfast in Campiello Novo.

Bologna ❺

✖ All'Osteria Bottega   Osteria €€

(☎051 58 51 11; Via Santa Caterina 51; meals
€36-41; ⏱12.30-2.30pm & 8-10.30pm Tue-Sat)
At Bologna's temple of culinary contentment,
owners Daniele and Valeria lavish attention
on every table between trips to the kitchen for
astonishing plates of *culatello di Zibello* ham,
tortellini in capon broth, Petroniana-style veal
cutlets (breaded and fried, then topped with
prosciutto di Parma and *parmigiano reggiano*,
and pan-sauteed in broth), off-menu speciality
pigeon and other Slow Food delights.

🛏 Bologna nel Cuore   B&B €€

(☎329 2193354; www.bolognanelcuore.it; Via
Cesare Battisti 29; s €90-120, d €125-145, apt
€130-145; P ❄ 🜚) This centrally located,
immaculate and well-loved B&B features a pair
of bright, high-ceilinged rooms with pretty tiled
bathrooms and endless mod cons, plus two
comfortable, spacious apartments with kitchen
and laundry facilities. Owner and art historian
Maria generously shares her knowledge of
Bologna and serves breakfasts featuring jams
made with fruit picked near her childhood home
in the Dolomites.

Florence ❻

✖ Trattoria Mario   Tuscan €

(☎055 21 85 50; www.trattoria-mario.com;
Via Rosina 2; meals €25; ⏱noon-3.30pm
Mon-Sat, closed 3 weeks Aug; ❄) Arrive by
noon to ensure a spot at this noisy, busy,
brilliant trattoria – a legend that retains its soul
(and allure with locals) despite being in every
guidebook. Charming Fabio, whose grandfather
opened the place in 1953, is front of house
while big brother Romeo and nephew Francesco
cook with speed in the kitchen. No advance
reservations; cash only.

🛏 Hotel Davanzati   Hotel €€

(☎055 28 66 66; www.hoteldavanzati.it;
Via Porta Rossa 5; s/d €202/252; ❄ @ 🜚)
Twenty-six steps lead up to this family-run
hotel. A labyrinth of enchanting rooms, frescoes
and modern comforts, it oozes charm – as do
Florentine brothers Tommaso and Riccardo, and

father Fabrizio, who run the show. Rooms come
with a mini iPad (meaning free wi-fi around
town), direct messaging with the hotel, handy
digital city guide and complimentary access to
a nearby gym.

Rome ❽

✖ Salumeria Roscioli   Ristorante €€€

(☎06 687 52 87; www.salumeriaroscioli.com;
Via dei Giubbonari 21; meals €55; ⏱12.30-4pm
& 7pm-midnight Mon-Sat; 🚇Via Arenula) The
name Roscioli has long been a byword for foodie
excellence in Rome, and this deli-restaurant
is the place to experience it. Tables are set
alongside the counter, laden with mouthwatering Italian and foreign delicacies, and in
a small bottle-lined space behind. The food,
including traditional Roman pastas, is top notch
and there are some truly outstanding wines.
Reservations essential.

🛏 Residenza Maritti   Guesthouse €€

(☎06 678 82 33; www.residenzamaritti.com; Via
Tor de' Conti 17; s €100, d €130-180, tr €150-200,
q €170-210; ❄ 🜚; Ⓜ Cavour) With stunning
views over the nearby forums and Vittoriano,
this hidden gem has 13 rooms spread across
three floors. Some are bright and modern;
others are more cosy with antiques, original
tiled floors and family furniture. There's a fully
equipped kitchen and a buffet breakfast is
served in the bistro next door.

Naples ❾

🛏 Hotel
Piazza Bellini   Boutique Hotel €€

(☎081 45 17 32; www.hotelpiazzabellini.com;
Via Santa Maria di Costantinopoli 101; d €90-190;
❄ @ 🜚; Ⓜ Dante) Only steps from the bars
and nightlife of Piazza Bellini, this sharp, hip
hotel occupies a 16th-century *palazzo*, its
pure-white spaces spiked with original majolica
tiles, vaulted ceilings and *piperno*-stone
paving. Rooms are modern and functional,
with designer fittings, fluffy duvets and chic
bathrooms with excellent showers. Four rooms
on the 5th and 6th floors feature panoramic
terraces.

Classic Trip

World Heritage Wonders

2

From Rome to Venice, this tour of Unesco World Heritage Sites takes in some of Italy's greatest hits, including the Colosseum and the Leaning Tower of Pisa, and some lesser-known treasures.

TRIP HIGHLIGHTS

`38 km` — ⑥

Padua

FINISH ⑧ — `870 km`

Verona
Experience opera, history and drama in romantic Verona

● Modena

● Florence

Pisa ●

② — `240 km`

Venice
Lose your heart in Italy's unique canal city

Siena
A gorgeous medieval city in the heart of Tuscany

`0 km`

Rome
Legends, history and masterpieces in the Eternal City

① START

14 DAYS
870KM / 540 MILES

GREAT FOR...

BEST TIME TO GO

April, May and September for ideal sightseeing weather and local produce.

 ESSENTIAL PHOTO

Roman Forum from the Palatino.

 BEST FOR ART

Florence's Galleria degli Uffizi.

Classic Trip

2 World Heritage Wonders

Topping the Unesco charts with 54 World Heritage Sites, Italy offers the full gamut, ranging from historic city centres and human-made masterpieces to snow-capped mountains and areas of outstanding natural beauty. This trip through central and northern Italy touches on the country's unparalleled artistic and architectural legacy, taking in ancient Roman ruins, priceless Renaissance paintings, great cathedrals and, to cap it all off, Venice's unique canal-scape.

TRIP HIGHLIGHT

1 Rome

An epic, monumental metropolis, Italy's capital is a city of thrilling beauty and high drama. Its historic centre, which according to Unesco has some of antiquity's most important monuments, has been a World Heritage Site since 1980, and the **Vatican**, technically a separate state but in reality located within Rome's city limits, has been on the Unesco list since 1984.

Of Rome's many ancient monuments, the most iconic is the **Colosseum** (Colosseo; ☑06 3996 7700; www.parcocolosseo. it; Piazza del Colosseo; adult/reduced incl Roman Forum & Palatino €12/7.50, SUPER ticket €18/13.50; ⊗8.30am-1hr before sunset; MColosseo), the towering 1st-century-AD amphitheatre where gladiators met in mortal combat and condemned criminals fought off wild beasts. Nearby, the **Palatine Hill** (Palatino; ☑06 3996 7700; www.parcocolos seo.it; Via di San Gregorio 30, Piazza di Santa Maria Nova;

adult/reduced incl Colosseum & Roman Forum €12/7.50, SUPER ticket €18/13.50; ⏱8.30am-1hr before sunset; some SUPER ticket sites Mon, Wed, Fri & morning Sun only; Ⓜ Colosseo) was the ancient city's most exclusive neighbourhood, as well as its oldest – Romulus and Remus supposedly founded the city here in 753 BC. From the Palatino, you can stroll down to the skeletal ruins of the **Roman Forum** (Foro Romano; ☎06 3996 7700; www.parcocolosseo.it; Largo della Salara Vecchia, Piazza di Santa Maria Nova; adult/reduced incl Colosseum & Palatino €12/7.50, SUPER ticket €18/13.50; ⏱8.30am-1hr before sunset; SUPER ticket sites Tue, Thu, Sat & afternoon Sun only; 🚌Via dei Fori Imperiali), the once-beating heart of the ancient city. All three sights are covered by a single ticket.

🔗 LINK YOUR TRIP

20 Etruscan Tuscany & Lazio

From Rome take the A12 autostrada up to Cerveteri and connect with this tour of ancient Etruscan treasures.

24 Tuscan Wine Tour

From Florence head south to Tuscany's Chianti wine country to indulge in some wine tasting at the area's historic vineyards.

To complete your tour of classical wonders search out the **Pantheon** (www.pantheonroma. com; Piazza della Rotonda; ☉8.30am-7.30pm Mon-Sat, 9am-6pm Sun; ▣Largo di Torre Argentina), the best preserved of Rome's ancient monuments. One of the most influential buildings in the world, this domed temple, now a church, is an extraordinary sight with its vast columned portico and soaring marble-clad interior.

✕ ⊨ p47, p60

The Drive » The easiest route to Siena, about three hours away, is via the A1 autostrada. Join this from the Rome ring road, the GRA (Grande Raccordo Anulare), and head north, past Orvieto's dramatic clifftop cathedral, to the Valdichiano exit. Take this and follow signs onto the Raccordo Siena-Bettolle (E78) for the last leg into Siena.

DETOUR: SAN GIMIGNANO

Start: ❷ Siena

Dubbed the medieval Manhattan thanks to its 14 11th-century towers, San Gimignano is a classic hilltop town and an easy detour from Siena. From the car park next to Porta San Giovanni, it's a short walk up to **Palazzo Comunale** (☎0577 28 63 00; www.sangimignanomusei.it; Piazza del Duomo 2; combined Civic Museums ticket adult/reduced €9/7; ☉10am-7pm Apr-Sep, 11am-5pm Oct-Mar), which houses the town's art gallery, the **Pinacoteca**, and tallest tower, the **Torre Grossa**. Nearby, the Romanesque basilica, known as the **Collegiata** (Duomo; Basilica di Santa Maria Assunta; ☎0577 28 63 00; www.duomosangimignano.it; Piazza del Duomo; adult/reduced €4/2; ☉10am-7pm Mon-Sat, 12.30-7pm Sun Apr-Oct, 10am-4.30pm Mon-Sat, 12.30-4.30pm Sun Nov-Mar, closed 2nd half Jan & 2nd half Nov), has some remarkable Ghirlandaio frescoes.

Before leaving town, be sure to sample the local Vernaccia wine at the **Vernaccia di San Gimignano Wine Experience** (☎0577 94 12 67; www.sangimignanomuseovernaccia.com; Via della Rocca 1; ☉11.30am-7.30pm Apr-Oct, to 6.30pm Nov & Mar, closed Dec-Feb) next to the Rocca (fortress).

San Gimignano is about 40km northwest of Siena. Head for Florence on the RA3 until Poggibonsi and then pick up the SS429.

TRIP HIGHLIGHT

❷ Siena

Siena is one of Italy's most enchanting medieval towns. Its walled centre, a beautifully preserved warren of dark lanes, Gothic *palazzi* (mansions) and pretty piazzas, is centred on **Piazza del Campo** (known as Il Campo), the sloping shell-shaped square that stages the city's annual horse race, Il Palio, on 2 July and 16 August.

On the piazza, the 102m-high **Torre del Mangia** (☎0577 29 26 15; ticket@comune.siena.it; Palazzo Pubblico, Piazza del Campo 1; adult/family €10/25; ☉10am-6.15pm Mar–mid-Oct, to 3.15pm mid-Oct–Feb) soars above the Gothic **Palazzo Pubblico** (Palazzo Comunale), home to the city's finest art museum, the **Museo Civico** (Civic Museum; ☎0577 29 26 15; Palazzo Pubblico, Piazza del Campo 1; adult/reduced €10/9, with Torre del Mangia €15, with Torre del Mangia & Complesso Museale di Santa Maria della Scala €20; ☉10am-6.15pm mid-Mar–Oct, to 5.15pm Nov–mid-Mar). Of Siena's churches, the one to see is the 13th-century **Duomo** (Cattedrale di Santa Maria Assunta; ☎0577 28 63 00; www.operaduomo.siena. it; Piazza Duomo; Mar-Oct €5, Nov-Feb free, when floor displayed €8; ☉10.30am-6.30pm Mon-Sat & 1.30-5.30pm Sun Mar-Oct, 10.30am-5pm Mon-Sat & 1.30-5pm Sun

Florence Fountain of Neptune, Piazza della Signoria

Nov-Feb), one of Italy's greatest Gothic churches. Highlights include the remarkable white, green and red facade, and, inside, the magnificent inlaid marble floor that illustrates historical and biblical stories.

p60, p275

The Drive » There are two alternatives to get to Florence. The quickest, which is via the fast RA3 Siena–Firenze Raccordo, takes about 1½ hours. But if you have the time, we recommend the scenic SR222, which snakes through the Chianti wine country, passing through quintessential hilltop towns and vine-laden slopes. Reckon on at least 2½ hours for this route.

3 Florence

Cradle of the Renaissance and home of Michelangelo, Machiavelli and the Medici, Florence (Firenze) is magnetic, romantic, unique and busy. A couple of days is not long here but it's enough for a breathless introduction to the city's top sights, many of which can be enjoyed on foot (p286).

Towering above the medieval skyline, the **Duomo** (Cattedrale di Santa Maria del Fiore; ☎055 230 28 85; www.museumflorence.com; Piazza del Duomo; ⏰10am-5pm Mon-Wed & Fri, to 4.30pm Thu & Sat, 1.30-4.45pm Sun) dominates the city centre with its famous red-tiled dome and striking facade. A short hop away, **Piazza della Signoria** opens onto the sculpture-filled **Loggia dei Lanzi** and the **Torre d'Arnolfo** above **Palazzo Vecchio** (☎055 276 85 58; www.musefirenze.it; Piazza della Signoria; adult/reduced museum €12.50/10, tower €12.50/10, museum & tower €17.50/15, museum & archaeological tour €16/13.50, archaeological tour €4, combination ticket €19.50/17.50; ⏰museum 9am-11pm Fri-Wed, to 2pm Thu Apr-Sep, 9am-7pm Fri-Wed, to 2pm Thu Oct-Mar, tower 9am-9pm Fri-Wed, to 2pm Thu Apr-Sep, 10am-5pm Fri-Wed, to 2pm Thu Oct-Mar), Florence's lavish City Hall.

Next to the *palazzo,* the **Galleria degli Uffizi** (Uffizi Gallery; ☎055 29 48 83; www.uffizi.it; Piazzale degli Uffizi 6; adult/reduced Mar-Oct €20/10, Nov-Feb €12/6; ⏰8.15am-6.50pm Tue-Sun) houses one of the world's great art collections, including works by Botticelli, Leonardo da Vinci, Michelangelo, Raphael and many other Renaissance maestros.

p47, p60, p257, p267

The Drive » From Florence it's about 1½ hours to Pisa along the A11 autostrada or just over an hour using the speedy, toll-free FI-PI-LI (SS67) linking the two cities. At the end of either route, follow signs to Pisa centro.

Classic Trip

WHY THIS IS A CLASSIC TRIP
DUNCAN GARWOOD, WRITER

Every one of the towns and cities on this drive is special. The great treasures of Rome, Florence and Venice are amazing but, for me, it's the lesser-known highlights that make this such an incredible trip – Siena's Gothic Duomo, Modena's stunning Romanesque cathedral, the Cappella degli Scrovegni in Padua, and Verona's gorgeous medieval centre.

Above: St Peter's Basilica, Rome
Left: Statue of Emperor Augustus, Rome
Right: Leaning Tower, Pisa

OLEG VORONISCHE/SHUTTERSTOCK ©

4 Pisa

Once a maritime republic to rival Genoa and Venice, Pisa now owes its fame to an architectural project gone horribly wrong. The **Leaning Tower** (Torre Pendente; ☎050 83 50 11; www.opapisa. it; Piazza del Duomo; €18; ⏰8.30am-10pm mid-Jun–Aug, 9am-8pm Apr–mid-Jun & Sep, to 7pm Oct & Mar, to 6pm Nov-Feb) is an extraordinary sight and one of Italy's most photographed monuments. The tower, originally erected as a *campanile* (bell tower) in the late 12th century, is one of three Romanesque buildings on the immaculate lawns of **Piazza dei Miracoli** (also known as Campo dei Miracoli or Piazza del Duomo).

The candy-striped **Duomo** (Duomo di Santa Maria Assunta; ☎050 83 50 11; www.opapisa.it; Piazza del Duomo; ⏰10am-8pm Mar-Oct, 10am-6pm or 7pm Nov-Feb), begun in 1063, has a graceful tiered facade and cavernous interior, while to its west, the cupcake-like **Battistero** (Battistero di San Giovanni; ☎050 83 50 11; www.opapisa. it; Piazza del Duomo; €5, combination ticket with Camposanto or Museo delle Sinopie €7, Camposanto & Museo delle Sinopie €8; ⏰8am-8pm Apr-Oct, 9am-6pm or 7pm Nov-Mar) is something of an architectural hybrid, with a Pisan-Romanesque lower section and a Gothic upper level and

55

dome. End your Piazza dei Miracoli foray with a saunter atop the city's old medieval walls, **Mura di Pisa** (📞050 098 74 80; www.muradipisa.it; Piazza del Duomo; adult/reduced €3/ free; ⏰9am-7pm summer, 10am-3.30pm winter; 👶).

 p61

The Drive » It's a 2½-hour drive up to Modena from Pisa. Head back towards Florence on the A11 and then pick up the A1 to Bologna. Continue as the road twists and falls through the wooded Apennines before flattening out near Bologna. Exit at Modena Sud (Modena South) and follow signs for the centro.

----

⑤ Modena

One of Italy's top foodie towns, Modena has a stunning medieval centre and a trio of Unesco-listed sights. First up is the gorgeous **Duomo** (Cattedrale Metropolitana di Santa Maria Assunta e San Geminiano; www.duomomo dena.it; Corso Duomo; ⏰7am-12.30pm & 3.30-7pm Mon, 7am-7pm Tue-Sun), which is widely considered to be Italy's finest Romanesque church. Features to look out for include the Gothic rose window and a series of bas-reliefs depicting scenes from Genesis.

Nearby, the 13th-century **Torre Ghirlandina** (www.unesco.modena.it; Corso Duomo; adult/reduced €3/2; ⏰9.30am-1pm & 3-7pm Tue-Fri, 9.30am-7pm Sat & Sun Apr-Sep, to 5.30pm Oct-Mar), an 87m-high tower topped by a Gothic spire, was named after Seville's Giralda bell tower by exiled Spanish Jews in the early 16th century. The last of the Unesco threesome is **Piazza Grande**, just south of the cathedral. The city's focal square, this is flanked by the porticoed **Palazzo Comunale**, Modena's elegant town hall.

✕ 🛏 p61, p283

WORLD HERITAGE SITES

With 54 World Heritage Sites, Italy has more than any other country. But what exactly is a World Heritage Site? Basically it's anywhere that Unesco's World Heritage Committee decides is of 'outstanding universal value' and inscribes on the World Heritage List. It could be a natural wonder such as the Great Barrier Reef in Australia or a human-made icon such as New York's Statue of Liberty, a historic city centre or a great work of art or architecture.

The list was set up in 1972 and has since grown to include 1121 sites from 167 countries. Italy first got in on the act in 1979 when it successfully nominated its first entry – the prehistoric rock drawings of the Valcamonica valley in northeastern Lombardy. The inscription process requires sites to be nominated by a country and then independently evaluated. If they pass scrutiny and meet at least one of 10 selection criteria, they get the green light at the World Heritage Committee's annual meeting. Once on the list, sites qualify for management support and access to the World Heritage Fund.

Italian nominations have generally fared well and since Rome's historic centre and the Chiesa di Santa Maria delle Grazie in Milan were inscribed in 1980, many of the nation's greatest attractions have made it onto the list – the historic centres of Florence, Naples, Siena and San Gimignano; the cities of Venice, Verona and Ferrara; the archaeological sites of Pompeii, Paestum and Agrigento; as well as natural beauties such as the Amalfi Coast, Aeolian Islands, Dolomites and Tuscany's Val d'Orcia.

Verona Arena

The Drive » From Modena reckon on about 1¼ hours to Verona, via the A22 and A4 autostradas. Follow the A22 as it traverses the flat Po valley plain, passing the medieval town of Mantua (Mantova; worth a quick break) before connecting with the A4. Turn off at Verona Sud and follow signs for the city centre.

TRIP HIGHLIGHT

⑥ Verona

A World Heritage Site since 2000, Verona's historic centre is a beautiful compilation of architectural styles and inspiring buildings. Chief among these is its stunning Roman amphitheatre, known as the **Arena** (☎045 800 32 04; Piazza Brà; adult/reduced €10/7.50; ☺8.30am-7.30pm Tue-Sun, 1.30-7.30pm Mon). Dating to the 1st century AD, this is Italy's third-largest amphitheatre after the Colosseum and Capua amphitheatre, and although it can no longer seat 30,000, it still draws sizeable crowds to its opera and music concerts.

Classic Trip

ITALY'S BEST TRIPS **2** WORLD HERITAGE WONDERS

But Verona isn't simply a relic of the past. A thriving regional city, it also hosts a fantastic modern art gallery, **Galleria d'Arte Moderna Achille Forti** (Palazzo della Ragione; ☎045 800 19 03; https://gam.comune.verona.it; Cortile Mercato Vecchio; adult/reduced €4/2.50, incl Torre dei Lamberti €8/5; ⏰10am-6pm Tue-Fri, 11am-7pm Sat & Sun), with a fabulous collection of under-appreciated Italian modernists such as Felice Casorati and Angelo Zamboni. It's also packed with excellent contemporary restaurants like **Locanda 4 Cuochi** (☎045 803 03 11; www.locanda4cuochi.it; Via Alberto Mario 12; meals €40, 3-course set menu €43; ⏰12.30-2.30pm & 7.30-10.30pm, closed lunch Mon & Tue; 📶) and wine bars, such as **Antica Bottega del Vino** (☎045 800 45 35; www.bottegavini.it; Vicolo Scudo di Francia 3; ⏰11am-1am), showcasing regional wines.

✂ 🏠 p61, p117, p181

The Drive » To Padua it's about an hour from Verona on the A4 Venice autostrada. Exit at Padova Ovest (Padua West) and join the SP47 after the toll booth. Follow this until you see, after a road bridge, a turnoff signposted to the centro.

----

❼ Padua

Travellers to Padua (Padova) usually make a beeline for the city's main attraction, the **Cappella degli Scrovegni** (Scrovegni Chapel; ☎049 201 00 20; www.cappelladegli scrovegni.it; Piazza Eremitani 8; adult/reduced €13/8, night ticket €8/6; ⏰9am-7pm, night ticket 7-10pm), but there's more to Padua than Giotto frescoes and it's actually the **Orto Botanico** (☎049 827 39 39; www.ortobotanicopd.it; Via dell'Orto Botanico 15; adult/reduced €10/8, with Padova-Card €5; ⏰9am-7pm Tue-Sun Apr-Sep, to 6pm Oct, to 5pm Nov-Mar) that represents Padua on Unesco's list of World Heritage Sites. The oldest botanical garden in the world, this dates to 1545 when a group of medical students planted some rare plants in order to study their medicinal properties. Discover Padua's outsized contribution to science and, in particular, medicine at the fascinating **Museum of Medical History** (Musme; www.musme.it; Via San Francesco 94; adult/reduced/child €10/8/6; ⏰2.30-7pm Tue-Fri, 9.30am-7pm Sat & Sun), housed in what was ostensibly the world's first hospital where medical students learnt clinical practice at a patient's beside.

The Drive » Traffic permitting, it's about 45 minutes from Padua to Venice, along the A4.

Pass through Mestre and over the Ponte della Libertà bridge to Interparking Venezia Tronchetto on the island of Tronchetto.

TRIP HIGHLIGHT

❽ Venice

The end of the road, quite literally, is Venice (Venezia). Of the city's many must-sees the most famous are on Piazza San Marco, including the **Basilica di San Marco** (St Mark's Basilica; ☎041 270 83 11; www.basilicasanmarco.it; Piazza San Marco; ⏰9.30am-5pm Mon-Sat, 2-5pm Sun summer, to 4.30pm Sun winter; 🚊San Marco), Venice's great showpiece church. Built originally to house the bones of St Mark, it's a truly awe-inspiring vision with its spangled spires, Byzantine domes, luminous mosaics and lavish marble work. For a bird's-eye view, head to the nearby **campanile** (www.basilicasanmarco.it; Piazza San Marco; adult/reduced €8/4; ⏰8.30am-9pm summer, 9.30am-5.30pm winter, last entry 45min before closing; 🚊San Marco).

Adjacent to the basilica, the **Palazzo Ducale** (Ducal Palace; ☎041 271 59 11; www.palazzoducale.visitmuve.it; Piazzetta San Marco 1; adult/reduced incl Museo Correr €20/13, with Museum Pass free; ⏰8.30am-7pm summer, to 5.30pm winter; 🚊San Zaccaria) was the official residence of Venice's doges (ruling dukes) from the 9th century. Inside, its lavishly decorated

ITALIAN ART & ARCHITECTURE

The Ancients
In pre-Roman times, the Greeks built theatres and proportionally perfect temples in their southern colonies at Agrigento, Syracuse and Paestum, whilst the Etruscans concentrated on funerary art, creating elaborate tombs at Tarquinia and Cerveteri. Coming in their wake, the Romans specialised in roads, aqueducts and monumental amphitheatres such as the Colosseum and Verona's Arena.

Romanesque
With the advent of Christianity in the 4th century, basilicas began to spring up, many with glittering Byzantine-style mosaics. The Romanesque period (c 1050–1200) saw the construction of fortified monasteries and robust, bulky churches such as Bari's Basilica di San Nicola and Modena's cathedral. Pisa's striking *duomo* (cathedral) displays a characteristic Tuscan variation on the style.

Gothic
Gothic architecture, epic in scale and typically embellished by gargoyles, pinnacles and statues, took on a more classical form in Italy. Assisi's Basilica di San Francesco is an outstanding early example, but for the full-blown Italian Gothic style check out the cathedrals in Florence, Venice, Siena and Orvieto.

Renaissance
From quiet beginnings in 14th-century Florence, the Renaissance erupted across Italy before spreading across Europe. In Italy, painters such as Giotto, Botticelli, Leonardo da Vinci and Raphael led the way, while architects Brunelleschi and Bramante rewrote the rule books with their beautifully proportioned basilicas. All-rounder Michelangelo worked his way into immortality, producing masterpieces such as *David* and the Sistine Chapel frescoes.

Baroque
Dominating the 17th century, the extravagant baroque style found fertile soil in Italy. Witness the Roman works of Gian Lorenzo Bernini and Francesco Borromini, Lecce's flamboyant *centro storico* (historic centre) and the magical baroque towns of southeastern Sicily.

Neoclassicism
Signalling a return to sober classical lines, neoclassicism majored in the late-18th and early-19th centuries. Signature works include Caserta's Palazzo Reale and La Scala opera house in Milan. In artistic terms, the most famous Italian exponent was Antonio Canova.

chambers harbour some seriously heavyweight art, including Tintoretto's gigantic *Paradiso* (Paradise) in the Sala del Maggiore Consiglio. Connecting the palace to the city dungeons, the **Ponte dei Sospiri** (Bridge of Sighs; ⛴San Zaccaria) was named after the sighs that prisoners (including Casanova) emitted en route from court to cell. If you're hungry, hit the streets on foot to get a real taste of the city (p200).

🍴 🛏 p46, p61, p117, p173

Classic Trip

Eating & Sleeping

Rome ❶

✖ La Ciambella · Italian €€

(☏06 683 29 30; www.la-ciambella.it; Via dell'Arco della Ciambella 20; meals €35-45; ⏱noon-11pm Tue-Sun; 🚉Largo di Torre Argentina) Near the Pantheon but as yet largely undiscovered by the tourist hordes, this friendly restaurant beats much of the neighbourhood competition. Its handsome, light-filled interior is set over the ruins of the Terme di Agrippa, visible through transparent floor panels, setting an attractive stage for interesting, imaginative food.

✖ Flavio al Velavevodetto · Roman €€

(☏06 574 41 94; www.ristorantevelavevodetto. it; Via di Monte Testaccio 97-99; meals €30-35; ⏱12.30-3pm & 7.45-11pm; 🚉Via Galvani) The pick of Testaccio's trattorias, this casual spot is celebrated locally for its earthy, no-nonsense *cucina romana* (Roman cuisine). For a taste, start with *carciofo alla giudia* (deep-fried artichoke) before moving onto *rigatoni alla carbonara* (pasta tubes wrapped in a silky egg sauce spiked with morsels of cured pig's cheek) and finishing up with tiramisu.

🛏 Arco del Lauro · Guesthouse €€

(☏06 9784 0350; www.arcodellauro.it; Via Arco de' Tolomei 27; r €120-175; ❄ @ 🛜; 🚉Viale di Trastevere, 🚉Viale di Trastevere) Perfectly placed on a peaceful cobbled lane on the 'quiet side' of Trastevere, this ground-floor guesthouse sports six gleaming white rooms with parquet floors, a modern low-key look and well-equipped bathrooms. Guests share a fridge, a complimentary fruit bowl and cakes. Breakfast (€5) is served in a nearby cafe. Daniele and Lorenzo, who run the place, could not be friendlier or more helpful.

Siena ❷

✖ Ristorante Enzo · Tuscan €€€

(☏0577 28 12 77; www.daenzo.net; Via Camollia 49; meals €52; ⏱noon-2.30pm & 7.30-10pm Tue-Sun) The epitome of refined Sienese dining, Da Enzo, as it is popularly called, welcomes guests with a complimentary glass of prosecco and follows up with Tuscan dishes made with skill and care. There's plenty of fish on the menu, as well as excellent handmade pasta and nonstandard meat dishes. The setting is equally impressive, with quality napery and glassware.

Florence ❸

✖ Il Teatro del Sale · Tuscan €€

(☏055 200 14 92; www.teatrodelsale.com; Via dei Macci 111r; brunch/dinner €20/30; ⏱noon-2.30pm & 7-11pm Tue-Fri, noon-3pm & 7-11pm Sat, noon-3pm Sun, closed Aug) Florentine chef Fabio Picchi is one of Florence's living treasures who steals the Sant'Ambrogio show with this eccentric, good-value, members-only club (everyone welcome, membership €7) inside an old theatre. He cooks up brunch and dinner, culminating at 9.30pm in a live performance of drama, music or comedy arranged by his wife, artistic director and comic actress Maria Cassi.

✖ Essenziale · Tuscan €€€

(☏333 7491973 055 247 69 56; www.essenziale. me; Piazza di Cestello 3r; 6-/8-course tasting menu €65/80; ⏱7-10pm Tue-Sat; 🛜) There's no finer showcase for modern Tuscan cuisine than this loft-style restaurant in a 19th-century warehouse. Preparing dishes at the kitchen bar in rolled-up shirt sleeves and navy butcher's apron is dazzling young chef Simone Cipriani. Order one of his tasting menus to sample the full range of his inventive, thoroughly modern cuisine inspired by classic Tuscan dishes.

🛏 Hotel Scoti   Pension €€

(📞055 29 21 28; www.hotelscoti.com; Via de' Tornabuoni 7; d/tr €140/165; 📶) Wedged between designer boutiques on Florence's smartest shopping strip, this hidden *pensione* is a fabulous mix of old-fashioned charm and value for money. Its traditionally styled rooms are spread across the 2nd floor of a 16th-century *palazzo;* some have lovely rooftop views. Guests can borrow hairdryers, bottle openers and so on, and the frescoed lounge (1780) is stunning. Optional breakfast €5 extra.

Pisa ④

🍴 Osteria dei Cavalieri   Tuscan €€

(📞050 58 08 58; www.osteriacavalieri.pisa.it; Via San Frediano 16; meals €25-30; 🕐12.30-2pm & 7.45-10pm Mon-Fri, 7.45-10pm Sat) When an *osteria* cooks up a tripe platter for antipasto, bone marrow with saffron-spiced rice as *primo* and feisty T-bone steaks as *secondo,* you know you've struck Tuscan foodie gold. A trio of inspired *piatti unico* (single dishes) promise a quick lunch, or linger over themed multicourse menus (including, unusually, a vegetarian menu) packed with timeless Tuscan faves.

Modena ⑤

🍴 Trattoria Ermes   Trattoria €

(📞059 23 80 65; Via Ganaceto 89; meals €20; 🕐noon-2.30pm Mon-Sat) In business since 1963, this fabulous, affordable little lunch spot is tucked into a single wood-panelled room at the northern edge of downtown Modena. Gregarious patron Ermes Rinaldi runs the place with his wife Bruna: she cooks, he juggles plates and orders while excessively bantering with the customers, though these days he often sits out for health reasons.

🛏 Hotel Cervetta 5   Hotel €€

(📞059 23 84 47; www.hotelcervetta5.com; Via Cervetta 5; s €80-104, d €120-150; ❊📶) Cervetta is about as hip as Modena gets without pandering to the convention crowd. Adjacent to the intimate Piazza Grande, it has quasi-boutique facilities, including rooms that complement the wonderfully soothing, candlelit lobby with rustic-chic additions like African iron light covers, unfinished concrete bathrooms and roped Edison lighting.

Verona ⑥

🍴 Café Carducci   Bistro €€

(📞045 803 06 04; www.cafecarducci.it; Via Carducci 12; meals €25-45; 🕐7am-3pm & 5-11pm Mon-Sat; ❊) A charming 1920s-style bistro where stylish diners relax in the mirror-lined interior at linen-topped tables set with candles and plates of exquisitely sweet salami and local cheeses. The menu is as classic as the surroundings, offering risotto in an Amarone reduction and black rice with scallops. In cherry season, don't miss the gelato with Bigarreau cherries doused in grappa.

Venice ⑧

🍴 All'Arco   Venetian €

(📞041 520 56 66; Calle de l'Ochialer 436; cicheti €2-2.50; 🕐9am-2.30pm Mon-Sat; 🚇Rialto Mercato) Search out this authentic neighbourhood bar for some of the best *cicheti* (Venetian tapas) in town. Armed with ingredients from the nearby Rialto Market, father-son team Francesco and Matteo serve miniature masterpieces to the scrum of eager patrons crowding the counter and spilling out onto the street. Even with copious prosecco, hardly any meal here tops €20.

🛏 Novecento   Boutique Hotel €€€

(📞041 241 37 65; www.novecento.biz; Calle del Dose 2683/84; d from €215; ❊📶; 🚇Giglio) Run by the Romanelli family for more than 50 years, this hotel is a home away from home. Nine individually designed rooms are inspired by designer Mario Fortuny and come finished with Turkish kilim pillows, velvet draperies and carved bedsteads. You can mingle with creative fellow travellers around the honesty bar, while the garden is a lovely spot in which to linger over breakfast.

Northern
Italy

FROM ALPINE PEAKS TO GLACIAL LAKES, coastal villages and Renaissance towns, northern Italy boasts natural wonders and artistic treasures. The area has been luring artists, celebrities and Mitteleuropeans since the days of the Grand Tour, and it's easy to see what draws them: art and architecture, an embarrassment of culinary riches, cult wines and a slew of sophisticated cities.

Our trips reveal the area in all its diversity – snaking mountain passes traverse the Dolomites and western Alps, coastal roads meander down the Italian Riviera, autostradas lead to historic cities such as Venice, Milan and Turin. Stunning scenery awaits around every turn as you wend your way to historic wineries, royal palaces and lakeside gardens.

Lago di Como Bellagio
MATT MUNRO/LONELY PLANET ©

Northern Italy

 DON'T MISS

Cappella degli Scrovegni

See the Renaissance blossoming through the tears in Giotto's moving frescoes for the Cappella degli Scrovegni. 🚗 🚶 📷

Portofino Peninsula

Steal a march on Cinque Terre hikers and walk the quiet pathways on the Portofino peninsula, ending with a harbourside meal at Ristorante Puny. 🚗

Truffles

Strike gastronomic gold in Alba, and dine on prized white truffles. 🚗

Terme Merano

Dip in and out of hot and cold pools amid stunning mountain scenery, just as Austrian royals, and Kafka, have done before you. 🚗

Walking the Alta Vie

Walk on the roof of the Dolomites through Alpine meadows strewn with wildflowers. 🚶

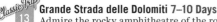

Savoy Palace Circuit

3

Bisected by the Po and overshadowed by the Alps, Turin has an air of importance, adorned as it is with sumptuous Savoy palaces, grand hunting lodges and Napoleonic boulevards.

TRIP HIGHLIGHTS

5 km

Venaria Reale
Spectacular Venaria Reale, Italy's Versailles

0 km

Turin
Franco-Italian Turin was the epicentre of Savoy power

6

5

1

7

START/ FINISH

Moncalieri

137 km

Basilica di Superga
The final resting place for 50 Savoy princes and princesses

Rivoli
Avant-garde art set against a baroque backdrop

8 km

Racconigi

3–4 DAYS
152KM / 94 MILES

GREAT FOR...

BEST TIME TO GO
April to October, when the castles are open for viewing.

ESSENTIAL PHOTO
The classical facade of the Basilica di Superga.

BEST FOR HISTORY
Palazzo Carignano, where key events leading to Italian unification took place.

3 Savoy Palace Circuit

The Savoys abandoned their old capital of Chambéry in France in 1563 and set up home in Turin (Torino). To make themselves comfortable they spent the next 300 years building an array of princely palaces (many of them designed by Sicilian architect and stage-set designer Filippo Juvarra), country retreats and a grand mausoleum. They encircle Turin like an extravagant baroque garland and make for fascinating day trips or an easy long-weekend tour.

Fiano

La Cassa

Pa
Regi
la Ma

San Gillio

Dora Riparia

E70 A32

5
Rivoli

Orbassano

Piossasco

Parco Na
di Stu

Volvera

Non

TRIP HIGHLIGHT

① Turin

Piazza Castello served as the seat of dynastic power for the House of Savoy. It is dominated by **Palazzo Madama** (☎011 443 35 01; www.palazzomadamatorino. it; Piazza Castello; adult/reduced €10/8; ☉10am-6pm Wed-Mon), a part-medieval, part-baroque castle built in the 13th century on the site of the old Roman gate and named after Madama Reale Maria Cristina (widow of Vittorio Amedeo I, also known as the Lion of Susa and nominally King of Cyprus and Jerusalem), who lived here in the 17th century.

Nearby statues of mythical twins Castor and Pollux guard the entrance to the **Palazzo Reale** (www.museireali. beniculturali.it; Piazza Castello; adult/reduced €12/2, 1st Sun of month Oct-Mar free; ☉9am-7pm Tue-Sun). Built for Carlo Emanuele II around 1646, its lavishly decorated rooms house an assortment of gilded furnishings and one of the greatest armouries in Europe, the **Armeria Reale**. Also in the palace is the **Galleria Sabauda**, which contains the Savoy art collection.

'The road through Memphis and Thebes passes through Turin', trumpeted French hieroglyphic decoder

0 ___ 5 k
0 ___ 2.5 mile

Jean-François Champollion in the 19th century, and he wasn't far wrong. The **Palazzo dell'Accademia delle Scienze** houses the most important collection of Egyptian treasure outside Cairo in the **Museo Egizio** (Egyptian Museum; ☎011 440 69 03; www.museoegizio.it; Via Accademia delle Scienze 6; adult/reduced €15/11; ⊙9am-6.30pm Tue-Sun, 9am-2pm Mon).

Opposite, **Palazzo Carignano** is where Carlo Alberto (1798–1849) and the first King of Italy, Vittorio Emanuele II (1820–78), were born, and it provided the seat for Italy's first parliament. Now it houses the unmissable **Museo Nazionale del Risorgimento Italiano** (☎011 562 11 47; www.museorisorgimentotorino.it; Via Accademia delle Scienze 5; adult/reduced €10/8; ⊙10am-6pm Tue-Sun),

§ LINK YOUR TRIP

1 Grand Tour
From Italy's first capital to a Grand Tour of the peninsula, continue from Turin to Genoa (Genova) on the A21 and A7.

4 Gourmet Piedmont
Head south of Turin on the A6 to tour the rich culinary hinterland of the Langhe, Piedmont's jealously guarded larder.

which charts the course of the modern nation state.

🍴 🛏 p46, p73, p81, p89

The Drive » Drive south along Corso Unitá d'Italia. This busy dual carriageway turns into Corso Trieste and then Via Custoza. Take a right for Moncalieri, beneath the A6 and across the river Po on Via Martiri della Libertá. Turn right on Via Arduino and you'll arrive at the castle after about 9km.

----

❷ Moncalieri

The 12th-century **Cas-tello di Moncalieri** (Piazza Baden Baden 4), the first fortress built by Thomas I of Savoy, is just south of the centre of Turin, com-manding the southern access to the city. The family then upped sticks and moved to more splendid accommodation in the city centre.

Since 1921 it has been the HQ for the *carabi-nieri* (military police), the police corps created by Victor Emanuele I of Savoy in 1726 as a police force for the island of Sardinia (briefly within Savoy dominion) and which later became Italy's first police force following unification in 1861. While the royal apartments can only be visited on a prebooked guided tour, you can wander around the gar-den and enjoy the view from the belvedere.

The Drive » Leave Moncalieri heading southeast, following

signs saying *tutte le direzioni* (all directions) and then pick up the A6 southbound towards Savona/Piacenza. Drive 15km on the autostrada, then exit for Carmagnola, which will put you first on the SP129 (as you skirt Carmagnola) and then on the SS20 towards Racconigi, a further 12km southwest.

----

❸ Racconigi

South of Moncalieri, the enormous **Castello di Racconigi** (www.ilcastello diracconigi.it; Via Morosini 3; adult/reduced €5/2.50; ☺9am-7pm Tue-Sun) was another 12th-century fortress, guarding the contested borderlands around Turin. Originally the domain of the Mar-quis of Saluzzo, the castle came into Savoy posses-sion through marriage and inheritance.

Inhabited by various branches of the family up until WWII, the castle was a favourite for sum-mering royals, hosting Tsar Nicholas II of Russia in 1918. In 1904 the last king of Italy, Umberto II, was born in the castle and in 1925 the grand wedding of Philip of Hesse and Mafalda of Savoy (p72) was hosted here. Tragically, Mafalda later died in the death camp of Buchenwald. Now you can wander the strangely intimate apartments of kings and queens – full of elegant furnishings, family pho-tos and personal objects – and enjoy the grand

portrait gallery with its 1875 dynastic portraits.

The Drive » The 38km drive north to Palazzina di Caccia Stupinigi retraces much of the previous journey, first on the SS20 and then the A6. However, after 14km on the autostrada, before you reach Moncalieri, take the exit for the E70 (Tangenziale) towards Aosta. Now heading northwest, drive a further 8.5km and then take the exit for Stupinigi. The Viale Torino runs right up to the *palazzina* (hunting lodge).

----

❹ Palazzina di Caccia di Stupinigi

The Savoy's finest hunt-ing park, the **Palazzina di Caccia di Stupinigi** (☎011 620 06 34; www.ordinemaurizi ano.it; Piazza Principe Amedeo 7; adult/reduced €12/8, park only €3; ☺10am-5.30pm Tue-Fri, to 6.30pm Sat & Sun, park open Mar-Nov) was cleverly acquired by the almost landless Emanuele Fili-berto, Duke of Savoy from 1553 to 1580. Known as *Testa di Ferro* ('Ironhead') due to his military prowess, Emanuele was the only child of Charles III, Duke of Savoy, and Beatrice of Portugal, who left him little more than his title when they died. However, through diligent service in the armies of the Austro-Hungarian Em-pire he slowly and surely reclaimed Savoyard lands, including the Stupinigi park and Turin, where he moved the fam-ily seat in 1563.

Turin Palazzo Carignano

The fabulous *palazzina* came later, thanks to Vittorio Amadeo II, who set Filippo Juvarra to work in 1729. He enlisted decorators from Venice to attend to the interiors covering the 137 rooms and 17 galleries in *trompe l'œil* hunting scenes such as the *Triumph of Diana* in the main salon. Now the rooms accommodate the **Museo di Arte e Ammobiliamento**, a fabulous museum of arts and furnishings, many of them original to the lodge.

The Drive >> Continue on the Turin periphery (E70) heading further northwest towards Fréjus for the 21km drive to Rivoli. You'll be on the E70 for 11km before exiting at Rosta/Avigliana. From here it's a short 4km drive before exiting on the SS25 towards Rivoli. Brown signs direct you to the castle.

- - - - - - - - - - - - - - -

TRIP HIGHLIGHT

⑤ Rivoli

Works by Franz Ackermann, Gilbert and George, and Sophie Calle would have been beyond the wildest imagination of the Savoy family, who used the 17th-century **Castello di Rivoli** as one of their country retreats.

Since 1984, the cutting edge of Turin's contemporary art scene has been housed here in the **Museo d'Arte Contemporanea** (☎011 956 52 22; www.castellodirivoli. org; Piazza Mafalda di Savoia; adult/reduced €8.50/6.50, Villa Cerruti incl shuttle & tour

adult/reduced €26.50/19.50; ⊙10am-5pm Tue-Fri, to 7pm Sat & Sun), creating shocking juxtapositions between the classical architecture and the art, such as the 1997 exhibition that showcased Maurizio Cattelan's taxidermy horse suspended from the rococo ceiling.

Rivoli's latest crown jewel is the **Villa Cerruti**, the former mansion-home of a reclusive art collector who amassed over €600 million worth of artistic treasures. Shuttle buses (with separate tickets purchased online well in advance) from the castle whisk visitors out to the villa for a guided tour of the lavish antique-filled home filled with works by Modigliani, Kandinsky, Giacometti, Picasso, Klee, de Chirico and Magritte.

✗ p73

The Drive >> Return to the Tangenziale via the SS25 and continue northeast in the direction of Aosta/Mont Blanc/Milano. This puts you on the A55/E64 for 9km. Then take the exit for Venaria and at the traffic lights turn left onto Corso Giuseppe Garibaldi, from where you'll see the palace signposted.

- - - - - - - - - - - - - - -

TRIP HIGHLIGHT

⑥ Venaria Reale

The **Reggia di Venaria Reale** (☎011 499 23 33; www.lavenaria.it; Piazza della Repubblica; admission incl exhibitions €25, Reggia & gardens €16, gardens only €5; ⊙9am-5pm Tue-Fri, to 6.30pm Sat & Sun) is a Unesco-listed palace complex built by Amadeo di Castellamonte for Carlo Emanuele II between 1667 and 1690. It's one of the biggest royal residences in the world and lengthy restoration works were concluded in late 2010. The full trajectory

MAFALDA OF SAVOY (1902–44)

Mafalda of Savoy was the second of four daughters of King Victor Emmanuel III of Italy and Elena of Montenegro. Known for her cultured, pious character, she made a grand marriage to Prince Philip, Landgrave of Hesse, grandson of German Emperor Frederick III and great-grandson of Queen Victoria of England. Affiliated with the German National Socialist (Nazi) movement, Philip, with his international connections, rose rapidly in the Nazi hierarchy, becoming a trusted member of the Reichstag and acting as an intermediary between Hitler and Mussolini. But Hitler distrusted the outspoken Mafalda and suspected her of working against the German war effort. When her father, Victor Emmanuel, ordered the arrest of Mussolini in July 1943 and signed the armistice with the Allies, the Gestapo reacted by arresting Mafalda for subversive activities and transferring her to Buchenwald concentration camp. There she was wounded during an Allied attack on the camp's munitions factory in 1944, and she later died of her wounds, beseeching fellow prisoners to remember her not as an Italian princess, but an Italian sister.

of the buildings stretches 2km. Highlights include the **Galleria Grande**, the **Cappella di Sant'Uberto** and the **Juvarra stables**.

Outside, there's more: 17th-century grottoes, the **Fontana del Cervo** (Stag Fountain), the **Rose Garden** and the 17th-century **Potager Garden**, all of which took eight years to restore and required the replanting of 50,000 plants. It's all set against the 30-sq-km La Mandria park.

✖ p73

The Drive ❱❱ Return to the A55/E64 and continue northeast for 6km, then take the Falchera exit for Torino Nord. Follow the signs for Torino Centro and merge southwards onto the A4 for 2.5km. Before you hit the river Po, turn left onto Lungo Stura Lazio, which skirts the river before crossing over it. The next 5km are through a natural park until you reach the suburb of Sassi where you turn left onto the Strada Comunale Superga.

- - - - - - - - - - - - - - - - - - - -

TRIP HIGHLIGHT

❼ Basilica di Superga

In 1706 Vittorio Amedeo II promised to build a basilica to honour the Virgin Mary if Turin was saved from besieging French and Spanish armies. The city was saved, so Duke Amadeo once again commissioned Juvarra to build the **Basilica di Superga** (www.basilicadisuperga.com; Strada della Basilica di Superga 75; adult/reduced €5/4; ⏱10am-1.30pm & 2.30-7pm Mar-Oct, to 6pm Nov-Feb, closed Wed year-round) on a hill across the Po river in 1717.

Magnificently sited as it is, with a crowning dome 65m high, it is visible for miles around and in due course it became the final resting place for 50 members of the Savoy family. Their lavish tombs make for interesting viewing. In their company, at the rear of the church, lies a tomb commemorating the Gran Torino football team, all of whom died in 1949 when their plane crashed into the basilica in thick fog.

The Drive ❱❱ To return to the city centre, descend down Strada Comunale Superga and take a left along Via Agudio for 3km. Cross the river right over Ponte Sassi onto Corso Belgio. Drive to the end of the road and turn right onto Corso Regina Margherita. At the roundabout take a left through the Royal Gardens to Piazza Castello.

Eating & Sleeping

Turin ❶

✖ Chiodi Latini   Vegetarian €

(☏011 026 00 53; www.chiodilatininewfood.
com; Via Bertola 20; lunch menu €12-18;
🕑8.45am-7.30pm Mon-Sat; 🛜 🍴) Chiodi Latini
serves elegantly prepared Slow Food fast. Amid
a sunny space with tall ceilings, upbeat jazz and
big windows facing onto a lively stretch of Via
Bertola, this inviting eatery serves excellent
creative vegetarian dishes that change daily:
think smoked lentil soup, flavour-packed grain
bowls and delectable Piemontese antipasti.

✖ Gaudenzio   Piedmontese €€

(☏011 860 02 42; www.gaudenziovinoecucina.
it; Via Gaudenzio Ferrari 2h; meals €30-55; 🕑7-
11pm Tue-Fri, noon-3pm & 7-11pm Sat, noon-3pm
Sun) Meet the gang who are intent on breaking
down Italy's beloved course structure. It's small
plates here – although there is a sliding scale of
small to large – and the innovative but sublimely
local dishes are some of the city's best. All wine
is natural and/or from small producers; in lieu of
a list, you and the sommelier will have a chat.

✖ Scannabue   Piedmontese €€

(☏011 669 66 93; www.scannabue.it; Largo
Saluzzo 25h; meals €30-42; 🕑12.30-2.30pm &
7.30-10.30pm) Scannabue, housed in a former
corner garage, is a retro-fitted bistro that has
a touch of Paris in its cast-iron doors and tiled
floors. There's a casual feel, but the cooking is
some of Turin's most lauded.

🛏 Via Stampatori   B&B €

(☏339 2581330; www.viastampatori.com;
Via Stampatori 4; d €110; 🛜 🌐) This utterly
lovely B&B occupies the top floor of a frescoed
Renaissance building, one of Turin's oldest. Its
bright, stylish and uniquely furnished rooms
overlook either a sunny terrace or a leafy inner
courtyard. The owner's personal collection
of 20th-century design is used throughout,
including in the two serene common areas. It's
central but blissfully quiet.

🛏 DuParc
Contemporary Suites   Design Hotel €€

(☏011 012 00 00; www.duparcsuites.com;
Corso Massimo d'Azeglio 21; r €95-175;
🅿 ❄ 🛜) A business-friendly location doesn't
mean this isn't a great choice for all travellers.
Staff are young, clued-up and friendly, and the
building's iconic modern lines are matched with
a fantastic contemporary art collection and
comfortable furnishings along with stunning
Italian lighting. Best of all, even the cheapest
rooms here are sumptuously large (50 sq m),
with king beds, huge baths and floor-to-ceiling
windows.

Rivoli ❺

✖ Combal Zero   Gastronomy €€€

(☏011 956 52 25; www.combal.org; Piazza
Mafalda di Savoia; meals €80-130, 8-course
tasting menu €180; 🕑8-10pm Tue-Sat) Davide
Scabin's tasting menus are theatrical, visual,
visceral and mischievous, but despite such
experimentation they are still deeply rooted in
Piemontese culinary traditions. The simple
modern space has glorious views across the
countryside as well as the surrounding Rivoli
castle.

Venaria Reale ❻

✖ Caffè degli Argenti   Cafe €

(www.lavenaria.it; Reggia di Venaria Reale, Piazza
della Repubblica 4; panini €4-8; 🕑10am-4.30pm
Tue-Fri, to 7.15pm Sat & Sun) Sip cups of molten
coffee in the glorious, gold-on-black Sala Cinese
of the Venaria Reale palace (p71). Also on order
are top-quality panini, pastries and gelato,
which can be enjoyed on the terrace overlooking
the Grand Parterre garden.

Gourmet Piedmont

Immersed in tradition as old as the towns that fostered it, Piedmont's cuisine is the toast of Italy. It is also home to the Slow Food movement, Alba truffles and big-hitting Barolo wines.

TRIP HIGHLIGHTS

0 km

Turin
Sample 'Sweet Moments in Turin' in Italy's chocolate capital

220 km

Asti
Raise a glass of Asti's signature fizz, Asti Spumante

1 START

7 FINISH

170 km

Alba
Sniff precious white truffles at Alba's truffle fair

● Bra

5

4

● Fossano

Barolo
Home town of the Ferrari of Italian red wines

● Cuneo

155 km

6 DAYS
220KM / 137 MILES

GREAT FOR...

BEST TIME TO GO

September to November for autumn food festivals.

ESSENTIAL PHOTO

Endless vistas of vines in Barolo or Barbaresco.

BEST FOR OENOPHILES

Sampling glasses of Barolo for only €3 at Castello Falletti.

dmont Shaved black truffle

75

4 Gourmet Piedmont

The hills, valleys and towns of Piedmont are northern Italy's specialist pantry, weighed down with sweet hazelnuts, rare white truffles, arborio rice and Nebbiolo grapes that metamorphose into Barolo and Barbaresco wines. Out here in the damp Po river basin they give out Michelin stars like overzealous schoolteachers give out house points, and with good reason. Trace a gourmet route, and counter the calorific overload with rural walks and bike rides.

TRIP HIGHLIGHT

❶ Turin

The innovative Torinese gave the world its first saleable hard chocolate, is home to one of its greatest mysteries (the Holy Shroud) and played a key role in the creation of the Italian state. You can follow the epic story in the **Museo Nazionale del Risorgimento Italiano** (☏011 562 11 47; www.museorisorgimentotorino. it; Via Accademia delle Scienze 5; adult/reduced €10/8; ◷10am-6pm Tue-Sun). Aside

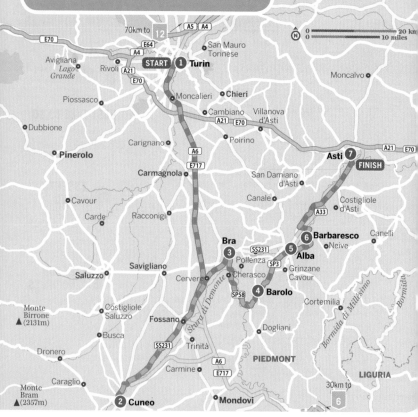

from the national narrative and the intriguing Shroud of Turin, which you can learn all about in **Museo della Sindone** (www.sindone.it; Via San Domenico 28; adult/reduced €8/6; ⊙9am-noon & 3-7pm), you've come to Turin for chocolate.

Planning your trip for November, when the **Cioccolatò** (www.ciocco lato.it) festival is in full swing, is a good start. Otherwise visit **Al Bicerin** (www.bicerin.it; Piazza della Consolata 5; ⊙8.30am-7.30pm Thu-Tue, closed Aug), named from *bicerin,* a caffeine-charged hot drink of chocolate, coffee and cream. Then there's **Guido Gobino** (☑011 566 07 07; www.guidogobino.it; Via Lagrange 1; ⊙3-8pm Mon, 10am-8pm Tue-Sun), one of Turin's favourite modern chocolatiers. Order a box of his tiny tile-like

LINK YOUR TRIP

Italian Riviera
From Bra continue south along the A6 to enjoy a tour of the olive groves and gardens along the Italian Riviera.

Valle d'Aosta
Cheese-lovers beware: the A5 from Turin takes you into the heart of the Valle d'Aosta, where days of hiking end with *fontina* fondues.

ganache chocolates or a bag of his classic *gianduiotto* (triangular chocolates made from *gianduja* – Turin's hazelnut paste). Beyond the chocolate, Turin is home to Slow Food's groundbreaking 'supermarket', **Eataly** (www.facebook.com/eatalytorino; Via Nizza 230; ⊙10am-10.30pm). Housed in a converted factory, it showcases a staggering array of sustainable food and beverages, and hosts regular tastings and cookery workshops.

✕ 🛏 p46, p73, p81, p89

The Drive ≫ Cuneo lies 100km south of Turin, virtually a straight shot down the A6 autostrada. Head out of Turin on Corso Unitá d'Italia and across the river Po. Then join the autostrada for 70km. Exit at Fossano and join the SS231 for the final 20km.

❷ Cuneo

A condensed version of Turin, Cuneo is a genteel

town with an impressive Renaissance square, the grand arcaded **Piazza Galimberti**, where market stalls set up every Tuesday. It's a good place for festivals, too, such as the **music festival** in June, the **Tour de France** in July and the impressive **Chestnut Fair** in October, which fills the town. The city's signature rum-filled chocolates, though, can be sampled year-round.

Cuneo also has some wonderfully dark and zealous churches. The oldest is the deconsecrated San Francisco convent and church, which today houses the **Museo Civico di Cuneo** (Via Santa María 10; adult/reduced €3/2; ⊙3.30-6.30pm Tue-Sun), tracking the history of the town and province.

✕ 🛏 p81, p89

The Drive ≫ The 44km journey to Bra retraces much of the previous drive along the SS231. Head back to Fossano, but instead of reconnecting with the A6, take the periphery north and continue northeast through Cervere, where the countryside opens out into green fields.

- - - - - - - - - - - - - - - - - -

❸ Bra

Up on the 1st floor of a recessed courtyard, the little **Osteria del Boccondivino** (📞0172 42 56 74; www.boccondivinoslow.it; Via Mendicità Istruita 14, Bra; meals €28-38, set menus €20-24; ⏰noon-2.30pm & 7-10pm Tue-Sat), lined with wine bottles, was the first restaurant to be opened by Slow Food in the 1980s. The food is predictably excellent, and the local Langhe menu changes daily. In the same courtyard you'll find the **Slow Food headquarters** (www.slowfood.it), which includes a small bookshop selling guides to all of Italy's Slow Food–accredited restaurants and heritage producers (see p77).

Just outside Bra, in the village of Pollenzo, 4km southeast, is the Slow Food **Università di Scienze Gastronomiche** (University of Gastronomic Sciences; www.unisg.it; Piazza Vittorio Emanuele 9). It offers three-year courses in gastronomy and food management. Next door is the **Banca del Vino** (📞0172 45 84 18; www.bancadelvino.it; Piazza Vittorio Emanuele II 13; ⏰10am-7pm Tue-Sat, to 1pm Sun), and a wine-cellar 'library' of Italian wines. Reserve

for guided tastings. Also nearby is the acclaimed **Guido Ristorante** (📞0173 62 61 62; www.guidoristorante. it; Via Alba 15, Serralunga d'Alba; tasting menus €75-100; ⏰7.30-10.30pm Tue-Sat, 12.30-2.30pm Sat & Sun, closed Jan & Aug) that people have been known to cross borders to visit, especially for the veal.

The Drive » From Bra to Barolo is a lovely 20km drive through the gentle Langhe hills. Head east along the SS231 for 3km before turning southeast onto the SP7, then the SP58. The latter passes through orchards and vineyards and offers up photogenic views of old stone farmhouses.

- - - - - - - - - - - - - - - - - -

TRIP HIGHLIGHT

❹ Barolo

Wine-lovers rejoice! This tiny 18-sq-km parcel of undulating land immediately southwest of Alba knocks out the Ferrari of Italian reds, Barolo. Many argue it is Italy's finest wine.

The eponymous village is dominated by the **Castello Falletti**, once owned by the powerful Falletti banking family. Today it houses the **Museo del Vino a Barolo** (www.wimubarolo.it; Castello Comunale Falletti di Barolo; adult/reduced €8/6;

Turin Sweets in a store

10.30am-7pm, closed Jan & Feb), where multimedia displays tell the story of wine through history, art, music, films and literature.

Tucked behind the castle, **Agrilab Wine Tasting Tour** (www.barolo winetastingtour.com; Piazza Falletti 2; tasting €1-4; 10am-6pm Tue-Fri, to 7pm Sat & Sun) lets you sample some 36 different wines (from €1 to €4 each), while listening to descriptions and historical tidbits about them.

🛏 p81

The Drive » The short 15km hop from Barolo to Alba is another pleasant drive through Barolo's vineyards as you head northeast along the SP3, which takes you all the way into the centre of Alba.

TRIP HIGHLIGHT

⑤ Alba

Alba's fertile hinterland, the vine-striped Langhe Hills, radiates out from the town, an undulating vegetable garden replete with grapes, hazelnut groves and vineyards. Exploring them on foot or with two wheels is a rare pleasure. Alba's **tourist office** (☎0173 35 8 33; www.langheroero.it; Piazza Risorgimento 2; 9am-6pm Mon-Fri, from 10am Sat & Sun) can organise an astounding number of Langhe/ Roero valley excursions, including a variety of cross-country walks through chestnut groves and vineyards, winery tours, cycling tours and truffle-hunting excursions (price depends on the group).

In October and November the town hosts its renowned **truffle fair** (every weekend), and the equally ecstatic *vendemia* (grape harvest).

🍴🛏 p81

The Drive » Barbaresco sits in the hills just 10km northeast

79

SNAILS, GLORIOUS SNAILS

Set within the Langhe's lush wine country, Cherasco, just south of Bra, is best known for *lumache* (snails). Snails in this neck of the woods are dished up *nudo* (shell-free). They can be pan-fried, roasted, dressed in an artichoke sauce or minced inside ravioli. Piedmontese specialities include *lumache al barbera* (snails simmered in Barbera wine and ground nuts) and *lumache alla Piemontese* (snails stewed with onions, nuts, anchovies and parsley in a tomato sauce).

Traditional trattorias serving such dishes include **Osteria della Rosa Rossa** (☎0172 48 81 33; Via San Pietro 31, Cherasco; meals €30-45; ☻12.30-2.30pm & 7.30-10pm Mon & Wed-Sat, 12.30-2.30pm Sun) in Alba.

of Alba. Exit Alba along Viale Cherasca and then pick up the narrow, winding SP3 as it loops through the pretty residential suburb of Altavilla and out into the countryside.

---

❻ Barbaresco

Only a few kilometres separate Barolo from Barbaresco, but a rainier microclimate and fewer ageing requirements have made the latter into a softer, more delicate red.

Sample it at the atmospheric **Enoteca Regionale del Barbaresco** (☎0173 63 52 51; www.enotecadelbarbaresco.it; Piazza del Municipio 7; ☻10am-7pm), housed inside a deconsecrated church. The *enoteca* (wine bar) also has information on walking trails in the vicinity.

If you haven't had your fill of wine yet, head a further 4km east to the pin-drop-quiet village of Neive, where you'll find the **Bottega dei Quattro Vini** (☎0173 67 71 95; www.bottegadei4vini.com; Piazza Italia 2; ☻10.30am-1.30pm & 3-8pm Fri-Tue). This two-room shop was set up by the local community to showcase the four 'DOC' wines (Dolcetto d'Alba, Barbaresco, Moscato and Barbera d'Alba) produced on Neive's hills.

The Drive ❯❯ The final 30km stretch to Asti leaves Barbaresco's vineyards behind on the SP3 and rejoins the A33 for an uninterrupted drive to Asti. Although it's a two-lane highway, it slices through more unspoilt farmland.

❼ Asti

Asti and Alba were fierce medieval rivals ruled over by feuding royal families, who built Asti's legendary 150 towers. Of these only 12 remain, and only the **Torre Troyana o Dell'Orologio** (☎0141 39 94 89; www.comune.asti.it; Piazza Medici; incl in Smarticket €10; ☻10am-1pm & 4-7pm Tue-Sun Apr-Sep) can be climbed (if you make a reservation). Asti's rivalry with Alba is still recalled in the annual **Palio d'Asti**, a bareback horse race on the third Sunday of September that commemorates a victorious battle.

The 10-day **Douja d'Or** (a *douja* being a terracotta wine jug unique to Asti), in the first or second week in September, is complemented by the **Delle Sagre** food festival on the second Sunday of September. Otherwise you can sample some fine regional fare and beautiful wines among the bottle-lined shelves of **Pompa Magna** (Via Aliberti 65; meals €20-30; ☻noon-2.30pm Tue-Sun, 6-10.30pm Thu-Sat).

Like Alba, the countryside around Asti contains precious black and white truffles. Asti's **truffle fair** is in November.

 p81

Eating & Sleeping

Turin ❶

✕ Perino Vesco — Bakery €

(☎011 068 60 56; www.perinovesco.it; Via Cavour 10; snacks from €5; ☺7.30am-7.30pm Mon-Sat) Cult Slow Food baker Andrea Perino turns out dense, fragrant *torta langarola* (hazelnut cake), naturally yeasted *panettone* and focaccia that draws sighs from homesick Ligurians. Join the queues for takeaway pizza and focaccia slices (grab a ticket upon entering) or head out the back and nab a seat for sandwiches, pizza slices, savoury tarts and coffee.

Cuneo ❷

✕ 4 Ciance — Piedmontese €€

(☎0171 48 90 27; www.4cianceristorante.it; Via Dronero 8c; meals €32-42, tasting menu €40; ☺12.30-2.30pm & 7.45-10pm Tue-Thu & Sat, 7.30-10.30pm Fri, 12.30-2.30pm Sun) A warm, unpretentious place where everything is made from scratch, including the bread. The chef's specialities showcase the Piedmont's quality produce in simple but elegant dishes like ravioli stuffed with borage and herbs with hazelnut butter, or lamb with broad beans and potatoes.

🛏 Hotel Ligure — Hotel €

(☎0171 63 45 45; www.ligurehotel.com; Via Savigliano 11; s/d/tr/q €65/80/110/130; P ✻ 🛜) In the heart of the old town, this two-star hotel is run by a charming, elegant family and has simple but spotless rooms and self-catering apartments for longer stays.

Barolo ❹

🛏 Hotel Barolo — Hotel €

(☎0173 5 63 54; www.hotelbarolo.it; Via Lomondo 2; s €80-100, d €120-200; P @ 🛜) Overlooked by the famous *enoteca*-castle, Hotel Barolo is an old-school place; sit back on the terrace with a glass of you-know-what, contemplating the 18th-century Piedmontese architecture that guards its shimmering swimming pool. Follow up with a meal at the in-house Brezza restaurant (it's been serving up truffles and the like for three generations, and making wine since 1885).

Alba ❺

✕ La Piola — Piedmontese €€

(☎0173 44 28 00; www.lapiola-alba.it; Piazza Risorgimento 4; meals €30-45; ☺12.15-2.30pm & 7.15-10pm Mon-Sat, closed Mon in summer) Part of the Ceretto family's small empire, La Piola offers a faithful menu of traditional Piedmontese dishes, but at the same time manages to be stylish, modern and relaxed (let's put it down to *sprezzatura* – the Italian art of studied nonchalance).The kitchen is overseen by one of Italy's most respected chefs, Enrico Crippa, from gastronomic Piazza Duomo upstairs.

🛏 Casa Dellatorre — B&B €€

(☎0173 44 12 04; Via Elvio Pertinace 20; d €130-170; ✻ 🛜) Three sisters run this central, upmarket B&B – which was once their family home – with love. Three classically decorated, antique-filled rooms share a flowery internal courtyard. Breakfast is served in the courtyard in summer, and in the sisters' pretty cafe in winter.

Asti ❼

✕ Osteria del Diavolo — Piedmontese €€

(☎0141 3 02 21; www.osteriadeldiavolo.it; Piazza San Martino 6; meals around €30; ☺7.30-10pm Mon-Fri, noon-2.30pm & 7.30-10pm Sat) For one of Asti's best dining experiences, book a table at this award-winning *osteria* that offers beautiful Piedmont and Ligurian dishes. *Cappon magro* (a stacked seafood and vegetable appetiser), braised beef cheek with Barbera wine and hearty seafood soup are among the standouts. You can dine outside on the small piazza on warm evenings.

Meandering the Maritime Alps

In the Susa valley and Maritime Alps you'll encounter a rich diversity of marmots, ibex and grouse. That's when you're not skiing the Via Lattea (Milky Way) or hiking old salt routes.

TRIP HIGHLIGHTS

38 km

Sacra di San Michele
Follow centuries of pilgrims up the 'Stairway of the Dead'

Susa

START

Avigliana

Cesana Torinese

Pinerolo

0 km

Turin
For forward-thinking design and Slow Food

30 km

Sestriere
Ski the Via Lattea from glamorous Sestriere

Saluzzo

77 km

Limone Piemonte
Gateway to the wild and wonderful Maritime Alps

Cuneo

FINISH

7 DAYS
277KM / 172 MILES

GREAT FOR...

BEST TIME TO GO

October to January for food fairs, hiking and skiing.

 ESSENTIAL PHOTO

The red-tiled rooftops of Saluzzo from the Torre Civica.

 BEST FOR SKIING

The 400 spotless kilometres of the Via Lattea.

mont Parco Naturale Alpi Marittime

Meandering the Maritime Alps

5

Shoehorned between the rice-growing plains of Piedmont and the sparkling coastline of Liguria lie the brooding Maritime Alps – a unique pocket of dramatically sculpted mountains that rise like a stony-faced border guard along the frontier of Italy and France. Traverse their valleys and peaks to gaze in mirror-like lakes, ski the spotless Via Lattea (Milky Way) and hike amid forests rich with chestnuts.

Parc National de la Vanoise

Col du Mt Cenis

Lac de Mont Cenis

FRANCE

Exilles · A32

Parco Regional du Gran Bosco di Salbertrand · E70 · Oulx · Sauze d'Oulx · SS24

Cesana Torinese · Milky Way · SS23 · ④ **Sestriere**

Claviere · Parco Regionale Val Troncea

Colle di Sestriere (2035m)

Parc Naturel Regional du Queyras

Mon (38

Monte Chersogno (3026m)

Tête de Siguret (3032m) · Col de Larche

Rocc la Me (2831

FRANCE

Mont Mounier (2817m)

TRIP HIGHLIGHT

❶ Turin

In 2008 Turin (Torino) held the title of European Capital of Design, and no wonder; the city's architecture mirrors its trajectory from the baroque elegance of the **Palazzo Reale** (www.museireali.beniculturali.it; Piazza Castello; adult/reduced €12/2, 1st Sun of month Oct-Mar free; ⊙9am-7pm Tue-Sun), seat of the monarchic House of Savoy, to the futuristic steel-and-glass **Mole Antonelliana**, symbol of the city's industrial rebirth and now the repository for the **Museo Nazionale del Cinema** (☎011 813 85 63; www.museocinema.

it; Via Montebello 20; adult/reduced €11/9, incl lift €15/12; ⊙9am-8pm Sun, Mon & Wed-Fri, to 11pm Sat). Take the lift to the roof terrace for 360-degree views.

From the Mole you may just be able to spy **Lingotto** (Via Nizza 294; MLingotto), Turin's former Fiat factory, redesigned by Renzo Piano into an exhibition centre. It also houses the 'treasure chest' rooftop gallery **Pinacoteca Giovanni e Marella Agnelli** (Lingotto; www.pinacoteca-agnelli.it; Via Nizza 230; adult/reduced €10/8; ⊙10am-7pm Tue-Sun; MLingotto), with masterpieces by Canaletto, Manet, Matisse and Picasso. Equally dazzling are the stalls in the famous Slow Food super-market,

Eataly (www.facebook.com/
eatalytorino; Via Nizza 230;
⏱10am-10.30pm) next door.

🛏 p46, p73, p81, p89

The Drive » Leave Turin
westwards along Corso Vittorio
Emanuele II following signs for
the A32/E70 to Bardonecchia/
Fréjus. Join the autostrada
for 11km and then take exit 2,
Avigliana Est. Follow the road
for 4km. At the roundabout turn
right up the Via Sacra (SP188)
to San Michele.

- - - - - - - - - - - - - - - - -

TRIP HIGHLIGHT

② Sacra di San Michele

Brooding above the A32,
once a key stretch of the
Via Francigena pilgrim
path from Canterbury
through Rome to Monte
Sant'Angelo in Puglia,
is the **Sacra di San
Michele** (www.sacradisan
michele.com; Via alla Sacra
14, Avigliana; adult/reduced
€8/6; ⏱9.30am-12.30pm

**LINK
YOUR
TRIP**

3 Savoy Palace Circuit

For more bombastic
Savoy palaces and castles,
continue from Rivoli on a
circuit around Turin on the
Tangenziale.

6 Italian Riviera

From Cuneo cut
across eastwards along the
A33 and then down the A6
to Savona for a cruise along
the Italian Riviera.

85

& 2.30-6pm, to 5pm mid-Oct–mid Mar). This Gothic-Romanesque abbey has kept sentry atop Monte Pirchiriano (962m) since the 10th century and exerted enormous power over abbeys throughout Italy, France and Spain, including Mont St Michel in France. It looks familiar, because Umberto Eco used it as the basis for the abbey in *The Name of the Rose*.

Approach as pilgrims would up the **Scalone dei Morti** (Stairway of the Dead), flanked by arches that would once have held the skeletons of dead monks. At the top enter through the whimsical, 12th-century Zodiac Door. Within the walls, the complex houses a frescoed church and the remnants of the monastery, crowned by the **Torre della Bell'Alda** (Tower of Beautiful Alda).

More beautiful though are the views down the Susa valley.

The Drive » Return to the A32 down the Via Sacra (SP188) for the 40km drive to Susa. Although you're on the autostrada the entire way, the journey passes through dense forests with snow-capped peaks slowly rising ahead of you. Just after Bussoleno, exit for Susa Est.

---

❸ Susa

The Romans marched up the **Val di Susa** and crossed the Alps to secure a passage to the French ports of Nice and Marseille. They enjoyed the thermal baths in Belvédère across the border in France, and grabbed Susa from the Gauls, thus securing the high passes of the Cottian Alps. You'll find evidence of them all over town, including the remnants of an **aqueduct**, a still-used **amphitheatre** and the triumphal **Arco d'Augusto**, dating from 9 BC.

Susa stands at the gateway to the Val di Susa, cut through by the Dora di Bardonecchia river and littered with stone towns such as Ex-illes, with its forbidding **Forte di Exilles**, said to be the keep of the Man in the Iron Mask between 1681 and 1687.

🛏 p89

The Drive » The 46km from Susa to Sestriere is a scenic mountain drive. Rejoin the A32, heading for Fréjus, for 20km (you'll pass the exit for Exilles after 12km). Exit at Oulx Est onto the SS24 and follow the gushing torrent of Dora-Riparia to Cesana Torinese (alternatively you can head uphill and base yourself in Sauze d'Oulx). When the road forks, veer left onto the SS23 for the final winding ascent to Sestriere.

DETOUR: RIVOLI

Start: ❶ Turin

Works by Franz Ackermann, Gilbert and George, and Frank Gehry now sit amid the splendour of **Castello di Rivoli**, once the home of Savoy princes and now the venue for the **Museo d'Arte Contemporanea** (📞011 956 52 22; www.castellodirivoli.org; Piazza Mafalda di Savoia; adult/reduced €8.50/6.50, Villa Cerruti incl shuttle & tour adult/reduced €26.50/19.50; ⏱10am-5pm Tue-Fri, to 7pm Sat & Sun). The startling contrasts between the historic house and the avant-garde art are worth the trip.

You can mix contemporary art with contemporary food at Combal Zero (p73).

TRIP HIGHLIGHT

❹ Sestriere

Developed in the 1930s by the Agnelli clan of Fiat, Sestriere ranks among Europe's most glamorous ski resorts due to its enviable location in the eastern realms of the **Via Lattea** (www.vialattea.it) ski area. This picturesque region nestled among mountain slopes incorporates some 400km of piste and seven interlinked ski resorts: Sestriere (2035m), Sauze d'Oulx (1509m), Sansi-

ARGALIS/GETTY IMAGES ©

Susa Arco d'Augusto

cario (1700m), Cesana Torinese (1350m), Pragelato (1524m) and Claviere (1760m) in Italy; and Montgenèvre (1850m) in neighbouring France.

Outside of ski season the **tourist office** (📞0122 75 54 44; www.turismo torino.org; Via Pinerolo/SS23; ⏰9am-1pm & 2-6pm) has information on every conceivable summer activity, including golfing on Europe's highest golf course, walking, free climbing and mountain biking.

 p89

The Drive » The longest journey on this tour is the 86km

out of the mountains to Saluzzo. Continue on the winding SS23 through mountain towns for 33km and descend southeast to Pinerolo. Then take the ramp to the SS589 (towards Cuneo), which brings you to Saluzzo after 29km.

- - - - - - - - - - - - - - - - -

5 Saluzzo

Situated at the foot of Monte Viso, Saluzzo was once a powerful marquisate that lasted four centuries until the Savoys won it in a 1601 treaty with France. Its historic significance – although diminished – has left a stirring legacy in its old centre.

The imposing castle, otherwise known as the **Castiglia di Saluzzo** (Castello dei Marchesi; Piazza Castello; adult/reduced €7/3.50; ⏰10am-1pm & 2-6pm Thu-Mon Mar-Oct, open Sun only Nov & Dec), overlooks the cobbled alleys and Gothic and Renaissance mansions of the old town, which cluster around the **Salita al Castello**, literally 'the ascent to the castle'. Nearby are the town hall and the **Torre Civica** (Via San Giovanni; adult/reduced €3/1.50; ⏰10.30am-12.30pm Fri, 10.30am-12.30pm & 3-6.30pm Sat & Sun), which you can climb for views

MARGUAREIS CIRCUIT

The Marguareis Circuit is a 35km, two-day hike that starts in Limone Piemonte and tracks up across the mountain passes and ridges to the **Rifugio Garelli** (📞0171 73 80 78; www.rifugiogarelli.com; dm €26, with half-board €49; ☺mid-Jun–mid-Sep). The peaks of the Argentera and Cime du Gélas massifs are clearly visible from the summit of **Punta Marguareis** (2651m), the highest point in the park. On day two, 4km of the trek passes through a mountainous nodule of France before swinging back round into Italy.

over the burnt-red-tiled rooftops.

 p89

The Drive » It's a scenic 54km drive from Saluzzo to Cuneo, first on the SP161 and then on the SP25 after Villafalletto. Dropping from mountains into low-lying plains and up again, the road passes through vineyards and orchards and across mountain torrents.

❻ Cuneo

Sitting on a promontory between the Gesso and Stura di Demonte rivers, Cuneo enjoys excellent Alpine views framed by the high pyramid-shaped peak of Monte Viso (3841m). To the southwest lie the Maritime Alps, a rugged outdoor-adventure playground. After a hard day out

hiking, you'll be thankful for the heart-warming buzz of a *cuneesi al rhum* – a large, rum-laced praline, which you can lay your hands on at 1920s-vintage chocolatier **Arione** (www.arionecuneo.it; Piazza Galimberti 14; cake €2-5; ☺8am-8pm Tue-Sat, 8am-1pm & 3.30-8pm Sun), located in magnificent **Piazza Galimberti**.

Cuneo also has some wonderful churches. The oldest is the deconsecrated San Francisco convent and church, which today houses the **Museo Civico di Cuneo** (Via Santa María 10; adult/reduced €3/2; ☺3.30-6.30pm Tue-Sun), tracking the history of the town and province.

✖ 🛏 p81, p89

The Drive » The final 28km to Limone Piemonte provide

another picturesque mountain road. Leave Cuneo heading southwest on the SS20 to Borgo San Dalmazzo, where you veer left (keeping on the SS20) across the Torrente Gesso and up into the mountains.

TRIP HIGHLIGHT

❼ Limone Piemonte

To the southwest of Cuneo lies the **Parco Naturale Alpi Marittime** (www.parcoalpimarittime.it). Despite their diminutive size, there's a palpable wilderness feel to be found among these Maritime peaks. The park is a walker's paradise, home to ibex, chamois and whistling marmots, which scurry around rocky crags covered in mist above a well-marked network of mountain trails, some of them old salt routes, others supply lines left over from two world wars.

The best-equipped town for access to the park is picturesque **Limone Piemonte** (www.limonepiemonte.it). One of the oldest Alpine ski stations, Limone has been in operation since 1907 and maintains 15 lifts and 80km of runs.

🛏 p89

Eating & Sleeping

Turin ❶

🛏 NH Collection
Torino Piazza Carlina   Design Hotel €€€

(☎011 860 16 11; www.nh-hotels.com; Piazza
Carlo Emanuele II; d €180-250; P ❄ 🛜)
Overlooking one of Turin's most beautiful
squares, this sprawling property occupies a
17th-century building, once the Albergo di Virtù,
a Savoy charitable institution (and home to the
famous political theorist Antonio Gramsci). The
decor is cutting edge, highly atmospheric and
deeply luxurious. There's a great downstairs
bar and guests have access to rooftop terraces
and a gym.

Susa ❸

🛏 Hotel Susa Stazione   Hotel €

(☎0122 62 22 26; www.hotelsusa.it; Corso Stati
Uniti 4/6; s/d €70/90; P 🛜) A handy all-round
base for the area and located directly opposite
Susa's train station, this cycle-friendly hotel has
12 pleasantly old-school rooms. Staff hand out
maps and itinerary proposals. Free ski shuttle
bus stop outside the door.

Cesana Torinese ❸

🛏 Casa Cesana   Hotel €€

(☎0122 8 94 62; www.hotelcasacesana.com;
Viale Bouvier, Cesana Torinese; s/d €60/120;
P ❄) Right across from Cesana Torinese's
ski lift, this timber chalet was built for the 2006
Olympics. Its rooms are light-filled and spotless,
there's a bustling restaurant open to non-
guests (meals around €25) and its bar is one of
the area's liveliest.

Sestriere ❹

✗ Pinky   Pizza €

(☎0122 43 21 47; Piazza Fraiteve 5n; pizzas
€6-10; ⊙ noon-1am) The perennially popular

pizzeria Pinky is a skiers' favourite, not to
mention a post-bar pit stop. During the season,
it also has live music.

Saluzzo ❺

✗ Le Quattro Stagioni   Piedmontese €

(☎0175 4 74 70; www.ristorantele4stagioni.
com; Via Volta 21; pizzas €8-11; ⊙ noon-2.30pm
& 7-11pm; 🍴) One of Saluzzo's iconic gathering
spots, Le Quattro Stagioni has a cavernous but
warmly lit dining room with vaulted ceilings, and
fresh flowers on the tables. A range of classic
Piedmontese dishes are on offer, but most
people are here for the outstanding pizzas –
fired up in a wood-burning oven, with gluten-free
and vegan options available.

Cuneo ❻

✗ Osteria
della Chiocciola   Gastronomy €€

(☎0171 6 62 77; www.osteriadellachiocciola.
it; Via Fossano 1; meals €30-35, degustation
€38; ⊙ restaurant 12.30-2pm & 7.30-10pm
Mon-Sat, enoteca 10am-3.30pm Mon-Sat) Slow
Food–affiliated Chiocciola's upstairs dining
room is the colour of buttercups and makes for
a soothing setting to linger over expertly crafted
local, seasonal dishes. Its weekday lunch menu
(meals €15 to €25) is a fabulous deal, or if on
the fly, you can stop by for a glass of wine with
cheese in the ground-floor *enoteca*.

Limone Piemonte ❼

🛏 Borgo Fantino   Apartment €

(☎0171 92 66 69; www.borgofantino.it; Corso
Nizza 54; 4-person apt €130-180; P 🛜) These
modern apartments in a low-slung structure
of wood and stone are both stylish and
comfortingly rustic. There's a communal games
room, a spa and a shuttle service to town and
the lifts. Apartments sleep up to four people.

Italian Riviera

Curving west in a broad arc, backed by the Maritime Alps, the Italian Riviera sweeps down from Genoa through ancient hamlets and terraced olive groves to the French border at Ventimiglia.

6

07 km

Alassio
The preferred holiday spot of presidents and artists

0 km

Genoa
For big-city grit and glamour

● Savona

● Cervo

Taggia

entimiglia
FINISH

San Remo
Italy's wannabe Monte Carlo

165 km

Finale Ligure
Provides a sandy shore nestled between two rivers

74 km

---

4 DAYS
214KM / 133 MILES

GREAT FOR...

BEST TIME TO GO
April, May and June for flowers and hiking; October for harvest.

ESSENTIAL PHOTO
Cascading terraces of exotic flowers at Giardini Botanici Hanbury.

BEST FINE DINING
Purple San Remo prawns on the terrace of San Giorgio.

6 Italian Riviera

The contrast between sun-washed, sophisticated coastal towns and a deeply rural, mountainous hinterland, full of heritage farms, olive oil producers and wineries, gave rise to the Riviera's 19th-century fame, when European expatriates outnumbered locals. They amused themselves in lavish botanical gardens, gambled in the casino of San Remo and dined in style in fine art-nouveau villas, much as you will on this tour.

TRIP HIGHLIGHT

❶ Genoa

Like Dr Jekyll and Mr Hyde, Genoa is a city with a split personality. At its centre, medieval *caruggi* (narrow streets) untangle outwards to the **Porto Antico** and teem with hawkers, merchants and office workers. Along Via Garibaldi and Via XXV Aprile is another Genoa, one of Unesco-sponsored palaces, smart shops and grand architectural gestures like **Piazza de Ferrari** with its monumental fountain, art nouveau **Palazzo Borsa** (once the city's stock exchange) and the neoclassical **Teatro Carlo Felice** (010 538 13 14; www.carlofelice.it; Passo Eugenio Montale 4).

Join the well-dressed *haute bourgeoisie* enjoying high-profile art exhibits in the grand Mannerist halls of the **Palazzo Ducale** (www. palazzoducale.genova.it; Piazza Giacomo Matteotti 9; price varies by exhibition; hours vary), then retire to sip a spritz amid 17th-century frescoes at **Les Rouges**

(329 3490644; 1st fl, Piazza Campetto 8a; 6-11.45pm Sun-Thu, to 12.45am Fri & Sat).

 p46, p97

The Drive ›› Exit Genoa westward, through a tangle of flyovers and tunnels, to access the A10 for the 56km drive to Savona. Once out of the suburbs the forested slopes of the Maritime Alps rise to your right and sea views peep out from the left as you duck through tunnels.

------

❷ Savona

Don't be put off by Savona's horrifying industrial sprawl; the Savonesi were a powerful maritime people and the town centre is unexpectedly graceful. Standing near the port are three of the many medieval towers that once studded the cityscape. Genoa's greatest rival, the town was savagely sacked in 1528, the castle dismantled and most of the population slaughtered, but somehow the **Fortezza del Priamàr** (Corso Mazzini 1; 9am-6.30pm mid-Sep–mid-Jun, to midnight mid-Jun–mid-Sep) and the **Cattedrale di Nostra Signora Assunta** (Piazza del Duomo; 7.30am-7.30pm) survived.

But you're not here for the architecture – you're here for the food. The covered **market** (Via Pietro Giuria; 7am-1.30pm Mon-Sat) is crammed with fruit-and-veg stalls and fish stands stacked with salt cod. **Grigiomar** (Via Pietro Giuria 42r; 8am-1pm Mon-Sat) salts its own local anchovies. Then there are the local specialities like the addictive *farinata di grano* (wheat-flour flat bread) at **Vino e Farinata** (Via Pia 15; meals €18-28; noon-2pm & 6-10pm Tue-Sat).

The Drive ›› Rejoin the A10 and leave the industrial chimneys of Savona behind you. For the first 13km the A10 continues with views of the sea, then at Spotorno it ducks inland for the final 15km to the Finale Ligure exit. Descend steeply for 3km to the Finale hamlets on the coast.

❽ LINK YOUR TRIP

4 Gourmet Piedmont
Up the A6 from food-town Savona is Slow Food HQ Bra and the start of a gourmet tour of the Langhe.

5 Meandering the Maritime Alps
From Ventimiglia slice through France on the D6204 to Limone Piemonte to start an adventure in the Maritime Alps.

TRIP HIGHLIGHT

❸ Finale Ligure

Finale Ligure comprises several seaside districts. The marina is narrow and charming, spreading along the sandy shore between two small rivers, the Porra and the Sciusa. A good place to pick up some picnic fare is **Salumeria Chiesa** (☏019 69 25 16; Via Pertica 15; small plates from €6; ⏰11am-2.30pm & 6-8.30pm May-Oct, closed Sun Nov-Apr), a delicatessen with a huge array of seafood salads, salamis, cheeses and gnocchi with pesto, of course.

Around 1.5km north of the seaside, **Finalborgo** is the old medieval centre. Its cobblestone streets are ripe for exploring, and you can stop for a meal or a pick-me-up at one of many charming restaurants with outdoor tables on the pavement.

Each year in March, Finalborgo's cloisters are home to the **Salone dell'Agroalimentare Ligure**, where local farmers hawk seasonal delicacies and vintages.

On Thursday it's worth driving 9km up the coast to picturesque **Noli** for the weekly outdoor market on Corso d'Italia.

✕ ⊨ p97

The Drive » Once again take the high road away from the coast and follow the A10 for a further 35km to Alassio. Near Albenga you'll cross the river Centa and the broad valley where dozens of hothouses dot the landscape.

TRIP HIGHLIGHT

❹ Alassio

Less than 100km from the French border, Alassio's popularity among the 18th- and 19th-century jet set has left it with an elegant colonial character. Its pastel-hued villas range around a broad, sandy beach, which stretches all the way to **Laigueglia** (4km to the south). American president Thomas Jefferson holidayed here in 1787 and Edward Elgar composed *In the South* inspired by his stay in 1904. **Il Muretto**, a ceramic-covered wall, records the names of 550 celebrities who've passed through.

Follow the local lead and promenade along Via XX Settembre or the unspoilt waterfront. Take coffee at **Antico Caffè Pasticceria Balzola** (www.balzola1902.com; Piazza Matteotti 26; pastries from

SAN GIORGIO

Cult restaurant **San Giorgio** (☏0183 40 01 75; Via A Volta 19, Cervo; meals €45-65; ⏰12.30-2pm & 7.30-10pm Wed-Mon, closed Jan) has been quietly wowing gourmets with its authentic Ligurian cooking since the 1950s when mother-and-son team Caterina and Alessandro opened the doors of their home in the *borgo* (medieval hamlet) of **Cervo Alta**. Dine out on the bougainvillea-draped terrace in summer, or in intimate dining rooms cluttered with family silverware and antiques in winter. Below the restaurant, in an old oil mill, is the less formal wine bar and deli **San Giorgino**.

Alassio Waterfront

€1.50; ✆9am-10pm Tue-Sun) and enjoy gelato on the beach beneath a stripy umbrella.

🛏 p97

The Drive » If you have time take the scenic coast road, SS1 (Via Roma), from Alassio through Laigueglia and Marina di Andora to Imperia. It is a shorter and more scenic jaunt when traffic is light. The alternative, when traffic is heavy, is to head back to the A10.

- - - - - - - - - - - - - - -

⑤ Imperia

Imperia consists of two small seaside towns, Oneglia and Porto Maurizio, on either side of the Impero river.

Oneglia, birthplace of Admiral Doria, the Genoese Republic's greatest naval hero, is the less attractive of the two, although **Piazza Dante**, with its arcaded walkways, is a pleasant place to grab a coffee. This is also where the great olive oil dynasties made their name. Visit the **Museo dell'Olivo** (www.museodellolivo.com; Via Garessio 13; adult/reduced €5/2.50; ✆9am-12.30pm & 3-6.30pm Mon-Sat), housed in a lovely art-nouveau mansion belonging to the heritage Fratelli Carli factory. The museum is surprisingly

extensive and details the history of the Italian Riviera industry from the 2nd century BC. Buy quality oil here or anywhere in town.

West of Oneglia is pirate haven **Porto Maurizio**, perched on a rocky spur that overlooks a yacht-filled harbour.

The Drive » Rejoining the A10 at Imperia, the landscape begins to change. The olive terraces are dense, spear-like cypresses and umbrella pines shade the hillsides, and the fragrant maquis (Mediterranean scrub) is prolific. Loop inland around Taggia and then descend slowly into San Remo.

6 San Remo

San Remo, Italy's wannabe Monte Carlo, is a sun-dappled Mediterranean resort with a grand belle-époque **casino** (www.casinosanremo.it; Corso degli Inglesi; ⊙10am-2.30am Sun-Thu, to 3.30am Fri & Sat) and lashings of Riviera-style grandeur.

During the mid-19th century the city became a magnet for European exiles such as Czar Nicolas of Russia, who favoured the town's balmy winters. They built an onion-domed **Russian Orthodox church** (Via Nuvoloni 2; admission €1; ⊙10am-12.30pm & 3-6pm) reminiscent of Moscow's St Basil's Cathedral, which still turns heads down by the seafront. Swedish inven-

tor Alfred Nobel also maintained a villa here, the **Villa Nobel** (Corso Felice Cavallotti 112), which now houses a museum dedicated to him.

Beyond the waterfront, San Remo hides a little-visited old town, a labyrinth of twisting lanes that cascade down the Italian Riviera hillside. Curling around the base is the **Italian Cycling Riviera**, a path that tracks the coast as far as Imperia. For bike hire, enquire at the **tourist office** (www.visitriviera.info; Corso Giuseppe Garibaldi; ⊙9.30am-1pm daily & 3-6.30pm Tue & Thu-Sat).

 p97

The Drive ⟫ For the final 17km stretch to Ventimiglia take the SS1 coastal road, which hugs the base of the mountains and offers uninterrupted sea views. In summer and at Easter,

however, when traffic is heavy, your best bet is the A10.

7 Ventimiglia

Despite its enviable position between the glitter of San Remo and the Côte d'Azur, Ventimiglia is a soulful but disorderly border town, its Roman past still evident in its bridges, amphitheatre and ruined baths. Now it's the huge **Friday market** (Lungo Roja Rossi; ⊙8am-3pm Fri) that draws the crowds.

If you can't find a souvenir here then consider one of the prized artisanal honeys produced by **Marco Ballestra** (☎333 7337412; Lungo Roja Rossi 5; ⊙9am-12.30pm & 3.30-7pm Tue-Sat), which has hives in the hills above the Valle Roya. There are over a dozen different types.

To end the tour head over to the pretty western suburb of Ponte San Ludovico to the **Giardini Botanici Hanbury** (www.giardinihanbury.com; Corso Montecarlo 43, La Mortola; adult/reduced €9/7.50; ⊙9.30am-6pm mid-Sep–mid-Jun, to 7pm mid-Jun–mid-Sep), the 18-hectare estate of English businessman Sir Thomas Hanbury; he planted it with an extravagant 5800 botanical species from five continents.

 p97

DETOUR: L'ENTROTERRA

Start: 7 Ventimiglia

The designation 'Riviera' omits the pleated, mountainous interior – *l'entroterra* – that makes up nine-tenths of the Italian Riviera. Harried by invasions, coast-dwellers took to these vertical landscapes over 1000 years ago, hewing their perched villages from the rock face of the Maritime Alps. You'll want to set aside two extra days to drive the coiling roads that rise up from Ventimiglia to Dolceacqua, Apricale and Pigna. If you do make the effort, book into gorgeous boutique hotel **Apricus Locanda** (☎339 6008622; www.apricuslocanda.com; Via IV Novembre 5, Apricale; d from €115; **P ⊠**); it's worth it for the breakfast and see-forever panoramas.

Eating & Sleeping

Genoa ❶

✖ Il Marin   Seafood €€€
(Eataly Genova; ✆010 869 87 22; www.eataly.
net; Porto Antico; meals €50-60, eight-course
menu €75; ⏱ noon-3pm & 7-10.30pm Wed-Mon)
Eating by the water often means a compromise
in quality, but Eataly's 3rd-floor fine-dining
space delivers both panoramic port views
and Genoa's most innovative seafood menu.
Rustic wooden tables, Renzo Piano–blessed
furniture and an open kitchen make for an easy,
relaxed glamour, while dishes use unusual
Mediterranean-sourced produce and look
gorgeous on the plate. Book ahead.

🛏 Palazzo Grillo   Design Hotel €€
(✆010 247 73 56; www.hotelpalazzogrillo.it;
Piazza delle Vigne 4; d €160-300; ❄ 🗺) In a
once derelict *palazzo*, Genovese locals Matteo
and Laura have created the extraordinary place
to stay that Genoa has been crying out for.
Stunning public spaces are dotted with spot-on
contemporary design pieces, character-filled
vintage finds and – look in any direction – original
15th-century frescoes. Rooms are simple but
superstylish with Vitra TVs and high ceilings.

Finale Ligure ❸

✖ Osteria ai Cuattru Canti   Osteria €€
(✆019 68 05 40; Via Torcelli 22; meals €25-35;
⏱ noon-2pm & 7.30-10pm Tue-Sun) Simple and
good Ligurian specialities are cooked up at this
rustic place in Finalborgo's historic centre.

🛏 Valleponci   Agriturismo €
(✆329 3154169; www.valleponci.it; Val Ponci 22,
Localita Verzi; d €80-100, apt €165) Only 4km
from the beach, Val Ponci feels deliciously wild,
tucked away in a rugged Ligurian valley. Horses
graze, grapevines bud and the restaurant turns
out fresh Ligurian dishes, with vegetables
and herbs from a kitchen garden. On weekend
evenings and Sunday lunch, there's live music
or classic vinyl. Rooms are simple but show the
keen eye of the Milanese escapee owners.

Alassio ❹

🛏 Villa della
Pergola   Boutique Hotel €€€
(✆0182 64 61 30; www.villadellapergola.com;
Via Privata Montagu 9/1, Alassio; d from €490;
P ❄ 🗺 ⛵) Sitting in a tropical garden that
rivals more famous Riviera gardens, with wow
sea views, this luxury hotel was one of the
homes of eminent Victorian, General McMurdo.
Built in 1875, the villa is in the then vogue
Anglo–Indian style with large airy rooms, broad
verandas and cascading terraces. Some suites
are furnished accordingly, while others take
more contemporary cues.

San Remo ❻

✖ A Cuvèa   Italian €
(Corso Giuseppe Garibaldi 110; meals €15-30;
⏱ noon-2.45pm & 7.15-9.45pm) This cosy,
warmly lit place lined with wine bottles
overflows with locals tucking into homemade
traditional dishes such as *tagliolini* with seafood
or *zimino di seppie* (cuttlefish stew); it also has
the most genial host in town. The set menus
(three courses with water, wine and coffee for
€25) are a fabulous deal, available at lunch and
dinner.

Ventimiglia ❼

✖ Pasta & Basta   Ligurian €€
(✆0184 23 08 78; www.pastaebastaventimiglia.
com; Via Marconi 20; meals €25-40; ⏱ noon-
3pm & 7.30-10pm Tue-Sun) Near the seafront
on the border side of town (overlooking the
new marina) you'll find elegant Pasta & Basta.
Various house-made fresh pasta can be mixed
and matched with a large menu of sauces,
including a good pesto or *salsa di noci* (walnut
purée), and washed down with a carafe of pale
and refreshing Pigato, a local white.

Cinematic Cinque Terre

From the Portofino peninsula, via the Cinque Terre's cliff-side villages to Portovenere, this trip exudes Riviera glamour. But amid billionaire motor yachts you'll find a hard-working community.

7

TRIP HIGHLIGHTS

0 km

Camogli
Painted villas perch above a bay of bobbing boats

Santa Margherita Ligure
1
ART
2
Chiavari

4

45 km

Sestri Levante
Retro Sestri has a broad bay and family-friendly facilities

5 **La Spezia**

Lerici
FINISH

Portofino
Possibly the world's most famous fishing village

15 km

Parco Nazionale delle Cinque Terre
Hike a unique, Unesco-listed coastline

97 km

5–7 DAYS
173KM / 107 MILES

GREAT FOR...

BEST TIME TO GO

Balmy days in April and October are perfect for hiking and swimming.

ESSENTIAL PHOTO

Views over pastel-coloured Camogli from San Rocco.

BEST FOR HIKING

Any one of the Cinque Terre's sanctuary walks.

7 Cinematic Cinque Terre

Challenged by a landscape of soaring mountains, Ligurian farmers have been reclaiming the Levante's wild slopes with neatly banded stone terraces for over 2000 years. The work that went into them took centuries and is comparable, it is said, to the building of the Great Wall of China. Planted with olives, grapes, basil and garlic, they snake from sea level to crest gravity-defying precipices and are now protected as a Unesco World Heritage Site.

TRIP HIGHLIGHT

❶ Camogli

Still an authentic fishing village with tall, *trompe l'œil* painted villas and a broad curving beach, Camogli's name is said to derive from *case delle mogli* (the wives' houses) for the women left behind by their fisherfolk husbands. In the 19th century it had the largest merchant fleet in the Mediterranean, but now it's a charming holiday spot for weekending Milanese who shop for

supplies in the Wednesday **mercato** (Via XX Settembre; ⊙8am-1pm).

Fishing traditions also continue here, such as the *tonnara di Punta Chiappa,* a large, complex fishing net between Camogli and San Fruttuoso, which is used for the trapping of tuna between April and September. It's been here since the 1600s and during the season it's pulled up by hand once or twice a day. Boats leave from Via Garibaldi to the **Punta Chiappa** where you can swim and sunbathe in summer. In

5km to
26
A15
● Pontremoli
TUSCANY

A15

A15

A12

ezia
A15
SS1
SP331

SS530
Lerici ⑦
6
FINISH
Tellaro
venere
Isola
Palmaria
Parco di
Montemarcello-
Magra
Isola del
Tino

May the village celebrates the **Sagra del Pesce** (Fish Festival) with a huge fry-up when hundreds of fish are cooked in 3m-wide pans along the busy waterfront.

For the best views in town, take a short drive up to **San Rocco di Camogli**, a small hamlet wrapped in olive groves with panoramic views. Trailheads crossing **Monte di Portofino** start here.

 p106

The Drive » Climb out of Camogli and pick up the SS1 in the direction of Santa Margherita Ligure. The cypress-lined road sweeps around the headland past gloriously grand villas. Just past San Lorenzo della Costa, exit right and descend steeply into Santa Margherita. When you hit the waterfront turn right on Corso Marconi (SP227), past Villa Durazzo, and follow the waterfront 5km to Portofino.

- - - - - - - - - - - - - - -

TRIP HIGHLIGHT

❷ Portofino

With its striking setting and pastel-hued villas framed by the dense

pine-covered slopes of the peninsula, Portofino ranks among the world's most famous fishing villages. A favourite destination of billionaires and celebrities, it has long been exclusive and expensive. In the late 16th century, aristocratic traveller Giambattista Confalonieri complained, 'You were charged not only for the room, but for the very air you breathed'.

Surprisingly, though, the best experience in Portofino is free: a hike along one of the 80km of trails that criss-cross the natural park (www.parco portofino.it). Enquire at the tourist office for maps. You can walk the full 18km from Portofino to Camogli, via San Fruttuoso. Otherwise take the Salita San Giorgio stairs from the harbour, past the **Chiesa di San Giorgio**, to Portofino's unusual **Castello Brown** (www.castellobrown.com; Via alla Penisola 13a; admission €5; ⊙10am-7pm daily summer, to 5pm Sat & Sun winter).

⑤ LINK YOUR TRIP

8 **Northern Cities**
Swap the coastal scenery for the cultural cities of the Po plain by driving north to Milan (Milano) on the A7.

26 **Foodie Emilia-Romagna**
From Lerici, head up the A15 to Parma to sample the gourmet hams, cheese and pasta of Emilia-Romagna.

In 1867 it became the private home of British diplomat Montague Yeats Brown, who no doubt derived endless pleasure from the spectacular views from its garden.

✗ ⊨ p106

The Drive » This short 9km seafront drive is fantastically scenic. Taking the only road out of town (SP227), follow its path back to Santa Margherita, where you can take a quick stroll in the gorgeous gardens of Villa Durazzo. The rest of the journey wends its way through Santa Margherita, which merges almost seamlessly with Rapallo.

❸ Rapallo

WB Yeats, Max Beerbohm and Ezra Pound all garnered inspiration in Rapallo and it's not difficult to see why. Set on a curving bay lined with striped umbrellas and palm trees, and backed by the 1900m Montallegro, Rapallo is the picture of Riviera living.

On Thursday the historic centre comes alive when weekly market stalls fill **Piazza Cile**. Otherwise stroll the gorgeous **Lungomare Vittorio Veneto**, explore temporary exhibitions in

the castle and take the 1934-vintage **cable car** (Piazzale Solari 2; one way/ return €5.50/8; ⊙9am-12.30pm & 2-6pm) up to the **Santuario Basilico di Montallegro** (612m), built on the spot where the Virgin Mary was reportedly sighted in 1557. Given the heavenly view, it's hardly surprising.

✗ ⊨ p106

The Drive » You can do the 25km drive from Rapallo to Sestri Levante all along the autostrada if you're pressed for time. Otherwise, it's worth taking the more scenic route out of Rapallo along the coast road (SS1) through Zoagli and

102

Portofino Harbour

rejoining the autostrada just before Chiavari (famous for its *farinata* flat bread). From here it's a further 13km to Sestri Levante.

- - - - - - - - - - - - - - -

TRIP HIGHLIGHT

❹ Sestri Levante

Set in a broad flat valley with a long sandy beach and two sheltered bays, Sestri, as the locals call it, has something of a 1950s feel. This might have something to do with the striped umbrellas that dot the beach, the old-style refreshment kiosks, play areas and amusements along the waterfront and the meandering cycle paths where well-dressed ladies pedal with brightly coloured towels in their baskets. Many of the beachfront apartments are owned by Milanese and Genovese families, so you can be sure of a high standard of restaurants, cafes and ice-cream shops in the densely packed historic centre, which sits squeezed between the incredibly photogenic **Baia del Silenzio** (Bay of Silence; off Via Portobello) and the **Baia della Favola** (Bay of Fairy Tales), the latter named after fairy-tale author Hans Christian Andersen, who lived in Sestri in the early 19th century.

✕ p107

The Drive » From Sestri head southeast onto the A12 autostrada for the 42km drive to the Monterosso al Mare. The first 13km are uneventful, but once you exit onto the SS566dir to Monterosso you descend steeply through the forested mountains along an improbable mountain road. The views, across deep valleys to the sea, are superb. There are two car parks on either side of the village: Fegina (€12 per day) and Loreto (€15 per day).

TRIP HIGHLIGHT

⑤ Parco Nazionale delle Cinque Terre

Five dramatically perched seaside villages – **Monterosso al Mare**, **Vernazza**, **Corniglia**, **Manarola** and **Riomaggiore** – make up the five communities of the Unesco-protected **Parco Nazionale delle Cinque Terre** (www.parconazionale 5terre.it). A site of genuine and marvellous beauty, it may not be the undiscovered Eden it was 100 years ago, but frankly – who cares? Sinuous paths traverse seemingly impregnable cliffs, while a 19th-century railway line cuts through coastal tunnels linking village to village. Cars are banned, so park in Monterosso or Riomaggiore, and take to the hills on foot or skirt the spectacular cliffs by boat.

Rooted in antiquity, the Cinque Terre's five towns date from the early medieval period, and include several castles and a quintet of illustrious parish churches. Buildings aside, the Cinque Terre's most unique feature is the steeply terraced cliffs banded by a complicated system of fields and gardens that have been chiselled, shaped and layered over the course of two millennia.

Since the 2011 floods, many of the Cinque Terre's walking paths have been in a delicate state. While most of the spectacular network of trails is open and you can plan some excellent village-to-village hikes along 30 numbered paths, only part of the iconic **Sentiero Azzurro** (Blue path, SVA on maps) is open. To hike this trail you must pay an admission charge (€7.50) or purchase a Cinque Terre card. All other trails are free.

From late March to October, the **Consorzio Marittimo Turistico Cinque Terre Golfo dei Poeti** (☎0187 73 29 87; www.navigazionegolfodeipoeti.it) runs daily shuttle boats between the villages.

✕ ⊨ p107

The Drive » If the roads are busy take the longer, 67km autostrada route via the A12 and A15. However, if you have more time you can take the more scenic, but winding SP51 and SS370 through the mountains of the Cinque Terre National Park until you hit the coast just south of La Spezia. From here turn southwards on the SS530 for the final 12km coastal drive into Portovenere.

SANCTUARY WALKS

Each of Cinque Terre's villages is associated with a sanctuary perched high on the cliff sides. Reaching these religious retreats used to be an act of penance, but these days the walks are for pure pleasure.

Monterosso to Santuario della Madonna di Soviore Follow trail No 509 up through forest to the Italian Riviera's oldest sanctuary.

Vernazza to Santuario della Madonna di Reggio Follow trail No 508 past 14 sculpted Stations of the Cross to this 11th-century chapel with a Romanesque facade.

Corniglia to Santuario della Madonna delle Grazie Ascend the spectacular Sella di Comeneco on trail No 587 to this church with its adored image of the Madonna and Child.

Manarola to Santuario della Madonna delle Salute The pick of all the sanctuary walks is this breathtaking traverse (trail No 506) through Cinque Terre's finest vineyards.

Riomaggiore to Santuario della Madonna di Montenero Trail No 593V ascends to this frescoed 18th-century chapel that sits atop an astounding viewpoint.

6 Portovenere

If the Cinque Terre had to pick an honorary sixth member, Portovenere would surely be it. Perched on the western promontory of the Gulf of Poets (Shelley and Byron were regulars here), the village's seven-storey houses form a citadel around **Castello Doria** (adult/reduced €5/3; ⊙10am-6pm Apr-Oct). No one knows the origins of the castle, although Portus Veneris was a Roman base en route from Gaul to Spain. The current structure dates from the 16th century and offers wonderful views from its terraced gardens. Just off the promontory you'll spy the tiny islands of Palmaria, Tino and Tinetto.

The wave-lashed **Chiesa di San Pietro** sits atop a Roman temple dedicated to the goddess Venus (born from the foam of the sea) from whom Portovenere takes its name. At the end of the quay a Cinque Terre panorama unfolds from the **Grotta Arpaia**. This is better known as the Grotto di Byron, as it was a favourite spot of Lord Byron, who once swam across the gulf to Lerici to visit his fellow romantic, Shelley.

 p107

The Drive » Head north to La Spezia via the SS530 and cross

✓ TOP TIP: CINQUE TERRE CARD

The best way to get around the Cinque Terre is with the Cinque Terre card (one/two days €7.50/14.50, four-person family card €19.60), which gives you unlimited use of the Sentiero Azzurro trail and electric village buses, as well as free use of normally fee-paying toilets at park offices. With the addition of train travel, a one-/two-day card is €16/29. A four-person family card costs €42/20 with/without train travel.

Cards are sold at all Cinque Terre **park information offices** (www.parconazionale5terre.it; ⊙8am-8pm summer, 8.30am-12.30pm & 1-5.30pm winter), located in the village train stations. If you just want to hike, you can also purchase a one-day hiking pass at the Sentiero Azzurro trailheads.

through town to exit eastwards on the SP331. Driving along waterfront boulevards lined with umbrella pines you'll pass La Spezia's marina, then go through suburbs such as San Terenzo, until at Pugliola you turn right onto the SP28 and climb up the villa-lined road into Lerici.

7 Lerici

Magnolia, yew and cedar trees grow in the 1930s public gardens at Lerici, an exclusive retreat of handsome villas that cling to the cliffs along its beach. In another age Byron and Shelley sought inspiration here and gave the Gulf of Poets its name. The Shelleys stayed at the waterfront **Villa Magni** (closed to visitors) in the early 1820s but sadly Percy drowned here when his boat sank off the coast in 1822.

From Lerici, you can head into the hillsides for a scenic 6km stroll passing high above the magnificent bay of Fiascherino, through abandoned villages like Barbazzano and **Portesone** (Via della Fonte; deserted during a medieval plague epidemic). You'll descend at **Tellaro**, a fishing hamlet with pink-and-orange houses cluttered about narrow lanes and tiny squares. Sit on the rocks at the **Chiesa San Giorgio** and imagine an octopus ringing the church bells – which, according to legend, it did to warn the villagers of a Saracen attack.

 p107

Eating & Sleeping

Camogli ➊

✖ La Cucina di Nonna Nina
Trattoria €€

(☎0185 77 38 35; www.nonnanina.it; Via F Molfino 126, San Rocco di Camogli; meals €35-50; ⏱12.30-3pm & 7.30-10.30pm Thu-Tue) In the leafy heights of San Rocco di Camogli you'll find the only Slow Food–recommended restaurant along the coast, named for grandmother Nina, whose heirloom recipes have been adapted with love by Paolo Delphin. Your culinary odyssey will include fabulous traditional dishes such as air-dried cod stewed with pine nuts, potatoes and local Taggiasca olives, and *rossetti* (minnow) and artichoke soup.

✖ Da Paolo
Seafood €€

(☎0185 77 35 95; www. ristorantedapaolocamogli.com; Via San Fortunato 14; meals €40-50; ⏱noon-2.30pm & 7.30-10.30pm Wed-Sun, 7.30-10.30pm Tue) Up a back lane from the waterfront, stylish Da Paolo has the town's best fish and seafood, all fresh off the boats and done in a variety of simple local styles. Order fish by the *etto* (100g) or plates of scampi or squid. Pastas include a fabulous fish ravioli.

⌂ Villa Rosmarino
B&B €€€

(☎0185 77 15 80; www.villarosmarino.com; Via Figari 38; d €240-290; ⏱Mar-Oct; P ✳ ⬆ ⬇) Villa Rosmarino's motto is 'you don't stay, you live' and it's apt. Simply taking in the views here is life affirming. This elegant pink 1907 villa is a typical Ligurian beauty on the outside, a calming oasis of modernity on the inside.

⌂ Hotel Cenobio dei Dogi
Hotel €€€

(☎0185 72 41; www.cenobio.com; Via Cuneo 34; s from €180, d €250-580; P ✳ ⬆ ⬇) The Cenobio's name means 'gathering place of the doges', and yes, the Genovese dukes used to holiday here aeons ago. A private beach and waterfront saltwater swimming pool signal you're in the Riviera, as do the 105 refined, classically furnished rooms. Note, you'll pay a premium for a sea view.

Portofino ➋

✖ Ristorante Puny
Ligurian €€

(☎0185 26 90 37; Piazza Martiri dell'Olivetta; meals €40-50; ⏱noon-3pm & 7-11pm Fri-Wed) Puny's harbourside location is the one you've come to Portofino for and the owners treat *everyone* like they're a visiting celeb. The food sticks loyally to Ligurian specialities, especially seafood.

⌂ Eight Hotels Paraggi
Hotel €€€

(☎0185 28 99 61; www.paraggi.eighthotels.it; Via Paraggi a Mare 8; d €550-960; ✳ ⬆) This low-key hotel has simple, luxurious rooms, but its real appeal is the location. Right on the perfect crescent of Paraggi beach, there's a sense of calm here that can be elusive around the cove in Portofino proper. Such beauty doesn't come cheap, however: rooms with balconies start at €750 per night.

Rapallo ➌

✖ uGiancu
Ligurian €€

(☎0185 26 05 05; www.ugiancu.it; Via San Massimo 78; meals €30-40; ⏱8-10.30pm Thu-Tue, noon-3pm Sun Dec-Oct) About 5km inland in the hamlet of San Massimo di Rapallo, this cult restaurant is run by comic-book collector Fausto Oneto, and half of his collection decorates the walls. Away from the coast, the cooking focuses on meat and vegetables, including an incredibly succulent herb-battered suckling lamb with field greens from the kitchen gardens.

✖ Vecchia Rapallo
Seafood €€

(☎0185 5 00 53; www.vecchiarapallo.com; Via Cairoli 20/24; meals €28-48; ⏱noon-2.30pm & 6-11pm summer, reduced hours winter) Seafood is the star here, and it's done well with the occasional creative touch. House-made stuffed pastas have particular appeal – sea bream ravioli comes with beetroot and prawn sauce, while a chard-filled variety is shaved with truffles. There's a cocktail and wine bar if you're just after a drink, too.

🛏 Europa Hotel
Design Spa 1877   Hotel €€

(📞0185 66 95 21; www.hoteleuropa-rapallo. com; Via Milite Ignoto 2; s €125-190, d €170-255; 🅿 ❄ 🛜) Close to the beach and with its own spa facilities – a thermal bath and steam room – this beautifully refurbished place is super relaxing. The modern rooms here have subtle design touches and are well appointed with marble bathrooms, double-insulated windows and high-quality bedding.

Sestri Levante ❹

✖ Osteria Mattana   Ligurian €

(📞0185 45 76 33; www.osteriamattana.com; Via XXV Aprile 34; meals €20-30; ⏱7-10.30pm daily May-Sep, closed Mon & also open noon-2.30pm Sat & Sun Oct-Apr) A cellar-like two-room restaurant beloved by locals, Osteria Mattana serves up hearty home-cooked dishes at outstanding prices. The chalkboard menu changes daily and might include cuttlefish stew with potatoes and artichokes, spaghetti with mussels and clams, or braised rabbit. Start off with *farinata* (chickpea flour flat bread) fired up from the wood-burning oven in front. Cash only.

Parco Nazionale delle Cinque Terre ❺

✖ La Scuna   Bar

(📞349 6355081; Via Fieschi 185; ⏱8.30am-11.30pm) Craft beer on draught, first-rate cocktails and creative appetisers make a great combo at this surprisingly hip little spot in this most traditional of regions. The best feature, however, is the jaw-dropping terrace, with its mesmerising views over a hill-studded stretch of coastline.

✖ Trattoria da Billy   Seafood €€

(📞0187 92 06 28; www.trattoriabilly.com; Via Rollandi 122; meals €30-40) Hidden off a narrow lane in the upper reaches of town, the Trattoria da Billy fires up some of the best seafood dishes anywhere in Cinque Terre. Start off with a mixed appetiser platter – featuring 12 different hot and cold dishes (octopus salad, lemon-drizzled

anchovies, tuna with sweet onion) – then tuck into lobster pasta or swordfish with black truffle. On clear days, book a table on the terrace for superb views. Reservations essential.

🛏 Il Magan   B&B €

(📞342 3505356; www.vernazzani5terre.it; Via Fieschi 204; r €100-120; 🛜) Four appealingly simple, rustic rooms all have spectacular views, including the single room; two have terraces. Private bathrooms are new, if basic, and breakfast is taken in the town's best bar, La Scuna. Il Magan also rents out an attractive modern apartment. A rare find.

🛏 La Mala   Boutique Hotel €€

(📞334 2875718; www.lamala.it; Via San Giovanni Battista 29; d €160-250; ❄ 🛜) These four rooms are some of Cinque Terre's nicest. Up in the cliff-side heights of the village, they are in a typical Ligurian house that's run by the grandson of the original owner. The fit-out is a clean-lined contemporary one, providing both comfort and a place to soak in some fabulous sea views, either from bed or a sunny terrace.

Portovenere ❻

✖ Anciua   Street Food €

(📞331 7719605; Via Cappellini 40; snacks from €6; ⏱11am-7pm) A perfect spot to pick up something to snack on while dangling your feet in the drink, this is Ligurian street food made with love. Grab a *panini* stuffed with anchovies or cod and olive paste, or pick up a whole spinach pie (aka *torta*) for a picnic. The slabs of sweet, fragrant rice-pudding cake are also highly recommended.

Lerici ❼

✖ Dal Pudu   Ligurian €

(Piazza Garibaldi 10, Lerici; mains €10-18; ⏱noon-3pm & 7-10pm) Just across from Piazza Garibaldi, Dal Pudu is a tiny storefront serving up some of the best seafood in town. A chalkboard menu lists the day's specials, which might include *stoccafisso* (a delectable fish stew), spaghetti with anchovies, lobster salad or lightly battered fried squid. Go early to score a seat at one of the three tables out front.

Northern Cities

8

The Po valley, with its waving cornfields and verdant rice paddies, hosts some of Italy's most prosperous towns, from the handsome walls of Bergamo to the romantic canals of Venice.

TRIP HIGHLIGHTS

395 km

Venice
Explore the drama and intrigue of the Palazzo Ducale

57 km

Verona
Shout 'Brava!' for opera diva encores at the Arena

Bergamo ●

Vicenza ●

6 Soave

7

8 FINISH

Milan
START

5

19 km

Mantua
Renowned for Mantegna's frescoes and fine dining

334 km

Padua
See the Renaissance dawning in Giotto's moving frescoes

7–10 DAYS
395KM / 245 MILES

GREAT FOR...

BEST TIME TO GO

September to May to avoid the crowds.

 ESSENTIAL PHOTO

The golden domes and precious mosaics of San Marco in Venice.

✓ **BEST FOR SURPRISES**

The little-known treasures in Bergamo's Accademia Carrara.

Piazza Duomo and the Duomo

8 Northern Cities

Ever since Julius Caesar granted Roman citizenship to the people of the plains, the Po valley has prospered. Wend your way through the cornfields from the Lombard powerhouse of Milan to Roman Brescia, the Gonzaga stronghold of Mantua and the serene Republic of Venice. This is a land of legends spun by Virgil, Dante and Shakespeare, where grand dynasties fought for power and patronised some of the world's finest art.

❶ Milan

From Charlemagne to Napoleon, and even Silvio Berlusconi, mercantile Milan (Milano) has always attracted the moneyed and the Machiavellian. Follow the city's changing fortunes through the frescoed halls of the **Castello Sforzesco** (☎ 02 8846 3703; www.milanocastello.it; Piazza Castello; adult/reduced €5/3; ☺ 9am-5.30pm Tue-Sun; Ⓜ Cairoli), some of them decorated by Leonardo da Vinci, where exquisite sculptures, paintings

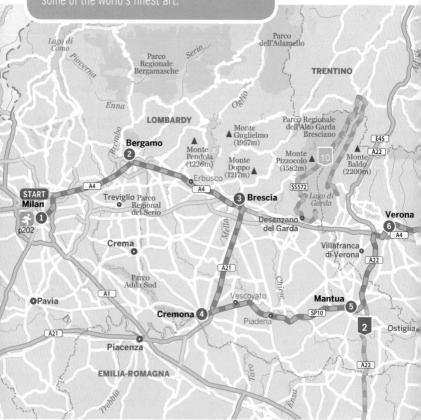

and weapons tell the turbulent tale of the city. From its ramparts, look out over the **Parco Sempione** and spy the pearly pinnacles of the **Duomo** (☏02 7202 3375; www.duomomilano.it; Piazza del Duomo; adult/reduced Duomo €3/2, roof terraces via stairs €10/5, lift €14/7, archaeological area €7/3 (incl Duomo); ⏱Duomo 8am-7pm, roof terraces & archaeological area 9am-7pm; Ⓜ Duomo). Begun in 1387, it took six centuries to build, and was rushed to completion in the 19th century so that Napoleon could crown himself

King of Italy in its cavernous interior.

True to Milan's spirit of free enterprise, one of the city's finest art collections is the private collection of **Museo Poldi Pezzoli** (☏02 79 48 89; www.museopoldipezzoli.it; Via Manzoni 12; adult/reduced €10/7; ⏱10am-6pm Wed-Mon; Ⓜ Montenapoleone), where priceless Bellinis and Botticellis hang in Pezzoli's 19th-century *palazzo* (mansion). From here walk around the city's nearby 'Golden Quadrangle' of designer shops (p202).

 p116

The Drive » Make your way northeast out of town along Corso Venezia, or via the ring road, depending on where you're staying in town. Merge with the A4 Milan–Brescia autostrada for an uneventful 56km drive to Bergamo.

- - - - - - - - - - - - - - - - -

2 Bergamo

Beautiful Bergamo, its domes and towers piled on a promontory at the foot of the Alps, is one of the most arresting urban views in Italy. Le Corbusier admired the incredible beauty of **Piazza Vecchia**, its magnificent ensemble of medieval and Renaissance buildings much influenced by Venetian fashions, with the lion of St Mark's emblazoned on the **Palazzo della Ragione**.

🔗 LINK YOUR TRIP

10 **A Weekend at Lago di Garda**

Got an urge for the outdoors? Jump off the A4 before Verona to Desenzano del Garda and mess around Lago di Garda for a weekend.

2 **World Heritage Wonders**

Further the tour of artistic and architectural blockbusters by continuing on the A22 from Mantua to Modena.

The city's Venetian **walls** were recognised by Unesco in 2017 for their historical value, and you can walk around them in a long morning gazing on hazy views of the *città bassa* (lower city) and the Lombard plains beyond.

Back in the centre, look through the arches of the Palazzo della Ragione for a glimpse of a second square, the **Piazza Duomo**, fronted by the extraordinary polychromatic marble facade of the **Cappella Colleoni** (Piazza del Duomo; ⊘9am-12.30pm & 2-6.30pm Mar-Oct, 9am-12.30pm & 2-4.30pm Tue-Sun Nov-Feb), the mausoleum-cum-chapel of Venice's most famous mercenary commander, Bartolomeo Colleoni (1696–1770).

✕ p116, p129

The Drive ≫ Leave Bergamo via the *città bassa* (lower city) southwards and rejoin the A4 in the direction of Brescia. Surprisingly, this 55km stretch is relatively scenic, especially as you drive through the wine region of Franciacorta.

- - - - - - - - - - - - - - -

❸ **Brescia**

Despite its seedy urban periphery, Brescia's old town contains the most important Roman ruins in Lombardy and an extraordinary, circular Roman church, the **Duomo Vecchio** (Old Cathedral; Piazza Paolo VI; ⊘9am-noon & 3-6pm Tue-Sat, 9-10.45am & 3-7pm Sun), built over the ancient Roman baths.

From here the Via dei Musei, the ancient *decumanus maximus* (east–west main street), leads to the heart of Brixia, the best-preserved Roman remains in northern Italy. The freshly reinvigorated **Brixia Parco Archeologico** (Via dei Musei; adult/reduced €8/6; ⊘9am-5pm Tue-Fri, 10am-6pm Sat & Sun) has recently opened a new underground wing containing a 1st-century-BC sanctuary with rescued mosaics and frescoes. They sit alongside the alfresco **Tempio Capitolino**, erected by Vespasian in AD 73 and preserved for posterity by a medieval mudslide. Next to the ruined temple is the unexcavated *cavea* (semicircular, tiered auditorium) of the **Teatro Romano.** If you have time, it's worth a peep in the **Santa Giulia** (Museo della Città; ☎030 297 78 33; www.bresciamusei.com; Via dei Musei 81; adult/reduced €10/7.50, combined ticket incl Tempio Capitolino €15/10; ⊘9am-5pm Tue-Fri, 10am-9pm Sat, 10am-6pm Sun), a vast monastery complex and museum that charts Brescian history, including more Roman remains.

✕ p116

The Drive ≫ Wend your way south out of Brescia's complicated suburbs following signs for the A21, which is smaller and less heavily trafficked than the A4. The 53km drive to Cremona goes through unspoilt farmland dotted with the occasional farmhouse.

- - - - - - - - - - - - - - -

❹ **Cremona**

Famous for its violins, nougat and the tallest bell tower in Italy (111m), Cremona is a charming stopover. The stout-hearted can climb the 502 steps to the top of the **Torrazzo** (bell tower; Piazza del Comune; adult/reduced €5/4, incl Baptistry €6/5; ⊘10am-1pm & 2.30-6pm, closed Mon winter), perusing a new 'vertical museum' dedicated to astronomy and clocks on the way. The **cathedral** (www.cattedraledicremona.it; Piazza del Comune; ⊘10.30am-noon & 3.30-5pm Mon-Sat, noon-12.30pm & 3-5pm Sun) next door is one of the most exuberant expressions of Lombard Romanesque architecture.

Aside from the views, Cremona made a name for itself as the violin capital of Europe, after Andrea Amati discovered in 1566 that with a bit of adjustment his old medieval fiddle could be made to sing the sweetest tunes. By the 18th century Andrea's son, Nicolò Amati, his pupil Antonio Stradivarius and Giuseppe Guarneri were crafting the best violins ever. See the originals in Cremona's state-of-the-art **Museo del Violino** (☎0372 08 08 09; www.museodelviolino.org; Piazza Marconi 5; adult/reduced €10/7; ⊘10am-6pm Tue-Sun). To hear them, head to the **Teatro Amilcare Ponchielli** (☎0372 02 20 01; www.teatroponchielli.it;

Venice Basilica di San Marco

Corso Vittorio Emanuele II 52; box office 10.30am-1.30pm & 4.30-7.30pm Mon-Sat); its season runs from October to June.

✖ 🛏 p46, p116

The Drive >> You're off the main roads between Cremona and Mantua. Take Via Mantova east out of town and join the SP10. The tree-lined single carriageway passes through cornfields and the small towns of Vescovato and Piadena before reaching the watery outskirts of Mantua after 67km.

- - - - - - - - - - - - - - - - - -

`TRIP HIGHLIGHT`

❺ Mantua

The Latin poet Virgil was born just outside Mantua

(Mantova) in 70 BC, and the modern town preserves its antique timeline in its art and architecture. Ruled by the Gonzaga dynasty for three centuries, the court attracted artists of the highest calibre, including Pisanello, Rubens and, more famously, Andrea Mantegna, who was court painter from 1460 until his death in 1506. It's their dazzling frescoes that decorate the **Palazzo Ducale** (☎041 241 18 97; www.ducalemantova. org; Piazza Sordello 40; adult/reduced €13/6.50; ⏲9.15am-7.15pm Tue-Sat, 8.30am-1.30pm Sun). During busy periods you may have to book to

see the biggest draw – Mantegna's 15th-century frescoes in the **Camera degli Sposi** (Bridal Chamber).

Hardly more modest in scale is the Gonzaga's suburban villa, the **Palazzo Te** (☎0376 36 58 86; www.palazzote.it; Viale Te 13; adult/reduced €12/8; ⏲1-7.30pm Mon, 9am-7.30pm Tue-Sun). Mainly used by Duke Federico II as a place of rendezvous with his mistress, Isabella Boschetti, it is decorated in playboy style with playful motifs and encoded love symbols.

✖ 🛏 p116

113

The Drive ≫ From Mantua head almost directly north for Verona. Leave town on Via Legnago, crossing the causeway that separates Lago di Mezzo from Lago Inferiore, then pick up the A22 autostrada for an easy 40km drive to Verona.

TRIP HIGHLIGHT

⑥ Verona

Shakespeare placed star-crossed Romeo and Juliet in Verona for good reason: romance, drama and fatal family feuds have been the city's hallmark for centuries.

From the 3rd century BC, Verona was a Roman trade centre, with ancient gates, a forum (now Piazza delle Erbe) and a grand **Roman Arena** (☑045 800 32 04; Piazza Brà; adult/reduced €10/7.50; ⏱8.30am-7.30pm Tue-Sun, 1.30-7.30pm Mon), which still hosts summer opera performances. But Shakespearean tragedy came with the territory.

After Mastino della Scala (aka Scaligeri) lost re-election to Verona's *comune* in 1262, he claimed absolute control, until murdered by his rivals. On the north side of **Piazza dei Signori** stands the early-Renaissance **Loggia del Consiglio**, the 15th-century city council. Through the archway you'll find the **Arche Scaligere** – elaborate Gothic tombs of the Scaligeri family, where murderers are interred next to the relatives they killed.

Paranoid for good reason, the fratricidal Cangrande II (1351–59) built the **Castelvecchio** (☑045 806 26 11; https://museodicastelvecchio.comune.verona.it; Corso Castelvecchio 2; adult/reduced €6/4.50, free with VeronaCard; ⏱1.30-7.30pm Mon, 8.30am-7.30pm Tue-Sun) to guard the river Adige, which snakes through town. Now it houses Verona's main museum with

works by Tiepolo, Carpaccio and Veronese.

To get an alternative view of the castle and the city, cast off on the river with **Adige Rafting** (☑347 8892498; www.adigerafting.it; Via del Perloso 14a; adult/reduced €25/18) for a thrilling two-hour Raft & Wine ride beneath a dozen bridges with pit stops for prosecco and plates of mountain cheese and prosciutto.

✖ ➤ p61, p117, p181

The Drive ≫ The 95km drive from Verona to Padua is once again along the A4. This stretch of road is heavily trafficked by heavy-goods vehicles. The only rewards are glimpses of Soave's crenellated castle to your left and the tall church spire of Monteforte d'Alpone. You could extend your trip with a stop to take in the World Heritage architecture of Vicenza.

TRIP HIGHLIGHT

⑦ Padua

Dante, da Vinci, Boccaccio and Vasari all honour Giotto as the artist who officially ended the Dark Ages. Giotto's startlingly humanist approach not only changed how people saw the heavenly company, it changed how they saw themselves; not as lowly vassals but as vessels for the divine, however flawed. This humanising approach was especially well suited to the **Cappella degli Scrovegni** (Scrovegni Chapel; ☑049 201 00 20; www.cappelladegliscrovegni.it; Piazza Eremitani 8; adult/reduced €13/8,

---

↱ **DETOUR: SOAVE**

Start: ⑥ Verona

East of Verona, Soave serves its namesake DOC white wine in a storybook setting. Built by Verona's fratricidal Scaligeri family, the **Castello di Soave** (☑045 768 00 36; www.castellodisoave.it; adult/reduced €7/4; ⏱9am-noon & 3-6.30pm Apr-Oct, to noon & 2-4pm Nov-Mar) encompasses an early-Renaissance villa, grassy courtyards and the Mastio, a defensive tower. More inviting is **1898 Cantina di Soave** (☑045 613 98 45; www.cantinasoave.it; Via Covergnino 7; ⏱9am-7pm Mon-Sat May-Sep, 8.30am-12.30pm & 2.30-7pm Mon-Sat Oct-Apr), a cooperative of 2000 Soave producers upholding the lemony, zesty DOC Soave Classico quality standards.

night ticket €8/6; ⏱9am-7pm, night ticket 7-10pm), the chapel in Padua (Padova) that Enrico Scrovegni commissioned in memory of his father, who as a moneylender was denied a Christian burial.

Afterwards, tour the **Musei Civici agli Eremitani** (☎049 820 45 51; Piazza Eremitani 8; adult/reduced €10/8; ⏱9am-7pm Tue-Sun) for pre-Roman Padua downstairs and a pantheon of Veneto artists upstairs.

✕ p117, p173

The Drive ≫ The 40km drive from Padua to Venice is through a tangle of suburban neighbourhoods and featureless areas of light industry along the A4 and then the A57.

- - - - - - - - - - - - - - - -

⑧ Venice

Like its signature landmark, the **Basilica di San Marco** (St Mark's Basilica; ☎041 270 83 11; www.basilicasanmarco.it; Piazza San Marco; ⏱9.30am-5pm Mon-Sat, 2-5pm Sun summer, to 4.30pm Sun winter; ⛴San Marco), the Venetian empire was dazzlingly cosmopolitan. Armenians, Turks, Greeks and Germans were neighbours along the **Grand Canal**, and Jewish communities persecuted elsewhere in Europe founded publishing houses and banks. By the mid-15th century, Venice (Venezia) was swathed in golden mosaics, imported silks and clouds of incense.

Underneath the lacy pink cladding the **Palazzo Ducale** (Ducal Palace; ☎041 271 59 11; www.palazzoducale.visitmuve.it; Piazzetta San Marco 1; adult/reduced incl Museo Correr €20/13, with Museum Pass free; ⏱8.30am-7pm summer, to 5.30pm winter; ⛴San Zaccaria) ran an uncompromising dictatorship. Discover state secrets on the **Itinerari Segreti** (☎041 4273 0892; adult/reduced €20/14; ⏱tours in English 9.55am, 10.45am & 11.35am), which takes you to the sinister Trial Chamber and Interrogation Room.

Centuries later, Napoleon took some of Venice's finest heirlooms to France. But the biggest treasure in the **Museo Correr** (☎041 240 52 11; www.correr.visitmuve.it; Piazza San Marco 52; adult/reduced incl Palazzo Ducale €20/13, with Museum Pass free; ⏱10am-7pm Apr-Oct, to 5pm Nov-Mar; ⛴San Marco) couldn't be lifted: Jacopo Sansovino's **Libreria Nazionale Marciana**, covered with larger-than-life philosophers by Veronese, Titian and Tintoretto.

For more visual commentary on Venetian high life, head for the **Gallerie dell'Accademia** (☎041 522 22 47; www.gallerieaccademia.it; Campo de la Carità 1050; adult/reduced €12/2; ⏱8.15am-2pm Mon, to 7.15pm Tue-Sun; ⛴Accademia), whose hallowed halls contain more murderous intrigue and forbidden romance than most Venetian parties. Alternatively, immerse yourself in the lagoon larder by walking around the city's markets and bars (p200).

✕ ⇞ p46, p61, p117, p173

THE ORIGINAL GHETTO

In medieval times, the Cannaregio island of **Ghetto Nuovo** housed a *getto* (foundry) – but its role as Venice's designated Jewish quarter from the 16th to 18th centuries gave the word its current meaning. In accordance with the Venetian Republic's 1516 decree, Jewish lenders, doctors and clothing merchants were allowed to attend to Venice's commercial interests by day, while at night and on Christian holidays, most were restricted to the gated island of Ghetto Nuovo.

When Jewish merchants fled the Spanish Inquisition for Venice in 1541, there was no place to go in the Ghetto but up: around **Campo del Ghetto Nuovo**, upper storeys housed new arrivals, synagogues and publishing houses. Despite a 10-year censorship order issued by the church in Rome in 1553, Jewish Venetian publishers contributed hundreds of titles popularising new Renaissance ideas on religion, humanist philosophy and medicine.

Eating & Sleeping

Milan ❶

✗ Trattoria da Pino   Milanese €

(📞02 7600 0532; Via Cerva 14; meals €20-25; 🕐noon-3pm Mon-Sat; Ⓜ San Babila) In a city full of fashion models in Michelin-starred restaurants, working-class da Pino offers the perfect antidote. Sit elbow-to-elbow at packed wooden tables and enjoy hearty plates of *bollito misto* (mixed boiled meats), sausages and potatoes, and comforting classic pastas. Arrive early or prepare to queue.

✗ Seta   Gastronomy €€€

(Mandarin Oriental; 📞02 8731 8897; www. mandarinoriental.com; Via Andegari 9; meals €110; 🕐12.30-2.30pm & 7.30-10.30pm Mon-Sat; 🅿 ❄ 📶; Ⓜ Montenapoleone) Smooth as the silk after which it's named, Seta is Michelin-starred dining at its best: beautiful, inventive and full of flavour surprises. Diners sit on their teal-coloured velvet chairs in keen anticipation of Antonio Guida's inspired dishes, such as blue lobster with *zabaglione* (egg and Marsala custard) and white miso. If weather permits, dine in the outdoor courtyard where you can glimpse the kitchen in action.

Bergamo ❷

✗ Noi   Italian €€

(📞035 23 77 50; www.noi-restaurant.it; Via Alberto Pitentino 6; meals €35-45; 🕐7.30pm-midnight Mon, 12.30-2.30pm & 7.30pm-midnight Tue-Sat; 📶) More esoteric than your average trattoria, Noi is a chameleonic restaurant that changes it spots between lunch and dinner (they even change the restaurant sign). Lunch (under the moniker 'Rame-noi') has an Asian-fusion theme with ramen noodles heading the bill, while at dinner, it returns to its Italian roots with five-course tasting menus endowing local food with fusion influences and presenting it like food art.

Brescia ❸

✗ La Vineria   Italian €€

(📞030 28 05 43; www.lavineriabrescia.it; Via X Giornate 4; meals €28-36; 🕐noon-3pm & 7-11pm Tue-Sat, noon-3pm Sun) Near the Piazza della Loggia, La Vineria serves up delectable regional cuisine at al fresco tables under a portico or in a classy dining room with vaulted ceilings. Try dishes like linguine with dried sardines and almond butter, or *bigoli* (thick spaghetti) with duck *ragù*. Not surprisingly, 'the winery' has good wine selections.

Cremona ❹

✗ Hosteria 700   Lombard €€

(📞0372 3 61 75; www.hosteria700.com; Piazza Gallina 1; meals €33-40; 🕐noon-2.45pm Wed-Mon, 7-11pm Wed-Sun) Behind the dilapidated facade lurks a diamond in the rough. Some of the vaulted rooms come with ceiling frescoes, dark timber tables come with ancient wooden chairs, and the hearty Lombard cuisine comes at a refreshingly competitive cost.

⌂ Hotel Continental   Hotel €

(📞0372 43 41 41; www. hotelcontinentalcremona.it; Piazza della Libertà 26; s/d from €70/97; 🅿 ❄ 📶) A short stroll outside the historic centre, the Hotel Continental is a self-proclaimed 'lifestyle' hotel that pricks your interest with a dynamically designed lobby replete with retro loungers, bookshelves, an honesty bar and a Nespresso machine. Take this as a gateway to more fun including a rooftop cocktail bar (negronis €6), a pizza restaurant (margheritas €4.50) and a modern gym.

Mantua ❺

✗ Osteria delle Quattro Tette   Osteria €

(📞0376 32 94 78; Vicolo Nazione 4; meals €10-15; 🕐12.30-2.30pm Mon-Sat) At the wonderfully esoteric *osteria* of the 'four breasts', you can pull up a pew (literally, an old church pew) and enjoy yet-to-be-exported Italian gems such as tripe and beans, horsemeat steak and sweet desserts smeared with alcoholic custard. This is a slice of gritty unwrapped Italy where service is fast, prices cheap and rough-hewn tables are spaced only centimetres apart.

🛏 C'a delle Erbe   B&B €€

(☎0376 22 61 61; www.cadelleerbe.it; Via Broletto 24; d €130-165; ❄️ 🛜) In this gorgeous 16th-century townhouse historic features have undergone a minimalist remodelling: exposed creamy stone walls surround pared-down furniture; whitewashed beams cohabit with lavish bathrooms and modern art. The pick of the bedrooms must be the one with the balcony overlooking the iconic Piazza delle Erbe, a candidate for the town's best room.

Verona ❻

✖ Pescheria I Masenini   Seafood €€€

(☎045 929 80 15; www.imasenini.com; Piazzetta Pescheria 9; meals €40-50; 🕐12.40-2pm & 7.40-10pm, closed Sun evening & Mon) Located on the piazza where Verona's Roman fish market once held sway, softly lit Masenini quietly serves up Verona's most imaginative, modern fish dishes. Inspired flavour combinations might see fresh sea-bass carpaccio paired with zesty green apple and pink pepper, black-ink gnocchi schmoozing with lobster *ragù*, or sliced amberjack delightfully matched with crumbed almonds, honey, spinach and raspberries.

🛏 Corte delle Pigne   B&B €€

(☎333 7584141; www.cortedellepigne.it; Via Pigna 6a; s €60-110, d €90-150, tr €110-170; 🅿️ ❄️ 🛜) In the heart of the historic centre, this tiny three-room B&B is set around a quiet internal courtyard. It offers tasteful rooms and plenty of personal touches: sweets jars, luxury toiletries and even a Jacuzzi for one lucky couple.

Soave ❻

✖ Locanda Lo Scudo   Italian €€

(☎045 768 07 66; www.loscudo.vr.it; Via Covergnino 9; meals €35; 🕐noon-2.30pm & 7.30-10.30pm Tue-Sat, to 2.30pm Sun; 🛜)

Just outside the medieval walls of Soave, Lo Scudo is half country inn and half high-powered gastronomy. Cult classics include a risotto of scallops and porcini mushrooms, though – if it's on the menu – only a fool would resist the extraordinary dish of tortelloni stuffed with local pumpkin, Grana Padano, cinnamon, mustard and Amaretto, and topped with crispy fried sage.

Padua ❼

✖ Caffè Pedrocchi   Cafe

(☎049 878 12 31; www.caffepedrocchi.it; Via VIII Febbraio 15; 🕐8am-midnight Sun-Thu, to 1am Fri & Sat) This unmissable piece of olde worlde European cafe culture takes you back to the days when Stendhal held court here. The cafe is divided into three rooms, each one sporting huge maps of the world, high ceilings, simple tables and waiters scurrying Central Europe–style. A white grand piano completes the scene.

✖ Da Nane della Giulia   Osteria €€

(☎049 66 07 42; Via Santa Sofia 1; meals €25-30; 🕐12.30-2pm & 7pm-midnight Wed-Sun; 🌿) Enter the blood-red, candlelit dining room of Padua's oldest tavern and you'll immediately be transported back to another era. Diners settle in at dark wooden tables beneath vaulted ceilings and peruse the seasonal, local menu. It includes traditional dishes such as chicken in red grappa with pancetta and polenta and vegetarian-friendly plates of white asparagus, courgettes and local cheese.

Venice ❽

✖ Osteria Trefanti   Venetian €€

(☎041 520 17 89; www.osteriatrefanti.it; Fondamenta del Rio Marin o dei Garzoti 888; meals €40-45; 🕐noon-2.30pm & 7-10.30pm Tue-Sun; 🛜; 🚤Riva de Biasio) La Serenissima's spice trade lives on at simple, elegant Trefanti, where gnocchi might get an intriguing kick from cinnamon, and turbot is flavoured with almond and coconut. Seafood is the focus; try the 'doge's fettucine', with mussels, scampi and clams. Furnished with recycled copper lamps, the space is small and deservedly popular – so book ahead.

Classic Trip

The Graceful Italian Lakes

Writers from Goethe to Hemingway have lavished praise on the Italian Lakes, dramatically ringed by snow-powdered mountains and garlanded by grand villas and exotic, tropical flora.

9

TRIP HIGHLIGHTS

6 km

Cannobio
The prettiest medieval hamlet on Lago Maggiore

3

Verbania
veno • **Laveno**

1
START

132 km

Bellagio
Bounded by classic gardens brimming with camellias

6

• **Lecco**

5

Bergamo
FINISH

Stresa
A perfect setting for sunsets over the Borromean palaces

km

Como
Silk souvenirs and lakeside swimming

113 km

5–7 DAYS
213KM / 132 MILES

GREAT FOR...

BEST TIME TO GO

April to June, when the camellias are in full bloom.

 ESSENTIAL PHOTO

The cascading gardens of Palazzo Borromeo.

 BEST FOR GLAMOUR

Touring Bellagio's headland in a mahogany cigarette boat.

Classic Trip

9 The Graceful Italian Lakes

Formed at the end of the last ice age, and a popular holiday spot since Roman times, the Italian Lakes have an enduring natural beauty. At Lago Maggiore the palaces of the Borromean Islands lie like a fleet of fine vessels in the gulf, while the siren call of Lago di Como draws Arabian sheikhs and James Bond location scouts to its discreet forested slopes.

:
TRIP HIGHLIGHT

1 Stresa

More than Como and Garda, Lago Maggiore has retained the belle-époque air of its early tourist heyday. Attracted by the mild climate and the easy access the new 1855 railway provided, the European *haute bourgeoisie* flocked to buy and build grand lakeside villas. The best of them are paraded in the small but select lakeside town of Stresa.

From here it's a short punt to the palace-punctuated Borromean Islands (Isole Borromee), Maggiore's star attractions. **Isola Bella** took the name of Carlo III's wife, the *bella* Isabella, in the 17th century, when its centrepiece, **Palazzo Borromeo** (0323 93 34 78; www.isoleborromee.it; Isola Bella; adult/child €17/9, incl Palazzo Madre €24/10.50; 9am-5.30pm mid-Mar–mid-Oct), was built. Construction of the villa and gardens was thought out in such a way that the island would have the

appearance of a vessel, with the villa at the prow and the gardens dripping down 10 tiered terraces at the rear. Inside, you'll find the work of countless old masters.

By contrast, **Isola Madre** eschews ostentation for a more romantic, familial atmosphere. The 16th- to 18th-century

120

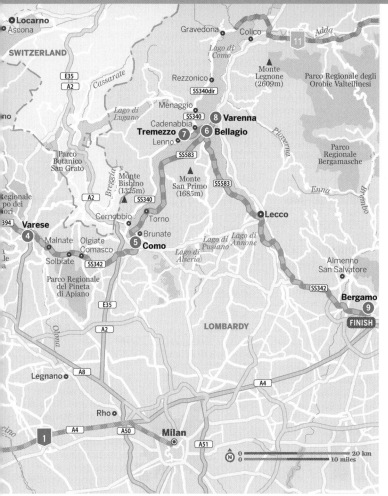

Palazzo Madre (📞0323
93 34 78; www.isoleborromee.
it; adult/child €13.50/7, incl
Palazzo Borromeo €24/10.50;
🕙9am-5.30pm mid-Mar–mid-
Oct) includes a 'horror'
theatre with a cast of
devilish marionettes,
while Chinese pheas-
ants stalk the English
gardens.

🍴 p129

**LINK
YOUR
TRIP**

1 Grand Tour
From Stresa take
the A8 to Milan (Milano),
from where you can
commence your own
Grand Tour of Italy.

11 Roof of Italy
From Como take
the SS340 to Gravedona,
from where you plunge
eastwards into the
Valtellina vineyards and
over the Alps to Merano.

The Drive » Leave Stresa westwards on the Via Sempione (SS33), skirting the edge of the lake for this short, 14km drive. Pass through Baveno and round the western edge of the gulf through the greenery of the Fondo Toce natural reserve. When you reach the junction with the SS34, turn right for Verbania.

2 Verbania

There are two Verbanias: Pallanza, a waterside maze of serpentine streets that serves as an embarkation point for the Borromean Islands, and Intra, the broader, newer ferry port. Between them sits the late-19th-century **Villa Taranto** (☎0323 55 66 67; www.villataranto.it; Via Vittorio Veneto 111, Verbania Pal-

lanza; adult/reduced €11/5.50; ☉8.30am-6.30pm Apr-Sep, 9am-4pm Oct; **P**). In 1931, royal archer and Scottish captain Neil McEacharn bought the villa from the Savoy family and started to plant some 20,000 species. With its rolling hillsides of purple rhododendrons and camellias, acres of tulip flowers and hothouses full of equatorial lilies it is considered one of Europe's finest botanical gardens. During the last week in April, **Settimana del Tulipano** takes place, when tens of thousands of tulips erupt in magnificent multicoloured bloom.

✖ p129

The Drive » Pick up the SS34 again, continuing in a northeasterly direction out of Verbania, through the suburbs of Intra and Pallanza. Once you've cleared the town the 20km to Cannobio are the

prettiest on the tour, shadowing the lakeshore the entire way with views across the water.

- - - - - - - - - - - - - - - -

TRIP HIGHLIGHT

3 Cannobio

Sheltered by a high mountain and sitting at the foot of the Cannobina valley, the medieval hamlet of Cannobio is located 5km from the Swiss border. It is a dreamy place. **Piazza di Vittorio Emanuele III**, lined with pastel-hued houses, is the location of a huge **Sunday market** that attracts visitors from Switzerland.

You can hire SUP boards, canoes and small sailing boats from **Tomaso Surf & Sail** (☎333 7000291; www. tomaso.com; Via Nazionale 7; ☉9.30am-7pm Jun-Sep, 11am-6pm Oct-May) next to the town lido. A good boat excursion is to the ruined **Castelli della Malpaga**, located on two rocky islets to the south of Cannobio. In summer it is a favourite picnic spot.

Alternatively, explore the wild beauty of the Valle Cannobina. Trails begin in town and snake alongside the surging Torrente Cannobino stream into the heavily wooded hillsides to Malesco. Just 2.5km along the valley, in Sant'Anna, the torrent forces its way powerfully through a narrow gorge known as the **Orrido di Sant'Anna**, crossed at its narrowest

---

DETOUR: LAGO D'ORTA

Start: 1 Stresa

Separated from Lago Maggiore by Monte Mottarone (1492m) and enveloped by thick, dark-green woodlands, Lago d'Orta would make a perfect elopers' getaway. At 13.4km long by 2.5km wide you can drive around the lake in a day. The focal point is the captivating medieval village of **Orta San Giulio**, which sits across from Isola San Giulio, where you'll spy the frescoed, 12th-century **Basilica di San Giulio** (☉9.30am-6pm Tue-Sun, 2-5pm Mon Apr-Sep, 9.30am-noon & 2-5pm Tue-Sun, 2-5pm Mon Oct-Mar). Come during the week and you'll have the place largely to yourself.

Stresa Isola Bella

part by a Romanesque bridge.

The Drive >> The next part of the journey involves retracing the previous 22km drive to Verbania-Intra to board the cross-lake ferry to Laveno. Ferries run every 20 minutes (one-way tickets cost €10.90 for standard-sized car and driver). Once in Laveno pick up the SP394dir and then the SP1var and SS394 for the 23km drive to Varese.

❹ Varese

Spread out to the south of the Campo dei Fiori hills, Varese is a prosperous provincial capital. From the 17th century onwards, Milanese nobles began to build second residences here, the most sumptuous being the **Palazzo Estense**, completed in 1771 for Francesco III d'Este, the governor of the Duchy of Milan. Although you cannot visit the palace you are free to wander the vast Italianate **gardens** (open 8am to dusk).

To the north of the city sits another great villa, **Villa Panza** (☎0332 28 39 60; www.fondoambiente.it; Piazza Litta 1; adult/reduced €15/7; ☺10am-6pm Tue-Sun), donated to the state in 1996. Part of the donation was 150 contemporary canvases collected by Giuseppe Panza di Biumo, mostly by post-WWII American artists. One of the finest rooms is the 1830 **Salone Impero** (Empire Hall), with heavy chandeliers and four canvases by David Simpson (b 1928).

The Drive >> The 28km drive from Varese to Como isn't terribly exciting, passing through a string of small towns and suburbs nestled in the wooded hills. The single-lane SS342 passes through Malnate, Solbiate and Olgiate Comasco before reaching Como.

TRIP HIGHLIGHT

❺ Como

Built on the wealth of its silk industry, Como is an elegant town and remains Europe's most important producer of silk products. The **Museo della Seta** (Silk Museum; ☎031 30 31 80; www.museosetacomo.com; Via Castelnuovo 9; adult/reduced €10/7; ☺10am-6pm Tue-Sun) unravels the town's industrial history, with early dyeing and printing equipment on display. At **A Picci** (☎031 26 13 69; Via Vittorio Emanuele II 54; ☺3-7.30pm Mon, 9am-12.30pm & 3-7.30pm Tue-Sat) you can buy top-quality scarves, ties and fabrics.

After wandering the medieval alleys of the historic centre take a stroll along **Passeggiata Lino Gelpi**, where you

123

Classic Trip

WHY THIS IS A CLASSIC TRIP
BRENDAN SAINSBURY, WRITER

Maggiore has always been my favourite Italian lake, where you can escape into the quiet woods of the Valle Cannobina and convalesce afterwards in a history-evoking belle-époque cafe in Stresa. And who doesn't have a soft spot for Como, where history buffs can vicariously become Napoleon, or James Bond in a gilded lakeside villa? Away from the water, Bergamo continues the classic theme, but with a little less pretension.

Above: Cappella Colleoni, Bergamo
Left: Villa Taranto, Verbania
Right: Bellagio

pass a series of waterfront mansions, finally arriving at **Villa Olmo** (☏031 25 23 52; www.villaolmocomo.it; Via Cantoni 1; gardens free, villa entry varies by exhibition; ⊙villa 10am-6pm Tue-Sun during exhibitions, gardens 7am-11pm Apr-Sep, to 8pm Oct-Mar). Set grandly facing the lake, this Como landmark was built in 1728 by the Odescalchi family, related to Pope Innocent XI, and now hosts blockbuster art shows. On Sundays you can continue your walk through the gardens of **Villa del Grumello** and the **Villa Sucota** on the so-called *Chilometro della Conoscenza* (Kilometre of Knowledge).

On the other side of Como's marina, the **Funicolare Como–Brunate** (☏031 30 36 08; www.funicolarecomo.it; Piazza de Gasperi 4; one way/return adult €3/5.50, reduced €2/3.20; ⊙half-hourly departures 6am-midnight summer, to 10.30pm winter) whisks you uphill to the quiet village of **Brunate** for splendid views across the lake.

✕ ⊨ p129

The Drive » The 32km drive from Como to Bellagio along the SS583 is spectacular. The narrow road swoops and twists around the lakeshore the entire way and rises up out of Como giving panoramic views over the lake. There are plenty of spots en route where you can pull over for photographs.

Classic Trip

TRIP HIGHLIGHT

⑥ Bellagio

It's impossible not to be charmed by Bellagio's waterfront of bobbing boats, its maze of stone staircases, cypress groves and showy gardens.

Bellagio is a place best absorbed slowly on your own. You can pick up three self-guided walking tour brochures from the **tourist office** (☏031 95 02 04; www.bel lagiolakecomo.com; Piazza Mazzini; ⌚9.30am-12.30pm & 1-5.30pm, reduced hours winter). The longest three-hour walk takes in neighbouring villages, including **Pescallo**, a small one-time fishing port about 1km from the centre, and **Loppia**, with the 11th-century Chiesa di Santa Maria, which is only visitable from the outside.

The walk to one of Como's finest mansions, **Villa Melzi d'Eril** (☏339 4573838; www.giardinidivil lamelzi.it; Lungo Lario Manzoni; adult/reduced €6.50/4; ⌚9.30am-6.30pm Mar-Oct), heads south along the lakeshore from the Bellagio ferry jetties, revealing views of ranks of gracious residences stacked up on the waterside hills. The grounds of the neoclassical Villa Melzi run right down to the lake and are adorned with classical statues couched in blushing azaleas.

For on-the-lake frollicks, **Barindelli's** (☏338 2110337; www.barindellitaxi boats.it; Piazza Mazzini; tours per hour €150) operates slick, mahogany cigarette boats in which you can tool around the headland on a sunset tour.

🛏 p129

The Drive » The best way to reach Tremezzo, without driving all the way around the bottom of the lake, is to take the ferry from Piazza Mazzini. One-way fares cost €4.60 and the journey takes 10 minutes, but for sightseeing you may

want to consider the one-day central lake ticket, covering Bellagio, Varenna, Tremezzo and Cadenabbia, for €15.

⑦ Tremezzo

Tremezzo is high on everyone's list for a visit to the 17th-century **Villa Carlotta** (☏0344 4 04 05; www.villacarlotta.it; Via Regina 2; adult/reduced €10/8; ⌚9am-6.30pm Mar-Sep, to 5.30pm Oct, 10am-4pm Nov & Dec), whose botanic gardens are filled with orange trees knitted into pergolas and some of Europe's finest rhododendrons, azaleas and camellias. The villa, which is strung with paintings and fine alabaster-white sculptures (especially lovely are those by Antonio Canova), takes its name from the Prussian princess who was given the palace in 1847 as a wedding present from her mother.

The Drive » As with the trip to Tremezzo, the best way to travel to Varenna is by passenger ferry either from Cadenabbia (1.3km north of Tremezzo's boat dock) or Bellagio.

⑧ Varenna

A mirror image of Bellagio across the water, Varenna is a beguiling village bursting with florid plantlife, narrow lanes and pastel-coloured houses stacked up on mountain slopes that defy the laws of physics.

SEAPLANES ON THE LAKE

For a touch of Hollywood glamour, check out **Aero Club Como** (☏031 57 44 95; www.aeroclubcomo.com; Viale Masia 44; 30min flight per person €90), which has been sending seaplanes out over the lakes since 1930. The 30-minute flight to Bellagio from Como costs €180 for two people. Longer excursions over Lago Maggiore are also possible. In summer you need to reserve at least three days in advance.

Varenna Lakefront restaurant

127

You can wander the flower-laden pathway from Piazzale Martiri della Libertà to the gardens of **Villa Cipressi** (☎0341 83 01 13; www.hotel villacipressi.it; Via IV Novembre 22; adult/child €6/3; ☉10am-6pm Mar-Oct), now a luxury hotel, or undertake a 40-minute walk up to the 13th-century **Castello di Vezio** (☎348 8242504; www.castellodivezio.it; Vezio, near Varenna; adult/reduced €4/3; ☉10am-7pm Mon-Fri, 10am-8pm Sat & Sun Jun-Aug, to 6pm Mar-May, Sep & Oct), high above the terracotta rooftops of Varenna. The castle was once part of a chain of early-warning medieval watchtowers. These days it hosts al fresco temporary exhibitions of avant-garde art and holds falconry displays in the afternoons

– daily except Tuesdays and Fridays. There's also a small cafe.

The Drive ≫ Departing Bellagio, pick up the SS583, but this time head southeast towards Lecco down the other 'leg' of Lago di Como. As with the stretch from Como to Bellagio, the road hugs the lake, offering spectacular views the whole 20km to Lecco. Once you reach Lecco head south out of town down Via Industriale and pick up the SS342 for the final 40km to Bergamo.

----

9 Bergamo

Although Milan's skyscrapers are visible on a clear day, historically Bergamo was more closely associated with Venice (Venezia). The Venetian-style architecture can be seen in **Piazza Vecchia** and, more stridently, in the **City Walls** that were included as part of a new Unesco World Heritage Site in 2017.

Behind this secular core sits the **Piazza del Duomo** with its modest baroque cathedral. A great deal more interesting is the **Basilica di Santa Maria Maggiore** (Piazza del Duomo; ☉9am-12.30pm & 2.30-6pm Mon-Fri, 9am-6pm Sat & Sun Apr-Oct, shorter hours Nov-Mar) next door. To its whirl of frescoed, Romanesque apses, begun in 1137, Gothic touches were added, as was the Renaissance **Cappella Colleoni** (Piazza del Duomo; ☉9am-12.30pm & 2-6.30pm Mar-Oct, 9am-12.30pm & 2-4.30pm Tue-Sun Nov-Feb), the mausoleum-cum-chapel of the famous mercenary commander, Bartolomeo Colleoni (1696–1770). Demolishing an entire apse of the basilica, he commissioned Giovanni Antonio Amadeo to create a tomb that is now considered a masterpiece of Lombard art.

Also like Venice, Bergamo has a grand art academy. The seminal **Accademia Carrara** (☎035 23 43 96; www.lacarrara.it; Piazza Carrara 82; adult/reduced €12/10; ☉9.30am-5.30pm Wed-Mon) is both school and museum, its stunning collection of 1800 Renaissance paintings amassed by local scholar Count Giacomo Carrara (1714–96).

✕ ⊨ p116, p129

p116, p129

LAGO MAGGIORE EXPRESS

The **Lago Maggiore Express** (☎091 756 04 00; www.lagomaggioreexpress.com; adult/child 1-day tour €34/17, 2-day tour €44/22) is a picturesque day trip you can do without the car. It includes train travel from Arona or Stresa to Domodossola, from where you get the charming *Centovalli* train, crossing 100 valleys, to Locarno in Switzerland and a ferry back to Stresa. The two-day version is perhaps better value if you have the time.

Eating & Sleeping

Stresa ❶

🍴 Ristorante Il Vicoletto   Ristorante €€

(📞0323 93 21 02; www.ristorantevicoletto.com; Vicolo del Pocivo 3; meals €32-38; 🕑noon-2pm & 7-10pm Fri-Wed) One of Stresa's most gourmet restaurants doesn't advertise itself from its modest perch up a narrow side street. It doesn't need to. Local word of mouth means the small interior is often full, with diners spilling out onto a heated front patio. Walk by and you'll see them demolishing cod carpaccio; saffron, asparagus and anchovy risotto; and lamb stewed in Nebbiolo wine.

Verbania ❷

🍴 Ristorante Milano   Modern Italian €€€

(📞0323 55 68 16; www.ristorantemilanolagomaggiore.it; Corso Zanitello 2, Verbania Pallanza; meals €68-80; 🕑noon-2pm & 7-9pm Wed-Mon; ❄) The setting really is hard to beat: Milano directly overlooks Pallanza's minuscule horseshoe-shaped harbour (200m south of the ferry jetty), with a scattering of tables sitting on lakeside lawns amid the trees. It's an idyllic if pricey spot to enjoy lake fish, local lamb and some innovative Italian cuisine, such as pigeon with pâté and red-currant reduction.

Como ❺

🍴 Osteria del Gallo   Italian €€

(📞031 27 25 91; www.osteriadelgallo-como.it; Via Vitani 16; meals €26-32; 🕑12.30-3pm Mon-Sat, 7-9pm Tue-Sat) An ageless *osteria* (casual tavern) that looks exactly the part. In the wood-lined checker-clothed dining room, wine bottles and other goodies fill the shelves, and diners sit at small timber tables to tuck into traditional local food. The menu is chalked up daily and might include a first course of *zuppa di ceci* (chickpea soup), followed by lightly fried lake fish.

🏨 Avenue Hotel   Boutique Hotel €€

(📞031 27 21 86; www.avenuehotel.it; Piazzolo Terragni 6; d €165-210, ste €250-290; P ❄ 🛜) An assured sense of style at this à la mode boutique hotel sees ultramodern, minimalist rooms team crisp white walls with shots of purple or fuchsia pink. Unusual art (two giant zebras in the breakfast room) melds with unusual design (square toilets) to leave a memorable impression, lent weight by warm but discreet service and fun extras (you can borrow bikes gratis).

Bellagio ❻

🏨 Hotel Silvio   Hotel €€

(📞031 95 03 22; www.bellagiosilvio.com; Via Carcano 10; d from €115; P ❄ 🛜 🏊) Located above the fishing hamlet of Loppia a short walk from the village, this family-run hotel is one of Bellagio's most relaxing spots. Here you can wake up in a contemporary Zen-like room and gaze out over the gardens of some of Lago di Como's most prestigious villas, then spend the morning at Bellagio's **lido** (📞031 95 11 95; www.lidodibellagio.com; Via Carcano 1; per half-/full day €6/10; 🕑10am-6.30pm Tue-Sun May, Jun & Sep, daily Jul & Aug); it's free for hotel guests.

Bergamo ❾

🍴 La Tana   Italian €€

(📞035 21 31 37; www.tanaristorante.it; Via San Lorenzo 25; meals €32-42; 🕑noon-2.30pm & 7-10pm Wed-Sun, 7-10pm Tue) In the upper town, tucked close to the Venetian walls, La Tana remains exceptionally popular for painstakingly prepared Bergamesque dishes served in a sun-drenched interior of exposed brick and colourful artwork, or out on the small front terrace.

A Weekend at Lago di Garda

10

Poets, politicians, divas and dictators: they've all been drawn to glorious Lago di Garda with mountains to the north, vine-clad hills to the south and a string of medieval towns encircling its shores.

TRIP HIGHLIGHTS

29 km

Salò
Refined Salò was capital of Mussolini's last republic

72 km

Riva del Garda
A landscaped lakefront backed by soaring mountains

5

Limone
sul Garda

Malcesine

3

6

108 km

Torri del Benaco
A pint-sized harbour overlooked by a Scaligero castle

Padenghe
sul Garda

Bardolino
FINISH

1 **START**

Sirmione
Roman ruins cascade down Sirmione's promontory

0 km

---

4 DAYS
135KM / 84 MILES

GREAT FOR...

BEST TIME TO GO

July for lake swimming and October for Bardolino's wine festival.

 ESSENTIAL PHOTO

Lakeside towns backed by mountains from aboard a boat.

☑ BEST FOR FAMILIES

Night swimming off pontoons floating along Riva's waterfront.

Lago di Garda is the largest of the Italian lakes, straddling the border between Lombardy and the Veneto. Vineyards, olive groves and citrus orchards range up the slopes and ensure the tables of Garda's trattorias are well stocked with fine products. Boats buzz across the water and paragliders utilise the thermals that caress Monte Baldo . All you need now is a vintage Alfa Romeo to blend in like an Italian.

Parco dell'Adamello

Lago d'Idro

Mo Capic (1977

Parco Re dell'A Garda Br

Lago di Valvestin

Garg

Monte Pizzocolo (1582m) ▲

Toscolano-Maderno

Gardone Riviera ④

Salò ③

SS572

Manerba del Garda

Padenghe sul Garda

Lago c Gard

START

Sirmione ①

Desenzano del Garda ②

A4

LOMBARDY

TRIP HIGHLIGHT

① Sirmione

Over the centuries impossibly pretty Sirmione has drawn the likes of Catullus and Maria Callas to its banks. The village sits astride a slender peninsula that juts out into the lake and is occupied in large part by the **Grotte di Catullo** (☎030 91 61 57; www.polomuseale. lombardia.beniculturali.it/index. php/grotte-di-catullo; Piazzale Orti Manara 4; adult/reduced €8/4, with Rocca Scaligera €12/6; ☻8.30am-7.30pm Mon & Wed-Sat, 9.30am-7pm Sun late Mar-late Oct, reduced hours rest of year), a misnomer for the ruins of an extensive Roman villa now comprising teetering stone arches

and tumbledown walls. There's no evidence that Catullus actually lived here, but who cares? The wraparound lake views from its terraced hillside are legendary. **Rocca Scaligera** (Castello Scaligero; adult/reduced €6/2, with Grotte di Catullo €12/6; ☻8.30am-7.30pm) is an enormous square-cut castle at the entrance to old Sirmione.

In true Roman style, there's an offshore thermal spring that pumps out water at a natural 37°C. Wallow lakeside in the contemporary outdoor pool at **Aquaria** (☎030 91 60 44; www. termedisirmione.com; Piazza Piatti; pools per 90min/day €19/53, treatments from €40; ☻pools 9am-10pm Sun-Wed, to midnight Thu-Sat Mar-Jun

& Sep-Dec, 9am-midnight daily Jul & Aug, hours vary Jan & Feb).

🍴 🛏 p137

The Drive » The first 7km from Sirmione to Desenzano del Garda is on the SS572 lake road. Exit Sirmione past the Garda Village campground and at the first major roundabout turn right towards Desenzano; total distance 11km.

- - - - - - - - - - - - - - - - -

❷ Desenzano del Garda

Known as the *porta del lago* (gateway to the lake), Desenzano may not be as pretty as other lakeside towns, but its ancient harbour, broad promenades and vibrant **Piazza Matteotti** make for pleasant wanderings. It is also a hub for summer nightlife.

Best of all are the mosaics in Desenzano's **Roman Villa** (☎030 914

🔗 LINK YOUR TRIP

8 **Northern Cities**
A 30-minute drive down the A22 and A4 from Bardolino brings you to Verona and the culture-heavy Northern Cities tour.

11 **Roof of Italy**
Climb out of the lake basin on the SS240 from Riva del Garda to Rovereto for a dose of modern art and an epic drive across Europe's highest pass.

133

35 47; Via Crocifisso 2; adult/ reduced €4/2; ⏰8.30am-7pm Tue-Sun mid-Mar–mid-Oct, to 5pm mid-Oct–mid-Mar). Wooden walkways lead directly over vivid scenes of chariot-riding, grape-gathering cherubs.

Stretching north of Desenzano, the rolling hills of the Valtenesi are etched with vine trellises and olive groves. **Frantoio Montecroce** (☏030 991 15 04; www.frantoiomontecroce.it; Viale Ettore Andreis 84; ⏰by appointment) offers tutored oil tastings.

The Drive » From Desenzano return to the SS572 and start to meander north right by the lakeshore. The first 6km to Padenghe sul Garda are some of the most scenic on the lake, lined with cypresses and umbrella pines with clear views over the water. Total distance to Salò is 19km.

TRIP HIGHLIGHT

3 Salò

Sedate and refined as Salò is today, in 1943 it was named the capital of the Social Republic of Italy as part of Mussolini's last-ditch efforts to organise Italian fascism in the face of advancing Allied forces. This episode, known as the Republic of Salò, saw more than 16 buildings turned into Mussolini's ministries and offices.

You can fill in more gaps in Salò's history at the relatively new **Museo di Salò** (Musa; www.museodisalo.it; Via Brunati 9; adult/reduced €14/11; ⏰10am-7pm, to 8pm Jun-Sep). Exhibits include objects relating to Mussolini, along with a collection of violins in honour of local-born luthier Gasparo di Salò (1542–1609), one of the world's earliest violin-makers.

✕ 🍽 p137

The Drive » Exit the medieval centre of Salò uphill on Via Umberto I and pick up the SS45bis heading north to Gardone. It's barely 7km along the narrow single carriageway, past old stone walls hiding lemon-coloured villas surrounded by luxuriant flora.

4 Gardone Riviera

In Gardone tour the home of Italy's most controversial poet, Gabriele d'Annunzio. Poet, soldier, hypochondriac and proto-fascist, d'Annunzio's home **Il Vittoriale degli Italiani** (☏0365 29 65 11; www.vittoriale.it; Piazza Vittoriale; gardens & museums adult/reduced €16/13; ⏰9am-8pm Apr-Oct, to 5pm Tue-Sun Nov-Mar; P) is as bombastic and extravagant as it is unsettling, and a perfect reflection of the man's enigmatic personality. He retreated to Gardone in 1922, claiming that he wanted to escape the world that made him sick.

For something less oppressive visit the flower-filled oasis of **Giardino Botanico Fondazione André Heller** (☏336 410877; www.hellergarden.com; Via Roma 2; adult/reduced €12/6; ⏰9am-7pm Mar-Nov). Hidden among the greenery are 30 pieces of contemporary sculpture.

🍽 p137

The Drive » Exit Gardone northeast on Corso Zanardelli for a long, scenic 43km drive north. At Tignale and Limone sul Garda you'll pass the stone pillars of Garda's lemon-houses. The final 12km from Limone to Riva del Garda are extraordinary, passing through dynamite-blasted tunnels dramatic enough to make this the location for the opening chase scene in Casino Royale.

DETOUR: LAGO DI LEDRO

Start: 5 Riva del Garda

From Riva take the SP37 and then the SS240 west into the mountains, past olive groves and vine-lined terraces. After 11km the road flattens and **Lago di Ledro** (www.vallediledro.com) comes into view. Only 2.5km long and 2km wide, this diminutive lake sits at an altitude of 650m and is set in a gorgeous valley beneath tree-covered mountains. **Molina di Ledro** is at the lake's eastern end, where thatched huts line up beside beaches and boat-hire pontoons.

Lago di Garda Malcesine

TRIP HIGHLIGHT

⑤ Riva del Garda

Even on a lake blessed by dramatic scenery, Riva del Garda still comes out on top. Encircled by towering rock faces and a looping landscaped waterfront, its appealing centre is a medley of grand architecture and wide squares. The town's strategic position was fought over for centuries and exhibits in the **Museo Alto Garda** (La Rocca; ☏0464 57 38 69; www.museoaltogarda.it; Piazza Cesare Battisti 3; adult/reduced €5/2.50; ⊙10am-6pm Tue-Sun mid-Mar–May & Oct, daily Jun-Sep) reflect this turbulent past. Riva makes a natural starting point for walks and bike rides, including trails around **Monte Rocchetta** (1575m), which looms over the northern end of the lake. Just south of town **La Strada del Ponale** (www.ponale.eu) is a walking path that ascends gently for 2.6km to **Ponale Alto Belvedere** (☏0464 56 73 21; Molina di Ledro; ⊙9am-6pm), a bar-restaurant where a couple of waterfalls are visible from the deck.

✕ ⋿ p137

TOP TIP: LAKE CRUISING

Fleets of ferries link many Lago di Garda communities, providing a series of scenic mini-cruises. They're run by **Navigazione sul Lago di Garda** (www.navigazionelaghi.it), which publishes English-language timetables online. A one-day, unlimited travel ticket costs €34.30/17.60 per adult/child. Car ferries cross year-round from Toscolano-Maderno on the west bank to Torri del Benaco on the east bank.

The Drive » From Riva pick up the SS240 around Torbole and then turn south on the SS249. Lake views abound through columned 'windows' as you pass through mountain tunnels, and to the left Monte Baldo rises above the lake. A cable car runs to the summit from Malcesine. The total distance from Riva to Torri del Benaco is 38km.

TRIP HIGHLIGHT

⑥ Torri del Benaco

Picturesque Torri del Benaco is one of the most appealing stops on the eastern bank. The 14th-century **Castello Scaligero** (☑045 629 61 11; www.museodelcastelloditorridelbenaco.it; Viale Fratelli Lavanda 2; adult/reduced €5/3; ☺9.30am-1pm & 4.30-7.30pm Tue-Sun mid-Jun–mid-Sep, 9.30am-12.30pm & 2.30-6pm Apr–mid-Jun & mid-Sep–Oct) overlooks a pint-sized harbour and packs a wealth of history into dozens of rooms, including exhibits on the lake's traditional industries of fishing, olive-oil production and lemon growing.

The Drive » From the waterfront at Torri del Benaco it's a short 7km drive to Garda, around the secluded Punta San Viglio headland. En route low stone walls or railings are all that stand between you and the water, while cypresses line front lawns to your left.

⑦ Garda

The bustling town of Garda lacks obvious charms, but it does possess the leafy headland of **Punta San Viglio**, a gorgeous crescent bay backed by olive trees 3km to the north. The privately owned **Parco Baia delle Sirene** (☑045 725 58 84; www.parcobaia dellesirene.it; Punta San Viglio; adult/reduced incl Punta San Viglio €13/6, cheaper after 2.30pm; ☺10am-7pm Apr & May, 9.30am-8pm Jun-Aug; ℗) has sunloungers and picnic tables beneath the trees.

The tiny headland is also the location of **Locanda San Vigilio** (☑045 725 66 88; www.punta-sanvigilio.it; Punta San Vigilio; d €270-375, ste €440-900; ℗✳@☒), with its excellent harbourside taverna, the perfect perch for Lago di Garda sunsets.

The Drive » The final 4km drive to Bardolino, continuing on the SS249, gives you your last fill of big views. Over the short distance the road rises up, giving you lofty views over the water before dropping down amid olive groves into Bardolino.

⑧ Bardolino

More than 70 vineyards and wine cellars grace the gentle hills that roll east from Bardolino's shores. They produce an impressive array of pink Chiaretto, ruby Classico, dry Superiore and young Novello.

One of the most atmospheric ways to savour their flavours is a tutored tasting (€5 per person) at the **Museo del Vino** (☑045 622 83 31; www.museodelvino.it; Via Costabella 9; ☺9am-12.30pm & 2.30-7pm mid-Mar–Sep, hours vary Oct–mid-Mar), which is housed within the **Zeni Winery**. Zeni has been crafting quality wines from Bardolino's morainic hills since 1870.

After this proverbial 'warm up', head into town (with designated driver) and hit the *amarone* and *valpolicella* varietals at **La Bottega del Vino** (☑348 6041800; Piazza Matteotti 46; ☺9.30am-2am).

Eating & Sleeping

Sirmione ❶

✖ Ristorante Il Girasole   Italian €€€
(☎030 91 91 82; Via Vittorio Emanuele 72; meals €40-55; ⏱noon-2.30pm & 7-10.30pm) Sirmione's best dining experience excels in congenial, well-organised service and traditional food skilfully executed. The three-ingredient *cacio e pepe* (pasta with cheese and pepper) topped with black truffles might be the simplest thing on the menu but it's also the most sublime, while the extra-crunchy breadsticks could be the best of the 100 or so you bite into in Italy.

⌂ Meublé Grifone   Hotel €
(☎030 91 60 14; www.gardalakegrifonehotel.eu; Via Gaetano Bocchio 4; s €70-85, d €95-115; ❄ 🔊) The location is superb: set right beside the shore, Grifone's many bedrooms directly overlook the lake and Sirmione's castle, meaning you get five-star views for two-star prices. Inside it's all old-school simplicity, but with large beds, air-con units and fans. It's family-run and super-accommodating. Breakfast and a balcony cost €10 extra each.

Salò ❸

✖ Al Cantinone   Trattoria €€
(☎0365 2 02 34; Piazza Sant'Antonio 19; meals €25-30; ⏱noon-2.30pm & 7-10pm Fri-Wed) It's well worth heading just a few streets back from the waterfront to track down this friendly neighbourhood trattoria, home to gingham tablecloths, fabulous cooking smells and a clutch of regulars playing cards in the corner. Good-value dishes draw on Salò's lake-meets-mountains setting.

⌂ Villa Arcadio   Villa €€€
(☎0365 4 22 81; www.hotelvillaarcadio.it; Via Navelli 2; d €150-270, ste €300-450; 🅿 ❄ @ 🔊 ⛵ 🐾) Perched above Salò and

surrounded by olive groves, this converted convent lays on restrained luxury in a semirural setting. Enjoy the vista of glassy lake and misty mountains from the cheese-wedge-shaped pool or retreat inside to frescoed rooms and ancient wood-beamed halls.

Gardone Riviera ❹

⌂ Locanda Agli Angeli   B&B €€
(☎0365 2 09 91; www.agliangeli.biz; Via Dosso 7; d from €105; 🅿 ❄ 🐾) It's a perfect hillside Lago di Garda bolthole: a beautifully restored, rustic-chic *locanda* (inn) with a kidney-shaped pool, a terrace dotted with armchairs and Italian-meets-Balinese decor. Ask for room 29 for a balcony with grandstand lake and hill views, but even the smaller bedrooms are full of charm.

Riva del Garda ❺

✖ Osteria Le Servite   Osteria €€
(☎0464 55 74 11; www.leservite.com; Via Passirone 68, Arco; meals €30-45; ⏱7-10.30pm Tue-Sun Apr-Sep, 7-10.30pm Wed-Sat Oct-Mar; 🅿 🐾) Tucked away in Arco's wine-growing region, this elegant little *osteria* (tavern) serves dishes that are so seasonal the menu changes weekly. You might be eating mimosa gnocchi, tender *salmerino* (Arctic char) or organic ravioli with *stracchino* cheese.

⌂ Hotel Garni Villa Maria   Hotel €
(☎0464 55 22 88; www.garnimaria.com; Viale dei Tigli; d €95, ste €120-160; 🅿 ❄ 🔊) Beautifully designed, uber-modern rooms make this small family-run hotel a superb deal. Pristine bedrooms have a Scandinavian vibe, with all-white linens, sleek modern bathrooms and accents of orange and lime green. There's a tiny roof garden, and bedrooms with balconies offer impressive mountain views.

Roof of Italy

Traversing the Alps, from Lago di Como through the Valtellina's vine-covered slopes and across the hair-raising Passo dello Stelvio to Merano, this is one of the north's most spectacular roads.

11

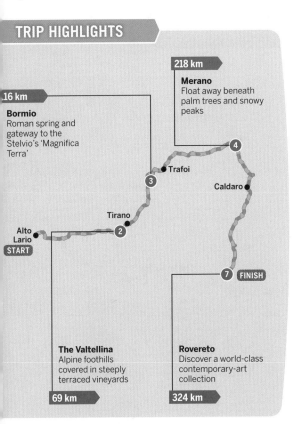

218 km

Merano
Float away beneath palm trees and snowy peaks

16 km

Bormio
Roman spring and gateway to the Stelvio's 'Magnifica Terra'

Trafoi

Caldaro

Tirano

Alto Lario
START

The Valtellina
Alpine foothills covered in steeply terraced vineyards

69 km

Rovereto
Discover a world-class contemporary-art collection

324 km

7 FINISH

6 DAYS
324KM / 201 MILES

GREAT FOR...

BEST TIME TO GO
June to September, when the Passo dello Stelvio is open.

ESSENTIAL PHOTO

Cloud-busting views on the Passo dello Stelvio.

BEST FOR WELL-BEING

Dipping in Merano's hot and cold spa pools surrounded by soaring mountain peaks.

11 Roof of Italy

Tracing the foothills of the Orobie Alps and the high passes of Parco Nazionale dello Stelvio, the borderlands of northern Italy offer up stunning wildernesses, stupendous scenery and warm welcomes in wooden farmhouses. Vineyards and orchards cloak the valleys of the Valtellina and Adige, while the region's historic cities – Merano, Trento and Rovereto – combine Austrian and Italian influences, creating a unique cultural and culinary melange.

1 Alto Lario

The towns of **Dongo**, **Gravedona** and **Sorico** once formed the independent republic of the Tre Pievi (Three Parishes) and were a hotbed of Cathar heresy. Now they're more popular with watersports enthusiasts than Inquisitors. Lake Lario is another name for Lago di Como (Lake Como), so the area takes its name from being at the top *(alto)* of the lake. Gravedona, the largest of the three towns, sits on

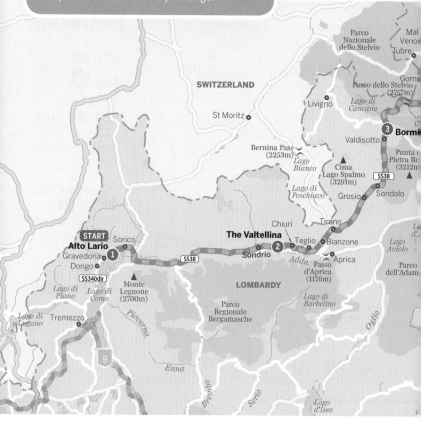

a gently curved bay with views across to Monte Legnone.

Up on the plateau at Peglio, **Chiesa di Sant'Eusebio** (Strada della Chiesa; ☺3-6pm Tue, Thu & Sun Jul, 3-6pm Tue-Thu & Sun Aug) offers lake views and masterly frescoes by Como painter Giovan Mauro della Rovere, better known as Il Fiammenghino (Little Fleming). He sought refuge here after murdering a man and did penance painting the vivid *Last Judgement*.

Sorico, the most northerly of the three towns, guards the mouth of the river Mera, which flows into shallow **Lago di Mezzola**, a bird-breeding nature reserve.

The Drive ≫ From Sorico take the SS340dir north. Cross over the waterway that connects Lago di Como and Lago di Mezzola and continue until you hit a T-junction. Turn right, and at the roundabout turn left onto the SS38 towards Morbegno. Continue for a further 36km, chasing the Adda river all the way to Sondrio.

TRIP HIGHLIGHT

❷ The Valtellina

The Valtellina cuts a broad swath down the Adda valley, where villages and vineyards hang precariously on the slopes of the Orobie Alps. The steep northern flank is carpeted by Nebbiolo grapes, which yield a light-red wine. Both body and alcohol content improve with altitude, so generations of Valtenesi built upwards, carrying the soil in woven baskets to high mountain terraces. Their rewards: a DOC classification for Valtellina Superiore since 1968. In **Sondrio**, it's possible, by appointment, to visit the cellars of **Arpepe** (☎0342 21 41 20;

LINK YOUR TRIP

9 **The Graceful Italian Lakes**

Take the scenic SS340dir to Tremezzo to tour Como's luxuriant gardens and Maggiore's Borromean palaces.

13 **Grande Strada delle Dolomiti**

Descend into Bolzano from Castello Firmiano on the SS42 and head east into the Dolomites for mountain hikes and gourmet dinners.

141

www.arpepe.com; Via Buon Consiglio 4), and in **Chiuro**, **Nino Negri** (📞0342 48 52 11; www.ninonegri.it; Via Ghibellini 3).

The prettiest town in the valley is **Tirano**, the departure point for the **Trenino Rosso del Bernina** (📞0342 70 62 63; www.treninorosso.it; Via Giuseppe Mazzini; adult/child return €61/15). This gravity-defying rail track traverses 196 bridges, crests the Bernina Pass (2253m) and crosses the Morteratsch glacier on the way to St Moritz in Switzerland.

 p145

The Drive ›› From Tirano it is 37 scenic kilometres to the heady heights of Bormio. Continue northeast on the SS38, still tracking the Adda river and rising up through the terraces, past small hamlets such as Grosio and Sondalo and into the snow-capped mountains.

---

❸ Bormio

Splendidly sited in a mountain basin at 1225m, Bormio was once the heart of a region dubbed Magnifica Terra. Most of the region's magnificent territory now lies within northern Italy's largest national park, the **Parco Nazionale dello Stelvio** (📞0473 83 04 30; www.parks.it/parco.nazionale. stelvio), an icy land of 100 glaciers that includes one of Europe's largest, the **Ghiacciaio dei Forni**.

The park is largely the preserve of walkers, who come for the network of well-organised mountain huts and marked trails – but there are a couple of well-serviced ski runs at **Solda** and the **Passo dello Stelvio** (2757m; p144), both of which offer year-round skiing.

DETOUR: MALLES & MARIENBERG

Start: ❸ Bormio

A short detour north off the main Bormio-to-Merano route via the scenic SS40 brings you to the old customs point of Malles. Aside from its handsome Gothic churches and historic centre, it's a convenient jumping-off point for nearby **Marienberg** (📞0473 84 39 80; www.marienberg.it; Schlinig 1, Malles (Mals); museum adult/reduced €5.50/3; ☉10am-5pm Mon-Sat mid-Mar–Oct & late Dec-early Jan), the highest Benedictine monastery in Europe. In the crypt are a series of superb Byzantine-Romanesque frescoes, which were only discovered in 1980. Their almost pristine condition makes them unique.

Back in Bormio's medieval centre, the **Bagni di Bormio** (📞0342 91 01 31; www.qcterme.com; Via Statale Stelvio; €48-54; ☉10am-11pm Mon-Thu, 10am-midnight Fri, 9am-midnight Sat, 9am-11pm Sun) were much loved by the likes of Pliny the Elder and Leonardo da Vinci. Hotel stays include unlimited spa access, but day passes are also available.

The Drive ›› The most difficult, and awe-inspiring, 96km is the road from Bormio to Merano, which crosses the cloud-covered Passo dello Stelvio, 25km from Bormio. Approaching along the SS38, the road rises through a series of switchbacks, some with very steep gradients, and descends via alarming hairpin bends to quaint Trafoi on the other side. From Trafoi continue on the SS38 to Merano. When the pass is closed, take the more circuitous 140km route through Switzerland via the SS301, Swiss route 28, SS41 and SS38.

---

❹ Merano

Merano is where 19th-century Mitteleuropeans came to soothe their weary bones, do a 'grape' cure, and, perhaps, embark on a dalliance or two. The Hapsburg-era spa was the hot destination of its day and the city's therapeutic traditions have served it well in the new millennium, with the striking modern redevelopment of the **Terme Merano** (📞0473 25 20 00; www.termemerano.it; Thermenplatz 9; bathing pass 2hr/all day from €13/19, with

Rovereto Bridge over the Adige river

sauna from $18/25; ⊘9am-10pm). Swim through the sluice towards 12 outdoor pools in summer and be met by a vision of palm-studded gardens and snow-topped mountains.

You could also give over an entire day to the botanical gardens at **Castel Trauttmansdorff** (✆0473 25 56 00; www.trauttmansdorff.it; St-Valentin-Strasse 51a; garden & museum adult/reduced €14/11; ⊘9am-7pm Apr–mid-Oct, to 5pm mid-Oct–mid-Nov, plus to 11pm Fri Jun-Aug), where exotic cacti and palms, and beds of lilies, irises and tulips all cascade down the hillside surrounding a castle where

Sissi (Empress Elisabeth) spent the summer.

✕ 🛏 p145

The Drive ›› From Merano to Bolzano and the Castello Firmiano, the SS38 becomes a dual-lane autostrada, so the next 30km are easy motorway driving as you leave the high mountains behind you.

----

❺ Castello Firmiano

Known as the 'Crown of Sigismund', the expansive walls and battlements of Castello Firmiano encircle the hilltop overlooking Bolzano and Appiano just like a princely coronet.

Fought over for 1000 years, it has long been a symbol of Tyrolean

independence and now houses the **Messner Mountain Museum** (MMM Firmian; ✆0471 63 12 64; www.messner-mountain-museum.it; Via Castel Firmiano 53; adult/reduced €12/10; ⊘10am-6pm Fri-Wed late Mar–mid-Nov), named after celebrated mountaineer Reinhold Messner. Exhibits explore humanity's relationship with the mountains, while the inspiring design suggests shifting altitudes and uneven mountain terrain.

South of the castle stretches the Südtiroler Weinstrasse (www.suedtiroler-weinstrasse.it), a wine road winding through the Adige valley

TOP TIP:
PASSO DELLO STELVIO

The high and hair-raising Passo dello Stelvio (www. stelvio.net) is only open from June to early October, and is always subject to closures dependent on early or late snow falls. For the rest of the year, you'll need to skirt around the pass to get to Merano by taking the SS301 to Livigno and then route 28 through Switzerland to Tubre and then on to Merano via the SS41 and SS38.

along the SP14 all the way to Trento. Producers line the route, although the hub of the region is **Caldaro**.

The Drive » South of Bolzano the autostrada carves a straight line through the midst of the Adige valley. It's a fast, scenic route with the mountains overlapping in descending order in front of you. If you have more time, however, the preferred route is to pick up the SP14 from the castle to Caldaro and follow the wine route all the way to Magrè, where you can stop and taste some of the prized Adige wines.

❻ Trento

During the tumultuous years of the Counter-Reformation, the Council of Trent convened here, dishing out far-reaching condemnations to up-pity Protestants. Modern Trento is less preachy: quietly confident and easy to like. Frescoed streets fan out from the **Duomo** (Cattedrale di San Vigilio; ☎0461 23 12 93; www.catte dralesanvigilio.it; Piazza del Du-omo; archaeological area adult/reduced €2/1; ☉cathedral

6.30am-6pm, archaeological area 10am-noon & 2.30-5.30pm Mon-Sat), which sits above a 6th-century temple and a paleo-Christian archaeological area.

On the opposite side of the square is the for-mer bishop's residence, now the **Museo Dioc-esano Tridentino** (Palazzo Pretorio; ☎0461 23 44 19; www.museodiocesanotriden tino.it; Piazza del Duomo 18; adult/reduced incl archaeolog-ical area €7/2; ☉10am-1pm & 2-6pm Wed-Mon Jun-Sep, 9.30am-12.30pm & 2-5.30pm Mon & Wed-Sat, 10am-1pm & 2-6pm Sun Oct-May), where illuminated manuscripts and paintings depict the Council of Trent.

Above it all, the mighty **Castello del Buonconsiglio** (☎0461 23 37 70; www.buonconsiglio. it; Via Clesio 5; adult/reduced €10/8, guided tour of Torre Aquila €2; ☉10am-6pm Tue-Sun May-Oct, 9.30am-5pm Tue-Sun Nov-Apr) is a reminder of the bloody history of these borderlands.

🍴 🛏 p145

The Drive » The final 30km drive south on the A22 leaves most of the majestic scenery behind, and the broad valley tapers out towards Rovereto.

TRIP HIGHLIGHT

❼ Rovereto

In the winter of 1769, Leopold Mozart and his soon-to-be-famous musi-cal son visited Rover-eto. Those on a musical pilgrimage come to visit the **Chiesa di San Marco** (Piazza San Marco; ☉8.30am-noon & 2-7pm), where the 13-year-old Wolfgang wowed the Roveretini, and for the annual fes-tival of classical music, **Festival Settenovecento** (www.settenovecento.it; ☉mid-Apr–mid-May).

The town that Mozart knew still has its tightly coiled streets, but it's the shock of the new that lures most to the **Museo di Arte Moderna e Contemporanea** (MART; ☎0464 43 88 87; www. mart.trento.it; Corso Bettini 43; adult/reduced €11/7, incl Casa d'Arte Futurista Depero & Galleria Civica di Trento €14/10; ☉10am-6pm Tue-Thu, Sat & Sun, to 9pm Fri), one of Italy's best 20th-century art museums. Designed by Ticinese architect Mario Botta, it is a fitting home for some huge 20th-century works, including Warhol's *Four Marilyns* (1962), several Picassos and a clutch of contemporary art stars.

🍴 p145

Eating & Sleeping

The Valtellina ❷

✖ Altavilla   Gastronomy €€

(☎0342 72 03 55; www.altavilla.info; Via ai Monti
46, Bianzone; meals €30-40; ⏱noon-2.30pm &
7-10pm Tue-Sun, daily Aug; 🅿🛜♿🎦) In this
charming Alpine guesthouse and restaurant
you'll find one of the region's gastronomic treats.
Owner and Slow Food connoisseur Anna Bertola
spreads a feast for her guests with traditional
mountain dishes like *sciàtt* (buckwheat fritters
stuffed with Bitto cheese) and *pizzoccheri*
(buckwheat pasta). The artisanal salami,
mountain venison and aged Bitto cheese are
particular highlights, as is the 500-label wine list.

✖ Osteria del Crotto   Osteria €€

(☎0342 61 48 00; www.osteriadelcrotto.it; Via
Pedemontana 22, Morbegno; meals €30-45;
⏱noon-3pm & 7.30-10pm Tue-Sat, noon-
3pm Sun, 7.30-10pm Mon) Osteria del Crotto
serves a whole slew of Slow Food Movement–
authenticated products such as *violino di capra
della Valchiavenna* (literally 'violin goat of the
Valchiavenna'), a traditional salami made from
the shank, which is sliced by resting it on the
shoulder and shaving it as a violin player would
move their bow.

Merano ❹

✖ Pur Südtirol   Deli €

(☎0473 01 21 40; www.pursuedtirol.com;
Freiheitsstrasse 35; snacks & light meals €5-13;
⏱9am-7.30pm Mon-Fri, to 2pm Sat; ♿) This
stylish regional showcase – now a chain with
branches in Bolzano and Brunico – has an
amazing selection of farm produce: wine,
cider, some 80 varieties of cheese, speck and
sausage, pastries and breads, tisanes and
body care. Everything is local (take Anton
Oberhöller's chocolate, flavoured with apple,
lemon balm or dark bread crisps).

🛏 Ottmanngut   Boutique Hotel €€€

(☎0473 44 96 56; www.ottmanngut.it;
Verdistrasse 18; s €132, d €264-314; 🛜) This
boutique hotel encapsulates Merano's mix of
stately sophistication, natural beauty and gently

bohemian backstory. The remodelled townhouse
has nine rooms scattered over three floors, and is
set among terraced vineyards a scant five-minute
walk from the arcades of the centre. Individually
furnished, antique-strewn rooms evoke different
moods, each highlighting the different landscape
glimpsed from the window.

Trento ❻

✖ Il Libertino   Alpine €€

(☎0461 26 00 85; Piazza Piedicastello 4-6; meals
€35-43; ⏱noon-2.30pm & 7-10.30pm Wed-Mon)
Stroll the bridge over the fast-flowing Adige to
this charming wood-panelled restaurant for
carefully prepared traditional dishessuch as
venison, chestnuts, radicchio, boar sausage and
river trout. There's also an encyclopedic wine list
of Trentino DOCs and a memorable *tavolozza di
dolci* (sampler of four scrumptious desserts).
Best of all, it's open for Sunday lunch.

🛏 Elisa B&B   B&B €

(☎0461 92 21 33; www.bbelisa.com; Viale
Rovereto 17; s/d from €65/90; ❄🛜) This is
a true B&B in an architect's beautiful family
home, with two private, stylish rooms and
breakfasts that are a feast of home-baked
cakes, freshly squeezed juice and artisanal
cheese. It's located in a smart residential
neighbourhood, a pleasant 15-minute stroll
from Trento's city centre, with lots of eating,
shopping and drinking options along the way.

Rovereto ❼

✖ Osteria del Pettirosso   Osteria €€

(☎0464 42 24 63; www.osteriadelpettirosso.
it; Corso Bettini 24; snacks €5-12, meals €25-30;
⏱11am-3.30pm & 5.30pm-1am Mon-Sat, 11am-
3.30pm Sun) There's a moody downstairs dining
room for evenings, but during the day join locals
for a blackboard menu of small-producer wines
by the glass, plates of cheese, *salumi* (cured
meats) or *canederli* (homemade dumplings),
a big salad, or one of the beautifully prepared
local dishes such as fillet of pork perfumed with
thyme and Garda lemon.

Valle d'Aosta

The Valle d'Aosta carves a deep and scenic path through the Alps to Mont Blanc (Monte Bianco). Explore an ancient, hybrid culture, sample Franco-Provençal food and eyeball epic peaks from cable cars.

12

TRIP HIGHLIGHTS

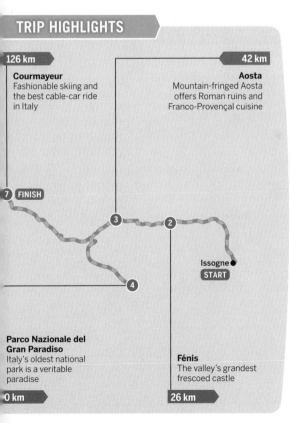

126 km

Courmayeur
Fashionable skiing and the best cable-car ride in Italy

42 km

Aosta
Mountain-fringed Aosta offers Roman ruins and Franco-Provençal cuisine

7 FINISH

3

2

Issogne ● **START**

4

Parco Nazionale del Gran Paradiso
Italy's oldest national park is a veritable paradise

Fénis
The valley's grandest frescoed castle

0 km

26 km

---

5 DAYS
126KM / 78 MILES

GREAT FOR...

BEST TIME TO GO
January to March for skiing; September for hiking.

ESSENTIAL PHOTO
Top-of-the-world views from the Funivie Monte Bianco.

BEST FOR SKIING
Courmayeur's slopes in the shadow of Mont Blanc.

12 Valle d'Aosta

Touring the Valle d'Aosta's castle-tipped peaks and glacial valley makes for one of Italy's most scenic drives. Courmayeur's fashion-parade of skiers hits the high slopes of Mont Blanc, while Valdostan farmers cultivate Alpine wines and ferment famous *fontina* cheeses in the pastures below. When the snow melts, the hiking in the Gran Paradiso park and along Aosta's high-altitude trails is even more sublime.

❶ Issogne

The Valle d'Aosta's peaks are crowned with castles, each within view of the next, so messages could be transferred up and down the valley via flag signals. Although many were little more than fortified barracks, as time progressed so their lordly inhabitants became more mindful of appearances. The **Castello di Issogne** (☎0125 92 93 73; www. lovevda.it; Piazza Castello, Issogne; adult/reduced €5/2; ⏰9am-7pm daily Apr-Sep, 10am-1pm & 2-5pm Oct-Mar,

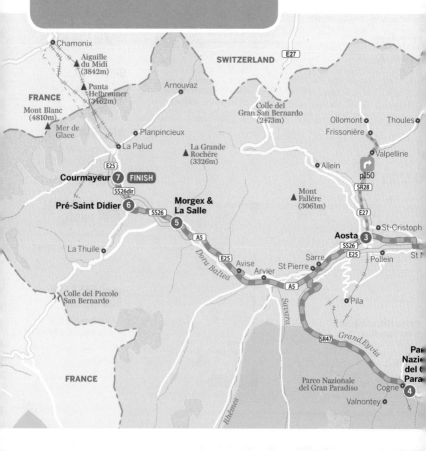

closed last 2 weeks of Oct), for example, sitting on the right bank of the Dora Baltea river and located on one of the only navigable routes over the Alps, is more of a signorial Renaissance residence, the interior decorated with rare Alpine frescoes. It looks quite different to the dour **Castello di Verrès** (☎0125 92 90 67; www. lovevda.it; Verrès; adult/reduced €3/2; ⏰9am-7pm daily Apr-Sep, 10am-1pm & 2-5pm Tue-Sun Oct-Mar), located on the opposite bank, with which it was in constant conflict.

The Drive ≫ From Issogne it's a 26km drive along the A5 autostrada to Fénis. The peaks of the lower Alps are already visible and frame your route. After Montjovet duck through a series of tunnels as you sweep westwards into the valley. Take the exit for Nus and follow signs for the castle.

- - - - - - - - - - - - - - - -

TRIP HIGHLIGHT

❷ Fénis

The finest castle in the Valle d'Aosta is without a doubt the magnificently restored **Castello di Fénis** (☎0165 76 42 63; www. lovevda.it; Fénis; adult/reduced €5/3.50; ⏰9am-7pm daily Apr-Sep, 10am-1pm & 2-5pm Tue-Sun Oct-Mar), owned by the powerful Challant clan from 1242 onwards. It features rich frescoes, including an impressive etching of St George slaying a fiery dragon. The castle is laid out in a pentagonal shape with square and cylindrical turrets lording it over the lush chestnut forests. It was never really used as a defensive post, but served as a plush residence for the Challants until 1716. The on-site **museum** allows access to a weaponry display, the kitchens, the battlements, the former residential quarters and the frescoed chapel.

The Drive ≫ Aosta is just 16km from the Castello di Fénis. Rejoin the A5/E25 for 8km through pretty mountainous forests. Then exit towards Aosta

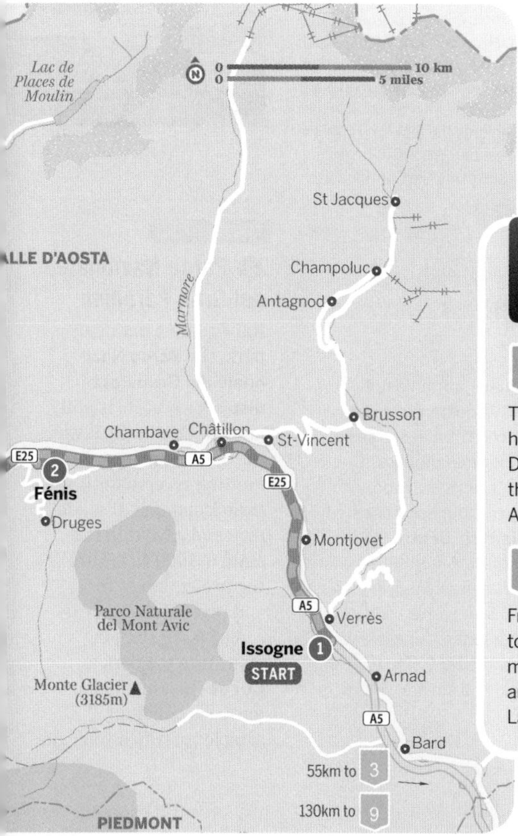

LINK YOUR TRIP

3 Savoy Palace Circuit

The Gran Paradiso was the hunting preserve of the Dukes of Savoy; pick up their trail in Turin, down the A5 from Issogne.

9 The Graceful Italian Lakes

From Alpine peaks to a Mediterranean microclimate, take the A5 and A4 from Issogne to Lago d'Orta.

Est onto the E27 for 1.2km, and after you pass through the toll booths follow signs for Aosta Centro, which is a further 4km.

- - - - - - - - - - - - - - - - -

TRIP HIGHLIGHT

❸ Aosta

Jagged Alpine peaks rise like marble cathedrals above the town of Aosta, a once-important Roman settlement that has sprawled rather untidily across the valley floor since the opening of the Mont Blanc tunnel in the 1960s. But its 2000-year-old centre still harbours Roman relics, such as the **Arco di Augusto** (Piazza Arco di Augusto), the **Roman bridge**, spanning the Buthier river since the 1st century, and the **Porta Praetoria**, the main gate to the Roman city. Even the **Roman Theatre** (Via Porta Praetoria; incl admission

to 3 other sites €7; ⊙9am-7pm Sep-Jun, to 8pm Jul & Aug) remains in use as a venue for summer concerts.

Otherwise, more Challant-commissioned artworks can be seen in the **Chiesa di Sant'Orso** (Via Sant'Orso; ⊙9am-5.30pm), which dates back to the 10th century.

For skiing and hiking on the slopes above, ascend the **Aosta-Pila cable car** (one way/return €4.50/7; ⊙9am-5.30pm mid-Jun–early Sep) to the 1800m-high resort of **Pila**.

✕ 🛏 p153

The Drive ≫ Leave Aosta heading westwards for the next scenic 26km to Cogne. You'll pick up the Viale Piccolo San Bernardino first for a couple of kilometres and then merge with the SS26. After about 3km turn left onto the SR47 and start the beautiful, mountain-hugging ascent into the Gran Paradiso.

FLAVIO VALLENARI/GETTY IMAGES ©

↱ DETOUR: VALPELLINE

Start: ❸ **Aosta**

Aosta's signature cheese is made from the full-cream, unpasteurised milk of Valdostan cows that have grazed on pastures up to 2700m above sea level, before being matured for three months in underground rock tunnels. You can learn more about the history, 'terroir' and production of Aostan cheeses at the **Valpelline Visitors' Centre** (☎0165 7 33 09; www.fontinacoop.it; Frissonière; €3; ⊙8.30am-12.30pm & 2.30-6.30pm Mon-Fri, 9am-noon & 3-6pm Sat & Sun mid-Jun-mid-Sep, closed Sat & Sun mid-Sep-mid-Jun). Follow the SR28 for 7km north to the Valpelline valley, turn east towards Ollomont and after 1.5km turn west along a mountain road to Frissonière, where the centre is located.

TRIP HIGHLIGHT

❹ Parco Nazionale del Gran Paradiso

Italy's oldest national park, the **Parco Nazionale del Gran Paradiso** (www.pngp.it), is aptly named. Originally it was the Savoy's own private hunting reserve until Vittorio Emanuele II made nice and gave it to the state in 1922 to ensure the protection of the endangered ibex.

The main stepping stone into the park is **Cogne** (1534m), famous for its lace-making, samples of which you can

Aosta Roman Theatre

buy at **Le Marché Aux Puces** (Rue Grand Paradis 4; ⏲9.30am-12.30pm & 3.30-7pm Thu-Tue). Easy walks in the park are possible, such as the 3km stroll to the village of **Lillaz** on trail 23, where there is a geological park and a waterfall that drops 150m. Trails 22 and 23 will get you to the village of **Valnontey**, where you can visit the **Giardino Alpino Paradisia** (☎0165 7 53 01; www.pngp. it; Frazione Valnontey 44, Cogne; adult/reduced €3/1.50; ⏲10am-5.30pm Jun & early Sep, to 6.30pm Jul & Aug), an Alpine garden displaying mountain flora and rare butterflies.

✗ ⌂ p153

The Drive » The longest drive on the tour is 42km to Morgex and La Salle. The first 20km involve retracing your route down the SR47 out of the mountains. When you reach the bottom follow signs to rejoin the A5/E25 autostrada in the direction of Mont Blanc. From here it's 18km to Morgex through the forested valley.

- - - - - - - - - - - - - - - - - - - -

❺ Morgex & La Salle

The ruined towers of **Châtelard**, which guard the road over the Piccolo San Bernardo pass, also cast a shadow over Europe's highest vineyards strung out between the two communes of Morgex and La Salle. The wines from these Alpine vines, produced almost exclusively from the Prié Blanc grape grown between 900m and 1200m, is light and fruity with overtones of mountain herbs and freshly cut hay.

Given the extremes of temperature at this altitude (some vines run almost to the snow line), vintners employ a unique system of cultivation called *pergola bassa* (low-level arbours), where vines are planted low to the ground to protect them.

SKIING MONTE BIANCO

Courmayeur offers some extraordinary skiing in the shadow of Mont Blanc. The two main ski areas – the Plan Checrouit and Pre de Pascal – are interlinked by 100km of runs. Three lifts leave from the valley floor: one from Courmayeur itself, one from the village of Dolonne and one from nearby Val Veny. They are run by Funivie Courmayeur Mont Blanc (www. courmayeur-montblanc.com).

Since 1983 the Aostan government has sought to preserve these ancient traditions by setting up the cooperative **Cave Mont Blanc de Morgex et La Salle** (☑0165 80 19 49; www.cavemontblanc. com; Strada des Iles 31, La Ruine-Morgex; ⊙10am-noon & 3.30-6.30pm Mon, Tue & Thu-Sat, 10am-noon Wed), which processes the grapes from the 90 or so local smallholdings. Aosta's **tourist office** (www.lovevda.it; Piazza Porta Praetoria 3; ⊙9am-7pm; 🗟) has an English-language booklet with information on individual cellars and the cooperative.

The Drive » From either La Salle or Morgex descend through the vineyards and rejoin the SS26 for the short 7km drive to Pré-Saint Didier. The road passes under the A5 and then wriggles alongside the river Thuile all the way to Pré.

❻ Pré-Saint Didier

Bubbling at a natural 37°C from the mountains' depths, where the river Thuile forces its

way through a narrow gorge into the Dora valley, the thermal waters at **Terme di Pré-Saint-Didier** (☑0165 86 72 72; www.qcterme.com; Allée des Thermes; admission €44-54; ⊙9.30am-9pm Mon-Thu, 8.30am-11pm Fri & Sat, 8am-9pm Sun) have been a source of therapeutic treatment since the bath-loving Romans were in town. In addition to saunas, whirlpools and toning waterfalls there's an indoor-outdoor thermal pool. It's lit by candles and torches on Saturday nights, when it is spectacular amid the snow and stars.

The Drive » The scenic drive to Courmayeur is on the SS26dir. Cross over the river Thuile in Pré and head westwards with the towering snow-capped peaks of the high passes in front of you. They're an awesome sight, especially in spring when they're framed by the deepest green conifers.

TRIP HIGHLIGHT

❼ Courmayeur

Flush up against France and linked by a dramatic

cable-car ride to its cross-border cousin in Chamonix, Courmayeur has grafted upmarket ski facilities onto an ancient Roman base. Its pièce de résistance is lofty **Mont Blanc**, western Europe's highest mountain, 4810m of solid rock and ice that rises like an impregnable wall above the Valle d'Aosta. Ride the **Funivie Monte Bianco** (Skyway; www.montebianco. com; Strada Statale 26; return €52, Pavillon du Mt Fréty return €28; ⊙8.30am-4pm) for transglacial views that will take your breath away.

First stop is the 2173m-high midstation **Pavillon du Mt Fréty**, where there's a restaurant and the **Mt Fréty Nature Oasis**. At the top of the ridge is **Punta Helbronner** (3462m). From Punta Helbronner another cable car (late May to late September) takes you on a spectacular 5km ride across the Italian border to the **Aiguille du Midi** (3842m) in France, from where the world's highest cable car transports you into Chamonix. The journey from Courmayeur to Chamonix costs €80 and the journey back to Courmayeur by bus is €15. It's pricey but spectacular.

🍴 🛏 p153

Eating & Sleeping

Aosta ❸

✖ Trattoria degli Artisti   Trattoria €€
(☎0165 4 09 60; www.trattoriadegliartisti.it; Via
Maillet 5-7; meals €25-33; ⏱12.30-2pm & 7.30-
10pm Tue-Sat; 🛜) Fabulous Valdostan cuisine is
dished up at this dark and cosy trattoria, tucked
down an alleyway off Via E Aubert. Antipasti
such as puff pastry filled with Valdostan fondue,
cured ham and regional salami are followed by
dishes such as roe venison with polenta, and
beef braised in Morgex et de La Salle white wine.

🛏 Le Rêve Charmant   Guesthouse €€
(☎0165 23 88 55; www.lerevecharmant.com;
Via Marché Vaudan 6; d €130-180; 🅿 ❄ 🛜)
Tucked away in a quiet historic alley, this six-
room hotel is full of traditional Aostan furniture
and decoration but keeps it simple and rather
stylish. A warm, welcoming lounge leads to
surprisingly spacious rooms that have beautiful
modern bathrooms and high ceilings. The young
owners are charming and service is top rate.

Parco Nazionale del Gran Paradiso ❹

✖ La Brasserie de Bon Bec   Alpine €€
(☎0165 74 92 88; Rue Bourgeois 72, Cogne;
meals €28-38; ⏱noon-2.30pm & 7-10pm Tue-
Sun) In a warmly lit dining room adorned with
old farm tools and glossy oil paintings, Bon Bec
serves up outstanding mountain cuisine. Start off
with house-smoked trout (sourced from nearby
Lillaz) or classic Valdostan polenta, before
moving on to grilled Angus beef or rich *tartiflette*
(a dish from the Savoy made with potatoes,
reblochon cheese, onions and lardons).

🛏 Hotel Ristorante Petit Dahu   Guesthouse €
(☎393 8285300; www.hotelpetitdahu.com;
Frazone Valnontey 27; d from €110; 🅿 🛜)

Straddling two traditional stone-and-wood
buildings, this friendly, family-run spot has cosy,
all-wood rooms in a peaceful location a short
stroll from the Cogne village centre. There's a
wonderful restaurant (open only to guests) that
features rustic mountain cooking using wild
Alpine herbs.

🛏 Hotel Bellevue   Heritage Hotel €€€
(☎0165 7 48 25; www.hotelbellevue.it; Rue
Grand Paradis 22; d €240-330, 2-person chalet
€360; ⏱mid-Dec–mid-Oct; 🅿 ☒) Overlooking
meadows, this green-shuttered mountain
hideaway evokes its 1920s origins with romantic
canopied timber 'cabin beds', weighty cowbells
strung from old beams, claw-foot baths and
the occasional open fire (it's definitely not for
minimalists). Afternoon tea is included in the
price, as is use of the health spa, and you can
also rent mountain bikes and snowshoes.

Courmayeur ❼

✖ La Terraza   International €€
(☎0165 84 33 30; www.ristorantelaterrazza.
com; Via Circonvallazione 73; meals €40-50;
⏱noon-2.30pm & 7-10.30pm) This attractive,
lively, central bar-restaurant-pizzeria has an
array of Valdostan dishes and local specialities
– including polenta with *fontina* and hazelnut
butter, trout with Aostan-white-wine sauce, and
onion soup baked in a crispy bread crust – plus
daily chalkboard specials. The free shot of
limoncello makes a nice finish.

🛏 Hotel Bouton d'Or   Hotel €€
(☎0165 84 67 29; www.hotelboutondor.
com; Strada Statale 26/10; s/d €110/180;
🅿 ❄ @ 🛜) Charmingly folksy Bouton d'Or
is in the centre of Courmayeur and not only
has incredible views of the imposing hulk of
Mont Blanc, but also a sauna, a lounge full
of interesting Alpine paraphernalia and, in
summer, a peaceful garden.

Classic Trip

Grande Strada delle Dolomiti

13

The Dolomites are one of the most beautiful mountain ranges in the world. Devotees come for skiing in winter, hiking and rock climbing in spring and summer, and harvest festivals in autumn.

TRIP HIGHLIGHTS

07 km

Alpe di Siusi
Europe's highest, and prettiest, alpine pastures

100 km

Parco Naturale Fanes-Sennes-Braies
Inspiration for Tolkien's Middle Earth in *The Lord of the Rings*

Bressanone ●

④

La Villa ●

③

Castelrotto ●

⑧

①

Passo Pordoi

Bolzano
A thriving provincial capital with an Austro-Hungarian flavour

Alta Badia
Michelin meals in mountain chalets are the norm in Alta Badia

km

65 km

**7–10 DAYS
207KM / 128 MILES**

GREAT FOR...

BEST TIME TO GO

December for Christmas markets and skiing; June for spring flowers.

ESSENTIAL PHOTO

The humpbacked Marmolada with a foreground of mountain flowers.

BEST FOR OUTDOORS

The villages of Alta Badia and the beautiful Lago di Braies.

Classic Trip

13 Grande Strada delle Dolomiti

Ranging across the South Tyrol, Alto Adige and Veneto, the Dolomites (Dolomiti) combine Austrian and Italian influences with the local Ladin culture. On this grand road trip *(grande strada)* your hosts may wear lederhosen, cure ham in their chimneys and use sleighs to travel from village to village. More recently a new generation of eco-chic hotels, cutting-edge spas and Michelin-starred restaurants has started grabbing the headlines, but overall these mountain peaks remain very low-key.

TRIP HIGHLIGHT

❶ Bolzano

Once a stop on the coach route between Italy and the flourishing Austro-Hungarian Empire, Bolzano has been a long-time conduit between cultures. The city's fine museums include the **Museo Archeologico dell'Alto Adige** (📞0471 32 01 00; www.iceman.it; Via Museo 43; adult/reduced €9/7; ⊙10am-6pm Tue-Sun), where the mummified remains of the 5300-year-

old iceman, Ötzi, are on display. He was found 3200m up the melting glacier on Hauslabjoch Pass in 1991, but how he got there remains a matter of some debate.

At the other end of the spectrum, the city's contemporary art museum, **Museion** (📞0471 22 34 13; www.museion.it; Piazza Piero Siena 1; adult/reduced €7/3.50, from 6pm Thu free; ⊙10am-6pm Tue, Wed & Fri-Sun, to 10pm Thu), is housed in a huge multifaceted glass cube, a surprising architectural assertion that

beautifully vignettes the old-town rooftops and surrounding mountains from within. There's an impressive permanent collection, and temporary shows highlight the local art scene's ongoing dialogue with Austria and Germany.

✕ p163

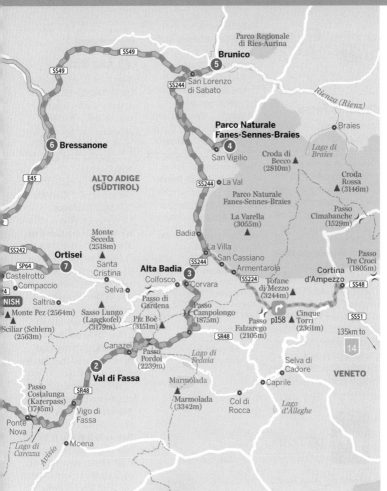

The Drive » Exit Bolzano on the SS241 to the Val di Fassa. The road is the start of a long ascent, the first section through a steep-sided canyon. At Ponte Nova the first peaks of the Dolomites come into view, and after 26km Lago di Carezza is visible on your right.

LINK YOUR TRIP

 A Weekend at Lago di Garda

Tool down the A22 to Lago di Garda and visit the vineyards and olive groves around its shores.

 A Venetian Sojourn

Drop down from Cortina d'Ampezzo on the SS51 and A27 for a tour of Venetian palaces and frescoes.

➋ Val di Fassa

Framed by the stirring peaks of the Gruppo del Sella to the north, the Catinaccio to the west and the Marmolada (3342m) to the southeast, the Fassa valley is a beautiful introduction to the rising mountain ranges. Amid the forests, the iridescent blue-green **Lago di Carezza** is known locally as *de lec ergobando* ('the lake of the rainbow'), as legend tells of a sorcerer who, trying to win the favour of the resident nymph, created a beautiful rainbow over the lake. Alas, the fearful nymph fled and in his fury the sorcerer shattered the rainbow in the lake, forever giving it its luminous colour.

The hub of the valley is the beautifully sited, but verging on over-developed, **Canazei** and, to a lesser extent, the riverside village of **Moena**. To access the **Gruppo del Sella** mountain range ascend to **Passo Pordoi** (2239m), where a cable car carries you to the **Sasso Pordoi** (2950m).

The Drive ≫ From Lago di Carezza it's 38km up a series of rapid switchbacks to Passo Pordoi. From the lofty summit, you'll have a view over the 33 hairpin bends that you'll be descending on the SR48. It's only 7km, but it's slow going and the views over meadows and villages are superb. At Arabba bear left on the SS244 for Corvara.

TRIP HIGHLIGHT

➌ Alta Badia

The area of Alta Badia (www.altabadia.org) is spectacularly located on the Sella Ronda massif, embraced by the peaks of Pelmo (3168m), Civetta (3218m) and the Marmolada.

In the valleys below, the villages of **Corvara** (1568m), **Colfosco** (1645m), **La Villa** (1433m), **Badia** (1324m), **San Cassiano** (1537m) and **La Val** (1348m) connect 130km of slopes over four mountain passes. Undoubtedly one of the Dolomites' premier ski destinations, the villages are all part of the **Dolomiti Superski network**, although the best access to the slopes is from Corvara.

In summer a cable car ascends into the Parco Naturale Fanes-Sennes-Braies from the **Passo Falzarego** (2105m). Alternatively, pick up trail No 12, near La Villa, or trail No 11, which joins the Alta Via pathway No 1 at the Capanna Alpina. Either will take you up to the Alpe di Fanes.

Horse-riding, mountain biking and hang-gliding are other popular valley activities.

🍴 🛏 p163

The Drive ≫ From Corvara the 27km to San Vigilio, the unofficial headquarters of the Fanes-Sennes-Braies park, is a pleasant, easy drive down the

DETOUR: CORTINA D'AMPEZZO

Start: ➌ **Alta Badia**

Thirty-four winding kilometres in the shadow of Tofane di Mezzo (3244m) from La Villa lies pricey, icy Cortina d'Ampezzo, the Italian supermodel of ski resorts. Sitting in a crescent-shaped glacial valley surrounded by wooded slopes, Cortina is undeniably beautiful, gaining international fame in the '60s and '70s when Elizabeth Taylor and Henry Fonda came to town to film *Ash Wednesday*. Unapologetically Italian in feel, ladies in fur coats *passeggiata* (stroll) along the Corso with their pampered pooches. Book a table at **SanBrite** (☎0436 86 38 82; www.sanbrite.it; Località Alverà; meals €50-80; ☺noon-2.30pm & 7.45-9.45pm Thu-Tue; **P**) for farm-to-table specialities in a cool, upcycled interior.

SS244. Chalets dot the hillsides and Alpine cows graze in the valleys, making for an idyllic scene. After 23km turn right on Via Longega for San Vigilio.

TRIP HIGHLIGHT

❹ Parco Naturale Fanes-Sennes-Braies

Hidden behind a wall of rocks northeast of Corvara is the Parco Naturale Fanes-Sennes-Braies, a 99-sq-km windswept plain, potent with Ladin legends that have resonated over the centuries, inspiring JRR Tolkien's Middle Earth in *The Lord of the Rings*. Not surprisingly, the valley and the high Fanes plateau, with its sculpted ridges and buttress towers of rock, are considered among the most evocative places in the Dolomites. Wordsworth considered it a heavenly environment and architect Le Corbusier envisioned the rocky pinnacles as a form of spectacular natural architecture.

For those up for a longer excursion, east down the Val Pusteria is the mystical **Lago di Braies**, a glassy lake set within an amphitheatre of stone. Crouched at its southern edge is 'Gate Mountain', **Sas dla Porta**, once thought to hide a gateway to the underworld.

The Drive ≫ Head back down the hill from San Vigilio to the SS244 and take a right for Brunico, 17km north. As you descend the valley the scenery,

LOCAL KNOWLEDGE: WALK THE HIGH PASSES

The Dolomites' *alte vie* – literally high ways – are high-altitude paths designed for experienced walkers, although most do not require mountaineering skills or equipment. From mid-June to mid-September a network of mountain huts offering food and accommodation lines the route. In high season (July and August) it's advisable to book in advance.

Alta Via No 1 Lago di Braies to Belluno, north to south

Alta Via No 2 Bressanone to Feltre, passing through Odle, the mythical Ladin kingdom

Alta Via No 3 Villabassa to Longarone

Alta Via No 4 San Candido to Pieve di Cadore

while still bucolic, is less dramatic. At picturesque San Lorenzo di Sabato you'll cross the milky Rio di Pusteria as you enter Brunico.

----

❺ Brunico

The Val Pusteria's big smoke, Brunico gets a bad rap from those who've only driven through its unremarkable main drag. The quintessentially Tyrolean historic centre, is, however, delightful.

Right by the town gate is **Acherer Patisserie & Blumen** (☎0474 41 00 30; www.acherer.com; Stadtgasse 8; items from €2; ☺9am-12.30pm & 2.30-7pm Mon-Fri, 8am-1pm & 2-6pm Sat), creator and purveyor of the region's best apple strudel and Sachertorte. The young owner reopened his grandfather's former bakery after apprenticing in Vienna.

On the outskirts of town, visit local wool manufacturer **Moessmer** (☎0474 53 31 11; www.moessmer.it; Walther von der Vogelweide Strasse 6; ☺9am-12.30pm & 2.30-6.30pm Mon-Fri, 9am-12.30pm Sat) for top-quality cashmere and Tyrolean tweeds from its outlet shop.

The Drive ≫ Exit Brunico onto the main SS49/E66 autostrada and follow the winding Rio di Pusteria river up the valley to Bressanone. After 21km you'll pass the frescoed Castello di Rodengo high up on your left, before dropping down through the vineyards of Varna into Bressanone.

----

❻ Bressanone

Beautiful Bressanone (Brixen), with its palace of the prince-bishops and illustrious history, is the artistic and cultural capital of the Val Pusteria.

The first **cathedral** (Duomo; Domplatz; ☺6am-

WHY THIS IS A CLASSIC TRIP
PAULA HARDY, WRITER

It's hard to overstate the incredible natural beauty of the Dolomites, whose shapes, colours and contours are endlessly varied. Walking the *alta vie* (high ways) you honestly feel like Heidi. I'll never forget sitting down at Gostner Schwaige, a mountain hut near Castelrotto, and being presented with a creamy soup served in a bowl made of bread that was sitting on a hay base sprinkled with still-fragrant wildflowers.

Above: Alpe di Siusi
Left: Lago di Carezza, Val di Fassa
Right: Cathedral, Bressanone

ROMAOSLO/GETTY IMAGES ©

MATT MUNRO/LONELY PLANET ©

6pm Apr-Oct & Dec, 6am-noon & 3-6pm Nov & Jan-Mar) was built here in the 10th century by the Bishop of Säben. Though rebuilt in the 18th century along baroque lines, it retains its fabulous 12th-century cloister, the cross-vaults decorated with superb 15th-century frescoes. Bressanone's prince-bishops obviously had an eye for art, and their Renaissance palace, the Hofburg – which now houses the **Museo Diocesano** (Museo Diocesano; ☎0472 83 05 05; www.hofburg.it; Hofburgplatz 2; adult/reduced €8/6; ⊙10am-6.30pm daily Jun-Aug, 10am-5pm Tue-Sun mid-Mar–May, Sep & Oct, 10am-5pm daily late Nov-early Jan) – was similarly decorated in lavish style. Amid the noble apartments you'll find treasures from the Middle Ages and a collection of *presepi* (wooden nativity scenes).

The Drive » From Bressanone you'll rejoin the main A22 autostrada south towards Modena. It winds through forested valleys for 20km, past Castello di Velturno on your right and above the river Isarco. Exit for the Val Gardena onto the SS242 for the scenic 15km climb to Ortisei at 1236m.

JUERGEN SACK/GETTY IMAGES ©

⑦ Ortisei

Ortisei is the main hub of the Val Gardena and the Alpe di Siusi mountain region. Like the Alta Badia and Val di Fassa, this is one of only five valleys where Ladin is a majority tongue, while

the villages of Ortisei (1236m), **Santa Cristina** (1428m) and **Selva** (1563m) are characterised by folksy architecture and a profusion of woodcarving shops. Ortisei's **Museum de Gherdëina** (☎0471 79 75 54; www.museumgherdeina. it; Via Rezia 83, Ortisei; adult/reduced €8/2.50; ⏱10am-12.30pm & 2-6pm Mon-Fri mid-May–Jun & Sep–mid-Oct, 10am-1pm & 2-6pm Mon-Sat Jul & Aug, 2-6pm Tue-Fri mid-Dec–Mar, closed rest of year) has a beautiful collection of wooden toys and sculptures, as does the local church, **St Ulrich**.

From the centre of Ortisei a high-speed cable car ascends the slopes of Alpe di Siusi, Europe's largest high-altitude Alpine meadow. To the northeast, another cable car ascends to **Monte Seceda** (2518m) with unforgettable views of the **Gruppo di Odle**, a cathedral-like series of mountain spires. From Seceda, trail No 2A passes through sloping pastures dotted with wooden *malghe* (shepherds' huts). Afterwards descend for traditional après-ski at the five-star **Hotel Adler** (www.adler-dolomiti.com).

 p163

The Drive ≫ The 15km drive to Siusi is staggeringly beautiful. Backtrack 1.2km west on the SS242 towards the autostrada, then veer left onto the SP64, passing through Castelrotto and continuing south on the SP24. The final climb to Alpe di Siusi between the villages of Siusi and Compaccio is off-limits to motorists for much of the year; whenever the Alpe di Siusi Cableway is running, you must park your car at the Siusi base station and take the cable car from there.

- - - - - - - - - - - - - - - - - -

TRIP HIGHLIGHT

8 Alpe di Siusi

There are few more beautiful juxtapositions than the undulating green pastures of the Alpe di Siusi – Europe's largest plateau – ending dramatically at the base of the Sciliar mountains. To the southeast lies the Catinaccio range; its German name 'Rosengarten' is an apt description of the eerie pink hue given off by the dolomite rock at sunset. Signposted by their onion-domed churches, the villages that dot the valleys – including **Castelrotto** (Kastelruth), **Fié allo Sciliar** (Völs am Schlern) and **Siusi** – are unexpectedly sophisticated.

Part of the Dolomiti Superski network, the gentle slopes of the Alpe di Siusi are even better hiking terrain, and average stamina will get you to the **Rifugio Bolzano** (☎0471 61 20 24; www.schlernhaus.it; dm €36-40, d €96; ⏱Jun–mid-Oct), one of the Alps' oldest mountain huts, which rests at 2457m, just under **Monte Pez** (2564m). Take the **Panorama chairlift** (☎0471 72 78 16; www.panoramaseiseralm.info; Via Saltria 1, Compaccio; one way/return €6/8.50; ⏱8.30am-5pm Dec-early Apr & late May–mid-Oct) from Compaccio to the Alpenhotel, from where it's a three-hour walk to the *rifugio* along paths S, No 5 and No 1.

Horses are also a big part of local culture, and there's nothing more picturesque than a chestnut Haflinger pony galloping across the pastures. **Gstatschhof Ponyhof** (☎0471 72 78 14; www.gstatschhof.com; Via Alpe di Siusi 39, Castelrotto) offers accommodation and summer programs.

 p163

✓ TOP TIP: SKI PASS

The **Dolomiti Superski** (www.dolomitisuperski.com) ski pass gives access to more than 1200km of pistes and 450 lifts spread over 12 resorts. Adult passes cost €55/155/290 for one/three/seven days.

Eating & Sleeping

Bolzano ❶

🍴 Zur Kaiserkron — Alpine €€

(📞0471 98 02 14; www.kaiserkron.bz; Piazza della Mostra 2; meals €40-50, lunch special 2/3 courses €30/35; 🕐noon-2pm & 7-9.30pm Mon-Sat) Refined but unfussy takes on regional favourites fill the menu at this calm and elegant dining room, and excellent produce is allowed to shine. From interesting starters such as risotto with taleggio cheese fondue and pioppini mushrooms to meaty mains – think charcoal-grilled chicken with rosemary potatoes and rainbow chard or veal cheeks with bok choy and ginger-carrot purée – everything is beautifully executed.

Alta Badia ❸

🍴 Restaurant Ladinia — Alpine €€

(📞0471 83 60 10; www.berghotelladinia. it; Pedecorvara 10, Corvara; meals €38-45; 🕐noon-2pm & 7-9pm, closed Apr & Nov) The dining room of Berghotel Ladinia is appealingly cosy, or you can soak up the sun on the protected terrace on warmer days. Mountain-style food is done in a fresh but unpretentious way: dishes such as salmon with mashed purple carrots and artichokes or roe deer medallions with caramelised walnuts, radicchio and apple sauce will reinvigorate even the most stew-and-dumpling-dulled palate.

🛏 Berghotel Ladinia — Boutique Hotel €€

(📞0471 83 60 10; www.berghotelladinia.it; Pedecorvara 10, Corvara; s/d incl half board from €112/164; 🅿 ❄ 🛜) The family owners of Hotel La Perla have taken over this traditional small hotel just up the hill from their luxurious place. Rooms are exquisitely simple and rustic, and the location is sublime. Four-course dinners at the hotel's own **restaurant** are included, or a food credit (€40 per person per day) can be used at any of La Perla's restaurants instead.

Ortisei ❼

🍴 Costamula — Alpine €€

(📞339 1467266; www.costamula.com; meals from €40; 🕐noon-3pm daily, 7pm-midnight Tue-Sat) Slip off the Lalongia slopes into the warren of cosy wood-panelled rooms at this painstakingly restored 17th-century *baita* (mountain cabin), and settle in for some of Val Gardena's finest Alpine fare, from spectacular *crafuncins* (rye pasta pockets stuffed with spinach and ricotta) to delicious apple strudel. Prices are high-end for a slope-side hut, but quality and views are both exceptional.

🛏 Chalet Gerard — Hotel €€€

(📞0471 79 52 74; www.chalet-gerard.com; Plan de Gralba 37, Selva; d with half board €220-380; 🛜) This modern family-run chalet, launched in the 1970s by award-winning skier Gerard Mussner and now lovingly managed by his two well-travelled daughters, enjoys stunning panoramic views from its perch 10 minutes' drive above Selva on the road to Passo Gardena. Supercute rooms are complemented by spots for cosy lolling by the (architect-designed) fire, a sauna and a mountain-facing outdoor hot tub.

Alpe di Siusi ❽

🍴 Gostner Schwaige — Alpine €€

(📞347 8368154; www.gostnerschwaige.com; Via Saltria 13, footpath No 3 from Compaccio; meals €35-45; 🕐8.30am-6pm late May–mid-Oct & mid-Dec–mid-Apr, dinner by reservation only from 7pm) Chef Franz Mulser gives new meaning to the tag 'locally sourced' at his mountain refuge (elevation 1930m) on the beautiful Alpe di Siusi. The butter and cheese come from the barn next door, while salads are decorated with flowers from the adjacent garden and pastures. Other innovative specialities include hay soup, home-cured meats and refreshing herb-infused soft drinks bottled on-site.

Classic Trip

A Venetian Sojourn

14

Pinch yourself, and you might expect to wake from this dream of pink palaces, teal waters and golden domes. Instead, you're in the Veneto, where gondoliers call Ooeee! and water laps at your feet.

TRIP HIGHLIGHTS

90 km

Asolo
Get your camera ready for the 'town of 100 vistas'

0 km

Venice
Cruise the Grand Canal for scene-stealing backdrops

7

Bassano del Grappa ● Riese Pio X

Treviso
FINISH

4

Mestre

1
START

2 ● Dolo

Vicenza
See European architecture change course in Vicenza

0 km

Brenta Riviera
Visit the country retreats of fashionable Venetians

35 km

5–6 DAYS
283KM / 176 MILES

GREAT FOR...

BEST TIME TO GO

April to June, and September for Carnival, the Biennale and the grape harvest.

ESSENTIAL PHOTO

The magical views of folding hillsides from Asolo.

✓ BEST FOR ART

From the avant-garde in Venice to Tiepolo frescoes in Palladian villas.

:e Grand Canal and Basilica di Santa Maria della Salute

165

Classic Trip

14 A Venetian Sojourn

Scan the Veneto coastline for signs of modern life — beach resorts, malls, traffic. But on closer inspection you'll catch the waft of fresh espresso from Piazza San Marco's 250-year-old cafes, faded villas on the Brenta Riviera and masterpieces everywhere: Titians in Venice, Palladios in Vicenza and Giottos in Padua (Padova). This calls for a toast with bubbly local *prosecco* — so raise your glass to *la bea vita* (the good life).

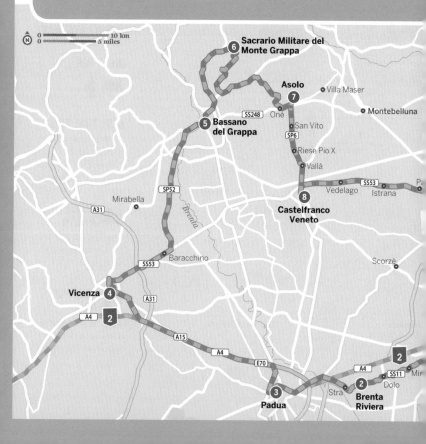

TRIP HIGHLIGHT

❶ Venice

Take the No 1 *vaporetto* (passenger ferry; €7.50) down the **Grand Canal** for scene-stealing backdrops featured in four James Bond films. It starts with controversy at the **Ponte della Costituzione** (Ponte di Calatrava), a luminous glass-and-steel bridge that cost triple the original €4-million estimate. Ahead are castle-like **Fondaco dei Turchi**, the historic Turkish trading house, and

Ca' d'Oro (☎041 522 23 49; www.cadoro.org; Calle di Ca' d'Oro 3932; adult/reduced €8.50/2; ☺8.15am-2pm Mon, to 7.15pm Tue-Sun, 2nd fl 10am-6pm Tue-Sun), a 1430 filigree Gothic marvel.

Points of Venetian pride include the Pescaria (p200), where fishmongers have been slinging lagoon crab for 700 years, before the marble marvel of the **Ponte di Rialto**. If you're feeling peckish, jump ashore for a gourmet food tour (p200).

The next two canal bends could cause architectural whiplash, with Renaissance **Palazzo Grimani** (☎call centre 041 520 03 45; www.palazzogrimani.org; Ramo Grimani 4858; adult/reduced €5/2, incl Ca' D'Oro €10/4; ☺10am-7pm Tue-Sun), followed by **Palazzo Grassi** (☎041 200 10 57; www.palazzograssi.it; Campo San Samuele 3231; adult/reduced incl Punta della Dogana €18/15; ☺10am-7pm Wed-Mon mid-Mar–Nov), site of contemporary-art sensations between Biennales,

and Baldassare Longhena's baroque jewel box **Ca' Rezzonico** (Museum of 18th-Century Venice; ☎041 241 01 00; www.visitmuve.it; Fondamenta Rezzonico 3136; adult/reduced €10/7.50, or with Museum Pass; ☺10am-5pm Wed-Mon).

Finally, stone lions flank the **Peggy Guggenheim Collection** (☎041 240 54 11; www.guggenheim-venice.it; Calle San Cristoforo 701; adult/reduced €15/9; ☺10am-6pm Wed-Mon), where the American heiress collected ideas, lovers and art. It's situated just before the dramatic dome of Longhena's **Basilica di Santa Maria della Salute** (Our Lady of Health Basilica; www.basilicasalutevenezia.it; Campo de la Salute 1; sacristy adult/reduced €4/2; ☺9.30am-noon & 3-5.30pm) comes into view.

✖ ⟷ p46, p61, p117, p173

The Drive ≫ Ironically the first 15km of the drive, from Venice to the Brenta Canal's most romantic villa, is the least attractive part of this route, which takes you through

A27

Piave

A27

A4

85km to
17

so
INISH

estre

START
❶ Venice

p200 Lido di Venezia

Adriatic Sea

⑤ LINK YOUR TRIP

17 **Trieste to Sappada**
Look eastwards down the A4 to Trieste and the borderlands with Slovenia, as many Venetians have done before you.

2 **World Heritage Wonders**
From the wonders of Venice to Unesco's list of World Heritage Sites, continue down the A4 from Vicenza to Verona.

the industrial wastelands of Mestre along the SS11. For Villa Pisani and Villa Foscarini Rossi continue a further 19km on the gradually more scenic Via Nazionale through Mira and Dolo.

TRIP HIGHLIGHT

❷ Brenta Riviera

Every 13 June for 300 years, summer officially kicked off with a traffic jam along the Grand Canal, as a flotilla of fashionable Venetians headed to their villas along the Brenta Riviera. Eighty villas still strike elegant poses, although private ownership and privacy hedges leave much to the imagination. Just four of them are open to the public as museums.

The most romantic of the four is the Palladio-designed, 1555–60 **Villa Foscari** (☎041 5203 9662; www.lamalcontenta.com; Via dei Turisti 9, Malcontenta; adult/reduced €10/8; ⊗9am-noon Tue, Wed & Fri-Sun Apr-Oct), also known as 'La Malcontenta' for the grande dame of the Foscari clan allegedly exiled here for adultery. Further downriver, at Stra, **Villa Pisani Nazionale** (☎049 50 20 74; www.villapisani.beniculturali.it; Via Doge Pisani 7, Stra; adult/reduced €10/5, park only €7.50/4.50; ⊗9am-8pm Tue-Sun Apr-Sep, to 6pm Oct, to 5pm Nov-Mar) strikes a Versailles-like pose with its 114 rooms, vast gardens and reflecting pools.

Well-heeled Venetians wouldn't dream of decamping to the Brenta without their favourite cobblers, sparking a local tradition of high-end shoemaking. Their art is commemorated with a Shoemakers' Museum in **Villa Foscarini Rossi** (☎049 980 10 91; www.museodellacalzatura.it; Via Doge Pisani 1/2, Stra; adult/reduced €7/5; ⊗9am-1pm & 2-6pm Mon-Fri, 2.30-6pm Sat & Sun Apr-Oct, 9am-1pm & 2-6pm Mon-Fri Nov-Mar).

🍴 p173

TOP TIP:
CRUISING THE
VENETIAN RIVIERA

Travel the length of the Brenta Canal on *Il Burchiello*, a luxury barge that lets you watch 50 villas drift by from velvet couches. Full-day cruises leave from Venice's Pontile della Pietà pier on Riva degli Schiavoni (Tuesday, Thursday and Saturday) or from Padua's Pontile del Portello pier (Wednesday, Friday and Sunday).

The Drive » From Stra it's a short 13km drive through the Padovan periphery into Padua. Leave Stra northwest on Via Venezia, cross beneath the A4 autostrada and follow the road round to merge with the Tangenziale Nord into Padua.

❸ Padua

The Brenta Canal once ran through Padua, 40km west of Venice, which was convenient for Padua-bound Venetians when the city came under Venetian dominion in 1405. Venetian governors set up house in the triple-decker, Gothic **Palazzo della Ragione** (☎049 820 50 06; Piazza delle Erbe; adult/reduced €6/4; ⊗9am-7pm Tue-Sun Feb-Oct, to 6pm Nov-Jan), its vast main hall frescoed by Giotto acolytes Giusto de' Menabuoi and Nicolò Mireto.

One illustrious Venetian, general Erasmo da Narni (aka Gattamelata or 'Honeyed Cat'), is commemorated with the 1453 bronze equestrian **Gattamelata statue** (Piazza del Santo) in front of the epic **Basilica di Sant'Antonio** (Il Santo; ☎049 822 56 52; www.basilicadelsanto.org; Piazza del Santo; ⊗6.20am-6.45pm Mon-Sat, to 7.45pm Sun). Not far from Gattamelata is the **Oratorio di San Giorgio** (☎049 822 56 52; www.santantonio.org; Piazza del Santo; adult/reduced €5/4; ⊗9am-1pm & 2-6pm Tue-Sun, to 5pm Oct-Mar), where Titian's 1511 portrait of St Anthony shows him calmly reattaching his own foot.

Padua holds a distinguished place in the history of art. The presence of the university at **Palazzo Bo** (☏049 827 39 39; www.unipd.it/en/guided tours; Via VIII Febbraio 2; adult/reduced €7/4; ⊙ see website for tour times) attracted big names such as Giotto, Fra Filippo Lippi, Donatello and even Mantegna. Padua was also the birthplace of Palladio, and Antonio Canova sculpted his first marble here for the **Prato della Valle** square. See the original in the **Musei Civici agli Eremitani** (☏049 820 45 51; Piazza Eremitani 8; adult/reduced €10/8; ⊙9am-7pm Tue-Sun) along with Giotto's heavenly vision in the **Cappella degli Scrovegni** (Scrovegni Chapel; ☏049 201 00 20; www.cappelladegli scrovegni.it; Piazza Eremitani 8; adult/reduced €13/8, night ticket €8/6; ⊙9am-7pm, night ticket 7-10pm).

✗ p117, p173

The Drive ≫ Leave Padua following signs for Verona and the A4 autostrada for the 42km drive northwest to Vicenza. Although the A4 is heavily trafficked, as you leave Padua behind the road becomes more scenic and you'll spy the Euganean hills to the south.

TRIP HIGHLIGHT

❹ Vicenza

When Andrea Palladio moved from Padua to Vicenza he began to produce some extraordinary buildings, marrying sophistication and rustic simplicity, reverent classicism and bold innovation. Go for a walk while you're here to see some of his finest works. His showstopper, **La Rotonda** (☏049 879 13 80; www.villalarotonda.it; Via della Rotonda 45; adult/child villa & gardens €10/5, gardens €5/free; ⊙villa 10am-noon & 3-6pm Wed & Sat mid-Mar–mid-Nov, gardens 10am-noon & 3-6pm Tue-Sun year-round), sits on a hill overlooking the city, its namesake dome and identical colonnaded facades giving it the ultimate classical proportions.

Walk up the narrow path opposite to **Villa Valmarana 'ai Nani'** (☏0444 32 18 03; www.villavalmarana.com; Via dei Nani 8; adult/reduced €10/6; ⊙10am-6pm Mar-Oct), which is nicknamed for the 17 dwarfs ('ai Nani) who guard the garden walls. In 1757 the entire interior was redecorated with frescoes by Giambattista Tiepolo and his son Giandomenico.

▶ p173

The Drive ≫ Pushing away from the autostrada, northwards towards Bassano del Grappa, the scenery becomes decidedly rural, passing through vineyards, cornfields and small towns. Drive 7km northeast on the SS53 and just past Baracchino turn left onto the SP52 for the final 20km to Bassano del Grappa.

❺ Bassano del Grappa

Bassano del Grappa sits with charming simplicity on the banks of the river Brenta as it winds its way free of the Alpine foothills. It is broached by the **Ponte degli Alpini**, Palladio's 1569 covered bridge. Fragile as it seems, it is designed to withstand the rush of spring meltwaters from Monte Grappa. It's always been critical in times of war: Napoleon bivouacked here for many months and in the Great War hundreds of soldiers were stationed here. Now the charming walled town is full of smart shops and restaurants and the largest collection of Dürer prints in the world, which can be seen at **Museo Civico** (☏0424 51 99 01; www.museibassano.it; Piazza Garibaldi 34; adult/reduced €7/5; ⊙10am-7pm Wed-Mon) and **Palazzo Sturm** (☏0424 51 99 40; www.museibassano.it; Via Schiavonetti 40; adult/reduced €5/3.50; ⊙9am-1pm & 3-6pm Mon-Sat, 10am-7pm Sun).

The town is also famous for its after-dinner firewater, grappa, which was invented here. Sample it at **Poli Museo della Grappa** (☏0424 52 44 26; www.poligrappa.com; Via Gamba 6; ⊙museum 9am-7.30pm, distillery guided tours 9am-1pm & 2-6pm Mon-Fri).

Classic Trip

MATT MUNRO/LONELY PLANET ©

WHY THIS IS A CLASSIC TRIP
PAULA HARDY, WRITER

This trip is a fantastic combination of grand-slam sites and delightful out-of-the-way surprises. Venice's marble palaces and Giotto's ground-breaking frescoes in the Scrovegni Chapel are understandably world famous, but who knows about the 1500 pairs of historic shoes in Villa Foscarini Rossi or the floor-to-ceiling frescoes at Villa Valmarana and Villa Maser? These places are quite wonderful, and what's more you'll often have them all to yourself.

Above: Treviso
Left: Grappa tasting, Bassano del Grappa
Right: Cappella degli Scrovegni, Padua

The Drive » Head out of Bassano on the SP59, crossing the Brenta river westwards. Then pick up the northbound SS47 before turning right onto the SP148. Once you leave the city limits you'll start the awesome climb up Monte Grappa through hairpin bends, enjoying ever more spectacular views.

❻ Sacrario Militare del Monte Grappa

No battle defines Italy's struggle in the Great War better than the 1917–18 battle of Monte Grappa (1776m). Despite being severely weakened after the battles of Caporetto and Isonzo, Italian Alpine brigades mounted a heroic stand atop this barren mountain and finally brought a halt to the Austro-Hungarian advance. The savage conflict claimed the lives of 22,910 troops, who are now entombed in this **mausoleum**, which caps the summit in a monumental modernist ziggurat and is studded with bronze plaques commemorating the deceased.

The Drive » The 39km south to Asolo is one of the most stunning drives in the itinerary. The drive down the SP140 descends through tight hairpin bends with sweeping views of the plains. At the bottom, pick up the SP26 eastwards and meander through the country to Asolo.

171

Classic Trip

NORTHERN ITALY **14** A VENETIAN SOJOURN

TRIP HIGHLIGHT

7 Asolo

East of Bassano rises Asolo, known as the 'town of 100 vistas' for its panoramic hillside location. It was once the haunt of the Romans and a personal gift from Venice to Caterina, 15th-century queen of Cyprus, in exchange for her abdication. A historic hit with writers, poet Robert Browning bought a house here and named his last work *Asolando* (1889).

Beneath Asolo's forested hilltop, Palladio and Veronese conspired to create the Veneto's finest monument to *la bea vita* at **Villa di Masèr** (Villa Barbaro; ✆0423 92 30 04; www.villadimaser.it; Via Cornuda 7, Maser; adult/reduced €9/7; ✆10am-6pm Tue-Sat, from 11am Sun Apr-Oct, 11am-5pm Sat & Sun Nov-Mar; **P**). Palladio set the arcaded villa into a verdant hillside, while inside Veronese imagined an Arcadian idyll in his floor-to-ceiling *trompe l'œil* frescoes.

✗ p173

The Drive » Descend from Asolo's sylvan heights and zigzag across the SS248 onto the SP6 towards Castelfranco Veneto for a 15km drive south through the small towns of San Vito, Riese Pio X and Vallà.

8 Castelfranco Veneto

Giorgio Barbarelli da Castelfranco (aka Giorgione) was one of the masters of the High Renaissance, and one of its most mysterious. Born in Castelfranco, he was a contemporary of Titian, but an early death from the plague in 1510 left an adoring public with just six acclaimed canvases. Like Titian, he is credited with revolutionising Renaissance painting, using a refined chiaroscuro technique called *sfumato* ('smokey') to blur hard lines and enhance the emotional quality of colour, light and perspective.

Luckily for Castelfranco, one of his few surviving works, an altarpiece known as *Castelfranco Madonna,* still hangs in the Cappella Costanza in the **Duomo** (www.chiesa castelfranco.it; Vicolo del Cristo 10, Castelfranco Veneto; ✆9am-noon & 3.30-6.30pm Mon-Sat, 3.30-6.30pm Sun). More of the Giorgione school of work can be viewed in the **Casa di Giorgione** (✆0423 73 56 26; www.museocasagiorgione. it; Piazza San Liberale, Castelfranco Veneto; adult/reduced €5/3; ✆9.30am-12.30pm & 2.30-6.30pm Fri-Sun, 9.30am-12.30pm Tue-Thu).

The Drive » At Castelfranco Veneto you're back on the SS53 again, this time heading 27km further east towards Treviso. Pass through Vedelago and on through flat, flat fields of corn to Istrana, Paese and then Treviso.

9 Treviso

Totally outdone by supermodel La Serenissima (Venice), Treviso seems becalmed beyond the tourist mayhem, its quiet canals, weeping willows and frescoed facades the backdrop to another midsized Italian town. So why drop in? Well, Treviso has made a handsome contribution to human happiness, giving us DēLonghi appliances, **Pinarello bicycles** (✆0422 54 38 21; www. pinarello.com; Borgo Mazzini 9; ✆9am-12.30pm & 3.30-7.30pm Tue-Sat, 3.30-7.30pm Mon), *radicchio Trevisano* (red radicchio, in season from December through February) and Italy's favourite dessert, tiramisu. Settle down to sample Treviso's culinary treats in vintage trattoria Toni del Spin (p173), where staff serve you risotto with white asparagus, sprinkled with wildflowers.

Afterwards, wander Treviso's pretty canals and visit the excellent modern-art museum, **Luigi Bailo** (✆0422 65 89 51; www.museicivicitreviso. it; Borgo Cavour 24; adult/reduced €6/4; ✆10am-6pm Tue-Sun), or enjoy Italy's foremost graphic poster collection at the **Museo Collezione Salce** (✆0422 59 19 36; www.collezionesalce. beniculturali.it; Via Carlo Alberto 31; adult/reduced €8/4; ✆10am-6pm Wed-Sun).

✗ p173

172

Eating & Sleeping

Venice ❶

✖ Osteria Bakàn
Italian €€

(☏041 564 76 58; Corte Maggiore 2314a; meals €36-44; ⏱8am-3pm & 6-10pm Wed-Mon; ⛴Santa Marta) A mix of local drinking den and surprisingly adventurous restaurant, Bakàn has bucketloads of atmosphere – with old beams and soft jazz inside, and tables on a tucked-away courtyard. The homemade pasta is excellent, or you could opt for the likes of *guance di vitello* (veal cheeks) or ginger prawns with pilaf rice.

🛏 Oltre Il Giardino
Boutique Hotel €€

(☏041 275 00 15; www.oltreilgiardino-venezia. com; Fondamenta Contarini 2542; d/ste from €180/280; ❄🛜; ⛴San Tomà) Live the dream in this garden villa, the 1920s home of Alma Mahler, the composer's widow. Hidden behind a lush walled garden, its six high-ceilinged guest rooms and suites marry historic charm with modern comfort: marquetry desks, candelabras and 19th-century poker chairs sit alongside flat-screen TVs and designer bathrooms, while outside, pomegranate trees flower.

Brenta Riviera ❷

✖ Osteria Da Conte
Venetian €€

(☏049 47 95 71; Via Caltana 133, Mira; meals €25-35; ⏱noon-2pm & 8-10pm Tue-Sat) An unlikely bastion of culinary sophistication lodged practically underneath an overpass, Da Conte has one of the most interesting wine lists in the region, plus creative takes on regional cuisine, from shrimps with black sesame and pumpkin puree to gnocchi in veal-cheek *ragù*. If it's on the menu, end your meal with the faultless *zabaglione* (egg and Marsala custard).

Padua ❸

✖ Osteria dei Fabbri
Osteria €€

(☏049 65 03 36; Via dei Fabbri 13; meals €30; ⏱noon-3pm & 7-11pm, closed Sun dinner) Rustic wooden tables, wine-filled tumblers and a single-sheet menu packed with hearty dishes keep things real at dei Fabbri. Slurp on superlative *zuppe* (soups) such as sweet red-onion soup, or tuck into comforting meat dishes such as oven-roasted pork shank with Marsala, sultanas and polenta.

Vicenza ❹

🛏 Hotel Palladio
Hotel €€

(☏0444 32 53 47; www.hotel-palladio.it; Contrà Oratorio dei Servi 25; s/d €110/170; 🅿❄🛜🐾) The top choice in central Vicenza, this renovated Renaissance *palazzo* delivers crisp, contemporary rooms with beamed ceilings, polished wooden floors and super-swish, glassed-in bathrooms with large power-showers. Staff are friendly, and breakfast is a generous buffet of cereal, pastries and cooked-to-order eggs and bacon.

Asolo ❼

✖ Due Mori
Italian €€€

(☏0423 95 09 53; www.2mori.it; Piazza Gabriele D'Annunzio 5; meals €40-50; ⏱12.30-2.30pm & 7.30-9.30pm Tue-Sun) If ever there was a table with a view, the dining room of Due Mori provides it, with floor-to-ceiling windows overlooking Asolo and the Veneto hillsides. Refined rustic dishes are cooked on a wood-burning stove that yields a delicious depth of flavour. Try the ravioli with poison-oak leaves and ricotta, or the rich guinea fowl *ragù*.

Treviso ❾

✖ Toni del Spin
Trattoria €€

(☏0422 54 38 29; www.ristorantetonidelspin. com; Via Inferiore 7; meals €35-50; ⏱noon-2.30pm & 7.15-10.30pm Tue-Sun, 7.15-10.30pm Mon) This trattoria has been a reference point since 1880, and the original wood-panelled dining room is reassuringly full of diners hunched over silky plates of risotto full of white asparagus and bowls of tagliatelle with duck *ragù*. In the evening, turn the corner into a second contemporary dining room where you'll find a slick bar serving the best of the region's labels from its 3000-bottle cellar.

Valpolicella Wine Country

15

The vineyards of Valpolicella are within easy reach of sunny Lago di Garda and romantic Verona. The Romans started the region's wine production and today Valpolicella produces some of Italy's best reds.

TRIP HIGHLIGHTS

54 km

Lazise
Bathe in thermal lakes equipped with hydromassage

27 km

Fumane
Admire the strange mannerist architecture of Villa della Torre

FINISH
Bardolino

Sant'Ambrogio di Valpolicella

3

Negrar

4

6

START
1

33 km

San Pietro in Cariano
Meet pioneering vintners breaking with tradition

Verona
Watch opera beneath the stars in Verona's Roman Arena

0 km

4 DAYS
70KM / 43 MILES

GREAT FOR...

BEST TIME TO GO
April and May for walking; autumn for harvest.

ESSENTIAL PHOTO
Views over the vineyards from Castelrotto.

BEST FOR FOODIES
A glass of Quintarelli's rich, red Amarone.

15 Valpolicella Wine Country

The 'valley of many cellars', from which Valpolicella gets its name, has been in the business of wine production since the ancient Greeks introduced their *passito* technique (using partially dried grapes) to create the blockbuster flavours still enjoyed in the region's Amarone and Recioto wines. Spread across 240 sq km, the vine-clad valleys are dotted with villas and ancient hamlets and harbour as much heritage and culture as they do wine.

TRIP HIGHLIGHT

❶ Verona

Strategically situated at the foot of the Italian-Austrian Alps, Verona has been a successful trade centre since Roman times. Its ancient gates, busy forum (now **Piazza delle Erbe**) and grand **Roman Arena** (☏045 800 32 04; Piazza Brà; adult/reduced €10/7.50; ☘8.30am-7.30pm Tue-Sun, 1.30-7.30pm Mon), which still serves as one of the world's great opera venues, are testament to its prosperity –

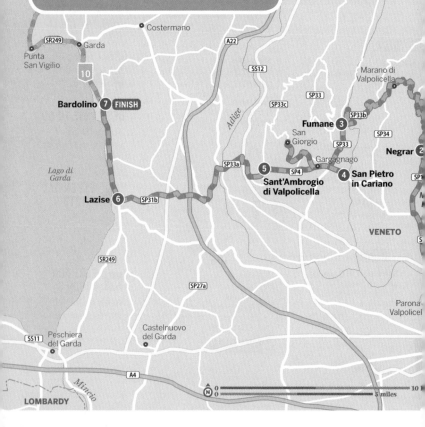

as is the city's handsome profile, which combines Renaissance gardens with the grand Gothic architecture of showcase churches, such as the **Basilica di Sant'Anastasia** (www.chieseverona.it; Piazza di Sant'Anastasia; €3, free with VeronaCard; ⏱9am-6pm Mon-Sat, 1-6pm Sun Mar-Oct, to 5pm Nov-Feb).

In summer people flock here to listen to opera beneath the stars, but in spring, food and wine professionals descend on the city for Italy's most important national wine fair, **Vinitaly** (www.vinitaly.com). Unsurprisingly, Verona is also big on *aperitivo* culture. **Antica Bottega del Vino** (☏045 800 45 35; www.bottegavini.it; Vicolo Scudo di Francia 3; ⏱11am-1am) is an oenophile institution, its 19th-century cellars filled with over 4000 labels.

✗ 🛏 p61, p117, p181

The Drive » Head northwest out of Verona on the SS12 crossing the river Adige before turning left onto the SP1. After 2.5km take the Arbizzano exit right onto the SP4, gradually leaving the suburbs behind and heading into the hills. At Arbizzano continue straight onto the SP12 towards Negrar.

- - - - - - - - - - - - - - - - -

❷ Negrar

Five communities compose the DOC quality-controlled heart of Valpolicella: Negrar, Marano di Valpolicella, San Pietro in Cariano, Fumane and Sant'Ambrogio di Valpolicella. Tiny Negrar, the so-called 'city of wine', is the largest and is set amid a patchwork of pergola vineyards,

crisscrossed by lines of *marogne* (dry-stone walls) typical of the region. Amarone acolytes flock to the iconic **Giuseppe Quintarelli** (☏045 750 00 16; giuseppe.quintarelli@tin.it; Via Cerè 1, Negrar; wine tastings per person €30; ⏱by appointment) estate, which, despite its modest appearance, produces one of the biggest, richest red wines this side of Porto.

Innovators, such as the fifth-generation vintners at **Damoli** (☏340 8762680; www.damolivini.com; Via Jago di Mezzo 5, Negrar; tastings per person €30; ⏱by appointment), are meticulous in their small-batch wine production, which includes a dryer style of Amarone, Checo, which has a leathery nose and rich, cherry flavour, alongside inventive new wines such as zippy Biancheté, an unusual white wine made from 100% Corvina grapes.

✗ p181

The Drive » Follow the SP12 north out of Negrar and

SP6

Grezzana

SP34b

SP6

46km to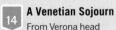

START

❶ Verona

Adige

🔗 **LINK YOUR TRIP**

10 **A Weekend at Lago di Garda**

From Bardolino continue on the SR249 and circumnavigate Lago di Garda for a spot of boating and wild swimming.

14 **A Venetian Sojourn**

From Verona head down the A4 to Vicenza for a dose of high-octane culture in the Venetian countryside.

after 3km turn left onto Via Ca' Righetto, climbing into the terraced hills before dropping down to Marano with its Romanesque church. From here take the SP33b to Fumane.

TRIP HIGHLIGHT

❸ Fumane

In Fumane you'll find Allegrini, one of the leading wineries of the region, where wine tastings are held in the fabulous 16th-century **Villa della Torre** (☎045 683 20 70; www.villadellatorre.it; Via della Torre 25, Fumane; villa guided tours €10, with wine tasting & snack €30-40; ⊘villa tours 11am & 4pm Mon-Sat by appointment; 🅿). Built for humanist scholar and law professor Giulio della

Torre (1480–1563), the villa has one of the earliest mannerist gardens in Italy. Mannerism was a rebellious strand of the Renaissance that produced some of the most intriguing interiors and garden landscapes of the period. The Italian word *maniera* means 'style' and mannerist art and architecture is highly stylised and fantastical.

On its surface the Villa della Torre and its garden appear to present a regular Renaissance scene, but look closer and you'll find grotesque masks spitting water at promenaders, fireplaces that look like roaring monsters and a grotto that resembles a snarling

hell's mouth. All of it together wittily suggests the veneer of civilisation is fragile, and despite humankind's best efforts, the primitive forces of nature are always lurking just beneath the surface.

🍴 p181

The Drive » Head south on the SP33 from Fumane for the short 6km drive to San Pietro in Cariano. Otherwise known as the 'Via della Valle', the route is lined with lush pergola vines. When you eventually hit a roundabout, take the third exit left into San Pietro.

TRIP HIGHLIGHT

❹ San Pietro in Cariano

At the heart of Valpolicella is San Pietro in Cariano, an ancient hamlet surrounded by elegant Palladian villas such as **San Giona** dating back to the period of Venetian domination. Traces of the town's Roman heritage are also visible in the 12th-century parish church of **Pieve di San Floriano** (Via della Pieve 49, Località San Floriano; ⊘7.30am-7.30pm), with its spare tripartite, tufa facade and serene, arcaded cloister.

But despite its impressive heritage San Pietro hasn't stayed stuck in the past. Take the strikingly contemporary, award-winning winery **Zýmē** (☎045 770 11 08; www.zyme. it; Via Cà del Pipa 1, San Pietro in Cariano; wine tastings €20;

DETOUR: VILLA MOSCONI BERTANI

Start: ❶ **Verona**

Before you reach Negrar take a quick 1.5km detour off the SP4 down Via Novare to the **Villa Mosconi Bertani** (☎045 602 07 44; www.mosconibertani.it; Via Novare, Arbizzano; tours €9, tastings €22-35; ⊘wine tastings & tours 2pm & 4pm Sun-Fri, & 10am Tue-Sun) in Arbizzano. Arguably one of the most beautifully sited villas in Valpolicella, this winery is one of the oldest continuously operating wine businesses in Italy. What's more, the lovely neoclassical residence, completed in 1769, with a phalanx of Greek gods perched on the facade and a grand, frescoed **Chamber of the Muses** designed for small operatic performances, is a listed historic landmark and is well worth a tour. Beyond the house are 8 hectares of English-style romantic gardens, lakes, orchards and Guyot vineyards to explore. Tours and tastings run regularly between April and October, but require prebooking.

Valpolicella Marano di Valpolicella

⊙ shop 9am-6pm Mon-Sat, tastings by appointment), which is headed up by Moreno Zurlo. It has a reputation for bold, big-blend wines, the most famous of which is Harlequin, a thrilling IGP wine made using 15 local grape varieties. In town, you can sample Amarone at **Montecari-ano Cellars** (☎045 683 83 35; www.montecariano.

it; Via Valena 3, San Pietro in Cariano; tastings per person €25; ⊙9am-12.30pm & 3-5pm Mon-Fri by appointment), **just off central Piazza San Giuseppe.**

🛏 p181

The Drive » A short 10km hop gets you from San Pietro in Cariano to Sant'Ambrogio via San Giorgio, a fraction (subdivision) of Sant'Ambrogio. Pick up the SP4 and head west

out of San Pietro. After 2km turn right on Via Case Sparse Conca d'Oro, which leads uphill to San Giorgio. Then retrace your steps to the SP4 and continue west to Sant'Ambrogio.

- - - - - - - - - - - - - - - -

❺ Sant'Ambrogio di Valpolicella

Part of the wealth of Valpolicella comes from the marble quarries at Sant'Ambrogio. The town was already quarrying Rosso Broccato and Bronzetto marble in the Roman period. Much of it went to build Verona's Arena and grand city gates, and even today the **Marble School** is the only one of its kind in Italy.

Perched 375m up on a hill, in San Giorgio di Valpolicella, the **Pieve di San Giorgio** (www.infoval policella.it; Piazza della Pieve 22, San Giorgio di Valpolicella; ☺7am-8pm summer, 8am-5pm winter) is the area's oldest Christian church, dating back to 712. Built in Romanesque style from local limestone, the interior displays some beautiful frescoed fragments. Behind the church you can pick up the **Sentiero della Salute**, a 2.5km (one hour) walk through the woods.

The Drive ≫ The next drive takes you out of the bucolic Valpolicella hills and across a tangle of autostradas running down the eastern shore of Lago di Garda. Exit Sant'Ambrogio west on the SP4 and then dog-leg across the SS12 onto the SP33a. Wend your way along here, merging with the SP27a and SP31b to Lazise, 11km away.

- - - - - - - - - - - - - - - - -

TRIP HIGHLIGHT

⑥ Lazise

Sitting at the foot of the gentle hills of Valpolicella on the shores of Lago di Garda is Lazise. Domi-

nated for centuries by the powerful and murderous Scaligeri clan from Verona, the town retains its impressive, turreted **castle** (privately owned) and encircling walls. Look out for the huge hole in the north wall of the main tower, made by a cannon during the 15th-century wars between Venice and Milan.

As an important medieval customs point, Lazise is surrounded by numerous grand villas such as **Villa dei Cedri**, set back from the waterfront in Colà. These days it is home to the fabulous **Parco Thermale del Garda** (☐045 759 09 88; www.villadeicedri.it; Piazza di Sopra 4, Colà; adult/reduced €26/17; ☺9.30am-11pm Sun-Fri, to 1am Sat), a 5.2-hectare natural spa with a couple of enormous thermal lakes fed by underground hot springs pumping out water at a balmy 33°C.

The Drive ≫ A short, lovely 6km lakeside drive takes you north up the SR249 from Lazise to Bardolino. To your left the large, blue expanse of the lake stretches out lazily while to your right ranks of olives and cypresses line the hillsides.

- - - - - - - - - - - - - - - - -

⑦ Bardolino

Prosperous Bardolino is a town in love with the grape. More than

70 vineyards grace the surrounding morainic hills interspersed with silvery olive groves, dark cypresses and cheerful pink oleanders. The tourist office has a map of local wine producers on the Strada del Vino (www.stradadelbardoli no.com).

The **Museo del Vino** (☐045 622 83 31; www.museo delvino.it; ☺9am-12.30pm & 2.30-7pm mid-Mar-Sep, hours vary Oct–mid-Mar) is set within the **Zeni Winery** (☐045 721 00 22; www.zeni.it; Via Costabella 9; ☺9am-12.30pm & 2.30-7pm) and offers a good insight into local production methods and grape varieties, coupled with free tastings and smell tests in a special Galleria Olfattiva. Wines to sample are the local Chiaretto and the young Novello, which rarely make it out of Italy. If you happen to be visiting in May, October or November you can probably catch one of the town's numerous **wine festivals**, when the waterfront fills up with food and wine stands, as well as musicians and dancers. Otherwise, plan to visit on a Thursday in order to catch the **weekly market**.

✗ p181

Eating & Sleeping

Verona ❶

✗ Locanda 4 Cuochi   Italian €€
(☎045 803 03 11; www.locanda4cuochi.it; Via Alberto Mario 12; meals €40, 3-course set menu €43; ⏱12.30-2.30pm & 7.30-10.30pm, closed lunch Mon & Tue; 🛜) With its open kitchen, urbane vibe and hotshot chefs, you're right to expect great things from Locanda. Culinary acrobatics play second fiddle to prime produce cooked with skill and subtle twists. Whether it's perfectly crisp suckling pig lacquered with liquorice, or an epilogue of *gianduja* ganache with sesame crumble and banana, you will be gastronomically impressed.

🛏 Agriturismo San Mattia   Agriturismo €€
(☎045 91 37 97; www.agriturismosanmattia.it; Via Santa Giuliana 2a; s €70-110, d €90-140, apt from €160; 🅿 ❄ 🛜) Make friends with the chickens, ducks and horses as you wander through San Mattia's olive groves, orchards and vineyards, then sit back on the patio and soak up the stunning views of Verona. Host Giovanni Ederle is the tour de force behind this 14-room farm, its popular Slow Food–focused restaurant and Valpolicella vintages. Located around 2km north of the city centre.

Negrar ❷

✗ Trattoria Caprini   Trattoria €€
(☎045 750 05 11; www.trattoriacaprini.it; Via Zanotti 9, Torbe; meals €30; ⏱noon-2.30pm & 7-10pm Thu-Tue) A little north of Negrar in the hamlet of Torbe, family-run Caprini serves heart-warming fare you wish your mamma could make. Many menu items are homemade, including the delicious *lasagnetta* with hand-rolled pasta, and a *ragù* of beef, tomato, porcini and *finferlo* mushrooms. Downstairs, beside the fire of the old *pistoria* (bakery), you can sample some 200 Valpolicella labels.

Fumane ❸

✗ Enoteca della Valpolicella   Venetian €€
(☎045 683 91 46; www.enotecadellavalpolicella.it; Via Osan 47, Fumane; meals €25-35; ⏱noon-2.30pm & 7pm-midnight Tue-Sat, to 3pm Sun) Gastronomes flock to the town of Fumane, just a few kilometres north of San Pietro in Cariano, where an ancient farmhouse has found renewed vigour as a rustically elegant restaurant. Put your trust in gracious owners Ada and Carlotta, who will eagerly guide you through the day's menu, a showcase for fresh, local produce.

San Pietro in Cariano ❹

🛏 La Caminella   B&B €€
(☎045 680 05 63; www.lacaminella.it; Via Don Gaspare Bertoni 24, San Pietro in Cariano; d/q €115/175; 🅿 ❄ 🛜 🖳) This pretty B&B is housed in an old stone structure once used for drying tobacco leaves. Now it's been transformed to provide chic accommodation in atmospheric rooms characterised by bare stone walls, terracotta-tiled floors and chic country-house furnishings. It's part of the relatively new Carilius winery, so there's wine tasting on the doorstep, as well as a pool.

Bardolino ❼

✗ Il Giardino delle Esperidi   Osteria €€
(☎045 621 04 77; Via Goffredo Mameli 1; meals €40-50; ⏱7-10pm Mon & Wed-Fri, noon-2.30pm & 7-10pm Sat & Sun) Holidaying gourmets should head for this intimate little *osteria*, where sourcing local delicacies is a labour of love for its sommelier-owner. The intensely flavoured baked truffles with *parmigiano reggiano* are legendary, and the highly seasonal menu may feature rarities such as nettle gnocchi or lamb fillet in Marsala reduction.

The Venetian Dolomites

It's hard to believe that in a few hours you can go from canals to the crisp Alpine clarity of Cortina d'Ampezzo — land of idyllic hikes, razor-sharp peaks and Italy's most fashion-conscious skiing.

TRIP HIGHLIGHTS

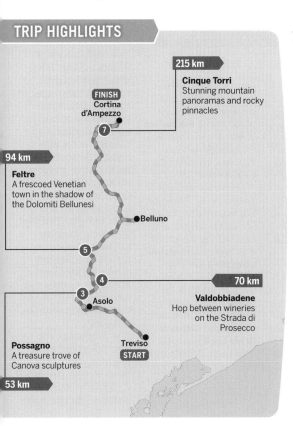

215 km

Cinque Torri
Stunning mountain panoramas and rocky pinnacles

FINISH
Cortina d'Ampezzo
⑦

94 km

Feltre
A frescoed Venetian town in the shadow of the Dolomiti Bellunesi

●Belluno

⑤

④

③ Asolo

70 km

Valdobbiadene
Hop between wineries on the Strada di Prosecco

Possagno
A treasure trove of Canova sculptures

Treviso
START

53 km

---

7 DAYS
231KM / 144 MILES

GREAT FOR...

BEST TIME TO GO
December to March for snow sports; July for mountain hikes.

 ESSENTIAL PHOTO
The five mythical peaks of the Cinque Torri at sunset.

 BEST FOR FOODIES
Refuelling after skiing on delicious, deep-fried Schiz cheese.

16 The Venetian Dolomites

A road trip through the Venetian Dolomites takes you through one of Italy's most sophisticated and least visited stretches of countryside. Some of the Veneto's finest country villas and medieval walled towns are to be found here, while a little further north prosecco vines dip and crest across the undulating foothills of the Alps. Crowning it all is the Italian supermodel of ski resorts, Cortina d'Ampezzo – fashionable, pricey and undeniably beautiful.

---

❶ Treviso

Treviso has everything you could want from a midsized Veneto city: medieval walls, pretty canals, narrow cobbled streets and frescoed churches. Despite this it receives few visitors, eclipsed by its more impressive neighbour – Venice. However, if you want to experience authentic Veneto life away from the tourist crowds, this is a great place to come.

Like its watery neighbour, Treviso is encircled by water. Its defensive walls are surrounded by a moat fed by the river Sile, which runs to the south of town. Grassy parks, weeping willows and waterwheels lend it a charming air, as does the island-bound **fish market** (Isolotto della Pescheria, Via Pescheria; ⊘7am-noon). Pick up a map from the **tourist office** (☏0422 54 76 32; www.marcatreviso.it; Via Fiumicelli 30; ⊘10am-1pm Mon, to 5pm Tue-Sat, to 4pm Sun) and follow one of the easy walking itineraries, then pop into the **duomo** (Cattedrale di San Pietro Apostolo; Piazza del Duomo; ⊘7.30am-1pm & 3.30-8pm summer, to 6.30pm winter) to see the local Titian, and fresco-filled **Chiesa di Santa Lucia** (www.santaluciatreviso.it; Piazza San Vito; ⊘8am-noon Mon-Fri, to noon & 4-6.30pm Sat, 9am-12.30pm & 4-6.30pm Sun), painted by local talent Tommaso da Modena.

For an authentic experience, visit a traditional *osteria* around Piazza dei Signori, such as **Osteria Dalla Gigia** (Via Barberia 20; snacks €1.30-3; ⊘9.30am-2pm & 4-8.30pm Mon-Sat) or **Dai Naneti** (Vicolo Broli 2; sandwiches €3-5; ⊘9am-2.30pm & 5.30-9pm Mon-Fri, 9.30am-2pm & 5.30-9pm Sat).

The Drive ❯❯ Head northwest out of Treviso on the regional road SR348 towards Montebelluno and then Asolo. It's a pleasant 37km drive through flat fields and small provincial towns.

---

❷ Asolo

Asolo with its view of 'a thousand hills' is one of the most beautiful villages in Italy (https://borghipiubelliditalia.it). It has always been wealthy, starting as a bishopric in the 10th century, then becoming the miniature kingdom of Caterina Cornaro, the Queen of Cyprus in 1489, who gave up her island home to Venice. She filled the town with artists and intellectuals such as Gentile Bellini and humanist Pietro Bembo, who lent it a refined and cosmopolitan air, which has lingered through the centuries.

In their wake came other bohemians such as American author Henry James, English poet Robert Browning, Russian composer Igor Stravinsky,

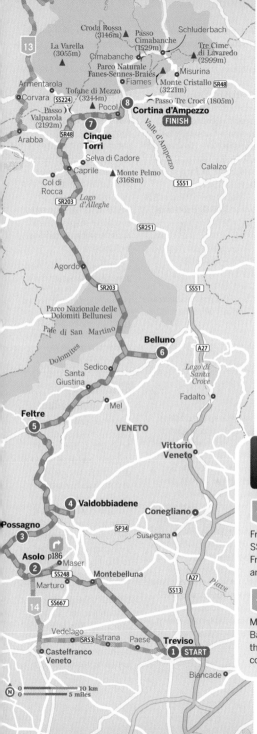

NORTHERN ITALY 16 THE VENETIAN DOLOMITES

Italian actress and the first woman to grace the cover of *Time* magazine, Eleonora Duse, and English adventurer Freya Stark. There's a small **museum** (☎0423 95 23 13; www.asolo.it; Via Regina Cornaro 74; adult/reduced €5/4; ⊙9.30am-12.30pm & 3-6pm Sat & Sun) and a **castle** (☎329 8508512; €2; ⊙10am-7pm Sat & Sun Apr-Jun, Sep & Oct, 10am-noon & 3-7pm Sat & Sun Jul & Aug, 10am-5pm Sat & Sun Nov-Mar), but the real pleasure here is to wander the romantic alleys and visit the garden of **Villa Freya** (☎0423 56 54 78; www.bella solo.it; Via Forestuzzo; adult/reduced €3/2; ⊙1st 3 Sat each month, closed Aug & Dec) with its dreamy views, then stop for lunch at **Villa Cipriani** (☎0423 52 34 11; www.villaciprianiasolo.com; Via Canova 298; meals €60; ⊙12.30-2.30pm & 8-10.30pm; ℗), once the home of

LINK YOUR TRIP

13 Grande Strada delle Dolomiti

From Cortina head up the SS224 to the Alta Badia. From here you can pick up an epic mountain road trip.

14 A Venetian Sojourn

Continue west from Maser on the SS248 to Bassano del Grappa and then loop around for more countryside culture.

185

Robert Browning and Lord Guinness, which also has a delightful spa and pool with the most enchanting view.

The Drive ≫ Descend south out of Asolo along Via Forestuzzo until you hit the SP6 where you turn right and then right again at the first roundabout. From here it's a pretty 9km drive up a leafy regional road all the way up to Possagno, which perches on a small hill capped by Antonio Canova's Palladian temple.

TRIP HIGHLIGHT

❸ Possagno

On the slopes of Monte Grappa, the dazzling, white neoclassical

Tempio peeps above the treetops as if some part of ancient Rome had come to holiday in the Veneto. It's the parish church of Possagno, where Italy's master-neoclassical sculptor, Antonio Canova, was born in 1757. Canova laid the first stone in 1819, and came to final rest here in 1822.

More interesting is his home and **Gypsotheca** (☎0423 54 43 23; www. museocanova.it; Via Canova 74, Possagno; adult/reduced €10/6; ⏱9.30am-6pm Tue-Sat, to 7pm Sun), a light-filled gallery designed by Carlo Scarpa to showcase Canova's working models

and plaster casts; you'll find it at the Museo Canova. The plaster casts reveal the laborious process through which Canova arrived at his glossy, seemingly effort-less marbles. Fascinating rough clay models give way to plaster figures cast in gesso, which were then used to map out the final marble in minute detail with small nails. It's the most complete display of an artist's working models in Europe.

The Drive ≫ The short 16km drive west to Valdobbiadene is delightful. Descend from hilltop Possagno on the SP26, through vineyards and green fields. Then take a left onto the SR348 and a right over the Piave river and into the vine-draped hills of prosecco country.

TRIP HIGHLIGHT

❹ Valdobbiadene

Prosecco can be traced back to the Romans. It was then known as 'Pucino' and was shipped directly to the court of Empress Livia from Aquileia, where it was produced with grapes from the Carso. During the Venetian Republic the vines were transferred to the Prosecco DOCG (quality-controlled) area, a small triangle of land between the towns of Valdobbiadene, Conegli-ano and Vittorio Veneto.

Valdobbiadene sits at the heart of prosecco country, vines dipping

---

DETOUR: MASER

Start: ❷ **Asolo**

Andrea Palladio managed to synthesise the classical past without doggedly copying it, creating buildings that were at once inviting, useful and incomparably elegant.

A prime example of this domestic perfection is Palladio's butter-yellow **Villa di Masèr** (Villa Barbaro; ☎0423 92 30 04; www.villadimaser.it; Via Cornuda 7, Maser; adult/reduced €9/7; ⏱10am-6pm Tue-Sat, from 11am Sun Apr-Oct, 11am-5pm Sat & Sun Nov-Mar; 🅿) set amid a prosecco vineyard in Maser. Inside, Paolo Veronese nearly upstages his collaborator with wildly imaginative *trompe l'œil* architecture of his own. Vines climb the walls of the Stanza di Baccho; an alert watchdog keeps one eye on the painted door of the Stanza di Canuccio (Little Dog Room); and in a corner of the frescoed grand salon, the painter has apparently forgotten his spattered shoes and broom. At the wine-tasting room by the villa's parking lot, you can raise a toast to Palladio and Veronese with the estate's own prosecco.

Dolomites Cinque Torri

and cresting across its hillsides. Take the **Strada di Prosecco** (www.coneglianovaldobbiadene.it) to discover some of the area's best wineries, such as **Cantina Bisol** (☏0423 90 47 37; www.bisol.it; Via Follo 33, Santo Stefano di Valdobbiadene; ☺10am-1pm & 3-6pm Mon-Sat, 10am-1pm Sun), where generations of the Bisol family have been tending Galera vines since 1542. Tastings take place in the atmospheric underground cellars; the signature labels are the award-winning Cartizze Dry and Jeio Brut.

✕ ⊨ p191

The Drive » Return to the northbound SR348 and take the next 24km alongside the Piave river at a leisurely pace. The views of the river, the vineyards and the approaching foothills of the Alps are timeless and very pretty when set against the blue, blue sky.

TRIP HIGHLIGHT

❺ Feltre

The 'painted city' of Feltre sits in a gorgeous natural setting at the foot of the Dolomites on the banks of the Piave. Since 1404, the city has been inextricably linked to Venice, demonstrating its unflinching loyalty to the Republic when

the Holy Roman army ransacked the city and massacred its inhabitants in 1510.

In reward for its faithfulness, Venice refinanced the city's reconstruction, paying for its frescoed and porticoed *palazzi* and elegant squares. Wander up **Via Mezzaterra** and **Via Lorenzo Luzzo** to admire the painted facades until you reach Piazza Maggiore, which is overlooked by the **Alboino Castle**. In August, one of the most famous historical re-enactments, **Palio di Feltre** (www.paliodifeltre.it; ☺1st weekend Aug), takes place here with hundreds of citizens dressed in Renaissance garb.

Also worth a look is the **Museo Civico** (☎0439 88 52 41; http://musei.comune.feltre.bl.it/MuseoCivico; Via Luzzo 23; adult/reduced €4/1.50; ⏱9.30am-6pm Tue-Sun mid-Jun–mid-Sep, 10.30am-12.30pm & 3-6pm Tue-Sun mid-Sep–mid-Jun), which houses an unusually fine art collection, including paintings by major Veneto artists such as Bellini, Cima da Conegliano and Palma il Giovane, while the nearby **Museo d'Arte Carlo Rizzarda** (☎0439 88 52 34; http://musei.comune.feltre.bl.it; Via Paradiso 8; adult/reduced €4/1.50; ⏱10.30am-12.30pm & 3-6pm Tue-Sun) contains modernist pieces by Egon Schiele, Picasso and Adolfo Wildt.

Finally, 5km south of Feltre, on the same road you drove in on, is the unmissable 12th-century, frescoed **Sanctuary of Vittore and Corona** (☎0439 21 15; www.santivittoreecorona.it; Località Anzù; ⏱9am-noon & 3-7pm summer, to 6pm winter), the patron saints of the town.

The Drive » Although a little busier, the 30km drive northeast to Belluno, up the valley, is equally scenic. The SS50 runs between the Piave river to the south and the snow-capped peaks of the Parco Nazionale delle Dolomiti Bellunesi to the north, climbing slowly to Belluno.

6 Belluno

Perched on high bluffs above the Piave river and backed majestically by the snowcapped Dolomites, Belluno makes a scenic and strategic base to explore the 315-sq-km **Parco Nazionale delle Dolomiti Bellunesi** (www.dolomitipark.it). And you'll be happy to fuel up for ski trails and hikes on the city's hearty cuisine, including Italy's most remarkable cheeses: Schiz (semisoft cow's-milk cheese, usually fried in butter) and the flaky, butter-yellow Malga Bellunense.

When you're not out on the slopes, the historical old town is its own attraction, mixing stunning views with Renaissance-era buildings. **Piazza dei Martiri** (Martyrs' Sq), Belluno's main pedestrian square, is named after four partisans hanged here during WWII. On sunny days and warm nights, its cafes overflow with young and old alike. Nearby, the Piazza del Duomo is framed by the early-16th-century Renaissance **Cattedrale di San Martino** (Piazza del Duomo; ⏱8.30am-8pm), the 16th-century **Palazzo Rosso** and the **Palazzo dei Vescovi**, with a striking 12th-century tower.

✕ 🛏 p191

DANIELPRUDEK/GETTY IMAGES ©

Dolomites Horses under Monte Pelmo

TOP TIP: PRIMAVERA DEL PROSECCO

Every May the 30 prosecco-producing villages in the DOC quality-controlled prosecco area participate in the **Primavera del Prosecco** (Prosecco Spring; www.primaveradelprosecco.it), putting on a weekend party with food stalls and all-day prosecco tasting.

The Drive » The two-hour (81km) drive from Belluno to the Cinque Torri is one of this trip's highlights. Cutting right through Parco Nazionale delle Dolomiti Bellunesi on the SR203, it offers stunning mountain panoramas and a nerve-tingling traverse of the Falzarego pass. Note: in winter, weather conditions may close the high passes. If so, take the A27 and SS51 directly to Cortina d'Ampezzo.

TRIP HIGHLIGHT

7 Cinque Torri

At the heart of the Dolomites, just 16km west of Cortina at the confluence of the Ampezzo, Badia and Cordevole valleys, is the gorgeous area of **Cinque Torri** (www.5torri.it). It is accessible from Cortina by buses – ski shuttles in winter (free to ski-pass holders) and a Dolomiti Bus service in summer – which connect with the lifts at Passo Falzerego.

Hard though it is to believe, some of the fiercest fighting of WWI took place in these idyllic mountains between Italian and Austro-Hungarian troops. Now you can wander over 5km of restored trenches in an enormous **open-air museum** (https://lagazuoi.it) between Lagazuoi and the Tre Sassi fort. Guided tours are offered by the Gruppo Guide Alpine, and in winter you can ski the 80km **Great War Ski Tour** (https://lagazuoi.it) with the Dolomiti Superski ski pass. En route, mountain refuges provide standout lunches with spectacular views.

🛏 p191

The Drive » Another super, swooping drive along mountain roads lined with conifers. At Cinque Torri, pick up the SS48 (Passo Falzarego) and wind your way slowly down the twisting route into Cortina d'Ampezzo, 16km away.

8 Cortina d'Ampezzo

The spiked peaks and emerald-green valleys of the Dolomites are so beautiful, and their ecosystem so unique, they've won Unesco protection. In winter, Cortina d'Ampezzo is the place to be, with fashion-conscious snow bunnies crowding its excellent slopes. In summer, it doubles as a stunning base for hiking, cycling and rock climbing.

Two cable cars whisk hikers and climbers from Cortina's town centre to a central departure point for chairlifts, cable cars and trails. They usually run from 9am to 5pm daily mid-December to April and resume June to October. Dolomiti Superski passes provide access to 12 runs in the area, and are sold at Cortina's **ski pass office** (📞0436 86 21 71; www.skipasscortina.com; Via Marconi 15; Valley Pass 1/3/7 days €50/144/269; ⏱8.30am-12.30pm & 3-6.30pm Mon-Fri).

Guide Alpine Cortina d'Ampezzo (📞0436 86 85 05; www.guidecortina.com; Corso Italia 69a; ⏱8.30-10.30am & 5-7pm Mon-Sat, 5-7pm Sun) runs rock-climbing courses and guided nature hikes.

Cortina's other highlight activity is hunting down its fabulous farm-to-table restaurants, such as Agriturismo El Brite de Larieto, in the surrounding larch forests.

🍴 🛏 p191

The Seattle Public Library
Southwest Branch
www.spl.org

Checked Out On: 10/29/2023 15:36
XXXXXXXXX3590

Item Title	Due Date
0010101811569	11/19/2023
Italy's best trips : 40 amazing road trips	
0010106787160	11/12/2023
A fever in the heartland : the Ku Klux Klan's plot to take over America : and the woman who stopped them	
0010087974449	11/19/2023
Cooking for Jeffrey	

# of items: 3

Renew items at www.spl.org/MyAccount
or 206-386-4190
Sign up for due date reminders
at www.spl.org/notifications

You're free to be you at the Library
Express who you are and choose what
you want to read, listen to or learn
www.spl.org/FreeTo
Northeast Branch and Northeast Lockers
will closed 11/1-12/10 for construction
All holds for Northeast will be rerouted to
Northgate

Eating & Sleeping

Valdobbiadene ❹

✗ Agriturismo Da Ottavio   Venetian €
(☎0423 98 11 13; Via Campion 2, San Giovanni di Valdobbiadene; meals €15-20; ⊙noon-3pm Sat, Sun & holidays, closed Sep; P) Prosecco is typically drunk with *sopressa*, a fresh local salami, as the sparkling spumante cleans the palate and refreshes the mouth. There's no better way to test this than at Da Ottavio, where everything on the table, *sopressa* and prosecco included, is homemade by the Spada family.

🛏 Azienda Agricola Campion   Farmstay €€
(☎0423 98 04 32; www.campionspumanti.it; Via Campion 2, San Giovanni di Valdobbiadene; s/d €85/110; ⊙tasting room 9am-noon & 2-6pm; P❄🛜♨🐾) Why not quit worrying about the challenges of prosecco tasting and driving, and instead bed down at this farmstay amid 14 hectares of vines in the heart of Valdobbiadene? The four rooms occupy converted farm buildings, with warm, rustic styling and the added perk of a kitchenette in each.

Belluno ❻

✗ Ristorante Taverna   Veneto €€
(☎0437 2 51 92; www.ristorantetaverna.it; Via Cipro 7; set menu €45; ⊙noon-2.30pm & 7.30-10pm Mon-Sat) Tucked away on Via Cipro, where Cypriot wine was once sold, this traditional tavern offers a warm welcome in its cosy, wood-panelled interior. While service can be slow – relax! – the food is worth the wait: plates come laden with polenta and Schiz cheese, delicate trout scooped out of mountain rivers and blueberry pappardelle with wild-boar *ragù*.

🛏 Parco Dolomiti Fisterre B&B   B&B €
(☎0437 93 20 16; Via Michele Cappellari 55; s/d €39/76; P🛜) This three-room B&B offers one of the warmest welcomes in the Dolomites, with extremely friendly and helpful owners, tasty breakfasts and a tranquil location just next to the Ardo river, 10 minutes on foot from the train

station. Bathrooms are shared and the check-in time is a little late (5pm), but these are small irritations.

Cinque Torri ❼

🛏 Rifugio Ristorante Peziè de Parù   Hut €
(☎0436 86 20 68; www.peziedeparu.it; Località Peziè de Parù, 1535m; d/q €95/120; ⊙Dec-Mar & Jul-Sep; P🛜) This idyllic Alpine hut sits in a meadow encircled by a crown of high peaks. In summer, guests lounge on the lawn with the cow, then retire to the terrace for bowls of *canederli* (dumplings) and glasses of bilberry-flavoured grappa. Three rustic-chic bedrooms with smart modern bathrooms and stunning views are also available for the lucky few who book ahead.

Cortina d'Ampezzo ❽

✗ Agriturismo El Brite de Larieto   Veneto €€
(☎368 7008083; www.elbritedelarieto.it; Passo Tre Croci, Località Larieto; meals €25-35; ⊙noon-3pm & 7-10pm, closed Thu out of season; P) This idyllic farm enjoys a sunny situation amid thick larch forest with fabulous views from its terrace and a quaint Alpine interior. It produces its own dairy products and vegetables and much of the meat on the menu. Cured charcuterie and *canederli* (dumplings) are a highlight. It's located 5km northwest of Cortina off the SR48 towards Passo Tre Croci.

🛏 Hotel Montana   Hotel €
(☎0436 86 21 26; www.cortina-hotel.com; Corso Italia 94; s €52-87, d €82-168; 🛜🐾) Right in the heart of Cortina, this friendly, vintage 1920s Alpine hotel offers simple but well-maintained rooms. Facilities include a ski room with a waxing table and rather nice boot warmer. In winter, there's a seven-night minimum (€310 to €570 per person), but call for last-minute cancellations. Reception areas double as gallery space for local artists. Pets are welcome.

Trieste to Sappada

Meander the borderlands of northeastern Italy and you'll find a curious mix of history and culture amid the alpine hillsides. Come with an open mind and prepare to be surprised.

17

TRIP HIGHLIGHTS

224 km

Sappada
Hike pristine trails and dine in historic *blockbau* chalets

NISH **7**

82 km

Il Collio
Sip Friulano amid the rolling hills of Il Collio

● Osoppo

San Daniele del Friuli ●   Cividale del Friuli ●

Udine ●

3

52 km

Aquileia
Once one of the largest and richest cities in the Roman Empire

2 Sistiana ●

0 km

1 START

Trieste
Commune with literary ghosts in Trieste's grand cafes

7 DAYS
224KM / 139 MILES

GREAT FOR...

BEST TIME TO GO
May to October for fine weather and the grape harvest.

ESSENTIAL PHOTO
Mosaic sea monsters and songbirds at Aquileia.

BEST FOR CULTURE
A true borderland: multilingual, multicultural and historically fascinating.

17 Trieste to Sappada

Influenced through the centuries by its Austrian and Slavic neighbours, a tour through Friuli Venezia Giulia reveals a place with a unique multicultural heritage. Starting in Trieste, the home of Habsburg princes and once Austria's seaside salon, climb the steep plateau to Cividale, the city of Julius Caesar, visit Europe's only school of mosaic in Spilimbergo, drink Hungarian-style Tocai in Collio and end in the linguistic mountain island of Sappada.

TRIP HIGHLIGHT

❶ Trieste

From as long ago as the 1300s, Trieste has faced east. It flourished under Habsburg patronage between 1382 and 1918, attracting writers and philosophers such as Thomas Mann and James Joyce to the busy cafes on **Piazza dell'Unità d'Italia**. There they enjoyed the city's fluid character where Latin, Slavic, Jewish and Germanic culture intermingled.

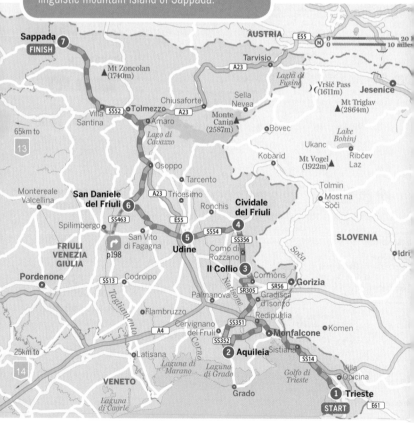

The neighbourhood of **Borgo Teresiano** reflects this cultural melange and on Via San Francesco d'Assisi you can tour Trieste's nationally important **Synagogue** (☑040 37 14 66; www.triestebraica. it; Via San Francesco d'Assisi 19; adult/reduced €3.50/2.50; ☺guided tours 4pm & 5.30pm Mon & Wed, 10am & 11.30am Tue, 10am, 11am & noon Sun) and the stunning Serbian Orthodox **Chiesa di Santo Spiridione** (☑040 63 13 28; www.comunitaserba. org; Via Filzi; ☺8.30am-12.30pm & 5-8pm Mon-Sat, 8.30am-12.30pm Sun).

Seven kilometres from the city centre, **Castello di Miramare** (☑040 22 41 43; www.castello-miramare. it; Viale Miramare; adult/reduced €8/2; ☺9am-7pm) is Trieste's bookend to Austrian rule, the fanci-

ful neo-Gothic home of Archduke Maximilian, commander in chief of Austria's Imperial Navy, who came to Trieste as an ambitious young aristocrat in the 1850s and was shot by firing squad in Mexico in 1867. The house is a reflection of his eccentric wanderlust.

✖ ⌂ p199

The Drive » Head northwest out of Trieste along Viale Miramare (SS14), where you'll keep sea views to your left for almost 20km. At Sistiana join the A4 (towards Venice) for 18km to Redipuglia, where you can visit Italy's largest war memorial. Then exit southwest towards Papariano and Aquileia for the final 16km run.

- - - - - - - - - - - - - - - -

TRIP HIGHLIGHT

❷ Aquileia

Colonised by Rome in 181 BC, Aquileia was one of the largest and richest cities of the empire. Levelled by Attila's Huns in AD 452, the city's inhabitants fled south and west where they founded Grado and then Venice. A smaller town rose in its place in the early Middle Ages with the construction of the present **basilica** (www. basilicadiaquileia.it; Piazza Capitolo; basilica complex adult/reduced €10/7.50; ☺9am-7pm Apr-Sep, to 6pm Mar & Oct, to 5pm Nov-Feb, bell tower Apr-Oct only), which is carpeted with one of the largest and most spectacular Roman-era mosaics in the world.

Beyond the basilica explore the scattered ruins of the **Porto Fluviale** (River Port; Via Sacra; ☺8.30am-1hr before sunset), the old port, and the standing columns of the ancient **Forum** on Via Giulia Augusta. Then visit the **Museo Archeologico Nazionale** (☑0431 9 10 35; www.museoarcheo logicoaquileia.beniculturali. it; Via Roma 1; adult/reduced €10/2; ☺10am-7pm Tue-Sun) for one of Italy's most important collections of Roman artefacts.

The Drive » A short 30km drive. Exit Aquileia north on the SS352 and after 3km veer off northeast onto the SS351 through open farmland towards Gradisca d'Isonzo. At Sagrado turn left onto the SR305 and head towards Borgnano where you'll turn right onto a small country road (SP16) that leads through vineyards to Cormòns.

- - - - - - - - - - - - - - - -

TRIP HIGHLIGHT

❸ Il Collio

Famed for its winemakers and country restaurants, the Collio produces some of the finest, mineral-rich white wines in Italy from local varietals such as Friulano, Malvasia Istriana and Ribolla Gialla. The area's vineyards are arranged like a quilt around the town of **Cormòns**, where the local wine shop, **Enoteca di Cormòns** (☑0481 63 03 71; www.enoteca-cormons. it; Piazza XXIV Maggio 21; ☺11am-10pm Wed-Mon), offers tastings with platters of Montasio cheese.

LINK YOUR TRIP

13 Grande Strada delle Dolomiti

From Sappada it's a super-scenic 57km drive, via the SR355, SS52 and SR48, through the mountains to Cortina d'Ampezzo.

14 A Venetian Sojourn

From Aquileia hop onto the A4 for a fast ride down to the Venetian lagoon, where golden domes and frescoed palaces await.

Even in high season, it is easy to drop in to dozens of family-run wineries and taste rare vintages with vintners such as **Renato Keber** (☎0481 63 98 44; www.renato keber.com; Località Zegla 15; ⏱by appt 10am-7pm Mon-Sat, 2-6pm Sun). Larger vineyards, offering international export, are **Venica & Venica** (☎0481 6 12 64; www.venica.it; Località Cerò 8, Dolegna del Collio; tastings per person €25-40; ⏱10am-5pm Mon-Sat).

If you feel peckish, drop into **La Subida** (☎0481 6 05 31; www.lasubida.it; Via Subida; meals €55-65; ⏱7-10pm Thu-Mon, plus noon-2.30pm Sat & Sun) or Michelin-starred **L'Argine a Vencò** (☎0481 199 98 82; www.largineavenco.it; Località Vencò, Dolegna del Collio; tasting menus €70-110; ⏱7.45pm-midnight Wed-Mon, plus 12.45-4pm Fri-Sun; P) where farm-to-table ingredients bring the landscape to the plate.

🛏 p199

The Drive » The next 18km to Cividale del Friuli are the most scenic on the trip. Rolling northwards from Cormòns on a country lane through the vineyards on the SS356, you'll pass through small villages such as Como di Rozzano, where Perusini offers tastings.

- - - - - - - - - - - - - - - -

❹ Cividale del Friuli

Founded by Julius Caesar in 50 BC as Forum de Lulii (ultimately 'Friuli'), Cividale's picturesque stone streets are worth a morning's quiet contemplation. Splitting the town in two is the **Ponte del Diavolo** (Devil's Bridge; Corso d'Aquileia), its central arch supported by a huge rock said to have been thrown into the river by the devil.

Cividale's most important sight is the **Tempietto Longobardo** (Oratorio di Santa Maria in Valle; ☎0432 70 08 67; www.tempiettolongobardo.it; Via Monastero Maggiore 34; adult/reduced €4/3; ⏱10am-1pm & 3-6pm Mon-Fri, 10am-6pm Sat & Sun summer, 10am-1pm & 2-5pm Mon-Fri, 10am-5pm Sat & Sun winter). Dating from the 8th century AD, its frescoes and ancient Lombard woodwork are both unusual and extremely moving. Afterwards head to the **Museo Cristiano** (Piazza del Duomo; museo adult/reduced €4/3; ⏱museo 10am-1pm & 3-6pm Wed-Sun) in the cathedral, where you can see the 8th-century stone Altar of Ratchis.

The Drive » Wend your way out of Cividale across the Natisone river on Via Fiore dei Liberti. To your right you'll get a great view of the Ponte del Diavolo. Then take a hard left onto Viale Udine, which becomes the SS54 and carries you 18km to Udine.

- - - - - - - - - - - - - - - -

❺ Udine

While reluctantly ceding its premier status to Trieste in the 1950s, Udine remains the spiritual,

MARIO SAVOIA/SHUTTERSTOCK ©

and gastronomic, capital of Friuli. At the heart of its walled medieval centre sits the **Piazza della Libertà**, dubbed the most beautiful Venetian square on the mainland.

Other Venetian echoes can be seen in the shimmering Tiepolo frescoes in the **cathedral** (www.cattedraleudine.it; Piazza del Duomo; ⏱8am-noon & 4-6pm) and the **Oratorio**

Il Collio Vineyards

della Purità (Piazza del
Duomo; ⏱10am-noon, ask
for key at cathedral if closed),
open for guided tours
only. The *Assumption*
on the ceiling was one of
Giambattista's very first
commissions, while the
eight biblical scenes in
chiaroscuro are by his
son Giandomenico. For
more Tiepolos and rare
views of the city framed
by the Alps beyond, walk
up the hill to the **castle**
(☎0432 127 25 91; www.
civicimuseiudine.it; adult/
reduced €5/2.50; ⏱10am-
6pm Tue-Sun). Local
legend has it that when
Attila the Hun plundered
Aquileia in AD 452, he
ordered his soldiers
to build the hill from
where he could witness
its destruction. Now
it houses the **Galleria
d'Arte Antica** (☎0432 27

15 91; Colle del Castello; adult/
reduced €5/2.50 incl Castello;
⏱10am-6pm Tue-Sun).

✖ 🛏 p199

The Drive)) A short 22km
meander down small provincial
roads through charming towns
like Martignacco and Fagagna.
Leave Udine westward on the
SR464. At Ciconicco turn right
(north) onto the SP10 then the
SP116 to San Daniele which sits
on a gentle hill overlooking the
broad Tagliamento river.

DETOUR: SPILIMBERGO

Start: ⑥ San Daniele del Friuli

The **mosaic school** (☎0427 22 74; https://scuolamosaicistifriuli.it; Via Corridoni 6) in Spilimbergo is one of the most fascinating places in Friuli. Although established in 1922 in a postwar effort to provide vocational skills for the poverty-stricken area, the mosaic tradition in Spilimbergo is centuries old. Artisans from this school decorated much of Renaissance Venice and have created some of the world's most celebrated mosaics, including those in the Foro Italico in Rome, the Church of the Holy Sepulchre in Jerusalem and in the subway station at Ground Zero in New York.

Prebooked tours take you through classrooms explaining the different styles of mosaic taught: Roman, Byzantine and some stunning free-form modern mosaics. What's more, the school itself forms a canvas with every floor, staircase, bathroom, wall and pillar covered in different styles of mosaic. As such, it represents a unique record of 20th-century mosaic work and wows at every turn.

⑥ San Daniele del Friuli

San Daniele del Friuli sits atop a rounded hill with a stunning view of the gently undulating surrounding landscape. Its 8000 inhabitants prepare Friuli's greatest gastronomic export, the dark, exquisitely sweet Prosciutto di San Daniele. Salt is the only method of preservation allowed and the 27 *prosciuttifici* (ham-curing plants) in the town are safeguarded by EU regulations. Learn the secrets of production and sample the ham at artisanal producer

La Casa del Prosciutto

(☎0432 95 74 22; www.lacasadelprosciutto.com; Via Ciconi 24; tours per person €40; ◷noon-3pm & 7-10pm Sat, 11am-5pm Sun).

In August, the town holds the **Aria di Festa** (Le Festa; www.ariadisandaniele.it), a four-day festival of open-house tours and tastings. For a list of *prosciuttifici* that are open year-round, visit the **tourist office** (☎0432 94 07 65; Via Roma 3; ◷9am-1pm & 2.30-6.30pm Mon-Fri, 10.30am-12.30pm & 3.30-6.30pm Sat & Sun).

✕ p199

The Drive » This 83km drive is the longest in the itinerary.

Head northeast out of San Daniele on the SR463. Join the A23 at Osoppo and exit 20km later at Amaro onto the SS52. Follow the Tagliamento river to Villa Santina and then turn right onto the SR355, which then climbs slowly for 37km up to Sappada.

TRIP HIGHLIGHT

⑦ Sappada

Voted one of the most beautiful villages in Italy and the winner of a sustainability award in 2019, Sappada (Plodn in dialect) is a picture-postcard alpine village set on a sunny slope surrounded by dramatic Dolomitic peaks. It's right on the border of the Veneto, Carnia and Carinthia (Austria) and was settled by families from East Tyrol. It remains a unique linguistic island and the inhabitants proudly maintain their unique culture and traditions.

Chief among these is **Plodar Vosenocht** (◷Feb-Mar), the annual masked Carnival, and **Sappa-Mukky** (◷Sep), when the cattle are brought down from the high mountain pastures. Otherwise, people in the know flock here for the fine dining restaurants, the pristine mountain hikes and the excellent skiing facilities in winter, making it a perfect place to end the tour.

🛏 p199

Eating & Sleeping

Trieste ❶

✗ De Scarpon   Friulian €€

(☏040 36 76 74; www.facebook.com/
descarpon; Via della Ginnastica 20; meals €25-
30; ⏱noon-2.15pm & 7-10pm Tue-Sun) No fuss,
no frills, just a large, vintage dining room with
tiled floors and walls huge with theatre posters,
and an utterly authentic Friulian menu. Fish is
the focus here, from the classic stockfish to the
bountiful seafood pasta, which comes served
in the pan. Other dishes worth trying are the
Barcola sardines and anything with mussels
from Duino.

🛏 B&B Lidia Polla Trieste   B&B €

(☏0334 7150231; www.atelierlidiapolla.com;
Via del Coroneo 1; s €70, d €90-100) A special
B&B where you'll find exquisite parquetry
floors, antique furniture and objects set against
contemporary textiles and a simple sensibility.
The quality of the linens, towels and bathrobes is
a rare find at this price. Bathrooms *are* in the hall,
but are exclusive to each room, plus one has a
claw-foot bath and all are beautiful.

Il Collio ❸

🛏 Perusini   Agriturismo €€

(☏0432 67 50 18; www.perusini.com; Via del
Torrione 13, Località Gramogliano, Corno di
Rosazzo; 1-bedroom apt €75-95, 2-bedroom
apt €140-160; P ❄) Calling the historic
Perusini Estate a 'farm stay' is something of
an understatement. Established by Giacomo
Perusini in the 18th century, the estate is
classified a historic winery and has been
instrumental in preserving several Friulian
varietals on the hills overlooking the Judrio
river. A number of farm buildings now provide
chic, rustic, self-catering accommodation on
the doorstep of the vineyards.

Udine ❺

✗ La Frasca   Friulian €€

(☏0432 67 51 50; www.lafrasca.com; Viale
Grado 10, Pavia di Udine; meals €35; ⏱noon-

3pm & 7-10pm Thu-Tue) A *frasca* is similar to
an *osmize*, a rustic place serving *salumi* (cured
meats) and wine, and takes its name from the
same practice of hanging a branch out as a
shingle. Walter Scarbolo's relaxed roadside
dining room has retained the *frasca* experience,
and his fans gather for his artisan cured meats,
menus that highlight a single seasonal crop,
and, naturally, the wonderful Scarbolo wines.

🛏 Dimora Montegnacco   B&B €

(☏333 3357540; www.dimoramontegnacco.it;
Via Cussignacco 48/3; d €65-85; P ❄ ⧬) This
charming B&B is housed in a lovely art nouveau
building in the city centre. Renovated by the two
architect-owners, the three double bedrooms
are artfully furnished and comfortable. All
of them overlook a delightful garden where
breakfast is served in summer beneath a bower
of wisteria. The owners are full of excellent
information, and there's private parking (€5
per day).

San Daniele del Friuli ❻

✗ Ai Bintars   Italian €€

(☏0432 95 73 22; www.aibintars.com; Via
Trento Trieste 67; meals €20-30; ⏱12.30-
2.30pm & 7.30-9.30pm Fri-Tue, 12.30-2.30pm
Wed; P) No menu, no fuss, no kerbside appeal;
simply serves the best prosciutto and salami
alongside small plates of marinated vegetables,
local cheeses and generous hunks of bread. You
won't find anything else on the menu.

Sappada ❼

🛏 B&B Graz Trojar Haus   B&B €

(☏0435 46 97 04; www.antichecasesappada.
com; Borgata Cima 73; d €80-100; P ⧬) One
of just two historic *blockbau* homes where
you can bed down for the night. Warm wooden
bedrooms are furnished with traditional carved
beds dressed with Alpine-style linens. Breakfast
is a spoiling affair of homemade goodies and
local produce and your hosts can give you tips
on activities in the local area.

STRETCH YOUR LEGS
VENICE

Start/Finish: Rialto Market

Distance: 3.5km

Duration: 3 hours

Venice's cosmopolitan outlook has kept the city ahead of the locavore curve and makes local cuisine anything but predictable. Tour the city's famous markets and backstreet *bacari* (hole-in-the-wall bars) to sample the unique fusion of flavours in Venice.

Take this walk on Trips

Rialto Market & Pescaria

Any tour through Venice's gourmet history starts at the 600-year-old **Rialto Market** (Rialto Mercato; ☏041 296 06 58; Campo de la Pescaria; ⏰7am-2pm; ⛴Rialto Mercato). Nearby fishmongers call out the day's catch at the **Pescaria** (Fish Market; Campo de la Pescaria; ⏰7am-2pm Tue-Sun; ⛴Rialto Mercato). You cannot take your car onto the lagoon islands so leave it in a secure garage in Mestre, such as **Garage Europa** (☏041 95 92 02; www.garageeuropa mestre.com; Corso del Popolo 55; per day €15; ⏰8am-10pm), and take the train to Venice Santa Lucia for a *vaporetto* (water taxi) to Rialto-Mercato.

The Walk » Around the corner from the Pescaria, on Ruga degli Spezieri, glimpse the treasures that made Venice's fortune: trade-route spices, in mounds in the windows of Drogheria Mascari (No 381). Down the road, duck into Calle dell'Arco.

All'Arco

At **All'Arco** (☏041 520 56 66; Calle de l'Ochialer 436; cicheti €2-2.50; ⏰9am-2.30pm Mon-Sat; ⛴Rialto Mercato) father and son chefs Francesco and Matteo invent Venice's best *cicheti,* the dainty bar snacks that are Venice's version of tapas. If you wait patiently, they'll invent a seasonal speciality for you.

The Walk » Pick up Calle Raspi and weave your way northwest over the Rio di San Cassiano, past Veneziastampa, on Campo Santa Maria Mater Domini, and on to Palazzo Mocenigo.

Palazzo Mocenigo

Costume dramas unfold in the **Palazzo Mocenigo** (☏041 72 17 98; www.mocenigo. visitmuve.it; Salizada San Stae 1992; adult/ reduced €8/5.50, with Museum Pass free; ⏰10am-4pm; ⛴San Stae), once the Mocenigos' swanky pad and now a showcase for the fashions of Venice's elite. Necklines plunge in the Red Living Room, lethal corsets come undone in the Contessa's bedroom and men's paisley knee-breeches show some leg in the dining room.

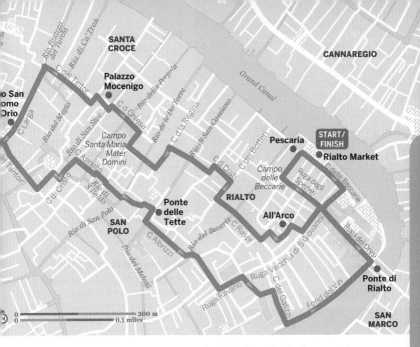

The Walk » Continue up Calle del Tentor and across the Ponte del Megio. Right after you cross the bridge turn left and then take the first right into the Campo San Giacomo da l'Orio.

Campo San Giacomo da l'Orio

You can pop your head into the church, but the real attraction of this *campo* (square) is **Al Prosecco** (☎041 524 02 22; www.alprosecco.com; Campo San Giacomo da l'Orio 1503; ☻10am-8pm Mon-Fri, to 5pm Sat; ☷San Stae), where from 10am they're popping corks and raising glasses of *vini naturi* (natural-process wines) and *ombre* (wine by the glass).

The Walk » Head southeast from Campo San Giacomo, quickly crossing a small canal and turn left on Calle di Cristo and then right down Calle Agnello, which will bring you to the high-arched Ponte delle Tette.

Ponte delle Tette

No one remembers the original name of the Ponte delle Tette, known since the 15th century as 'Tits Bridge'. Back in those days, the shadowy porticoes flanking this bridge were a designated red-light zone where prostitutes displayed their wares. Fees were set by the state and posted in Rialto brothels.

The Walk » Continue down Calle Albrizzi across the Rio del Becarie at Ponte Storte and dog-leg down Ruga Ravano and Calle del Galizzi towards the waterfront. Turn left along the Fond del Vin and you'll be greeted by the splendid Ponte di Rialto.

Ponte di Rialto

An amazing feat of engineering in its day (1592), Antonio da Ponte's marble Ponte di Rialto was for centuries the only land link across the Grand Canal. The southern side faces San Marco, and when shutterbugs clear out around sunset it offers a romantic long view of gondolas pulling up to Grand Canal *palazzi* (mansions).

The Walk » To return to the Rialto Market head northwest up Ruga dei Oresi, past the Hotel San Salvadore and right down Ruga Vecchia di San Giovanni.

STRETCH YOUR LEGS
MILAN

Start/Finish: Pasticceria Cova

Distance: 1.8km

Duration: 2 hours

A stroll around the Quadrilatero d'Oro, the world's most famous shopping district, is a must. Even if you don't have the slightest urge to sling a swag of glossy shopping bags over your arm, the elaborate windows and people-watching are priceless.

Take this walk on Trips

Pasticceria Cova

Coffee and pastries at **Pasticceria Cova** (📞02 7600 5599; www.pasticceriacova.com; Via Monte Napoleone 8; 🕐7.45am-8.30pm Mon-Sat, 9.30am-7.30pm Sun; Ⓜ Montenapoleone) provide a glimpse into the world of the Quadrilatero, where fashion-industry divas, tourists and wealthy Milanese all come to sit and sup on velvet-cushioned banquettes. This is one of the oldest cafes in Milan, opened in 1817 by Antonio Cova, a soldier of Napoleon.

The Walk ⟫ Cova sits on the corner of Via Monte Napoleone and Via Sant'Andrea. Walk northwest up Monte Napoleone past the lavish designer window displays, many of which appear in old aristocratic palazzi (mansions).

Via Monte Napoleone

Via Monte Napoleone has always been synonymous with elegance and money and now it's the most important street of the Quad, lined with global marques such as Etro, Armani, Gucci and Prada.

The Walk ⟫ Halfway up Via Monte Napoleone, you'll spot the Acqua di Parma store at the narrow opening of Via Gesù. Head down past the luxurious-looking Brioni store; in front of the Four Seasons is the Bagatti Valsecchi museum.

Four Seasons

The Quad's most luxurious hotel is the **Four Seasons** on Via Gesù. The neoclassical facade hides a 15th-century convent complete with frescoes and an arcaded cloister. Dine here at one of the outdoor tables of **La Veranda** (📞02 7 70 88; www.fourseasons.com/milan; Via Gesù 6/8; meals €80-90; 🕐7-11am, noon-4.30pm & 7-11pm; P ❄ 🍴 🛉; Ⓜ Montenapoleone). Opposite is the **Museo Bagatti Valsecchi** (📞02 7600 6132; www.museobagattival secchi.org; Via Gesù 5; adult/reduced €10/7; 🕐1-5.45pm Tue-Sun; Ⓜ Montenapoleone), stuffed with Renaissance furnishings and paintings.

The Walk ⟫ Retrace your steps and head northwest to where Via Monte Napoleone intersects with bigger, busier Via Manzoni. Turn left here and after a few metres you'll find Alessi on your left.

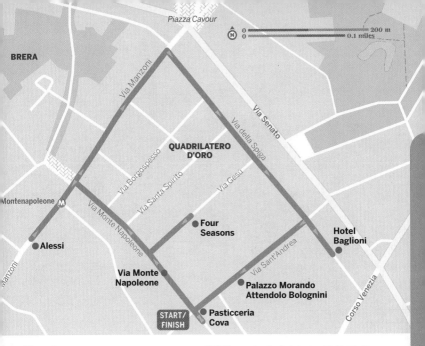

Alessi

Established on the shores of Lago d'Orta in Omegna in 1921, **Alessi** (02 79 57 26; www.alessi.com; Via Manzoni 14-16; 10am-7pm; MMontenapoleone) has gone on to transform modern homes with tens of thousands of crafted utensils. Some of the best examples now reside in the V&A in London and New York's MoMA, but you can just pop into Milan's flagship store refitted by Martí Guixé.

The Walk » Exit Alessi and turn right, retracing your footsteps. Continue past Via Monte Napoleone, past the Teatro Manzoni and take the next right down Via della Spiga. Walk almost the whole length of it, past Sermoneta and Tiffany, to reach the back door of Hotel Baglioni.

Hotel Baglioni

Who wouldn't love shopping on pedestrianised Via della Spiga, where fashion and 19th-century charm go hand in hand? But if the cobbles are making those killer heels pinch, take the back door into **Hotel Baglioni** (02

7 70 77; www.baglionihotels.com; Via Senato 5; 7am-1am; ; MSan Babila) for a Campari and soda in its cafe, which has art deco touches.

The Walk » Exit the Baglioni back entrance onto Via della Spiga, turn right and walk to Via Sant'Andrea and take a left. Walk a few metres down Via Sant'Andrea and you'll see the sign for the Palazzo Morando.

Palazzo Morando Attendolo Bolognini

For a glimpse of the Quad as it was during its 18th-century heyday, wander around the **Palazzo Morando Attendolo Bolognini**. Its **Costume Moda Immagine** (02 8846 5735; www.costumemodaimmagine .mi.it; Via Sant'Andrea 6; admission varies; 9am-1pm & 2-5.30pm Tue-Sun; MSan Babila) exhibits the collections of Contessa Bolognini, while other rooms house the **Museo di Milano** civic art collection.

The Walk » It's a short walk back to Cova from the Palazzo Morando. Turn left down Via Sant'Andrea and you'll find it just past Via Bagutta on your left.

Central Italy

AS FLORENCE'S RENAISSANCE SKYLINE FADES INTO THE BACKGROUND THE OPEN ROAD BECKONS. Motoring through Tuscany's voluptuous, wine-rich hills is one of Italy's great driving experiences and one of the many on offer in this fascinating part of the country.

To the north of Tuscany, Emilia-Romagna is a paradise for foodies, while to the east and south, Umbria, Le Marche and Abruzzo are made for slow travel with their wooded peaks, hilltop towns and wild landscapes. Travel to Italy's green, rural heart and you'll come across artistic treasures, ancient Roman ruins and Etruscan tombs. And all the while the road leads inexorably, often tortuously, towards Rome, the Eternal City.

Tuscany Val d'Orcia
JAROSLAW PAWLAK/SHUTTERSTOCK ©

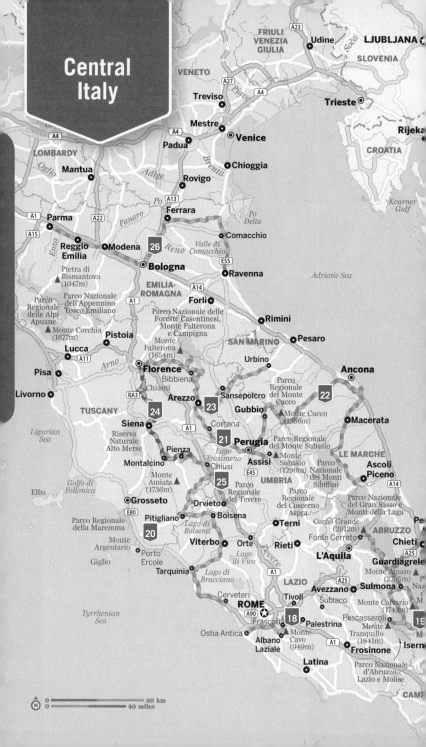

DON'T MISS

Necropolis Tarquinia

The frescoed Etruscan tombs at Tarquinia's Unesco-listed Necropolis are remarkable, yet they rarely attract big crowds. 20

Santo Stefano di Sessanio

It's a thrilling drive up to this atmospheric *borgo* (medieval hamlet) in Abruzzo's Parco Nazionale del Gran Sasso e Monti della Laga. 19

Palazzo Ducale, Urbino

The palatial residence of an art-loving Renaissance aristocrat dominates Urbino's charming historic centre. 23

Ostia Antica

Overshadowed by more famous ruins in Rome, this is one of central Italy's most compelling archaeological sites. 18

Montalcino

Crowned by a 14th-century fort, this hilltop town produces one of Italy's top red wines. 24

Roaming Around Rome

18

Rome's little-explored hinterland is a real eye-opener, with verdant scenery and thrilling cultural treasures – haunting ancient ruins, hilltop villas and landscaped Renaissance gardens.

TRIP HIGHLIGHTS

7 km

Villa Adriana
Explore the remnants of Hadrian's lavish country residence

101 km

Tivoli
Fountains, frescoes and landscaped Renaissance gardens

6 FINISH
5

● Palestrina

3
●Grottaferrata
●Marino
Castel Gandolfo

45 km

Frascati
Food, wine, aristocratic villas and ancient artefacts

START

Ostia Antica
The beautifully preserved ruins of ancient Rome's seaport

0 km

3 DAYS
101KM / 62 MILES

GREAT FOR...

BEST TIME TO GO
Spring's good for the ancient sites, early summer for romantic views.

 ESSENTIAL PHOTO
Fountains at Tivoli's Villa d'Este.

✓ **BEST FOR WINE BUFFS**
Frascati's traditional cellars.

i Villa Adriana

18 Roaming Around Rome

While Rome (Roma) hogs the limelight, the area around the capital makes for an absorbing drive with its wealth of historic sights. Headline acts include the remarkably well-preserved ruins of ancient Rome's port at Ostia Antica, and Emperor Hadrian's vast palace complex at Tivoli. Tivoli is one of several hilltop towns featured on this trip, along with the wine town of Frascati and the former papal retreat of Castel Gandolfo.

TRIP HIGHLIGHT

① Ostia Antica

One of Lazio's prize sights, the ruins of ancient Rome's seaport are wonderfully complete, like a smaller version of Pompeii. Ostia was founded in the 4th century BC at the mouth of the Tiber and developed into a major port with a population of around 50,000. Decline set in after the fall of the Roman Empire and it was gradually abandoned, its citizens driven off by barbarian

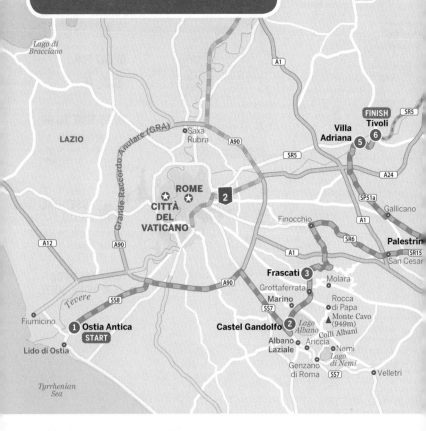

raids and outbreaks of malaria. Over subsequent centuries, it was slowly buried in river silt, hence its survival.

The **Area Archeologici di Ostia Antica** (📞06 5635 8099; www.ostia antica.beniculturali.it/; Viale dei Romagnoli 717; adult/reduced €10/5; 🕑8.30am-7.15pm Tue-Sun summer, last admission 6.15pm, shorter hours winter) is a vast site and you'll need several hours to do it justice. The main thoroughfare, the **Decumanus Maximus**, leads from the entrance at Porta Romana to

highlights such as the **Terme di Nettuno** (Baths of Neptune), whose floor features a famous mosaic of Neptune driving his seahorse chariot. Nearby, the steeply stacked **Teatro** was built by Agrippa and later enlarged to hold 4000 people. Behind the amphitheatre, the **Piazzale delle Corporazioni** (Forum of the Corporations) housed merchant guilds and is decorated with well-preserved mosaics. Further towards Porta Marina, the **Thermopolium** is an ancient cafe with a bar and fresco advertising the bill of fare.

🍴 p215

The Drive » Head back towards Rome and take the Grande Raccordo Anulare (GRA; A90) for Naples. Exit at the Ciampino Airport turnoff and continue up Via Appia (SS7), until you come to traffic lights halfway up a long climb. Make a left turn to Lago Albano and follow this road up under the towering umbrella pines to

Castel Gandolfo at the top. All told, it's about 36km.

- - - - - - - - - - - - - - - - - -

➋ Castel Gandolfo

One of the prettiest towns in the Castelli Romani, an area of wooded, wine-rich hills south of Rome, Castel Gandolfo makes for a memorable stop. It's not a big place but what it lacks in size it makes up for in atmosphere, and on a warm summer's evening there's no better place for a romantic tête-à-tête. Sightseeing action is centred on the **Palazzo Apostolico** (📞06 6988 3145; www.museivaticani.va; Piazza della Libertà; adult/reduced €11/5; 🕑8.30am-2pm Mon-Fri, to 5.30pm Sat, 10am-3pm Sun), a 17th-century palace that for centuries served as the pope's summer residence, and the **Giardini di Villa Barberini** (Villa Barberini Gardens; 📞06 6988 3145; www. museivaticani.va; Via Rosselli; tours adult/reduced €20/15, Sat morning walk €12/5;

ABRUZZO

A24

p214

Subiaco

A1

160km to 27

Segni

10 km
5 miles

LINK
YOUR
TRIP

2 **World Heritage Wonders**

From Ostia Antica head into Rome along Via Ostiense to join up with this tour of Italy's greatest hits.

27 **Shadow of Vesuvius**

Take the A1 autostrada from near Frascati and head down to Naples (Napoli), the starting point for this exploration of Vesuvius, Pompeii and other classic sites.

⏱9.30am-2.30pm). A stop here is as much about admiring the gorgeous views over Lago Albano and enjoying al fresco meals as sightseeing.

🍴 p215

The Drive ≫ To Frascati, it's a pretty straightforward 9km drive. From Castel Gandolfo follow the road for Marino, enjoying glimpses of Lago Albano off to your right, and then Grottaferrata. Here you'll come to a roundabout. Take the third exit and Frascati is 4km further on.

- - - - - - - - - - - - - - - - - -

TRIP HIGHLIGHT

❸ Frascati

Best known for its crisp white wine, Frascati is a popular day-trip destination. On hot summer weekends Romans pile into town to hang out in the elegant historic centre and fill up on *porchetta* (herb-roasted pork) and local wine. You can follow suit by filling up from the food stalls on **Piazza del Mercato** or searching out the traditional *cantinas* (originally wine and olive-oil cellars, now informal restaurants) that pepper the centre's narrow lanes. Once you've explored the town and admired the sweeping views from the tree-lined avenue at the bottom of Piazza Marconi, head up to **Villa Aldobrandini**. Designed by Giacomo della Porta and built by Carlo Maderno, this regal 16th-

PAVEL068/GETTY IMAGES ©

century villa sits haughtily above town in a stunning hillside position. The villa itself is closed to the public but you can visit the impressive early baroque **gardens** (☎06 942 25 60; Via Cardinal Massai 18; ⏱8.30am-5.30pm Mon-Fri) dramatically landscaped into the wooded hill.

🍴 🛏 p215

The Drive ≫ Take Viale Catone from the top of Piazza Marconi, following the green signs for the autostrada. Continue down to Finocchio where you'll hit the fast-flowing SR6 (Via Casilina). Turn right onto the Casilina and after San Cesareo turn left

onto the SR155 for a twisting climb up to Palestrina's historic centre. It's just under 30km from Frascati.

- - - - - - - - - - - - - - - - - -

❹ Palestrina

The pretty town of Palestrina stands on the slopes of Monte Ginestro, one of the foothills of the Apennines. In ancient times Praeneste, as it was then known, was a favourite summer retreat for wealthy Romans and the site of a much-revered temple dedicated to the goddess of fortune. Little remains of the 2nd-century BC **Santuario della Fortuna**

Primigenia, but much of what is now Palestrina's historic centre was built over its six giant terraces. Nowadays, the town's main act is the fantastic **Museo Archeologico Nazionale di Palestrina** (☎06 953 81 00; Piazza della Cortina; admission incl sanctuary adult/reduced €5/2.50; ☺9am-8pm, sanctuary 9am-1hr before sunset), housed in the 17th-century Palazzo Colonna Barberini. The museum's collection comprises ancient sculpture, funerary artefacts, and some huge Roman mosaics, but its crowning glory is the breathtaking *Mosaico Nilotico*, a detailed 2nd-century-BC mosaic depicting the flooding of the Nile and everyday life in ancient Egypt.

The Drive » It takes just over half an hour to travel the 21km or so to Villa Adriana. Exit Palestrina and head northwest towards Gallicano. Here, follow the signs to Tivoli, continuing past the shrubbery and bucolic green fields until you see Villa Adriana signposted a few kilometres short of Tivoli.

- - - - - - - - - - - - - - - - -

❺ Villa Adriana

The Emperor Hadrian's sprawling 2nd-century country estate, **Villa Adriana** (☎0774 38 27 33; www.villaadriana.benicul turali.it; Largo Marguerite Yourcenar 1; adult/reduced €10/5; ☺8.30am-1hr before sunset), was one of ancient Rome's grandest properties, lavish even by the decadent standards of the day. Hadrian personally designed much of the complex, taking inspiration from buildings he'd seen around the world. The **pecile**, the large pool area near the walls, is a reproduction of a building in Athens. Similarly, the **canopo** is a copy of a sanctuary in the Egyptian town of Canopus, with a narrow

DETOUR: SUBIACO

Start: ❻ Tivoli

Remote-feeling and dramatic, Subiaco is well worth the trip to see its two breathtaking Benedictine monasteries. The **Monastero di San Benedetto** (Santuario del Sacro Speco; 📞0774 8 50 39; www.benedettini-subiaco.org; ⊙9am-12.30pm & 3-6pm) is carved into the rock over the cave where St Benedict holed up for three years to meditate and pray. As well as a setting described by Petrarch as 'the edge of Paradise', it has an interior covered in 13th- to 15th-century frescoes.

Halfway down the hill from San Benedetto is the **Monastero di Santa Scolastica** (📞0774 8 55 69; www.benedettini-subiaco.org; ⊙9am-12.30pm & 3.30-7pm summer, to 6.15pm winter), the only one of the 13 monasteries built by St Benedict still standing in the Valley of the Amiene. If you decide to stay, its **Foresteria** (📞0774 8 55 69; www. benedettini-subiaco.org; B&B/half-board per person €37/51; P) is a great place to spend a contemplative night. But book ahead, as Benedictine clergy from around the world often make the pilgrimage here to work in the monastery's famous **library** and **archive**. There's also a restaurant offering simple meals for €20 to €25.

120m-long pool flanked by sculptural figures.

To the northeast of the *pecile*, the **Teatro Marittimo** is one of the site's signature buildings. A circular mini-villa set in an artificial pool, this was Hadrian's personal refuge and could only be accessed by swing bridges.

There are also several bath complexes, temples and barracks.

Parking (€3) is available at the site.

The Drive » Pick up Via Tiburtina (SR5), the main Rome–Tivoli road, and head up to Tivoli *centro*. It's a steep, twisting 4km climb up to the town centre.

TRIP HIGHLIGHT

❻ Tivoli

Tivoli's elevated historic centre is an attractive, if often busy, spot. Its main attraction is the Unesco-protected **Villa d'Este** (📞0774 33 29 20; www.villadestetivoli.info; Piazza Trento 5; adult/reduced €10/5; ⊙8.30am-7.45pm Tue-Sun, from 2pm Mon, gardens close sunset, ticket office closes 6.45pm), a one-time Benedictine convent that Lucrezia Borgia's son, Cardinal Ippolito d'Este, transformed into a pleasure palace in the late-16th century. It later provided inspiration for Franz Liszt, who

composed *The Fountains of the Villa d'Este* after spending time here between 1865 and 1886.

Before heading out to the gardens, take time to admire the villa's Mannerist frescoes. Outside, the manicured **gardens** feature water-spouting gargoyles and shady lanes flanked by lofty cypresses and extravagant fountains, all powered by gravity alone. Look out for the Bernini-designed **Fountain of the Organ**, which uses water pressure to play music through a concealed organ, and the 130m-long **Avenue of the Hundred Fountains**.

✕ ⌷ p215

Eating & Sleeping

Ostia Antica ❶

✗ Ristorante Monumento   Italian €€
(📞06 565 00 21; www.ristorantemonumento.it;
Piazza Umberto I 8; meals €30-35; 🕑12.30-
3.30pm & 8-11pm Tue-Sun) In Ostia's tiny
medieval centre, this historic restaurant started
life in the 19th century, catering to the labourers
working on reclaiming the local marshlands.
Nowadays, it does a brisk business feeding
sightseers from the nearby ruins. Particularly
good are seafood dishes such as *spaghetti alle
vongole* (with clams). Bookings recommended,
particularly at weekends.

Castel Gandolfo ❷

✗ Antico Ristorante
Pagnanelli   Ristorante €€€
(📞06 936 00 04; www.pagnanelli.it; Via Gramsci
4; meals €60; 🕑noon-3.30pm & 6.30-11.45pm)
A local landmark for more than a century,
this colourful wisteria-clad restaurant oozes
romance, particularly on warm summer nights
when the views over Lago Albano melt the
heart. The seasonally driven Italian food rises
to the occasion too, especially when paired with
outstanding wine from the terrific list – bottles
are racked in an amazing cellar carved into tufa
rock.

Frascati ❸

✗ Cantina Simonetti   Osteria €
(📞347 6300269; Piazza San Rocco 4; meals
€25; 🕑8pm-midnight Tue-Sun summer, 1-4pm
Sat & Sun & 8pm-midnight Wed-Sun winter)
For an authentic *vino e cucina* (wine and
food) experience, search out this traditional
cantina and sit down to a mountainous meal of
porchetta, cold cuts, cheese and Roman pastas,

all accompanied by jugs of local white wine. In
keeping with the food, the decor is rough-and-
ready rustic with strings of hanging garlic and
plain wooden tables.

🛏 Cacciani   Hotel €
(📞06 940 19 91; www.cacciani.it; Via Diaz 13; s
€69-79, d €85-95; ❄🛜) This is the family-run
hotel of the **Cacciani** (📞06 942 03 78; meals
€50; 🕑12.30-2.30pm & 8-10.30pm, closed
Sun dinner & Mon) restaurant. It's well placed
for exploring the historic centre and comes
with sunny, simply decorated rooms, some
with balconies and views down to the town of
Ciampino and, on a clear day, the sea. The buffet
breakfast is served in the restaurant.

Tivoli ❻

✗ Sibilla   Ristorante €€€
(📞0774 33 52 81; www.ristorantesibilla.com;
Via della Sibilla 50; meals €40-50; 🕑12.30-
3pm & 7.30-10.30pm Tue-Sun) With tables
set by the 2nd-century BC Tempio di Vesta
and water cascading down the green river
gorge below, this elegant restaurant sets a
wonderfully romantic stage for sophisticated
dining. Expect classic Italian food prepared
with fresh, seasonal ingredients and paired with
superlative wine.

🛏 Residenze
Gregoriane   Boutique Hotel €€€
(📞0774 43 69 03, 347 7136854; www.
residenzegregoriane.it; Via Domenico Giuliani
92; ste €230-250; ❄🛜🛗) Steeped in history,
the Residenze Gregoriane offers a night to
remember. Its four suites, all decorated in
classic antique style, occupy the 16th-century
Palazzo Mancini-Torlonia. Frescoes adorn the
historic building, many by the same artists
who worked on Villa d'Este (p214), and there's
a magnificent internal courtyard adorned with
ceramic tiles and seashell mosaics.

Abruzzo's Wild Landscapes

This crinkled mountain region offers superb driving and spectacular scenery. Roads snake through silent valleys and stone-clad villages, over highland plains and past thick forests.

19

TRIP HIGHLIGHTS

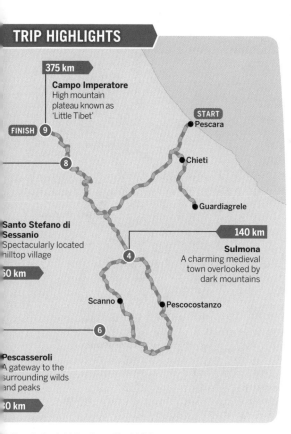

375 km

Campo Imperatore
High mountain plateau known as 'Little Tibet'

FINISH 9

START
●Pescara

●Chieti

●Guardiagrele

Santo Stefano di Sessanio
Spectacularly located hilltop village

50 km

4

140 km

Sulmona
A charming medieval town overlooked by dark mountains

Scanno ●

8

● Pescocostanzo

6

Pescasseroli
A gateway to the surrounding wilds and peaks

30 km

6 DAYS
375KM / 233 MILES

GREAT FOR...

BEST TIME TO GO
June, July and September for perfect weather and clear views.

ESSENTIAL PHOTO

Corno Grande from Campo Imperatore.

BEST FOR HIKING

The hills around Pescasseroli.

19 Abruzzo's Wild Landscapes

Although little more than an hour's drive from Rome, Abruzzo is largely unknown to foreign visitors. Yet with its mountain scenery and rural, back-country charm, it's ideal for a road trip. This route takes in the best of the region's three national parks, winding over green hills and past ancient beech woods populated by wolves and bears, as snow-capped summits shimmer in the distance. Cultural gems also await, such as the charming medieval town of Sulmona.

❶ Pescara

Before heading into the wild interior spend a day relaxing on the beach in Pescara, Abruzzo's largest city. Action centres on the animated seafront although there are a couple of small museums worth a look – the **Museo delle Genti d'Abruzzo** (☎085 451 00 26; www.gentidabruzzo.com; Via delle Caserme 24; adult/reduced €6/3; ⏰9am-1pm Mon-Fri, 9am-1pm & 4.30-7.30pm Sat, 4.30-7.30pm Sun), which illustrates regional rural culture, and the **Museo**

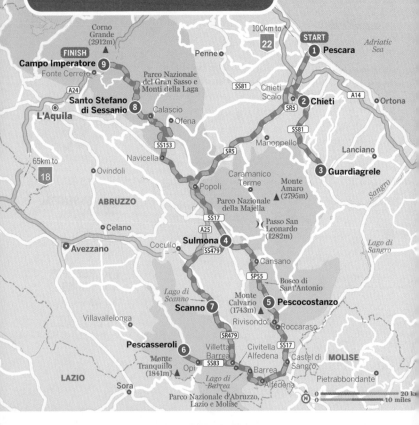

Casa Natale Gabriele D'Annunzio (☎085 6 03 91; Corso Manthonè 116; admission €4; ⏰8.30am-7.30pm), birthplace of controversial fascist poet Gabriele D'Annunzio.

Pescara also offers top-notch seafood and a youthful and energetic *aperitivo* scene.

✕ 🛏 p223

The Drive ❯❯ From central Pescara it's about half an hour to Chieti. Follow the green signs to the autostrada (motorway), which direct you onto the Raccordo Pescara-Chieti, a fast-moving dual carriageway that runs past factories and warehouses towards the distant mountains. Exit for Chieti and follow signs for Chieti *centro* and then the Civetta and Museo Archeologico Nazionale.

LINK YOUR TRIP

18 Roaming Around Rome

From Fonte Cerreto take the A24 for about 105km southwest to Tivoli, one of the gems in Rome's fascinating hinterland.

22 Green Heart of Italy

Pick up the A24 near Fonte Cerreto and continue for 140km southwest to Frascati, and a tour of the wine-rich Castelli Romani.

TOP TIP: ARRIVING IN SULMONA

Try to time your arrival in Sulmona between 1.30pm and 5.30pm, when traffic restrictions are lifted and you can drive into the historic centre. It makes getting to your hotel much easier.

---

❷ Chieti

Overlooking the Aterno valley, hilltop Chieti dates back to pre-Roman times, to the era of feuding Italic tribes. Two museums showcase the town's ancient history. The most important is the **Museo Archeologico Nazionale d'Abruzzo Villa Frigerj** (☎0871 40 43 92; www.archeoabruzzo. beniculturali.it; Via Costanzi 2, Villa Comunale; adult/reduced €4/2; ⏰8.30am-7.30pm Tue-Sat, 8.30am-2pm Sun), home to the 6th-century-BC 'Warrior of Capestrano', the most important pre-Roman find in central Italy and a much-publicised regional icon. Uphill from the Frigerj, the **Museo Archeologico Nazionale d'Abruzzo – La Civitella** (☎0871 6 31 37; www.archeoabruzzo.benicul turali.it; Via Pianell; adult/reduced €4/2; ⏰8.30am-7.30pm Tue-Sat, 2-8pm Sun) is built around a Roman amphitheatre.

The Drive ❯❯ Descend from Chieti's centre until you see signs for Guardiagrele and the SS81 off to the left. The road twists and turns slowly

for the first few kilometres but eventually broadens out and becomes quicker as it runs past woods and vineyards up to Guardiagrele, about 26km (40 minutes) away.

---

❸ Guardiagrele

Described as Abruzzo's terrace by poet Gabriele D'Annunzio, this ancient *borgo* (medieval town) on the eastern flank of the **Parco Nazionale della Majella** (www.parcomajella. it) commands sweeping views. Admire these and the striking **Collegiata di Santa Maria Maggiore** (Piazza di Santa Maria Maggiore, Guardiagrele; ⏰7am-noon & 4-7pm Mon-Fri) with its elegant Gothic doorway that frames a Romanesque facade topped by a collection of nine bells exposed to the elements.

The Drive ❯❯ To Sulmona it's about 1½ hours from Guardiagrele. Double back to Chieti on the SS81, then follow signs for the autostrada towards L'Aquila then the SR5 to Chieti Scalo and Manoppello. Pass through Popoli and continue on the SS17 until you see Sulmona signposted about 18km on.

TRIP HIGHLIGHT

❹ Sulmona

Overlooked by the grey Morrone massif, Sulmona is a midsized medieval town famous for its *confetti* (sweets traditionally given to guests at Italian weddings). Action is focused on **Corso Ovidio**, named after the local-born poet Ovid, and **Piazza Garibaldi**, a breezy piazza accessed through a 13th-century **aqueduct**. Here on the square, you can peruse religious and contemporary art at the **Museo Diocesano di Arte Sacra** (☎0864 21 29 62; Piazza Garibaldi; adult/reduced €4/2; ☉9am-1pm & 3.30-6.30pm Tue-Sun).

At the other end of Corso Ovidio, **Palazzo dell'Annunziata** sits above a 1st-century-BC Roman *domus* (villa), remains of which can be seen at the **Museo Civico** (☎0864 21 02 16; Palazzo dell'Annunziata, Corso Ovidio; adult/reduced €4/2; ☉9am-1pm & 3.30-6.30pm Tue-Sun).

🍴 🛏 p223

The Drive » The 50-minute run over to Pescocostanzo takes you through some beautiful mountain terrain, via the Bosco di Sant'Antonio (ideal for a picnic). From Sulmona head towards Cansano and follow the road as it ascends the increasingly rocky landscape. At Cansano take the SP55 for Pescocostanzo.

❺ Pescocostanzo

Surrounded by lush highland meadows, Pescocostanzo (elevation 1400m) is a characteristic hilltop town whose historical core has changed little in over 500 years. Of particular note is the **Collegiata di Santa Maria del Colle** (☎0864 64 14 30; Via Diomede 1; ☉hours vary), an atmospheric Romanesque church with a lavish baroque interior. Nearby, **Piazza del Municipio** is flanked by a number of impressive *palazzi* (mansions), including **Palazzo Comunale** with its distinctive clock tower, and **Palazzo Fanzago** (Piazza Municipio; ☉11am-1pm & 5-8pm Sat & Sun), designed by baroque architect Cosimo Fanzago in 1624.

History apart, Pescocostanzo also offers skiing on **Monte Calvario** and summer hiking in the **Bosco di Sant'Antonio**.

The Drive » Reckon on about 75 minutes to Pescasseroli. Continue past Rivisondoli to the SS17, then turn south towards Roccaraso. After Castel di Sangro head right onto the SS83. This beautiful road swoops and dips its way through Alfedena, Barrea, past the artificial Lago di Barrea, and on to Villetta Barrea, Opi and Pescasseroli.

TRIP HIGHLIGHT

❻ Pescasseroli

Deep in the heart of the Marsican mountains, Pescasseroli is the main centre of the **Parco Nazionale d'Abruzzo, Lazio e Molise** (www.parcoabruzzo. it), the oldest and most popular of Abruzzo's national parks. Hiking

Scanno Historic centre

opportunities abound with clearly marked paths for all levels. In winter there's a small ski station that's popular with locals. You'll be lucky to see bears or wolves in the wild here (though they exist); however, you can view rescued animals at Pescasseroli's **Centro Visita** (📞0863 911 32 21; www.

parcoabruzzo.it; Viale Colli dell'Oro, Pescasseroli; adult/reduced €6/4; ⏱10am-5.30pm) and learn about wolves in Civitella Alfedena's **Museo del Lupo Appenninico** (Appenine Wolf Museum; 📞0864 89 01 41; Via Santa Lucia, Civitella Alfedena; adult/reduced €3/2; ⏱10am-1.30pm & 3-6.30pm Apr-Sep, to 5.30pm Oct-Mar).

🛏 p223

The Drive ⟫ To Scanno it takes about an hour. Double back to Villetta Barrea and turn left onto the SR479. Wind your way up through a pine forest and past grassy slopes to the Passo Godi, a mountain pass set at 1630m. From here, the road starts its slow, tortuous descent to Scanno.

ABRUZZO WILDLIFE

Abruzzo's three national parks – Parco Nazionale del Gran Sasso e Monti della Laga; Parco Nazionale della Majella; and Parco Nazionale d'Abruzzo, Lazio e Molise – are home to thousands of animal species. Most famous of all is the critically endangered Marsican brown bear, of which there are an estimated 50 or so in the Parco Nazionale d'Abruzzo, Lazio e Molise. Apennine wolves also prowl the deep woods, sometimes emerging in winter when thick snow forces them to approach villages in search of food. Other notable animals include the Abruzzi chamois and red deer, and, overhead, golden eagles and peregrine hawks.

❼ Scanno

A tangle of steep alleyways and sturdy, grey-stone houses, prepossessing Scanno is an atmospheric *borgo* known for its finely worked filigree gold jewellery. Explore the pint-sized historic centre and then head down to Lago di Scanno – a couple of kilometres out of town on the road to Sulmona – for a cool lakeside drink.

✗ p223

The Drive ❯❯ This two-hour leg can be broken up by overnighting in Sulmona, 31km from Scanno through the narrow, steep-sided Gole di Sagittario. From Sulmona pick up the SS17 to Popoli and then follow signs for L'Aquila, climbing steadily to Navicella. Here, take the SS153 towards Pescara. Exit for Ofena and climb the snaking road past Calascio and on to Santo Stefano di Sessanio.

TRIP HIGHLIGHT

❽ Santo Stefano di Sessanio

If you really want to slip away from it all, you can't get much more remote than this picturesque village high in the **Parco Nazionale del Gran Sasso e Monti della Laga** (www.gransassolagapark.it). Once a 16th-century Medici stronghold, it suffered damage in the 2009 earthquake when its emblematic Medici tower collapsed (it's being rebuilt). Notwithstanding, exploring Santo Stefano's ancient mossy streets with their smattering of local shops and 'diffused' accommodation is a peaceful joy. The helpful **Centro Visite** (✆0862 89 91 17, 347 3159855; www.centrovisitesantostefanodisessanio.it; Via del Municipio; ⏰10am-7pm summer, to 3pm Sat & Sun winter) also

contains a small museum about the national park.

🛏 p223

The Drive ❯❯ From Santo Stefano, Campo Imperatore is signposted as 13km. It's actually more like 20km (20 minutes), but you'll forget about such things as the awesome scenery unfolds ahead of you. Just follow the road and its continuation, the SS17bis, and admire the views.

TRIP HIGHLIGHT

❾ Campo Imperatore

The high point – quite literally – of this trip is the highland plain known as Campo Imperatore (average elevation 1800m). Often referred to as Italy's 'Little Tibet', this magnificent grassy plateau provides spectacular views of **Corno Grande** (2912m), the highest mountain in the Apennines. You can climb the mountain on the 11.5km *via normale* (normal route) or just hang around the cable-car station admiring the art-deco Hotel Campo Imperatore (currently being refurbished) from where German paratroopers famously rescued Mussolini in 1943.

From Campo Imperatore, signs direct you down to **Fonte Cerreto**, a small cluster of hotels set around a *funivia* (cable car) station, and the nearby A24 autostrada.

Eating & Sleeping

Pescara ❶

🍴 La Cucineria — Abruzzese €€

(📞335 5459990; Via Clemente de Cesaris 26; meals €28-35; ⏰12.30-2.30pm & 7.30-10.30pm Mon-Sat, 7.30-10.30pm Sun) Sitting pretty in a city full of seafood, Cucineria relies more on the fat of the *terra* (land) with *chitarrina* (Abruzzo's spaghetti) tossed with mountain herbs and sun-dried tomatoes, cheesy Roman favourite *cacio e pepe*, and a whole section of the menu dedicated to different *focaccie* made with locally milled flour that's been left to rise for 72 hours.

🛏 G Hotel — Boutique Hotel €€

(📞085 2 76 89; www.ghotelpescara.it; Via Stazione Ferroviaria 100; s/d €105/130; 🅿 ❄ 📶 🐾) The G is the Alfa Romeo of Pescara's hotels: smart, well designed and quietly luxurious, but at the same time, not ridiculously expensive. Located a mere 100m dash from the train station, it instantly impresses with a large modern-minimalist lobby-lounge where generous *aperitivo* snacks are rolled out every afternoon. Tech-savvy rooms have huge mirrors, rain showers, crisp duvets and atmospheric lighting.

Sulmona ❹

🍴 Il Vecchio Muro — Abruzzese €€

(📞0864 5 05 95; Via M D'Eramo 20; meals €28; ⏰12.45-2.30pm & 7.45-10.30pm, closed Wed Oct-Apr) One of Sulmona's best restaurants, the 'old wall' is notable for spot-on Abruzzese fare such as wholewheat pasta with lentils and *guanciale* (cured pork jowl). The rest of the menu – especially the bits involving sausage and mushroom – is wonderfully executed, and even the pizza is well above average.

🛏 Legacy Casa Residencia — B&B €

(📞377 9766036; www.legacycasaresidencia.it; Vico dell'Ospedale 54; d/apt €75/135; 🅿 ❄ 📶) A beautifully curated and professionally run B&B right in the centre of Sulmona with a choice of double rooms or miniapartments. All the accommodation skilfully combines convenience and comfort with the distinct sense that you're in the heart of traditional Italy. The apartments can be let on self-catering and (discounted) weekly bases and cooking, painting and hiking packages are available.

Pescasseroli ❻

🛏 Pensione Al Castello — Pension €

(📞0863 91 07 57; Viale D'Annunzio 1, Pescasseroli; d with breakfast/half-board €75/95) Just off the main square in Pescasseroli, this long-established, family-run *pensione* has all you need for a post-hiking day of relaxation. Its large, sunny rooms have white tiled floors and pleasant wooden furniture.

Scanno ❼

🍴 Pizzeria Trattoria Vecchio Mulino — Trattoria €

(📞0864 74 72 19; Via Silla 50; pizzas/meals from €8/28; ⏰noon-3pm & 7pm-midnight, closed Wed winter) This old-school eatery is a good bet for a classic wood-fired pizza, lentil soups, pastas (perhaps ravioli with mushroom and ricotta) and roasted *salsicce* (sausage). In summer the pretty street-side terrace provides a good perch from which to people-watch (read: tourist-watch). The excellent bread and pasta are homemade and the cheeses are all local.

Santo Stefano di Sessanio ❽

🛏 Sextantio — Design Hotel €€

(📞0862 89 91 12; www.sextantio.it; Via Principe Umberto; d/ste from €162/320; 📶) This enchanting *albergo diffuso*, with 28 distinctive rooms and suites scattered throughout the village, was what helped rescue Santo Stefano from oblivion. Designed to reignite Italy's lesser-known settlements without scrimping on luxury, it marries traditional handmade bedspreads and rustic furniture with underfloor heating, mood lighting and divinely deep bathtubs. Everything was restored using local materials.

Etruscan Tuscany & Lazio

20

From Tuscan treasures and rugged hilltop towns to tufa-carved tombs and raunchy frescoes, this tour takes you into the heart of ancient Etruria, the land the Etruscans once called home.

TRIP HIGHLIGHTS

START
Chiusi

66 km

Sovana
Explore monumental tombs and ancient Etruscan roads

2
3

Bolsena

73 km

Pitigliano
A rocky, dramatically sited hill town

Viterbo

6

231 km

Cerveteri
Walk around a veritable town of the dead

Tarquinia
Delve into amazing frescoed tombs

178 km

7

FINISH

3–4 DAYS
231KM / 144 MILES

GREAT FOR...

BEST TIME TO GO

Early summer is good for sightseeing and the sea.

 ESSENTIAL PHOTO

Pitigliano rising out of the rock.

BEST FOR HIKING

Etruscan trails around Sovana and Pitigliano.

Etruscan Tuscany & Lazio

Long before Rome came into existence, the Etruscans had forged a great civilisation in the pitted, rugged hills of southern Tuscany, Umbria and northern Lazio. This trip leads through these little-known parts of the country, opening the window onto dramatic natural scenery and spectacular Etruscan treasures. From Tuscany's pock-marked peaks to the haunting tombs that litter Lazio's soft green slopes, it's a beguiling ride.

❶ Chiusi

Located in Tuscany's Etruscan heartland, in territory where archaeologists still regularly unearth tombs, Chiusi has an outstanding collection of ancient finds. Housed in the **Museo Archeologico Etrusco di Chiusi** (☎0578 2 01 77; www.facebook.com/museoetrusco.dichiusi; Via Porsenna 93; adult/reduced €6/3; ⊙9am-8pm), these include a bevy of 9th- to 2nd-century BC ceramics, pottery, jewellery and cinerary urns. Don't miss the extraordinary '*pietra fetida*' (sulphur stone) funerary sphinx and bust of a grieving woman, both dating from the 6th century BC. The museum ticket also covers entry to two Etruscan tombs in the nearby countryside – free shuttle buses run from the museum to the tombs between April and September.

✖ p231

The Drive » Reckon on 66km for this first leg. From Chiusi, head south through Chiusi Scalo to pick up the southbound SP308. Follow this country road until Piazze where the road bears left and becomes the SP321. Continue onto the SR2 and then the rural SP22 for the last few kilometres to Sovana.

TRIP HIGHLIGHT

❷ Sovana

Tuscany's most significant Etruscan tombs are

San Quirico d'Orcia

TUSCANY

Terme di Saturnia
Sovana ❷
Montemerano
Pitig
Manciano
SS74

SS1

Tyrrhenian Sea

concentrated in the **Ne-cropoli di Sovana** (☎0564 61 40 74; www.leviecave.it; admission €5; ⏱10am-7pm summer, to 6pm Oct, to 5pm Sat & Sun Nov-Mar; P), an archaeological park encompassing land around the villages of Sovana, Sorano and Vitozza. At Sovana, the best finds are situated just 1.5km west of the village. Here you'll find four major tombs, including the monumental **Tomba Ildebranda**, with traces of carved columns and stairs, as well as two stretches of original Etruscan road – **Via del Cavone** and **Via Cava di Poggio Prisca**.

The village itself has a pretty main street and two beautiful Romanesque churches – the **Cattedrale di San Pietro** (Via del Duomo; adult/12-17yr/under 12yr €2/1/free;

LINK YOUR TRIP

18 Roaming Around Rome

At Cerveteri, pick up the A12 autostrada and continue south 45km, via Fiumicino, to Ostia Antica, Rome's very own Pompeii.

25 Tuscan Landscapes

From Bolsena, head northeast to join the SR71 for the 20km drive to Orvieto, one of the stars of this fabulously scenic trip.

⊘10am-1pm & 2.30-7pm Apr-Oct, 10am-1pm & 2.30-5.30pm Nov–early Jan, 10am-1pm & 2.30-6pm mid-Feb–Mar, weekends only early-Jan–mid-Feb), with its austere vaulted interior, and the **Chiesa di Santa Maria Maggiore** (Piazza del Pretorio; ⊘9am-5pm), notable for its 16th-century apse frescoes.

 p231

The Drive » Head east out of Sovana and after a couple of kilometres go right on the SP46. This winding road twists through scorched open peaks and occasional pockets of woodland as it wends its way to Pitigliano, about 7km away.

- - - - - - - - - - - - - - - -

TRIP HIGHLIGHT

❸ Pitigliano

Sprouting from a towering tufa outcrop and surrounded by dramatic gorges on three sides, Pitigliano is a lovely knot of twisting stairways, cobbled alleys and quaint stone houses. In the middle of it all, the **Museo Civico Archeologico di Pitigliano** (🖉389 5933592; Piazza della Fortezza; adult/reduced €3/2; ⊘10am-6pm Fri-Sun Jun, 10am-7pm Tue-Sun Jul-Sep, 9am-5pm Fri-Sun Oct, 10am-5pm Sat & Sun Nov, hours vary rest of year) has a small but rich collection of local Etruscan finds, including some huge *bucchero* (black earthenware pottery) dating from the 6th century BC.

The town also has an interesting Jewish history – at one point it was

dubbed 'Little Jerusalem' – which you can find out about at **La Piccola Gerusalemme** (Little Jerusalem; 🖉0564 61 42 30; www.lapicco lagerusalemme.it; Vicolo Manin 30; adult/reduced €5/4; ⊘10am-1pm & 2.30-6pm Sun-Fri summer, 10am-12.30pm & 2-3.30pm Sun-Fri winter).

🛏 p231

The Drive » Head east on the SR74 until the road forks. Bear right onto the SP489 for Gradoli and follow through the increasingly lush countryside until you hit the fast-flowing SR2 (Via Cassia). Go right and skirt the northern banks of Lago di Bolsena into Bolsena town. All told it's about 30km.

- - - - - - - - - - - - - - - -

❹ Bolsena

The main town on **Lago di Bolsena**, Italy's largest volcanic lake, Bolsena was a major medieval pilgrimage destination after a miracle supposedly took place here in 1263, leading Pope Urban IV to establish the festival of Corpus Domini. Other than the lake, the main reason to stop by is to visit the **Rocca Monaldeschi**, a 13th-century fortress that dominates the skyline and houses a small collection of locally unearthed artefacts in the **Museo Territoriale del Lago di Bolsena** (🖉0761 79 86 30; www.simu labo.it; Piazza Monaldeschi 1, Bolsena; adult/reduced €5/3.50; ⊘3-7pm Mon, 10am-

1pm & 3-7pm Tue-Fri, 10am-7pm Sat & Sun).

The Drive » It's a straightforward 31km drive to Viterbo along the SR2. This takes you down Lago di Bolsena's eastern side, past orchards, vineyards and olive groves through the medieval town of Montefiascone and on to Viterbo.

- - - - - - - - - - - - - - - -

❺ Viterbo

Founded by the Etruscans and later taken over by the Romans, Viterbo became an important medieval centre, and in the 13th century was briefly the seat of the papacy.

Its Etruscan past is chronicled at the **Museo Nazionale Etrusco** (🖉0761 32 59 29; Piazza della Rocca; adult/reduced €6/2; ⊘8.30am-7.30pm Tue-Sun), one of several interesting sights in the town's well-preserved *centro storico*. To the south, the Renaissance **Piazza del Plebiscito** is overlooked by **Palazzo dei Priori** (Piazza del Plebiscito 14, Via Ascenzi 1; ⊘9am-1pm & 3-6.30pm Mon-Fri, 9am-noon & 3-7pm Sat, 9am-noon Sun), Viterbo's city hall, which has some fine 16th-century frescoes.

Southwest of here, **Piazza San Lorenzo** was the medieval city's religious heart, where cardinals came to vote for their popes and pray in the 12th-century **Cattedrale di San Lorenzo**

Cerveteri Necropoli di Banditaccia

(www.archeoares.it/cattedrale-di-san-lorenzo; Piazza San Lorenzo; ⊗10am-7pm summer, 10am-1pm & 3-6pm winter). Next door, the **Museo del Colle del Duomo** (☑320 7911328; www.archeoares.it/museo-colle-del-duomo; Piazza San Lorenzo 8; €3, incl Cattedrale & Palazzo dei Papi adult/reduced €9/7; ⊗10am-7pm summer, 10am-1pm & 3-6pm winter) displays a small collection of archaeological artefacts and religious art. Also on the piazza is the **Palazzo dei Papi** (☑320 7911328; www.archeoares.it/palazzo-dei-papi-2; Piazza San Lorenzo; incl Cattedrale & Museo Colle del Duomo adult/reduced

€9/7; ⊗10am-7pm summer, 10am-1pm & 3-6pm winter), a handsome Gothic palace that was built for the popes who lived in Viterbo from 1257 to 1281. Its main feature is the **Sala del Conclave**, scene of the first and longest ever papal conclave.

✗ ☐ p231

The Drive ≫ Exit Viterbo and pick up the SS675 heading towards Rome. Continue on this fast dual carriageway until the turnoff for SR2 (Via Cassia). Take this and continue to Vetralla, where you should go right onto the SS1bis (Via Aurelia bis) and continue on to Tarquinia. It's about 44km in total.

- - - - - - - - - - - - - - - - - -

TRIP HIGHLIGHT

➏ Tarquinia

The pick of Lazio's Etruscan towns, Tarquinia is a gem. Its highlight is the 7th-century BC **Necropoli di Tarquinia** (Necropoli dei Monterozzi; ☑0766 85 63 08; www.polomusealelazio.beni culturali.it/index.php?it/145/antichit; Via Ripagretta; adult/reduced €6/2, incl museum €10/4; ⊗8.30am-7.30pm Tue-Sun summer, to 1hr before sunset winter), one of Italy's most important Etruscan sites. Some 6000 tombs have been excavated here since 1489, of which 22 are currently open to

229

THE ETRUSCANS

Of the many Italic tribes that emerged from the Stone Age, the Etruscans left the most enduring mark. By the 7th century BC their city-states – places such as Caere (modern-day Cerveteri), Tarquinii (Tarquinia), Veii (Veio), Perusia (Perugia), Volaterrae (Volterra) and Arretium (Arezzo) – were the dominant forces in central Italy.

Debate rages about their origins – Roman historian Herodotus claimed they came to Italy from Asia Minor to escape famine – but what is not disputed is that they gave rise to a sophisticated society based on agriculture, trade and mineral mining. They were skilled architects, and although little remains of their buildings, archaeologists have found evidence of aqueducts, bridges and sewers, as well as temples. In artistic terms, they were known for their jewellery and tomb decoration, producing elaborate stone sarcophagi and bright, vivid frescoes.

For much of their existence, the Etruscans were rivals of the Greeks, who had colonised much of southern Italy from the 8th century BC, but in the end it was the Romans who finally conquered them. In 396 BC they lost the key town of Veii, and by the 2nd century BC they and their land had largely been incorporated into the rapidly expanding Roman Republic.

---

the public, including the **Tomba della Caccia e della Pesca**, the richly decorated **Tomba dei Leopardi**, and the **Tomba della Fustigazione** with its erotic depiction of ancient S&M.

In the *centro storico*, the **Museo Archeologico Nazionale Tarquiniense** (☐0766 85 60 36; www.polomusealelazio.benicul turali.it/index.php?it/145/antichit; Via Cavour 1; adult/reduced €6/2, incl necropolis €10/4; ⏰8.30am-7.30pm Tue-Sun) is a delightful museum, showcasing some wonderful Etruscan artefacts, including a breathtaking terracotta frieze of winged horses (the *Cavalli Alati*).

✕ p231

The Drive » The easiest way to Cerveteri, about 53km away, is by the A12 autostrada. Take this towards Rome/Civitavecchia and exit at the Cerveteri/Ladispoli turnoff. After the toll booth, head left into town.

TRIP HIGHLIGHT

❼ Cerveteri

Cerveteri, or Kysry to the Etruscans and Caere to Latin-speakers, was one of the most important commercial centres in the Mediterranean from the 7th to the 5th century BC. Its main sight is the Unesco-listed **Necropoli di Banditaccia** (☐06 994 00 01; www.polomu sealelazio.beniculturali.it/index.php?it/145/antichit; Via della Necropoli 43/45; adult/reduced €6/2, incl museum

€10/4; ⏰8.30am-1hr before sunset Tue-Sun) just outside town. This 12-hectare site is a veritable city of the dead, with streets, squares and terraces of *tumuli* (circular tombs cut into the earth and capped by turf). Look out for the 6th-century BC **Tomba dei Rilievi**, which retains traces of painted reliefs.

In Cerveteri itself, the **Museo Nazionale Cerite** (☐06 994 13 54; www.polomusealelazio.beniculturali.it/index.php?en/145/antiquity; Piazza Santa Maria 1; adult/reduced €6/2, incl necropolis €10/4; ⏰8.30am-7.30pm Tue-Sun) displays finds from the tombs, including the *Euphronios Krater*, a celebrated 1st-century BC vase.

Eating & Sleeping

Chiusi ❶

✖ Il Grillo è Buoncantore Tuscan €€

(📞0578 2 01 12; https://ilgrilloebuoncantore.
wixsite.com/ristorante; Piazza XX Settembre
10; meals €30, pizzas €6-10; ⏱noon-2.30pm &
7-11pm, closed Mon in winter; 🌼🍴) Chef and
sommelier Tiziana Tacchi is passionate about
the cuisine and wine of the Chiusi region and
showcases both in this acclaimed Slow Food
destination. The menu is grounded in local
tradition but Tiziana's creations are executed
with a contemporary sensibility and the
results are truly delectable (the antipasti are a
knockout). No pizzas at lunch.

Sovana ❷

✖ Vino al Vino Tuscan €

(📞0564 61 71 08; www.facebook.com/enoteca.
vinoalvino; Via del Duomo 10; cheese & salumi
plates €15, soup €8; ⏱10.30am-9pm Wed-Mon
mid-Mar–Dec, 10.30am-9pm Sat & Sun Jan–mid-
Mar; 🍴) Mellow jazz plays on the soundtrack,
art adorns every wall and the vibe is friendly
at this hybrid cafe and *enoteca* (wine bar) on
Sovana's main street. The speciality-roast
coffee is good; cakes (sourced in Pitigliano)
are even better. At lunch or dinner, glasses of
wine and tasting plates of local produce reign
supreme. Vegan and vegetarian soups and
bruschette are available.

Pitigliano ❸

🛏 La Casa degli Archi Apartment €€

(📞349 4986298; www.lacasadegliarchi.com; r
€129-149; 🛜) These apartment rentals sleeping
between two and six guests make great bases
for those visiting the region. Casa degli Archi
is highly recommended and two of the three
apartments in a second building, Case Nuove,

are also good – the third, Casa Capitano,
has a strangely sloping low roof and isn't as
comfortable. Reception is in Via Roma.

Viterbo ❺

✖ Il Gargolo Ristorantino Italian €€

(📞0761 95 88 30; Piazza della Morte 14; meals
€30; ⏱noon-3pm & 7.30-11pm) A casual meal
on an atmospheric piazza is one of the joys of
eating out in Italy, and that's exactly what you
get at Il Gargolo. Its al fresco tables, shaded by
leafy trees, are a wonderful place to tuck into
scrumptious pastas – try the *tonnarelli* (thick
square spaghetti) with pecorino, *guanciale*
(cured pig's cheek) and black truffle – and rich,
creamy desserts.

🛏 B&B Centro Storico B&B €

(📞389 2386283; Via Romanelli 24; s €68-82,
d €59-82, q €84-107; 🌼🛜) A great little
bolthole in the heart of the historic centre. Its
three cool, tastefully attired rooms, including
a mini-apartment for four, are up a steep set of
stairs (no lift) on the 1st floor of a 14th-century
palazzo, about 200m from Piazza del Plebiscito.
Kettles are provided, along with some lovely
homemade biscuits; otherwise breakfast is
served in a nearby bar.

Tarquinia ❻

✖ Il Cavatappi Lazio €€

(📞0766 84 23 03; www.cavatappirestaurant.it;
Via dei Granari 2; meals €25-30; ⏱12.30-2pm
Fri-Sun year-round, also 7.30-10pm Wed-Mon
summer, 7-10pm Wed-Mon winter) Tarquinia
has several decent eateries, including this
family-run restaurant in the *centro storico*. Bag
a table in the tastefully cluttered interior or on
the summer terrace, and dive into generous
helpings of earthy regional food – cured meat
and cheese platters, seasonal veggie soups and
flavoursome grilled steaks.

Monasteries of Tuscany & Umbria

This trip takes in world-famous basilicas, remote hermitages and secluded sanctuaries as it leads from Assisi to a 15th-century Florentine monastery frescoed by Fra' Angelico.

21

5 DAYS
262KM / 163 MILES

GREAT FOR...

BEST TIME TO GO
Summer and early autumn are best for monastic visits.

ESSENTIAL PHOTO
The towered castle at Poppi.

BEST FOR HIKING
The forests around the Santuario della Verna.

21

Monasteries of Tuscany & Umbria

Away from the crowds and bright lights, an austere 11th-century monastery sits in silence surrounded by forest and rocky mountainsides. Welcome to the Monastero & Sacro Eremo di Camaldoli, one of the starkly beautiful monasteries that you'll discover on this tour of central Umbria and Tuscany. Most people don't venture into the remote and densely forested locations where these monasteries are set, but they set the scene for a gripping drive.

TRIP HIGHLIGHT

❶ Assisi

Both the birthplace and the final resting place of St Francis, this medieval hilltop town is a major destination for millions of pilgrims. Its biggest drawcard is the **Basilica di San Francesco** (www.sanfrancescoassisi.org; Piazza Superiore di San Francesco; ⊘ basilica superiore 8.30am-6.50pm, basilica inferiore 6am-6.50pm summer, shorter hours winter), which comprises two gloriously frescoed churches – the Gothic

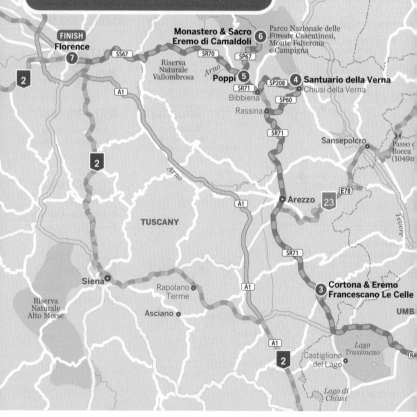

Basilica Superiore (upper church), which was built between 1230 and 1253 and features a celebrated fresco cycle by Giotto, and the dimly lit **Basilica Inferiore (lower church)**, with frescoes by Simone Martini, Cimabue and Pietro Lorenzetti.

At the other end of the *centro storico* (historic centre), the 13th-century **Basilica di Santa Chiara** (www.assisisantachiara.it; Piazza Santa Chiara; ⏰6.30am-noon & 2-7pm summer, to 6pm winter) is the last resting place of St Clare, a con-

temporary of St Francis and founder of the Order of the Poor Ladies, aka the Poor Clares.

 p239

The Drive » From Assisi you can get to Perugia in about 40 minutes, but if you've got time it's worth stopping off to admire the basilica at Santa Maria degli Angeli. From Assisi head down the snaking road to Santa Maria degli Angeli and pick up the fast-running SS75 to Perugia.

- - - - - - - - - - - - - - - -

❷ Perugia

With its hilltop medieval centre and international student population, Perugia is as close as Umbria gets to a heaving metropolis – which isn't all that close. Action is focused on the main strip, **Corso Vannucci**, and **Piazza IV Novembre**, home to the austere 14th-century **Cattedrale di San Lorenzo** (☎075 572 38 32; Piazza IV Novembre; ⏰7.30am-12.30pm & 3.30-6.45pm Mon-Sat, 8am-12.45pm & 4-7pm Sun) with its unfinished two-tone facade.

Over the square, the 13th-century **Palazzo dei Priori** houses Perugia's

best museums, including the **Galleria Nazionale dell'Umbria** (☎075 572 10 09; www.gallerianazionaleum bria.it; Palazzo dei Priori, Corso Vannucci 19; adult/reduced €8/4; ⏰8.30am-7.30pm Tue-Sun year-round, plus from noon Mon mid-Mar–Oct), with a collection containing works by local heroes Perugino and Pinturicchio. Close to the *palazzo* (mansion), the impressive **Nobile Collegio del Cambio** (Exchange Hall; ☎075 572 85 99; www.collegiodel cambio.it; Palazzo dei Priori, Corso Vannucci 25; €4.50, incl Nobile Collegio della Mercanzia €5.50; ⏰9am-12.30pm & 2.30-5.30pm Mon-Sat, 9am-1pm Sun) also has some wonderful frescoes by Perugino.

 p239, p249

The Drive » From Perugia it's just under an hour's drive to Cortona. Pick up the RA6 Raccordo Autostradale Bettolle-Perugia and head west, skirting Lago Trasimeno before joining the northbound SR71 at the lake's northwestern corner. From there the pace slackens as the road cuts through vineyards and sunflower fields up to Cortona.

LINK YOUR TRIP

2 **World Heritage Wonders**

From Florence, head 73km south to Siena, one of the stars of this classic trip.

23 **Piero della Francesca Trail**

Push north from Cortona to Arezzo and join up with this art-based trail that runs from Urbino to Florence.

DETOUR: GUBBIO

Start: ② Perugia

Stacked on the steep slopes of an Umbrian mountainside, the medieval town of Gubbio is well worth a visit. Highlights include **Piazza Grande**, with grandstand views over the surrounding countryside, and the **Museo Civico Palazzo dei Consoli** (☎075 927 42 98; www.palazzodeiconsoli.it; Palazzo dei Consoli, Piazza Grande; adult/reduced €10/5; ◎10am-1pm & 3-6pm Mon-Fri, 10am-6pm Sat & Sun, shorter hours winter), where you'll find Gubbio's most famous treasures – the Iguvine Tablets. Dating to between 300 BC and 100 BC, these bronze tablets are inscribed with ancient text, the finest existing samples of the ancient Umbrian language.

For a change of scene, and yet more views, take the **Funivia Colle Eletto** (☎075 927 38 81; www.funiviagubbio.it; Via San Girolamo; adult/reduced one way €4/3, return €6/4; ◎9am-8pm daily Jul & Aug, shorter hours rest of year) up to the **Basilica di Sant'Ubaldo** high above on Monte Ingino.

Gubbio is just over an hour's drive northeast of Perugia on the SR298.

TRIP HIGHLIGHT

❸ Cortona & Eremo Francescano Le Celle

A stunning hilltop town, and the setting for the film *Under the Tuscan Sun,* Cortona has a remarkable artistic pedigree. Fra' Angelico lived and worked here in the late 14th century, and fellow artists Luca Signorelli and Pietro da Cortona were both born within its walls – all three are represented in the excellent **Museo Diocesano di Arte Sacra** (☎0575 6 28 30; Piazza del Duomo 1; adult/reduced €5/3; ◎10am-6.30pm daily Apr-Oct, 11am-4pm Tue-Fri, 10am-5pm Sat & Sun Nov-Mar).

Three kilometres north of town in dense woodland, the Franciscan hermitage called **Eremo Francescano Le Celle** (☎0575 60 33 62; Strada dei Cappuccini 1; ◎7am-7pm) sits next to a picturesque stream. It's a wonderfully tranquil spot, disturbed only by the bells calling the resident friars to mass in the cave-like **Chiesa Cella di San Francesco**.

🍴 p239

The Drive ›› The 1¾-hour drive to the Santuario della Verna takes you deep into the heart of the Casentino hills. From Cortona head north on the SR71. About 25km beyond Arezzo, in Rassina, follow signs right and continue up the densely wooded slopes to Chiusi della Verna. The sanctuary is about 3km above Chiusi.

TRIP HIGHLIGHT

❹ Santuario della Verna

St Francis of Assisi is said to have received the stigmata at the **Santuario della Verna** (☎0575 53 41; www.laverna.it; Via del Santuario 45, Chiusi della Verna; ◎sanctuary 6.30am-10pm summer, to 7.30pm winter,

Florence Fresco in Museo di San Marco

Cappella delle Stimmate 8am-7pm summer, to 5pm winter, Museo della Verna 10am-noon & 1-4pm Sat & Sun, daily Jul & Aug) on the southeastern edge of the **Parco Nazionale delle Foreste Casentinesi Monte Falterona e Campigna** (www.parcoforestecasentinesi.it). The sanctuary, which is dramatically positioned on a windswept mountainside, holds some fine glazed ceramics by Andrea Della Robbia and his studio, including a magnificent *Crucifixion* in the **Cappella delle Stimmate**, the 13th-century chapel built on the spot where the saint supposedly received the stigmata.

The Drive » Allow about 45 minutes to Poppi from the sanctuary. The first leg, along the SP208, winds through the lush tree-covered mountains to Bibbiena, from where it's an easy 5km north on the SR71. You'll know you're near when you see Poppi's castle up on your left.

- - - - - - - - - - - - - - -

❺ Poppi

Perched high above the Arno plain, Poppi is crowned by the **Castello dei Conti Guidi** (📞0575 52 05 16; www.buonconte. com; Piazza della Repubblica 1; adult/reduced €7/4; ⏰10am-4.30pm Thu-Sun, extended hours summer). Inside the 13th-century structure, you'll find a fairytale courtyard, a library full of medieval manuscripts, and a chapel with frescoes by Taddeo Gaddi, including a gruesome depiction of *Herod's Feast* with a dancing Salome and headless John the Baptist.

✕ 🛏 p239

The Drive » Camaldoli is about 13km from Poppi. Take SP67 (Via Camaldoli) and follow it up through the forest until you come to a fork in the road – the hermitage is uphill to the right; the monastery is downhill to the left.

ST FRANCIS OF ASSISI

The son of a wealthy merchant and a French noblewoman, Francesco was born in Assisi in 1181. He enjoyed a carefree youth, but in his mid-20s he went off to fight against Perugia and spent a year in an enemy prison. Illness followed and after a series of holy visions he decided to renounce his possessions and live a humble life in imitation of Christ, preaching and helping the poor. He travelled widely, performing miracles (curing the sick, communicating with animals) and establishing monasteries until his death in 1226. He was canonised two years later.

Today, various places claim links with the saint, including Gubbio where he supposedly brokered a deal between the townsfolk and a man-eating wolf, and Rome where Pope Innocent III allowed him to found the Franciscan order at the Basilica di San Giovanni in Laterano.

6 Monastero & Sacro Eremo di Camaldoli

The 11th-century **Sacro Eremo e Monastero di Camaldoli** (Camaldoli Hermitage & Monastery; ☑0575 55 60 12 (Monastery), 0575 55 60 21 (Eremo); www.camaldoli. it; Località Camaldoli 14, Camaldoli; ⊙ hermitage 6-11am & 3-6pm, monastery 8am-noon & 2.30-6pm, pharmacy 9am-12.30pm & 2-6pm) sits immersed in thick forest on the southern fringes of the Parco Nazionale delle Foreste Casentinesi Monte Falterona e Campigna. Home to a small group of Benedic-

tine monks, it has some wonderful art: in the monastery's **church** you'll find three paintings by Vasari: *Deposition from the Cross; Virgin with Child, St John the Baptist and St Girolamo;* and a Nativity; while at the hermitage, the small church harbours an exquisite altarpiece by Andrea Della Robbia.

For a souvenir, pop into the 16th-century **pharmacy** and pick up soap, perfumes and other items made by the resident monks.

The Drive » From the Monastero di Camaldoli, it's a 1½-hour drive to the Florentine monastery now housing the

Museo di San Marco. From Camaldoli, double back along the SP67 and then head west along the SR70 through Poppi and then over the Passo della Consuma, a scenic mountain pass in the Tuscan section of the Appenine mountains, before following the river Arno through Pontassieve and into Florence's historic centre.

TRIP HIGHLIGHT

7 Museo di San Marco, Florence

This 15th-century Dominican monastery located next to the Chiesa di San Marco in the Florentine neighbourhhod of the same name is one of the city's most spiritually uplifting **museums** (☑055 238 86 08; Piazza San Marco 3; adult/reduced €4/2; ⊙8.15am-1.50pm Mon-Fri, to 4.50pm Sat & Sun, closed 1st, 3rd & 5th Sun, 2nd & 4th Mon of month), showcasing frescoes by Fra' Angelico ('Il Beato Angelico', or 'The Blessed Angelic One'), an artist and monk who was made a saint by Pope John Paul II in 1984. Major works here include Fra' Angelico's haunting *Annunciation* (c1440) on the staircase leading to the monks' cells, one of the best-loved of all Renaissance artworks.

✕ ⊨ p47, p60, p257, p267

Eating & Sleeping

Assisi ❶

✖ Osteria La
Piazzetta dell'Erba   Osteria €€

(📞075 81 53 52; www.osterialapiazzetta.it; Via San Gabriele dell'Addolorata 15a; meals €30-35; 🕑12.30-2.30pm & 7.30-10pm Tue-Sun; 🛜) Tables at this local favourite are always highly coveted: in winter in the cosy stone-vaulted interior, in summer outside on a small, flower-strewn square. The big draw is the kitchen's inventive cuisine and a seasonally driven menu that's flecked with Asian and European influences (hummus, sauerkraut and wasabi regularly pop up in dishes).

🛏 Gallery Hotel Sorella Luna   Hotel €€

(📞075 81 61 94; www.hotelsorellaluna.it; Via Frate Elia 3; r €53-150; ❄🛜) This artistic hideaway, about 200m from the Basilica di San Francesco and five minutes' walk from the Parcheggio Piazza Giovanni Paolo II, is a real find. Its 15 rooms are bright and tastefully low-key with white walls, unobtrusive modern furniture and smooth brick-tiled floors. Breakfast is a further plus and well worth getting up for.

Perugia ❷

✖ La Taverna   Ristorante €€

(📞075 572 41 28; www.ristorantelataverna.com; Via delle Streghe 8; meals €35-40; 🕑12.30-2.30pm & 7.30-10.30pm; 🛜) La Taverna consistently wins the praise of local foodies. Brick vaults and candlelit tables create an intimate backdrop for Chef Claudio Brugolossi's seasonal dishes, from homemade ravioli with black truffles to diverse *secondi* (expertly grilled steaks, lamb stew with flat bread, chicken curry), all paired with superb wines.

🛏 Castello di Monterone   Hotel €€€

(📞075 572 42 14; www.castellomonterone.com; Strada Montevile 3; r €110-250; 🅿❄🛜🏊) This fairy-tale castle comes with all the turreted, ivy-clad, vaulted trappings you would imagine. Its 18 individually designed rooms have been finished to great effect, with low timber-beamed

ceilings, exposed stone, custom wood furniture, handmade wrought-iron beds, antiques and the odd Etruscan and medieval artefact. Superior rooms come with views over the rolling countryside to Perugia's centre, 3km away.

Cortona ❸

✖ La Bucaccia   Tuscan €€

(📞0575 60 60 39; www.labucaccia.it; Via Ghibellina 17; meals €38; 🕑12.30-2.30pm & 7-10.30pm Tue-Sun) Occupying the medieval stable of a Renaissance *palazzo*, Cortona's best-regarded restaurant has close-set tables where diners enjoy refined versions of Cortonese specialities – beef, game and handmade pasta feature on the menu. Owner Romano Magi ripens his own cheeses and starting or ending your meal with a cheese course is recommended. There's an excellent wine list, too. Reservations essential.

Poppi ❺

✖ La Vite   Tuscan €€

(📞0575 56 09 62; www.ristorantelavite.net; Piazza della Repubblica, Soci; meals €25; 🕑noon-2.30pm & 6.30-10.30pm Wed-Mon) This easy dine in Soci, 5km east of Poppi, is run by young dynamic sommelier Barbara and chef Cesare. It's a real favourite with locals – and travellers – hungry for a good-value feast of top-quality Tuscan food with great wine. Don't skimp on *dolci* (dessert) – all homemade and fabulous. Kudos for the pretty summertime patio garden.

🛏 Borgo Corsignano   Agriturismo €€

(📞0575 50 02 94; www.borgocorsignano.it; Via Corsignano, Corsignano; d/q from €150/300; 🅿@🛜🏊) At home in a *borgo* (medieval hamlet) once home to Camaldoli monks, this gorgeous country hotel is the Casentino's finest accommodation option. A 5km drive from Poppi, it has a mix of self-catering apartments and houses spread lavishly among 13 old stone properties. Voluptuous sculptures collected by the art-loving owners pepper the vast grounds, and sweeping mountain views are magnificent.

Green Heart of Italy

22

From handsome hill towns to otherworldly caves and the wild green peaks of the Monti Sibillini, this trip weaves through the rural heartland of Umbria and Le Marche.

TRIP HIGHLIGHTS

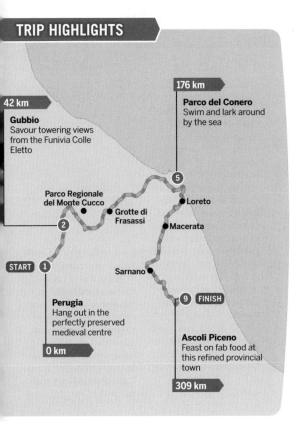

176 km

Parco del Conero
Swim and lark around by the sea

42 km

Gubbio
Savour towering views from the Funivia Colle Eletto

Parco Regionale del Monte Cucco

2

5

● Loreto

Grotte di Frasassi

● Macerata

START **1**

Sarnano ●

9 FINISH

Perugia
Hang out in the perfectly preserved medieval centre

0 km

Ascoli Piceno
Feast on fab food at this refined provincial town

309 km

4–5 DAYS
309KM / 192 MILES

GREAT FOR...

BEST TIME TO GO

June to September for wildflowers, arts festivals and hiking.

ESSENTIAL PHOTO

The plunging coastline around Sirolo in the Parco del Conero.

BEST FOR FOOD

Veal-stuffed olive all'ascolana in their hometown, Ascoli Piceno.

Green Heart of Italy

Few places are as off the beaten track as this swath of central Italy. Here small rural roads run past sun-ripened wheat fields while dark mountains brood in the distance and medieval hill towns cling onto wooded slopes. But it's not all nature and stunning scenery – there's also culture aplenty with several fine art galleries, striking basilicas and opera in the summer sun.

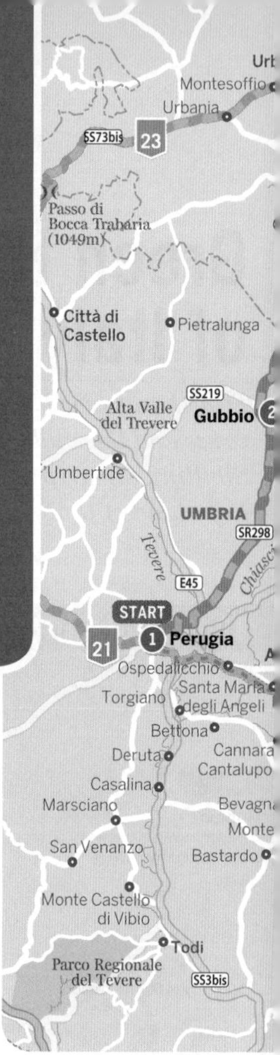

TRIP HIGHLIGHT

❶ Perugia

With a pristine medieval centre and an international student population, Perugia is Umbria's largest and most cosmopolitan city. Its *centro storico* (historic centre), seemingly little changed in more than 400 years, rises in a helter-skelter of cobbled alleys, arched stairways and piazzas framed by solemn churches and magnificent Gothic *palazzi* (mansions).

Flanking the main strip, **Corso Vannucci**, the 14th-century Gothic **Palazzo dei Priori** (Corso Vannucci 19) was the headquarters of the local mag-

istracy, but now houses Umbria's foremost art gallery, the **Galleria Nazionale dell'Umbria** (🖉075 572 10 09; www.gallerianazionaleumbria.it; Palazzo dei Priori, Corso Vannucci 19; adult/reduced €8/4; ⊗8.30am-7.30pm Tue-Sun year-round, plus from noon Mon mid-Mar–Oct) and its impressive collection of Italian masterpieces. Of particular note are the Renaissance works of hometown heroes Pinturicchio and Perugino.

Also in the Palazzo is the **Nobile Collegio del Cambio** (Exchange Hall; 🖉075 572 85 99; www.collegiodelcambio.it; Palazzo dei Priori, Corso Vannucci 25; €4.50, incl Nobile Collegio della Mercanzia €5.50; ⊗9am-12.30pm & 2.30-5.30pm Mon-Sat, 9am-

1pm Sun), home to yet more Perugino paintings.

At the end of Corso Vannucci, **Piazza IV Novembre** is a local hangout where people gather to chat, soak up the sun and watch street entertainers in the shadow of the city's cathedral, the **Cattedrale di San Lorenzo** (🖉075 572 38 32; Piazza IV

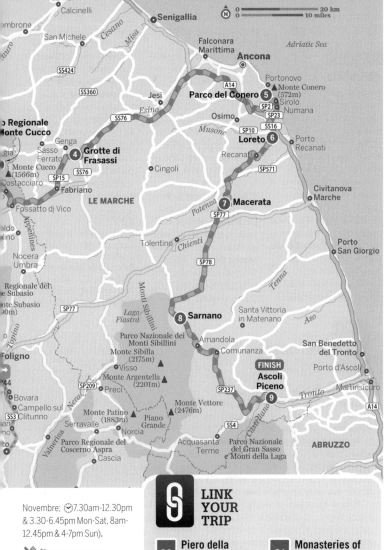

Novembre; ⊙7.30am-12.30pm
& 3.30-6.45pm Mon-Sat, 8am-
12.45pm & 4-7pm Sun).

✕ ⊨ p239, p249

The Drive ⟫ From east of town
pick up the northbound SS3bis
and after less than a kilometre
bear right onto the SR298. This
easygoing country road climbs
and twists and turns through
verdant hills and past cultivated
fields up to Gubbio. Although

§ LINK YOUR TRIP

23 Piero della Francesca Trail

Some 62km north of
Gubbio, Urbino is the
starting point for this
art-lovers's pilgrimage
through Tuscany.

21 Monasteries of Tuscany & Umbria

Head west from Perugia
to join this tour of
monasteries in the
forests and forgotten
mountains of Tuscany
and Umbria.

it's only 42km you should allow about an hour for the drive.

TRIP HIGHLIGHT

2 Gubbio

Angular, sober, and imposing, Gubbio appears like something out of a medieval fresco. Tightly packed grey buildings cluster together on the steep slopes of Monte Ingino in a picturesque jumble of tiled roofs, Gothic towers and 14th-century turrets. There are unforgettable views from the open-air **Funivia Colle Eletto** (☑075 927 38 81; www.funiviagubbio.it; Via San Girolamo; adult/reduced one way €4/3, return €6/4;

🕑9am-8pm Jul & Aug, shorter hours rest of year) – like a glorified ski lift with precarious-looking metal baskets – as it hauls you up to the **Basilica di Sant'Ubaldo** (Via Monte Ingino 5; 🕑basilica 8am-6pm, museum 10am-12.30pm & 2.30-5.30pm Mon-Fri, 10am-12.30pm & 3-6pm Sat & Sun), a fine medieval church displaying the body of St Ubaldo.

Once back on terra firma, head over to **Piazza Grande**, Gubbio's panoramic showpiece square, to enjoy yet more panoramas and visit the **Museo Civico** (☑075 927 42 98; www.palazzodeiconsoli.it; Palazzo dei Consoli, Piazza Grande; adult/reduced €10/5;

🕑10am-1pm & 3-6pm Mon-Fri, 10am-6pm Sat & Sun, shorter hours winter). Occupying the 14th-century Palazzo dei Consoli, this museum has a picture gallery, archaeological artefacts and, most notably, seven bronze tablets known as the Iguvine Tablets (also called the Eugubian Tablets). These are considered the best existing samples of ancient Umbrian script.

🍴 p249

The Drive » The 19km drive to Costacciaro takes you east to the Parco Regionale del Monte Cucco, via the SR298 and spectacular SS3. This scenic road winds down the eastern fringes of the park, with mood-

DETOUR:
SPOLETO

Start: 1 Perugia

Presided over by a formidable medieval fortress and backed by the broad-shouldered Apennines, their summits iced with snow in winter, the hill town of Spoleto is visually stunning.

At its heart is the pretty, pale-stone **Duomo** (Cattedrale di Santa Maria Assunta; www.duomospoleto.it; Piazza del Duomo; 🕑10.30am-6pm Mon-Sat, from 12.30pm Sun summer, 10.30am-5pm Mon-Sat, from 12.30pm Sun winter), originally built in the 11th century and subsequently enriched by the addition of a Renaissance portico in the 15th century. Inside, marvel at a rainbow swirl of mosaic frescoes by Filippo Lippi and assistants.

For a different view of things, head up to the **Rocca Albornoziana** (☑0743 22 49 52; Piazza Campello; adult/reduced €7.50/3.75; 🕑9.30am-7pm Tue-Sun, to 1.30pm Mon summer, to 6pm Tue-Sun winter), a glowering 14th-century former papal fortress that now houses the **Museo Nazionale del Ducato**, a small museum dedicated to the Duchy of Spoleto.

Before leaving town, make sure to photograph the medieval **Ponte delle Torri** (Via Giro del Ponte), a 10-arch bridge that leaps spectacularly across a steeply wooded gorge – a scene beautifully captured by Turner in his 1840 oil painting.

Spoleto is worth visiting any time, but come in summer and you'll find it a hive of cultural activity as it hosts the mammoth, 17-day **Festival dei Due Mondi** (☑0743 77 64 44; www.festivaldispoleto.it; Via Filitteria 1; 🕑late Jun–mid-Jul, box office 10am-1pm & 3-6pm mid-Apr–mid-Jun, 10am-7pm mid-Jun–Jul).

To get to Spoleto, it's a 65km drive south from Perugia via the SS75 and SS3.

CENTRAL ITALY **22** GREEN HEART OF ITALY

lifting views on almost every corner, passing quaint mountain hamlets and woods where wolves, lynx and wild boar roam.

③ Parco Regionale del Monte Cucco

In Umbria's wild north-eastern fringes near the regional border with Le Marche, the **Parco Regionale del Monte Cucco** (📞075 917 10 46; www.discovermontecucco.it; Costacciaro; ⏰info point 9am-12.30pm & 3-5pm) is a gorgeous swathe of wildflower-speckled meadows, gentle slopes brushed with beech, yew and silver fir trees, waterfalls, deep ravines and karst cave systems, all topped off by the oft-snowcapped **Monte Cucco** (1566m). Outdoor escapades beckon, and if you have the time, there's everything from hiking on 120km of waymarked trails to horse riding, hang-gliding and cross country skiing.

A highlight is the **Grotta Monte Cucco** (📞351 2827335; www.grottamontecucco.umbria.it; Località Pian di Monte; tours adult/reduced from €14/12; ⏰info point 9am-1pm daily Jul & Aug, shorter hours spring & autumn), one of Europe's most spectacular limestone caves, with 30km of galleries reaching depths of 900m. Those up for a challenge can delve into its underground forest of stalactites and stalagmites on a guided two-to three-hour 'discovery'

tour. For more details on the caves and park, stop by the info point in the nearby village of **Costacciaro**.

The Drive » Push on down the park's eastern flank on the SS3 to pick up the eastbound SS76 near Fossato di Vico. Continue on this fast road to Fabriano where you'll need to join the SP15. Head on to Frazione Pianello near Genga where a right will lead on to the Grotte. All in, it's about 40km.

④ Grotte di Frasassi

Further subterranean displays await at the **Grotte di Frasassi** (📞800 166250; www.frasassi.com; adult/reduced €18/12; ⏰10am-6pm summer, to 5pm winter; 🅿), one of Europe's largest cave systems, near the village of Genga.

This karst wonderland, gouged out by the river Sentino and discovered by a team of climbers in 1971, can be explored on a 75-minute, 1.5km guided tour of its rock stars. First up is the Ancona Abyss, a cavernous 200m-high, 180m-long chamber, which could comfortably accommodate Milan cathedral. Your gaze will be drawn to a fairy forest of dripping stalactites and giant 20m-long stalagmites, some of which took 1.4 million years to form. Highlights here include the Niagara, a petrified cascade of pure calcite, and a crystallised lake. Further on, in the Gran Canyon, look out for parallel stalactites resembling pipe organs and

---

PARCO NAZIONALE DEI MONTI SIBILLINI

Straddling the Le Marche–Umbria border in rugged splendour, the wild and wonderfully unspoiled **Parco Nazionale dei Monti Sibillini** (www.sibillini.net) never looks less than extraordinary, whether visited in winter, when its peaks are dusted with snow, or in summer, when its highland meadows are carpeted with poppies and cornflowers.

The 700-sq-km park has some of central Italy's most dramatic landscapes, with great glacier-carved valleys, beautifully preserved hilltop hamlets, beech forests where deer roam, and mountains, 10 of which tower above 2000m.

The park is a magnet for hikers and outdoor enthusiasts, with an expansive network of walking trails, mountain-biking circuits and a series of summer *rifugi* (mountain huts) offering basic accommodation. Most trails are now open after the 2016 earthquakes but a number of *rifugi* remain closed – check www.sibillini.net for updates.

waxy stalagmites that rise up like melted candles.

Make sure to wear comfortable shoes and take an extra layer of clothing, as the 14°C temperature can feel nippy, even in summer.

The Drive » From the caves, head to Camponocecchio to rejoin the SS76. Continue northeast on this dual carriageway as it traverses farmland to pick up the southbound A14 autostrada near Chiaravalle. Push on towards Pescara until the Ancona-Sud Osimo exit. From there take the SP2 to Sirolo in the Parco del Conero, some 75km from the Grotte.

TRIP HIGHLIGHT

❺ Parco del Conero

Just south of Ancona, Le Marche's main city and port, the Parco del Conero has a stunning stretch of coastline. Limestone cliffs soar above the cobalt-blue Adriatic as crescent-shaped, white pebble bays hide behind fragrant woods of pine, oak, beech, broom and oleander trees. Walking trails thread through the 60 sq km regional park, which is remarkably still off the radar for many travellers and retains a peaceful, unspoilt air found nowhere else along Le Marche's coast. Its highest peak is the 572m-high **Monte Conero**, which takes a spectacular nosedive into the sea and provides fertile soil for the vineyards that taper down its slopes, giving rise to the excellent, full-

bodied Rosso Conero red wine.

In the south of the park, the cliff-backed resort of **Sirolo** is one of several that makes a fine base for exploring the area. A boat trip is the best way to cove hop.

🛏 p249

The Drive » It's just short of 15km to Loreto. South of Sirolo pick up the SP23 and head inland. It's a slow, country drive, past hedgerows and sunflower fields, to near Crocette where you should turn left onto the SS16 and follow signs to Loreto.

❻ Loreto

Straddling a hilltop and visible from miles around, Loreto is dominated by the domed **Basilica della Santa Casa** (www.santuariolore to.it; Piazza della Madonna; ⏰6.15am-7.30pm summer, to 7pm winter). This magnificent sanctuary, built between 1469 and 1587, is a stunning hybrid of Gothic and Renaissance architectural styles. Inside, the chief focus is the Santa Casa di Loreto, a tiny brick house that's said to be where the Virgin Mary grew up. Each year, thousands of pilgrims flock to the Casa, now enclosed in an ornately sculpted marble screen by Bramante, to glimpse a bejewelled black statue of the Virgin and pray in the candlelit twilight. According to legend, a host of angels brought the house from

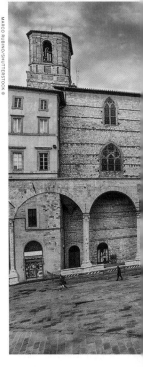

Nazareth in 1294 after the Crusaders were expelled from Palestine.

🍴 p249

The Drive » More back country roads await on the 28km stretch to Macerata. From Loreto head south to pick up the SP571. Continue on to Fontenoce where you should bear left on to the SP77, which will take you on to the village of Sambucheto. Go left here and continue through the bucolic green scenery to Macerata.

❼ Macerata

Straddling low-rise hills, Macerata combines charming hill-town scenery with the verve of student life – its uni-

Perugia Piazza IV Novembre

versity is one of Europe's oldest, dating to 1290. Its old town, a jumbled maze of cobblestone streets and honey-coloured *palazzi,* springs to life in summer for the month-long **Macerata Opera Festival** (☏0733 23 07 35; www. sferisterio.it; Arena Sferisterio; ⊗Jul & Aug), one of Italy's foremost musical events during which big name opera stars take to the stage at the stunning outdoor **Arena Sferisterio** (☏0733 27 17 09; www.mac eratamusei.it; Piazza Mazzini 10; adult/reduced €10/8, incl Palazzo Buonaccorsi, Palazzo Ricci & City Tour; ⊗10.30am-1pm & 2.30-5.30pm Tue-Sun).

Of the numerous Renaissance *palazzi* in the *centro storico,* the **Loggia dei Mercanti** (Piazza della Libertà) stands out. An arcaded building commissioned for Cardinal Alessandro Farnese and built in 1505, it originally housed travelling merchants selling their wares. A short walk away, the fabulous **Musei Civici di Palazzo Buonaccorsi** (☏0733 25 63 61; www.mac eratamusei.it; Via Don Minzoni 24; adult/reduced €10/8, incl Arena Sferisterio, Palazzo Ricci & City Tour; ⊗10.30am-1pm & 2.30-5.30pm Tue-Sun) harbour an eclectic collection of horse-drawn carriages

and artworks. A real highlight are the dynamic paintings of Ivo Pannaggi, one of the driving forces behind Italian futurism in the 1920s and '30s.

The Drive ⟩⟩ Exit Macerata and head south on the SP77 to Sforzacosta where you'll need to hook up with the SP78. Continue southwards, past the ancient Roman ruins of Urbs Salvia, and on to Sarnano, 40km away.

- - - - - - - - - - - - - - -

❽ Sarnano

Spilling photogenically down a hillside, its medieval heart a maze of narrow cobbled lanes, Sarnano looks every inch the prototype Italian hill

Macerata Arena Sferisterio

town, particularly when its red-brick facades glow warmly in the late-afternoon sun. There are no must-see sights but it makes a charming, hospitable base for exploring the Monti Sibillini range, much of which is encompassed in the **Parco Nazionale dei Monti Sibillini** (www.sibillini.net).

Sarnano is the main gateway to the Sassotetto-Santa Maria Maddalena ski resort, about 15km to the west. In winter, alpine and cross-country skiing, snowboarding and snowshoeing are all available on its 11km of pistes. In warmer weather you can take to the hills on 100km of waymarked hiking and cycling trails. For more dramatic thrills, Sarnano is also a popular paragliding site.

The Drive » Driving this 50km leg you'll understand why this part of Italy is referred to as the country's green heart. The SP237 runs past overhanging trees and overgrown hedgerows before opening up to reveal wooded peaks as far as the eye can see. Continue for about 46km and then join the eastbound SS4 for the last few kilometres into Ascoli.

TRIP HIGHLIGHT

9 Ascoli Piceno

The charming town of Ascoli Piceno marks the end of the road. With a continuous history dating from the 9th century BC, it's like the long-lost cousin of ancient Rome and a small Marchigiani village, heavy on history and food – it's famous as the birthplace of Italy's much-loved *olive all'ascolana* (veal-stuffed fried olives).

In the centre of town, the harmonious and lovely **Piazza del Popolo** has been Ascoli's *salotto* (drawing room) since Roman times. An elegant rectangular square, it's flanked by the 13th-century **Palazzo dei Capitani del Popolo** and the beautiful **Chiesa di San Francesco** (Via del Trivio 49; ⊘7am-12.30pm & 3.30-8pm). Virtually annexed to the church is the Loggia dei Mercanti, built in the 16th century by the powerful guild of wool merchants to hide their rough-and-tumble artisan shops.

To finish on a high note, Ascoli's fine **Pinacoteca** (☑0736 29 82 13; www.ascolimusei.it; Piazza Arringo 7; adult/reduced €8/5; ⊘10am-7pm Tue-Sun summer, 10am-1pm & 3-6pm Tue-Fri, 11am-6pm Sat & Sun winter) holds an outstanding display of art, sculpture, and religious artefacts including paintings by Titian, Carlo Crivelli and Guido Reni.

✕ p249

Eating & Sleeping

Perugia ❶

✕ Osteria a Priori — Umbrian €€

(☏075 572 70 98; www.osteriaapriori.it; Via dei Priori 39; meals €30-35; ☺12.30-2.30pm & 7.30-10pm Mon-Sat; 🛜) Located above an *enoteca* (wine bar/shop), this fashionable *osteria* (tavern) specialises in local wines and fresh regional cuisine prepared with seasonal ingredients. Umbrian cheeses and cured meats feature alongside black truffles, Chianina beef and autumnal mushrooms. Reservations recommended.

🛏 B&B San Fiorenzo — B&B €

(☏393 3869987; www.sanfiorenzo.com; Via Alessi 45; d €70-90, q €100-120, apt per week €450-560; 🛜) Buried in Perugia's medieval centre is this charming B&B, where Luigi and Monica make you welcome in one of three suites, each with its independent entrance. Mod cons and marble bathrooms have been skilfully incorporated into spacious quarters with brick vaulting, lime-washed walls and antique furnishings; the Maior suite even has a shower built into an 11th-century well.

Gubbio ❷

✕ Taverna del Lupo — Umbrian €€€

(☏075 927 43 68; www.tavernadellupo.it; Via Ansidei 21; fixed-price menu €19.50, meals €35-55; ☺noon-3pm & 7-11pm; 🛜👪) Soft light casts flattering shadows across the barrel-vaulted interior of this sophisticated restaurant, serving Umbrian cuisine with a pinch of creativity and a dash of medieval charm. It's a class act, with tables draped in white linen, polished service and an expertly curated wine list.

Parco del Conero ❺

🛏 Acanto Country House — Guesthouse €€

(☏071 933 11 95; www.acantocountryhouse. com; Via Ancarano 18, Sirolo; s €70, d €90-140, ste €100-150;) Set back from Sirolo's beaches and surrounded by cornfields, meadows and olive groves, this converted farmhouse is a gorgeous country hideaway. Named after flowers like peony and rose, its rooms have been designed with the utmost attention to detail, with gleaming wood floors, exposed stone and embroidered bedspreads. Outside, you can relax in the gardens and enjoy bucolic views from the panoramic saltwater pool.

Loreto ❻

✕ Ristorante Andreina — Italian €€€

(☏071 97 01 24; www.ristoranteandreina.it; Via Buffolareccia 14; tasting menus €75-100, meals €60-70; ☺noon-3pm & 8-10.30pm, closed lunch Tue & Wed) The basilica isn't the only place pilgrims seek out in Loreto: Michelin-starred Ristorante Andreina draws foodies from far and wide for its grilled meats prepared with a gourmet twist. Lamb, partridge, guinea fowl, suckling pig, tuna – they all get the grill treatment here and, trust us, chef Errico Recanati is the man you want running your grill.

Ascoli Piceno ❾

✕ Vittoria Ristorante — Ristorante €

(☏0736 25 95 35; www.vittoriaristorante.it; Via dei Bonaccorsi 7; meals €20-25, weekday fixed-price menu €15; ☺noon-2.30pm & 7.30-10.30pm, closed Wed & Sun) This welcoming spot is a great example of what Italy does so well: a casual, friendly restaurant, in this case decorated with white arches and bright lights, cooking up fabulous local food at honest prices. The menu includes Ascoli's renowned fried olives and a brilliant *amatriciana* (pancetta and tomato sauce), here served with *mezze maniche* (thick pasta rings).

Piero della Francesca Trail

23

Follow in the footsteps of the Renaissance painter Piero della Francesca as you wind your way from medieval Urbino to Florence, stopping en route to admire his greatest works.

TRIP HIGHLIGHTS

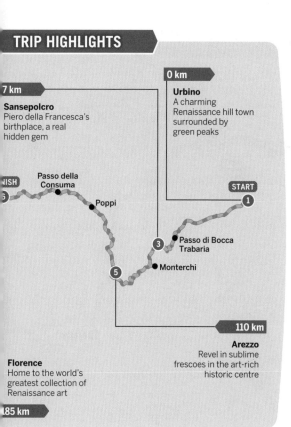

0 km

Urbino
A charming Renaissance hill town surrounded by green peaks

7 km

Sansepolcro
Piero della Francesca's birthplace, a real hidden gem

Passo della Consuma

NISH

Poppi

START
1

3 ● Passo di Bocca Trabaria

5 ● Monterchi

110 km

Arezzo
Revel in sublime frescoes in the art-rich historic centre

Florence
Home to the world's greatest collection of Renaissance art

185 km

7 DAYS
185KM / 115 MILES

GREAT FOR...

BEST TIME TO GO

June to September for summer pageantry.

ESSENTIAL PHOTO

Views from the Passo della Consuma.

BEST FOR FILM BUFFS

Arezzo's Piazza Grande, a location for scenes in *La vita è bella* (Life is Beautiful).

23 Piero della Francesca Trail

The Piero della Francesca trail was first advocated by the British author Aldous Huxley in *The Best Picture,* a 1925 essay he wrote in praise of della Francesca's *Resurrezione* (Resurrection). The roads have improved since Huxley's day but the trail remains a labour of love for art fans – it leads through dramatic Apennine scenery, over mountain passes and on to bustling medieval towns, culminating in Italy's revered Renaissance time capsule, Florence (Firenze).

TRIP HIGHLIGHT

1 Urbino

Hidden away in hilly Le Marche, the charming town of Urbino was a key player in the Renaissance art world. Its ruler, the Duca Federico da Montefeltro, was a major patron and many of the top artists and intellectuals of the day spent time here at his behest. Piero della Francesca arrived in 1469 and, along with a crack team of artists and architects, worked on the duke's palatial

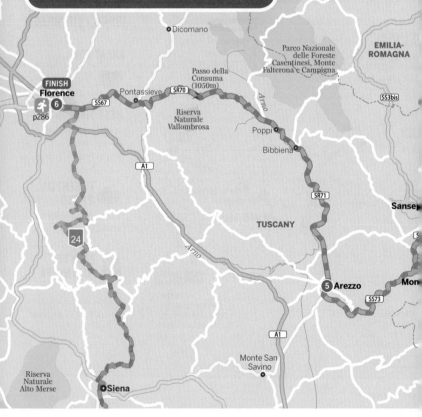

residence, the Palazzo Ducale. This magnificent palace now houses the **Galleria Nazionale delle Marche** (📞0722 32 26 25; www.gallerianazionalemarche. it; Piazza Duca Federico; adult/ reduced €8/5; ⏰8.30am-7.15pm Tue-Sun, to 2pm Mon) and its rich collection of Renaissance paintings, including Piero della Francesca's great *Flagellazione di Cristo* (Flagellation of Christ).

A short walk away, you can pay homage to Urbino's greatest son at the **Casa Natale di Raffaello** (📞0722 32 01 05; www.casaraffaello.com; Via Raffaello 57; €3.50; ⏰9am-1pm & 3-7pm Mon-Sat, 10am-1pm & 3-6pm Sun Mar-Oct, 9am-2pm Mon-Sat, 10am-1pm Sun Nov-Feb), the house where superstar painter Raphael was born in 1483.

✕ 🛏 p257

The Drive >> The 50km (one hour) drive up to the Passo di Bocca Trabaria involves hundreds of hairpin bends and tortuous climbing as it traverses a magnificent swath of Apennine mountains. From Urbino pick up the SS73bis and head through Montesoffio and Urbania before climbing up to the pass.

----

❷ Passo di Bocca Trabaria

The Bocca Trabaria mountain pass (1049m) divides the Valtiberina (Tiber valley), on the Urbino side, from the upper Valle del Metauro (Metauro valley). It's a magnificent spot, well worth a quick pause, with sweeping views over the Apennines and several hiking trails heading into the surrounding mountains.

The Drive >> Allow about half an hour for the 20km descent from Bocca Trabaria to Sansepolcro. For the first 15km or so the winding road plunges down the valley slopes to San Giustino, from where it's an easy hop northwest to Sansepolcro.

EMILIA-ROMAGNA

96 km to 26

Montesoffio

❶ **Urbino** **START**

SS73bis

Urbania

SS73bis

LE MARCHE

Metauro

Passo di ❷ **Bocca Trabaria** **(1049m)**

●Cagli

UMBRIA

Parco Regionale del Monte Cucco

SS3bis

0   20 km
0   10 miles

253

🔗 **LINK YOUR TRIP**

24 **Tuscan Wine Tour**
From Florence head south on the SR222 to the Castello di Verrazzano, one of the historic Chianti vineyards on this classic wine tour.

26 **Foodie Emilia-Romagna**
Head 125km north from Urbino via the A14 autostrada to connect with Ravenna and this tasty trip through Emilia-Romagna.

TRIP HIGHLIGHT

❸ Sansepolcro

Birthplace of Piero della Francesca and home to two of his greatest works, Sansepolcro is an authentic hidden gem. Its unspoiled historic centre is littered with *palazzi* (mansions) and churches harbouring great works of art, including the 14th-century **Cattedrale di San Giovanni Evangelista** (Duomo di Sansepolcro; Via Giacomo Matteotti 4; ☺10am-noon & 4-7pm), which contains an *Ascension* by Perugino. The highlight, though, is the **Museo Civico** (☎0575 73 22 18; www. museociviciosansepolcro. it; Via Niccolò Aggiunti 65; adult/reduced €10/8.50, with Casa di Piero della Francesca €11/9.50; ☺10am-1.30pm & 2.30-6.40pm mid-Jun–mid-Sep, 10am-1pm & 2.30-5.40pm mid-Sep–mid-Jun), whose small but top-notch

collection includes della Francesca's *Resurrection* (1458–74) and *Madonna della Misericordia* (Madonna of Mercy) polyptych (1445–56) as well as two fresco fragments portraying *San Ludovico* (Saint Ludovic, 1460) and *San Giuliano* (Saint Julian, 1460).

🍴 p257

The Drive » Head southwest from Sansepolcro along the SS73 following signs for Arezzo. After roughly 12km of easy driving through pleasant green countryside, turn left onto the SP42 and continue for 3km to Monterchi. It takes about 25 minutes.

❹ Monterchi

This unassuming village has one of Piero della Francesca's best-loved works, the *Madonna del Parto* (Pregnant Madonna, c 1460). Housed in its own museum, the **Museo della Madonna del Parto** (Pregnant Madonna Museum;

☎0575 7 07 13; www.madon nadelparto.it; Via della Reglia 1, Monterchi; adult/reduced €6.50/5; ☺9am-1pm & 2-7pm Apr-Oct, to 5pm Wed-Mon Nov-Mar), it depicts a heavily pregnant Madonna wearing a simple blue gown and standing in a tent, flanked by two angels who hold back the tent's curtains as a framing device. In a nice touch, pregnant women get free entry to the museum.

The Drive » Take the SP221 out of Monterchi until you hit the SS73. Turn left and follow the fast-running road, which opens to four lanes in certain tracts, as it snakes through thickly wooded hills up to Arezzo.

PIERO DELLA FRANCESCA

Though many details about his life are hazy, it's believed that Piero della Francesca was born around 1415 in Sansepolcro and died in 1492. Trained as a painter from the age of 15, his distinctive use of perspective, mastery of light and skilful synthesis of form and colour set him apart from his artistic contemporaries. His most famous works are the *Leggenda della Vera Croce* (Legend of the True Cross) in Arezzo, and *Resurrezione* (Resurrection) in Sansepolcro, but he is most fondly remembered for his luminous *Madonna del Parto* (Pregnant Madonna) in Monterchi.

Arezzo Piazza Grande

TRIP HIGHLIGHT

5 Arezzo

The biggest town in eastern Tuscany, Arezzo has a distinguished cultural history. Petrarch and art historian Giorgio Vasari were both born here, and, between 1452 and 1466, Piero della Francesca painted one of his greatest works, the *Leggenda della Vera Croce* (Legend of the True Cross) fresco cycle in the Basilica di San Francesco's **Cappella Bacci** (☎0575 35 27 27; www.pierodellafrancesca.it; Piazza San Francesco; adult/reduced €8/5; ⊙9am-6pm Mon-Fri, to 5.30pm Sat, 1-5.30pm Sun, extended hours summer).

Once you've seen that, take time to admire the magnificent Romanesque facade of the **Chiesa di Santa Maria della Pieve** (Corso Italia 7; ⊙8am-12.30pm & 3-6.30pm) en route to the **Duomo** (Cattedrale di SS Donato e Pietro; Piazza del Duomo; ⊙7am-12.30pm & 3-6.30pm) and yet another della Francesca fresco – his *Mary Magdalene* (c 1460).

Film buffs should also stop by **Piazza Grande**, where scenes were filmed for Roberto Benigni's *La vita è bella* (Life is Beautiful), and where the city celebrates its big annual festival, the **Giostra del Saracino** (Joust of the Saracino), on the third or fourth Saturday of June and the first Sunday of September.

✖ p257

The Drive » The quickest route to Florence is via the A1 autostrada, but you'll enjoy the scenery more if you follow the SR71 up the Casentino valley and on to the medieval castle town of Poppi. At Poppi pick up the SR70 to tackle the heavily forested Passo della Consuma (1050m) and descend to Pontassieve and the SS67 into Florence. Allow about 2¾ hours.

255

THE RENAISSANCE

Bridging the gap between the Middle Ages and the modern world, the Renaissance (*il Rinascimento*) emerged in 14th-century Florence and quickly spread throughout Italy.

The Early Days

Giotto di Bondone (1267–1337) is generally considered the first great Renaissance artist, and with his exploration of perspective and a new interest in realistic portraiture, he inspired artists such as Lorenzo Ghiberti (1378–1455) and Donatello (c 1382–1466). In architectural terms, the key man was Filippo Brunelleschi (1377–1446), whose dome on Florence's Duomo was one of the era's blockbuster achievements. Of the following generation, Sandro Botticelli (c 1444–1510) was a major player and his *Birth of Venus* (c 1485) was one of the most successful attempts to resolve the great conundrum of the age – how to give a painting both a realistic perspective and a harmonious composition.

The High Renaissance

By the early 16th century, the focus had shifted to Rome and Venice. Leading the way in Rome was Donato Bramante (1444–1514), whose classical architectural style greatly influenced the Veneto-born Andrea Palladio (1508–80). One of Bramante's great rivals was Michelangelo Buonarroti (1475–1564), whose legendary genius was behind the Sistine Chapel frescoes, the dome over St Peter's Basilica, and the *David* sculpture. Other headline acts included Leonardo da Vinci (1452–1519), who developed a painting technique (sfumato) enabling him to modulate his contours using colour; and Raphael (1483–1520), who more than any other painter mastered the art of depicting large groups of people in a realistic and harmonious way.

TRIP HIGHLIGHT

⑥ Florence

The last port of call is Florence, the city where the Renaissance kicked off in the late 14th century. Paying the way was the Medici family, who sponsored the great artists of the day and whose collection today graces the **Galleria degli Uffizi** (Uffizi Gallery; ☎055 29 48 83; www.uffizi.it; Piazzale degli Uffizi 6; adult/reduced Mar-Oct €20/10, Nov-Feb €12/6; ☉8.15am-6.50pm Tue-Sun).

Here you can admire Piero della Francesca's famous portrait of the red-robed *Duke and Duchess of Urbino* (1465–72) alongside works by Renaissance giants, from Giotto and Cimabue to Botticelli, Leonardo da Vinci, Raphael and Titian.

Elsewhere in town, you'll find spiritually uplifting works by Fra' Angelico in the wonderful **Museo di San Marco** (☎055 238 86 08; Piazza San Marco 3; adult/reduced €4/2; ☉8.15am-1.50pm Mon-Fri, to 4.50pm Sat & Sun, closed 1st, 3rd & 5th Sun, 2nd & 4th Mon of month), and superb frescoes by Masaccio, Masolino da Panicale and Filippino Lippi at the **Cappella Brancacci** (☎055 238 21 95; www.musei civicifiorentini.comune.fi.it; Piazza del Carmine 14; adult/reduced Wed-Fri €8/6, Sat-Mon €10/7; ☉10am-5pm Wed-Sat & Mon, 1-5pm Sun), over the river in the Basilica di Santa Maria del Carmine. The historic centre is a great place to explore on foot (p286).

✖️🛏️ p47, p60, p257, p267

Eating & Sleeping

Urbino 1

Antica Osteria da la Stella — Osteria €€€

(☎0722 32 02 28; www.anticaosteriadalastella.com; Via Santa Margherita 1; meals €45-50; ⏲12.30-2.15pm & 7.30-10.30pm, closed Sun dinner & Mon lunch; 📶) Duck down a quiet side street to this elegant, wood-beamed restaurant, occupying what was once a 15th-century inn patronised by the likes of Piero della Francesca. Legendary in these parts, it serves a menu of updated regional dishes prepared with seasonal, locally sourced ingredients and dreamy, homemade pastas. Skipping dessert is unwise.

B&B Albornoz — B&B €

(☎347 2987897; www.bbalbornoz.com; Via dei Maceri 23; s/d €50/80; 📶) Wedged in a quiet old-town corner, this B&B offers boutique style for a pinch of the price. A spiral staircase links three contemporary designed studio flats, with murals, funky lighting and bold artworks, from the monochromatic *You and Me* to the floral, lilac-kissed romance of *Osaka*. All come with kitchenettes and espresso machines.

Sansepolcro 3

Ristorante Da Ventura — Tuscan €€

(☎0575 74 25 60; www.albergodaventura.it; Via Niccolò Aggiunti 30; meals €30; ⏲12.30-2.15pm & 7.30-9.45pm Tue-Sat, 12.30-2.15pm Sun; 🥕) This old-world eatery is a culinary joy. Trolleys laden with feisty joints of pork, beef stewed in Chianti Classico and roasted veal shank are pushed from table to table, bow-tied waiters intent on piling plates high. Vegetarians are well catered for with a feast of a mixed house antipasti followed by black truffle omelette or buttered *tagliatelle* (ribbon pasta).

Arezzo 5

Antica Osteria Agania — Tuscan €

(☎0575 29 53 81; www.agania.com; Via Mazzini 10; meals €20; ⏲noon-3pm & 6-10.30pm Tue-Sun) Operated by the Ludovichi family since 1905, Agania serves the type of die-hard traditional fare that remains the cornerstone of Tuscan dining. Specialities include sensational antipasti (with lots of vegetarian options), rustic soups, homemade pasta and *secondi* ranging from *lumache* (snails) to *grifi* (lambs' cheeks) with polenta, *baccalà* (cod) with chickpeas, and sausages with beans.

Florence 6

Osteria Il Buongustai — Osteria €

(☎055 29 13 04; www.facebook.com/ibuongustaifirenze; Via dei Cerchi 15r; meals €15-20; ⏲9.30am-3.30pm Mon-Sat) Run with breathtaking speed and grace by Laura and Lucia, 'The Gourmand' is unmissable. Lunchtimes heave with locals and savvy students who flock here to fill up on tasty Tuscan home cooking at a snip of other restaurant prices. The place is brilliantly no frills – watch women in hair caps at work in the kitchen, share a table and pay in cash. No credit cards.

Hotel Orto de' Medici — Hotel €€€

(☎055 48 34 27; www.ortodeimedici.it; Via San Gallo 30; d from €220; ❄ @ 📶) This four-star hotel in San Marco redefines elegance with its majestic ceilings, chic oyster-grey colour scheme and contemporary furnishings, set off to perfection by the historic *palazzo* in which it languishes. Hunt down the odd remaining 19th-century fresco, and don't miss the garden with lemon trees in terracotta pots and rambling ivy. To splurge, go for a room with its own flowery terrace.

Classic Trip

Tuscan Wine Tour

24

Tuscany has its fair share of highlights, but few can match the indulgence of a drive through its wine country – an intoxicating blend of scenery, acclaimed restaurants and ruby-red wine.

TRIP HIGHLIGHTS

START
Florence

34 km

Greve in Chianti
Taste Tuscany's best at Greve's vast cellar

4 ● 3

● Panzano in Chianti

● Radda in Chianti

Badia a Passignano
Idyllically located wine estate and medieval abbey

6

km

67 km

Castello di Ama
Enjoy modern art and excellent Chianti Classico

● Siena

FINISH
Montepulciano

8 km

7

Montalcino
A fortified hill town, home of Brunello di Montalcino

4 DAYS
185KM / 115 MILES

GREAT FOR...

BEST TIME TO GO

Autumn for earthy hues and the grape harvest.

ESSENTIAL PHOTO

Val di Chiana and Val d'Orcia panoramas from Montepulciano's upper town.

BEST FOR GOURMETS

Tuscan *bistecca* (steak) in Panzano in Chianti.

nti Wine tasting

24 Tuscan Wine Tour

Meandering through Tuscany's bucolic wine districts, this classic Chianti tour offers a taste of life in the slow lane. Once out of Florence (Firenze), you'll find yourself on quiet back roads driving through wooded hills and immaculate vineyards, stopping off at wine estates and hilltop towns to sample the local vintages. En route, you'll enjoy soul-stirring scenery, farmhouse food and some captivating towns.

Arno

START
Florence ①
A1
p286

SR2

Castello di Verrazzano ②
Badia a Passignano
④
Greve in Chianti SP1
Panzano in Chian

Riserva
Naturale
Alto Merse

0 ————— 10 km
0 ————— 5 miles

① Florence

Whet your appetite for the road ahead with a one-day cooking course at the **Cucina Lorenzo de' Medici** (☏334 3040551; www.cucinaldm.com; Piazza del Mercato Centrale, Mercato Centrale), one of Florence's many cookery schools. Once you're done at the stove, sneak out to visit the **Chiesa e Museo di Orsanmichele** (Via dell'Arte della Lana; ⊙ church 10am-4.50pm daily, closed Mon Aug, museum 10am-4.50pm Mon, 10am-12.30pm Sat), an inspirational 14th-century church and one of Florence's lesser-known gems. Over the river, you can stock up on Tuscan wines and gourmet foods at **Obsequium** (☏055 21 68 49; www.obsequium.it; Borgo San Jacopo 17/39; ⊙11am-9pm Mon-Sat, from noon Sun), a well-stocked wine shop on the ground floor of a medieval tower. Or, explore the old town on foot (p286) before you hit the road.

✕ 🏠 p47, p60, p257, p267

The Drive » From Florence it's about an hour to Verrazzano.

Head south along the scenic SR222 (Via Chiantigiana) towards Greve. When you get to Greti, you'll see a shop selling wine from the Castello di Verrazzano and, just before it, a right turn up to the castle.

 Castello di Verrazzano

Some 26km south of Florence, the **Castello di Verrazzano** (☏0558 5 42 43; www.verrazzano.com; Via Citille, Greti; tours €21-68; ☺9.30am-6pm Mon-Sat, 10am-1pm & 3-6.30pm Sun) lords it over a 230-hectare estate where Chianti Classico, Vin Santo, grappa, honey, olive oil and balsamic vinegar are produced. In a previous life, the castle was home to Giovanni di Verrazzano (1485–1528), an adventurer who explored the North American coast and is commemorated in New York by

LINK YOUR TRIP

23 Piero della Francesca Trail

Starting in Florence, you can join this trail of revered Renaissance frescoes.

26 Foodie Emilia-Romagna

Also from Florence, continue 120km north on the A1 to Bologna and a tour of Emilia-Romagna's great food towns.

the Verrazzano-Narrows bridge linking Staten Island to Brooklyn.

At the *castello*, you can choose from a range of guided tours, which include a tasting and can also include lunch with the estate wines. Book ahead.

The Drive » From the castello it's a simple 10-minute drive to Greve in Chianti. Double back to the SR222 in Greti, turn right and follow for about 3km.

TRIP HIGHLIGHT

③ Greve in Chianti

The main town in the Chianti Fiorentino, the northernmost of the two Chianti districts, Greve in Chianti has been an important wine centre for centuries. It has an

amiable market-town air, and several eateries and *enoteche* (wine bars) that showcase the best Chianti food and drink. To stock up on picnic supplies, head to **Antica Macelleria Falorni** (☎0558 5 30 29; www.falorni. it; Piazza Giacomo Matteotti 71; ⊗9am-1pm & 3-7pm Mon-Sat, from 10am Sun), an atmospheric butcher's shop-cum-bistro that the Bencistà Falorni family have been running since

TUSCAN REDS

Something of a viticultural powerhouse, Tuscany excites wine buffs with its myriad full-bodied, highly respected reds. Like all Italian wines, these are classified according to strict guidelines, with the best denominated *Denominazione di Origine Controllata e Garantita* (DOCG), followed by *Denominazione di Origine Controllata* (DOC) and *Indicazione di Geografica Tipica* (IGT).

Chianti
Cheery, full and dry, contemporary Chianti gets the thumbs up from wine critics. Produced in eight subzones from Sangiovese and a mix of other grape varieties, Chianti Classico is the best known, with its Gallo Nero (Black Cockerel) emblem, which once symbolised the medieval Chianti League. Young, fun Chianti Colli Senesi from the Siena hills is the largest subzone; Chianti delle Colline Pisane is light and soft in style; and Chianti Rùfina comes from the hills east of Florence.

Brunello di Montalcino
Brunello is among Italy's most prized wines. The product of Sangiovese grapes, it must be aged for a minimum of 24 months in oak barrels and four months in bottles, and cannot be released until five years after the vintage. Intense and complex with an ethereal fragrance, it is best paired with game, wild boar and roasts. Brunello grape rejects go into Rosso di Montalcino, Brunello's substantially cheaper but wholly drinkable kid sister.

Vino Nobile di Montepulciano
Prugnolo Gentile grapes (a clone of Sangiovese) form the backbone of the distinguished Vino Nobile di Montepulciano. Its intense but delicate nose and dry, vaguely tannic taste make it the perfect companion to red meat and mature cheese.

Super Tuscans
Developed in the 1970s, the Super Tuscans are wines that fall outside the traditional classification categories. As a result they are often made with a combination of local and imported grape varieties, such as Merlot and Cabernet. Sassacaia, Solaia, Bolgheri, Tignanello and Luce are all super-hot Super Tuscans.

the early 19th century and which specialises in delicious *finocchiona briciolona* (pork salami made with fennel seeds and Chianti wine). The family also run the Enoteca Falorni, the town's top cellar, where you can sample all sorts of local wine.

The Drive » From Greve turn off the main through road, Viale Giovanni di Verrazzano, near the Esso petrol station, and head up towards Montefioralle. Continue on as the road climbs past olive groves and through woods to Badia a Passignano, about 15 minutes away.

TRIP HIGHLIGHT

④ Badia a Passignano

Encircled by cypress trees and surrounded by swaths of olive groves and vineyards, the 11th-century **Chiesa di San Michele Arcangelo** (Abbey of Passignano; Via di Passignano; ⏱10am-noon & 3-5pm Mon-Wed, Fri & Sat, 3-5pm

WINE TASTING GOES HIGH TECH

One of Tuscany's biggest cellars, the **Enoteca Falorni** (☎0558 54 64 04; www.enotecafalorni.it; Piazza delle Cantine 2-6; tastings by glass €0.60-30; ⏱10.30am-7.30pm Apr-May, to 8pm Jun-Sep, 10am-7pm Thu-Mon Oct-Mar, closed 3 weeks Jan) in Greve in Chianti stocks more than 1000 labels, of which around 100 are available for tasting. It's a lovely, brick-arched place, but wine tasting here is a very modern experience, thanks to a sophisticated wine-dispensing system that preserves wine in an open bottle for up to three weeks and allows tasters to serve themselves by the glass. Leave your credit-card as a guarantee or buy a nonrefundable prepaid wine card (€5 to €100) to test your tipples of choice at the various 'tasting islands' dotted around the cellar. Curated tastings are also available.

Sun) at Passignano sits at the heart of a historic wine estate run by the Antinoris, one of Tuscany's oldest and most prestigious winemaking families. The estate offers a range of guided tours, tastings and cookery courses. Most require prior booking, but you can just turn up at the estate's wine shop,

La Bottega (☎0558 07 12 78; www.osteriadipassignano. com; Via di Passignano 33; ⏱10am-7.30pm Mon-Sat), to taste and buy Antinori wines and olive oil.

✗ ⊨ p267

The Drive » From Badia a Passignano, double back towards Greve and pick up the signposted SP118 for a pleasant 15-minute drive along the narrow tree-shaded road to Panzano.

TOP TIP: DRIVING IN CHIANTI

To cut down on driving stress, purchase a copy of *Le strade del Gallo Nero* (€2.50), a useful map that shows major and secondary roads and has a comprehensive list of wine estates. It's available at the tourist office in Greve and at **Casa Chianti Classico** (☎0577 73 81 87; www.chianticlassico.com; Monastery of Santa Maria al Prato, Circonvallazione Santa Maria 18; self-guided tour with glass of wine €7; ⏱tours & tastings 11am-7pm Tue-Sat, to 5pm Sun mid-Mar–Oct), the headquarters of the Consorzio di Chianti Classico in Radda.

⑤ Panzano in Chianti

The quiet medieval town of Panzano is an essential stop on any gourmet's tour of Tuscany. Here you can stock up on meaty picnic fare at **L'Antica Macelleria Cecchini** (☎0558 5 20 20; www.dario cecchini.com; Via XX Luglio 11; ⏱9am-4pm), a celebrated butcher's shop run by

WHY THIS IS A CLASSIC TRIP
DUNCAN GARWOOD, WRITER

The best Italian wine I've ever tasted was a Brunello di Montalcino. I bought it directly from a producer after a tasting in the Val d'Orcia and it was a revelation. It was just so thrilling to be drinking wine in the place it had been made. And it's this, combined with the inspiring scenery and magnificent food, that makes this tour of Tuscan wineries so uplifting.

Above: Wine cellar, Val d'Orcia
Left: Wine selection, Montalcino
Right: Stone house. Chianti

the poetry-spouting guru of Tuscan meat, Dario Cecchini. Alternatively, you can dine at one of his three eateries: the **Officina della Bistecca** (📞0558 5 20 20; Via XX Luglio 11; set menu adult/under 10yr €50/25; 🕐 sittings at 1pm & 8pm), which serves a simple set menu based on *bistecca;* **Solociccia** (📞0558 5 27 27; Via XX Luglio; set meat menu adult/under 10yr €30/15; 🕐 sittings at 1pm, 7pm, 8pm & 9pm), where guests share a communal table to sample meat dishes other than *bistecca;* and **Dario DOC** (📞0558 5 21 76; Via XX Luglio 11; burgers €10 or €15 Mon-Fri, €15 Sat, meat sushi €20; 🕐 noon-3pm Mon-Sat), a casual daytime eatery. Book ahead for the Officina and Solociccia.

The Drive » From Panzano, it's about 20km to the Castello di Ama. Strike south on the SR222 towards Radda in Chianti, enjoying views off to the right as you wend your way through the green countryside. At Croce, just beyond Radda, turn left and head towards Lecchi and San Sano. The Castello di Ama is signposted after a further 7km.

- - - - - - - - - - - - - - - - - -

TRIP HIGHLIGHT

⑥ Castello di Ama

To indulge in some contemporary-art appreciation between wine tastings, make for **Castello di Ama** (📞0577 74 60 69; www.castellodiama.com; Località Ama; guided tours adult/under 16yr €15/free; 🕐 enoteca 10am-7pm, tours by

Classic Trip

appointment) near Lecchi. This highly regarded wine estate produces a fine Chianti Classico and has an original sculpture park showcasing 14 site-specific works by artists including Louise Bourgeois, Chen Zhen, Anish Kapoor, Kendell Geers and Daniel Buren. Book ahead.

The Drive » Reckon on about 1½ hours to Montalcino from the *castello*. Double back to the SP408 and head south to Lecchi and then on towards Siena. Skirt around the east of Siena and pick up the SR2 (Via Cassia) to Buonconvento and hilltop Montalcino, off to the right of the main road.

TRIP HIGHLIGHT

❼ Montalcino

Montalcino, a pretty medieval town perched above the Val d'Orcia, is home to one of Italy's great wines, Brunello di Montalcino (and the more modest, but still very palatable, Rosso di Montalcino). There are plenty of *enoteche* where you can taste and buy, including one in the **Fortezza** (☎0577 84 92 11; Piazzale Fortezza; courtyard free, ramparts adult/reduced €4/2; ☺9am-8pm Apr-Oct, 10am-6pm Nov-Mar), the 14th-century fortress that dominates the town's skyline.

For a historical insight into the town's winemaking past, head to the **Museo della Comunità di Montalcino e del**

Brunello (☎0577 84 61 04; www.fattoriadeibarbi.it/ museo-del-brunello; Fattoria dei Barbi, Località Podernovi 170; adult/reduced €5/2.50; ☺10am-12.30pm & 2.30-6pm Thu-Tue Easter-late Nov), a small museum at the Fattoria dei Barbi wine estate, one of the oldest in the region.

✖ p267

The Drive » From Montalcino, head downhill and then, after about 8km, turn onto the SR2. At San Quirico d'Orcia pick up the SP146, a fabulously scenic road that weaves along the Val d'Orcia through rolling green hills, past the pretty town of Pienza, to Montepulciano. Allow about an hour.

❽ Montepulciano

Set atop a narrow ridge of volcanic rock, the Renaissance centre of Montepulciano produces the celebrated red wine Vino Nobile. To sample it, head up the main street, called in stages Via di Gracciano nel Corso, Via di Voltaia del Corso and Via dell'Opio nel Corso, to the **Enoliteca Consortile** (www.enolitecavinonobile. it; Fortezza di Montepulciano, Via San Donato 21; ☺2-6pm Mon, Wed & Thu, 11am-6pm Fri, 10.30am-7pm Sat & Sun), a modern tasting room operated by local wine producers. Housed on the ground floor of the town's Medicean fortress, it offers over 70 wines for tasting and purchase.

✖ ⌂ p267, p275

DETOUR: ABBAZIA DI SANT'ANTIMO

Start: ❼ **Montalcino**

The striking Romanesque **Abbazia di Sant'Antimo** (☎0577 28 63 00; www.antimo.it; Castelnuovo dell'Abate; ☺10am-7pm Apr-Oct, to 5pm Nov-Mar) lies in an isolated valley just below the village of Castelnuovo dell'Abate, 10.5km from Montalcino.

According to tradition, Charlemagne founded the original monastery in 781. The exterior, built in pale travertine stone, is simple but for the stone carvings, which include various fantastical animals. Inside, look for the polychrome 13th-century *Madonna and Child* and 12th-century *Crucifixion* above the main altar. The abbey's church, crypt, upper loggia, chapel, pharmacy and garden can be visited with a rented video guide (€6).

Eating & Sleeping

Florence ❶

🍴 Il Santo Bevitore — Tuscan €€

(📞055 21 12 64; www.ilsantobevitore.com; Via di Santo Spirito 64-66r; meals €40; ⏰12.30-2.30pm & 7.30-11.30pm, closed Sun lunch & Aug) Reserve or arrive right on 7.30pm to snag the last table at this ever-popular address, an ode to stylish dining where gastronomes eat by candlelight in a vaulted, whitewashed, bottle-lined interior. The menu is a creative reinvention of seasonal classics: pumpkin gnocchi with hazelnuts, coffee and green-veined blue di Capra (goat cheese), *tagliatelle* with hare *ragù,* garlic cream and sweet Carmignano figs...

Badia a Passignano ❹

🍴 L'Antica Scuderia — Tuscan €€

(📞0558 07 16 23, 335 8252669; www.ristorolanticascuderia.com; Via di Passignano 17; meals €45, pizza €12-20; ⏰12.30-2.30pm & 7.30-10.30pm Wed-Mon; ❄🛜♿) The large terrace at this restaurant overlooks one of the Antinori vineyards and is perfect for summer dining. In winter, the elegant dining room comes into its own. Lunch features antipasti, pastas and traditional grilled meats, while dinner sees plenty of pizza-oven action. Kids love the playground set; adults love the fact that it keeps the kids occupied. Huge wine list.

🛏 Fattoria di Rignana — Agriturismo €€

(📞0558 5 20 65; www.rignana.it; Via di Rignana 15, Rignana; d from €95; ⏰Apr-Nov; 🅿@🛜♿🐾) The historic farmhouse of this wine estate has its very own chapel and bell tower, which reveal themselves after you brave a long, rutted access road. You'll also find glorious views, a large swimming pool and a nearby eatery. Sleep in rustic en suite rooms in the estate's *fattoria* (farmhouse). Find it 4km from Badia a Passignano.

Montalcino ❼

🍴 Re di Macchia — Tuscan €€

(📞0577 84 61 16; redimacchia@alice.it; Via Soccorso Saloni 21; meals €35, set menus €27; ⏰noon-2pm & 7-9pm Fri-Wed; 🍴) Husband-and-wife team Roberta and Antonio run this relaxed eatery in the centre of town with great aplomb. Roberta's cooking is much more sophisticated than the Tuscan average but retains the usual laudable focus on local, seasonal produce. Antonio's excellent and affordable wine list is one of the best in town. The four-course set menus (one vegetarian) offer excellent value.

Montepulciano ❽

🍴 La Dogana — Italian €€

(📞339 5405196; www.ladoganaenoteca.it; Strada Lauretana Nord 75, Valiano; 3-/5-course set lunch €25/40, meals €34; ⏰11am-3.30pm & 6-10pm Wed-Mon, closed Jan) Chef and cookbook writer Sunshine Manitto presides over the kitchen of this chic *enoteca* overlooking the Palazzo Vecchio Winery, 13km northeast of Montepulciano. Windows frame vistas of vines and cypress trees, but the best seats in the house are on the grassed rear terrace. The menu showcases seasonal produce (much of it grown in the kitchen garden). When here, be sure to try a glass of Palazzo Vecchio wine (try the Terra Rossa). You can also enjoy a tasting of three/six Palazzo Vecchio wines (€15/25) or take a cooking class (€165 including wine tasting and lunch or dinner) here.

🛏 Locanda San Francesco — B&B €€€

(📞0578 75 87 25; www.locandasanfrancesco.it; Piazza San Francesco 3; r €220-260; ⏰closed mid-Jan–early Feb; 🅿❄@🛜) The only downside to this four-room luxury B&B is that once you check in, you might never want to leave. The feel is elegant but also homey: refined furnishings meet well-stocked bookshelves; restrained fabrics are teamed with fluffy bathrobes. The best room has superb views over the Val d'Orcia on one side and Val di Chiana on the other. Excellent breakfast.

Tuscan Landscapes

Rolling hills capped by medieval towns, golden wheat fields and snaking lines of cypress trees – immerse yourself in Tuscan scenery on this trip through the region's southern stretches.

25

TRIP HIGHLIGHTS

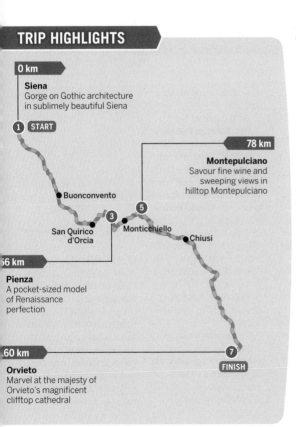

0 km

Siena
Gorge on Gothic architecture in sublimely beautiful Siena

1 **START**

Buonconvento

3

San Quirico d'Orcia

5

Monticchiello

Chiusi

78 km

Montepulciano
Savour fine wine and sweeping views in hilltop Montepulciano

56 km

Pienza
A pocket-sized model of Renaissance perfection

160 km

Orvieto
Marvel at the majesty of Orvieto's magnificent clifftop cathedral

7

FINISH

3–4 DAYS
160KM / 99 MILES

GREAT FOR...

BEST TIME TO GO

May to September for blue skies and fab photos.

ESSENTIAL PHOTO

The Val d'Orcia between San Quirico d'Orcia and Pienza.

BEST FOR

RENAISSANCE ARCHITECTURE

Montepulciano's historic centre.

START
1 Siena
SP43
TUSCANY
Riserva Naturale Alto Merse
Buonconvent
E78

25 Tuscan Landscapes

Ever since medieval pilgrims discovered Tuscany en route from Canterbury to Rome, the region has been captivating travellers. This trip strikes south from Siena, running through the Crete Senesi, an area of clay hills scored by deep ravines, to the Unesco-listed Val d'Orcia, whose soothing hills and billowing plains are punctuated by delightful Renaissance towns. The end of the road is Orvieto, home to one of Italy's most feted Gothic cathedrals.

- - - - - - - - - - - - - - - - - -

TRIP HIGHLIGHT

1 Siena

With its medieval *palazzi* (mansions) and humbling Gothic architecture, Siena's historic centre is a sight to compare with any in Tuscany. To admire it from above, climb to the top of the **Torre del Mangia** (☑0577 29 26 15; ticket@comune.siena.it; Palazzo Pubblico, Piazza del Campo 1; adult/family €10/25; ☉10am-6.15pm Mar–mid-Oct, to 3.15pm mid-Oct–Feb), the slender 14th-century tower that rises above **Piazza del Campo**, and look down on a sea of red-tiled roofs and, beyond, to the green, undulating countryside

that awaits you on this trip.

At the foot of the tower, **Palazzo Pubblico** (Palazzo Comunale; Piazza del Campo) is a magnificent example of Sienese Gothic architecture and home to the city's best art museum, the **Museo Civico** (Civic Museum; ☑0577 29 26 15; Palazzo Pubblico, Piazza del Campo 1; adult/reduced €10/9, with Torre del Mangia €15, with Torre del Mangia & Complesso Museale di Santa Maria della Scala €20; ☉10am-6.15pm mid-Mar–Oct, to 5.15pm Nov–mid-Mar).

To the southwest of Palazzo Pubblico, another inspiring spectacle awaits. Siena's 13th-century **duomo** (Cattedrale di Santa Maria Assunta;

☑0577 28 63 00; www.opera duomo.siena.it; Piazza Duomo; Mar-Oct €5, Nov-Feb free, when floor displayed €8; ☉10.30am-6.30pm Mon-Sat & 1.30-5.30pm Sun Mar-Oct, 10.30am-5pm Mon-Sat & 1.30-5pm Sun Nov-Feb) is one of Italy's greatest Gothic churches, and its magnificent facade of white, green and red polychrome marble is

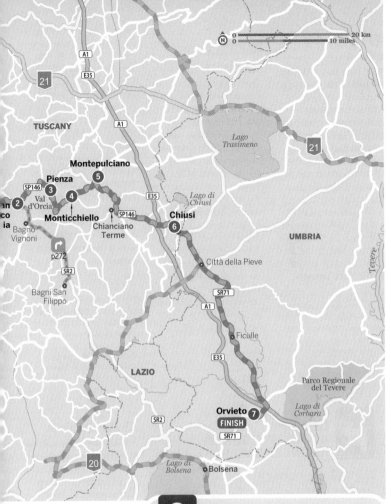

TUSCANY

Lago Trasimeno

Montepulciano

Pienza

Val d'Orcia

Monticchiello

Chianciano Terme

Chiusi

UMBRIA

Città della Pieve

Bagno Vignoni

p272

Bagni San Filippo

Ficulle

LAZIO

Parco Regionale del Tevere

Lago di Corbara

Orvieto **FINISH**

Lago di Bolsena

Bolsena

Tevere

one you'll remember long after you've left town.

✕ 🛏 p60, p275

The Drive » The first leg down to San Quirico d'Orcia, about an hour's drive, takes you down the scenic SR2 via the market town of Buonconvento. En route you'll pass cultivated fields and swaths of curvaceous green plains.

LINK YOUR TRIP

20 **Etruscan Tuscany & Lazio**

From Orvieto continue 20km southwest to Bolsena and join up with this Etruscan treasure hunt.

21 **Monasteries of Tuscany & Umbria**

Head east from Montepulciano along the SP438 to visit a string of ancient, isolated monasteries.

271

❷ San Quirico d'Orcia

First stop in the Unesco-protected Val d'Orcia is" San Quirico d'Orcia. A fortified medieval town and one-time stopover on the Via Francigena pilgrim route between Canterbury and Rome, it's now a lovely, low-key village. There are no great must-see sights, but it's a pleasant place for a stroll, with a graceful Romanesque **Collegiata** (church) and formal Renaissance gardens known as the **Horti Leononi**.

The Drive » From San Quirico d'Orcia it's a quick 15-minute drive to Pienza along the SP146. This is one of the trip's most beautiful stretches, offering unfettered views over seas of undulating grasslands peppered by stone farmhouses and lines of elegant cypress trees.

**DETOUR:
BAGNO VIGNONI &
BAGNI SAN FILIPPO**

Start: ❷ **San Quirico d'Orcia**

Some 9km south of San Quirico d'Orcia along the SP53, hot sulphurous water (around 49°C) bubbles up into a picturesque pool in the centre of **Bagno Vignoni**. You can't actually enter the pool, but there are various spa complexes offering a full range of treatments. For free hot-water frolics continue 18km further along the SR2 to the tiny village of **Bagni San Filippo**, where there are thermal cascades in an open-air reserve. You'll find these just uphill from Hotel le Terme – follow a sign marked 'Fosso Bianco' down a lane for about 150m and you'll come to a series of mini pools, fed by hot, tumbling cascades of water. Not unlike a free, al fresco spa, it's a pleasant if slightly whiffy spot for a picnic.

TRIP HIGHLIGHT
❸ Pienza

One of the most popular tourist destinations in the Val d'Orcia, pint-sized Pienza has a Renaissance centre that has changed little since local boy Pope Pius II had it built between 1459 and 1462. Action is centred on Piazza Pio II, where the solemn **duomo** (Concattedrale di Santa Maria Assunta; Piazza Pio II; ⊙7.30am-1pm & 2-7pm) is flanked by two Renaissance *palazzi* – on the right, **Palazzo Piccolomini** (0577 28 63 00; www.palazzopiccolomini pienza.it; Piazza Pio II; adult/reduced with guided tour €7/5; ⊙10am-6pm Tue-Sun mid-Mar–mid-Oct, to 4pm mid-Oct–mid-Mar, closed mid-Jan–mid-Feb & 2nd half Nov), the

former papal residence; on the left, Palazzo Vescovile, home to the **Museo Diocesano** (☎0578 74 99 05; www.palazzoborgia.it; Corso il Rossellino 30; adult/reduced €4.50/3; ⊙10.30am-1.30pm & 2.30-6pm Wed-Mon mid-Mar–Oct, 10am-1pm & 2-5pm Sat & Sun Nov–mid-Mar) and an intriguing miscellany of artworks, manuscripts, tapestries and miniatures. Before leaving town make sure you pick up some of the local *pecorino* cheese for which the area is justly famous.

✖ p275

The Drive » From Pienza strike south on the SP18 and head into the heart of the countryside, enjoying more bucolic scenery as you go. After 6km or so you'll see a sign to Monticchiello off to the left. Take this road and continue for another 4km.

❹ Monticchiello

A 15-minute drive south-east from Pienza brings you to Monticchiello, a sleepy medieval hilltop village with two good eateries. Choose between **Osteria La Porta** (☎0578 75 51 63; www.osterialaporta. it; Via del Piano 1; meals €45; ⊙9am-midnight), just inside the main gate, which has a small terrace with panoramic views of the Val d'Orcia; and stylish **Ristorante Daria** (☎0578 75 51 70; www. ristorantedaria.it; Via San Luigi 3; €40; ⊙12.15-2.30pm &

Pienza Piazza Pio II

7.15-10pm Thu-Tue), a short walk away, which offers a menu of dishes that successfully marry rustic inspiration and refined execution.

The Drive » Take the SP88 and follow it as it ploughs on through fields and light woodland to the main SP146. Go left and continue past orderly vineyards and olive groves up to San Biagio and 2km further

on to Montepulciano. All told it takes about 20 minutes.

- - - - - - - - - - - - - - - - - -

TRIP HIGHLIGHT

⑤ Montepulciano

Famous for its Vino Nobile wine, Montepulciano is a steeply stacked hill town harbouring a wealth of *palazzi* and fine buildings, as well as grandstand views

over the Val di Chiana and Val d'Orcia. The main street, aka the Corso, climbs steeply, passing **Caffè Poliziano** (☑0578 75 86 15; www. caffepoliziano.it; Via di Voltaia 27; ⊙7am-9pm Mon-Fri, to 10.30pm Sat, to 9pm Sun; ⑦), which has been operating since 1868, as it leads to the **Cantine Contucci** (☑0578 75 70 06;

273

THE PALIO

Siena's Palio is one of Italy's most spectacular annual events. Dating from the Middle Ages, it comprises a series of colourful pageants and a wild horse race on 2 July and 16 August. Ten of Siena's 17 *contrade* (town districts) compete for the coveted *palio* (silk banner).

From about 5pm, representatives from each *contrada* parade around the Campo in historical costume, all bearing their individual banners. Then, at 7.30pm in July and 7pm in August, the race gets the green light. For scarcely one exhilarating minute, the 10 horses and their bareback riders tear three times around the temporarily constructed dirt racetrack with a speed and violence that makes spectators' hair stand on end.

www.contucci.it; Via del Teatro 1; ⊙10am-12.30pm & 2.30-6pm), one of a number of historic wine cellars in town. Nearby **Piazza Grande** is flanked by the 14th-century **Palazzo Comunale** (terrace & tower adult/reduced €5/2.50, terrace only €2.50; ⊙10am-6pm Apr-Christmas) and the late-16th-century **duomo** (Cattedrale di Santa Maria Assunta; www.montepulcianochiusipienza.it; ⊙8am-7pm).

✕ p267, 275

The Drive » Reckon on about 40 minutes to cover the 25km to Chiusi. From Montepulciano head southeast along the SP146 to Chianciano Terme, a popular spa town. Continue on towards the A1 autostrada, and Chiusi is just on the other side of the highway.

---

⑥ Chiusi

Once an important Etruscan centre, Chiusi is now a sleepy country town. Its main attractions are the Etruscan tombs dotted around the surrounding countryside, two of which are included in the ticket price of the impressive **Museo Archeologico Etrusco di Chiusi** (☎0578 2 01 77; www.facebook.com/museoetrusco.dichiusi; Via Porsenna 93; adult/reduced €6/3; ⊙9am-8pm) in the town centre. The museum has a bevy of ceramics, pottery, jewellery and cinerary urns dating from between the 9th and 2nd centuries BC.

The Drive » You have two choices for Orvieto. The quick route is on the A1 autostrada (about 45 minutes), but it's a more interesting drive along the SR71 (1½ hours). This

passes through Città della Pieve, birthplace of the painter Perugino, and Ficulle, known since Roman times for its artisans.

TRIP HIGHLIGHT
⑦ Orvieto

Over the regional border in Umbria, the precariously perched town of Orvieto has one of Italy's finest Gothic cathedrals. The **Duomo di Orvieto** (☎0763 34 24 77; www.opsm.it; Piazza Duomo 26; €4, incl Museo dell'Opera del Duomo di Orvieto €5; ⊙9.30am-7pm Mon-Sat, 1-5.30pm Sun summer, shorter hours winter) took 30 years to plan and three centuries to complete. Work began in 1290, originally to a Romanesque design, but as construction proceeded, Gothic features were incorporated into the structure. Highlights include the richly coloured facade, and, in the **Cappella di San Brizio**, Luca Signorelli's fresco cycle *The Last Judgement*.

Across the piazza from the cathedral, the **Museo Claudio Faina e Civico** (☎0763 34 15 11; www.museofaina.it; Piazza Duomo 29; adult/reduced €4.50/3; ⊙9.30am-6pm summer, 10am-5pm winter, closed Mon Nov-Feb) houses an important collection of Etruscan archaeological artefacts.

✕ 🛏 p275

Eating & Sleeping

Siena

✕ Morbidi — Deli €

(📞0577 28 02 68; www.morbidi.com; Via Banchi di Sopra 75; lunch buffet €12; ⊙8am-8pm Mon-Wed, to 9pm Thu & Fri, to 3pm Sat) Famed for top-quality produce, Morbidi's excellent-value basement lunch buffet (12.15pm to 2.30pm Monday to Saturday) includes freshly prepared antipasti, salads, risotto, pasta and dessert. Bottled water is supplied; wine and coffee cost extra. Buy your ticket upstairs before heading down. It also offers an *aperitivo* buffet from 6pm (€7 to €13 Monday to Thursday, €8 to €14 Friday and Saturday).

🛏 Campo Regio Relais — Boutique Hotel €€€

(📞0577 22 20 73; www.camporegio.com; Via della Sapienza 25; r €220-450; ⊙mid-Mar–early Jan; ❋ 🛜) Siena's most charming boutique hotel has only six rooms, each individually decorated and luxuriously equipped (opt for deluxe room five, which has a private terrace). An excellent breakfast is served in the sumptuously decorated lounge or on the main terrace, which has a sensational view across the Fontebranda valley and across to the Torre del Mangia and the *duomo*.

Pienza ❸

✕ Townhouse Caffè — Italian €€

(📞0578 74 90 05; www.la-bandita.com/townhouse/the-restaurant; Via San Andrea 8; meals €40; ⊙noon-2.30pm Tue-Sun, 7.30-10pm daily mid-Mar–early Jan; 🛜 🍴) The menu at this chic eatery is pared back in more ways than one: there are around four choices per course, presentation is minimalist and the emphasis is on the quality of the produce rather than clever culinary tricks – bravo! In summer, guests dine in an atmospheric medieval courtyard; in winter, the action moves into a two-room space with open kitchen.

Montepulciano ❺

✕ La Grotta — Tuscan €€

(📞0578 75 74 79; www.lagrottamontepulciano.it; Via di San Biagio 15; meals €43; ⊙12.30-2pm & 7.30-10pm Thu-Tue, closed mid-Jan–late Mar) Located just below Montepulciano, overlooking the Renaissance splendour of the **Chiesa di San Biago** (📞0577 28 63 00; www.tempiosanbiagio.it; Via di San Biagio; incl audio guide €3.50; ⊙10am-6pm Mar-May & Oct, 9.30am-7pm Jun-Sep, 10am-5pm Sat & Sun Nov-Feb), the town's best restaurant serves traditional dishes with refined flavour and presentation. Service is exemplary, and the courtyard garden is a lovely place to enjoy a six-course tasting menu (€53) or your choice from the à la carte menu. Bookings advisable.

Orvieto ❼

✕ I Sette Consoli — Italian €€

(📞0763 34 39 11; www.isetteconsoli.it; Piazza Sant'Angelo 1a; meals €40-45, tasting menu €45; ⊙12.30-3pm & 7.30-10pm, closed Wed & Sun dinner) This refined restaurant walks the culinary high wire in Orvieto, serving inventive, artfully presented dishes, from joyful starters such as *panzanella* (a bread-based salad typical of central Italy) with vegetables and anchovies to pasta so light it almost floats off the fork. In good weather, try to get a table in the back garden. Dress for dinner and reserve ahead.

🛏 B&B Ripa Medici — B&B €

(📞328 7469620, 0763 34 13 43; www.ripamedici.com; Vicolo Ripa Medici 14; s €50, d €75-90; 🅿 ❋ 🛜) Hugging the walls on the edge of Orvieto's old town, this gracious B&B takes the concept of a 'room with a view' to another level, gazing out across undulating countryside. But the dreamy views are just one of its attractions. The immaculate guest room and two apartments ooze charm and are lovingly furnished with antique pieces, timber beams and English farmhouse decor.

Foodie Emilia-Romagna

Experience the best of cucina italiana on this tour of Italy's culinary heartland. As well as great food and wine, you'll come across artistic treasures and medieval cities at every turn.

26

TRIP HIGHLIGHTS

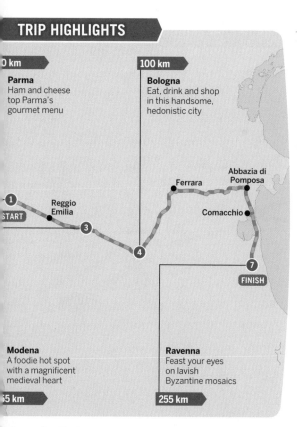

0 km

Parma
Ham and cheese top Parma's gourmet menu

100 km

Bologna
Eat, drink and shop in this handsome, hedonistic city

Abbazia di Pomposa

Ferrara

1
START

Reggio Emilia

Comacchio

3

4

7
FINISH

Modena
A foodie hot spot with a magnificent medieval heart

Ravenna
Feast your eyes on lavish Byzantine mosaics

5 km

255 km

7 DAYS
255KM / 158 MILES

GREAT FOR...

BEST TIME TO GO

Autumn is ideal for fresh seasonal produce.

ESSENTIAL PHOTO

Food stalls and delis in Bologna's Quadrilatero district.

BEST FOR ART LOVERS

Ravenna's sparkling mosaics.

26 Foodie Emilia-Romagna

Sandwiched between Tuscany and the Veneto, Emilia-Romagna is a foodie's dream destination. Many of Italy's signature dishes originated here, and its regional specialities are revered across the country. This tasty trip takes in the region's main culinary centres of Parma, Modena and Bologna, as well as the charming Renaissance town of Ferrara, and art-rich Ravenna, celebrated for its glorious Byzantine mosaics.

TRIP HIGHLIGHT

❶ Parma

Handsome and prosperous, Parma is one of Italy's culinary hot spots, producing the country's finest ham *(prosciutto di Parma)* and its most revered cheese *(parmigiano reggiano)*. To stock up on these, as well as local Lambrusco wines and other regional delicacies, head to the **Salumeria Garibaldi** (www.salumeria garibaldi.com; Via Garibaldi 42; ⏰8am-8pm Mon-Sat), a

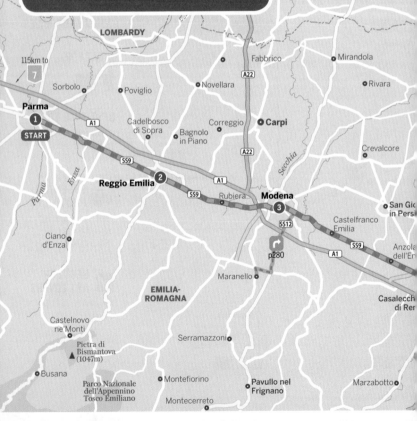

divine deli in the historic centre.

Once you've sated your appetite, sate your soul at the city's 12th-century **Duomo** (Cattedrale di Santa Maria Assunta; www.piazza duomoparma.com; Piazza del Duomo; ⊙7.30am-7.15pm), with its classic Lombard-Romanesque facade and ornate baroque interior. Nearby, the octagonal **Battistero** (www.piazza duomoparma.com; Piazza del Duomo; adult/reduced incl Museo Diocesano €8/6; ⊙10am-6pm Apr-Oct, to 5pm Nov-Mar) displays a hybrid Romanesque-Gothic look in pink and white marble. Parma's main art collection, which includes works by locals Parmigianino and Correggio alongside paintings by Fra' Angelico, El Greco and a piece attributed to Leonardo da Vinci, are in the **Galleria Nazionale** (www.pilotta.beniculturali.it; Piazza della Pilotta 5; adult/reduced incl Teatro Farnese & Museo Archeologico Nazionale €10/5; ⊙8.30am-7pm Tue-Sat, 1-7pm Sun), one of several museums in the monumental **Palazzo**

LINK YOUR TRIP

7 **Cinematic Cinque Terre**
From Parma head 120km along the A15 autostrada to La Spezia, gateway to the spectacular Cinque Terre coastline.

8 **Northern Cities**
From Ferrara take the A13 autostrada for 75km to Padua, home of one of Italy's great Renaissance masterpieces.

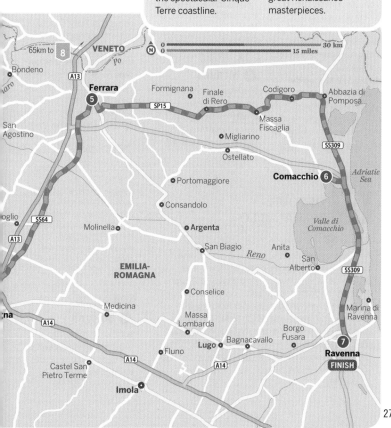

della Pilotta (www.pilotta. beniculturali.it; Piazza della Pilotta; ⏲8.30am-7pm Tue-Sat, 1-7pm Sun).

 p283

The Drive » From Parma, it's a straightforward 50-minute drive southeast on the SS9 (Via Emilia) through fairly uninspiring flat farmland to Reggio Emilia. If you're in a hurry, the quicker A1 autostrada covers the same route.

❷ Reggio Emilia

Genteel Reggio Emilia puts the *reggiano* in *parmigiano reggiano* (Parmesan cheese). Apart from its cheese, the city is best known as the birthplace of the Italian flag – the famous red, white and green tricolour – whose history is chronicled at the **Museo del Tricolore** (www.musei.re.it/ sedi/museo-del-tricolore; Piazza Prampolini 1; ⏲9am-noon Tue-Fri, 10am-1pm & 4-7pm Sat & Sun Sep-Jun, 9-11pm Tue-

Sun Jul & Aug). There are several other museums and galleries in town, including the **Galleria Parmeggiani** (www.musei. re.it/sedi/galleria-parmeggiani; Corso Cairoli 2; ⏲9am-noon Tue-Fri, 10am-1pm & 4-7pm Sat & Sun Sep-Jun, 9am-noon & 9pm-midnight Tue-Sat, 9pm-midnight Sun Jul & Aug), which has some interesting Italian, Flemish and Spanish paintings.

✕ p283

The Drive » The run down to Modena takes about an hour on the SS9. The scenery is much like the first leg from Parma – flat fields, petrol stations, agricultural buildings and the occasional stone farmhouse. At Modena head for the *centro*.

TRIP HIGHLIGHT

❸ Modena

Modena is one of Italy's great gastro centres, the creative force behind *aceto balsamico* (balsamic vinegar), *zamponi*

(pig's trotters), *cotechino* (stuffed pork sausage) and sparkling Lambrusco wines. You'll find shops all over town selling local delicacies, including **La Consorteria 1966** (www. facebook.com/laconsorteria 1966; Piazza Mazzini 9; ⏲11am-6pm Mon-Sat).

Modena also has a wonderfully suggestive medieval core, centred on **Piazza Grande** and the **Duomo** (Cattedrale Metropolitana di Santa Maria Assunta e San Geminiano; www.duomo dimodena.it; Corso Duomo; ⏲7am-12.30pm & 3.30-7pm Mon, 7am-7pm Tue-Sun), considered by many to be the finest Romanesque church in Italy. Inseparable from the cathedral is the early-13th-century tower, the **Torre Ghirlandina** (www.unesco.modena.it; Corso Duomo; adult/reduced €3/2; ⏲9.30am-1pm & 3-7pm Tue-Fri, 9.30am-7pm Sat & Sun Apr-Sep, to 5.30pm Oct-Mar).

✕ p61, 283

The Drive » From Modena take the SS9 southeast to Bologna. It's only about 45km away, but traffic is often heavy and it can take up to 1½ hours to get there. Bologna's centre is closed to most traffic, so if you're staying downtown, contact your hotel to ask about parking.

TRIP HIGHLIGHT

❹ Bologna

Emilia-Romagna's vibrant regional capital, Bologna is a city with serious culinary

---

↱ DETOUR: MARANELLO

Start: ❸ Modena

A mecca for petrolheads, Maranello is the home town of Ferrari. The world's sportiest cars have been manufactured here since the early 1940s, and although the factory is off-limits (unless you happen to own a Ferrari), you can get your fix ogling the flaming red autos on display at the **Museo Ferrari** (www.museomaranello.ferrari.com; Via Ferrari 43, Maranello; adult/reduced €17/15; ⏲9.30am-7pm Apr-Oct, to 6pm Nov-Mar). Maranello is 17km south of Modena on the SS12.

Ravenna Mosaic in Basilica di Sant'Apollinare Nuovo

credentials. It's most famous for inspiring the eponymous bolognese sauce with its own (and tastier) dish known as *ragù*, but it also gifted the world lasagne, *mortadella* and tortellini (pockets of meat-stuffed pasta). These and other local goodies appear on menus across the city, but for a real gastro treat, sniff out the fabulous old-style delis in the bustling **Quadrilatero** district.

Overshadowing the Quadrilatero's medieval streets are **Le Due Torri** (The Two Towers; Piazza di Porta Ravegnana), Bologna's two leaning towers. If vertigo is not a problem, you can climb the taller of the two, the 97.6m-high **Torre degli Asinelli** (www.duetorribologna.com; Piazza di Porta Ravegnana; adult/reduced €5/3;

⊙9.30am-7.30pm Mar–5 Nov, to 5.45pm 6 Nov–Feb), and survey the historic centre from on high. The big barn-like structure you'll see to the northwest is the **Basilica di San Petronio** (☏051 648 06 11; www.basilicadisan petronio.org; Piazza Maggiore; photo pass €2; ⊙7.45am-1.30pm & 3-6.30pm Mon-Fri, 7.45am-6.30pm Sat & Sun), the world's fifth-largest basilica, which lords it over **Piazza Maggiore**, Bologna's striking showpiece square.

✕ p47, p283

The Drive » Head north out of Bologna along Via Stalingrado and follow the SS64. This leads through orderly farmland and neat villages to Ferrara, about 1½ hours away. In Ferrara, turn left after the river and head for the *centro storico* (historic centre) car park on Via Darsena.

----

⑤ Ferrara

Ferrara was once the seat of the powerful Este family (1260–1598), and although it is often bypassed by travellers, it's an attractive place with an austere Unesco-listed cityscape and compact historic centre. In food terms, specialities include the town's uniquely shaped bread, known as *coppia ferrarese,* and *cappellacci di zucca* (hat-shaped pasta stuffed with pumpkin, herbs and nutmeg).

The town centre, which is easily explored on foot, is focused on **Castello Estense** (www. castelloestense.it; Viale Cavour; adult/reduced €8/6; ⊙9.30am-5.30pm Tue-Sun Oct-Feb, 9.30am-5.30pm Mar-Sep), a martial 14th-century castle complete with moat

VIA EMILIA

For the first half of the trip from Parma to Bologna you follow the region's most famous road, the ruler-straight Via Emilia. Built by the Romans in the 2nd century BC, it ran for 206km through the Po river valley connecting the region's main cities – Placentia (Piacenza), Parma, Regium (Reggio Emilia), Mutina (Modena), Bononia (Bologna) and Ariminum (Rimini). Within decades of completion, it had opened up Italy's fertile northern hinterland to economic expansion, and converted the rich river plain into the empire's proverbial breadbasket – a position it still enjoys today.

and drawbridge. Linked to the castle by an elevated passageway is the 13th-century crenellated **Palazzo Municipale** (Palazzo Ducale; Piazza del Municipio 1; ◷9am-1pm Mon, Wed & Fri, to 1pm & 3-5pm Tue & Thu), now largely occupied by administrative offices. Opposite, Ferrara's pink-and-white, 12th-century **Duomo** (Cattedrale di San Giorgio; Piazza Cattedrale; ◷7.30am-noon & 3.30-6.30pm Mon-Sat, 7.30am-12.30pm & 3.30-7pm Sun) sports a graphic three-tier facade, combining Romanesque and Gothic styles.

The Drive » Head east out of Ferrara on the SP15 and continue on the straight road past immaculate vineyards into the tiny village of Massa Fiscaglia. Bear left here and continue on to Codigoro and the Abbazia di Pomposa (well worth a quick stop). From the abbey it's a straight 20-minute run down the SS309 to Comacchio.

⑥ Comacchio

Resembling a mini Venice with its canals and brick bridges, Comacchio is the main centre in the Po delta (Foci del Po). This area of dense pine forests and extensive wetlands, much of it protected in the **Parco del Delta del Po** (www.parcodeltapo.it), offers superlative birdwatching and excellent cycling. Foodies can try the prized local speciality, eel, which is served at the many restaurants on Comacchio's canals. Don't miss the excellent **Museo Delta Antico** (www.museodeltaantico.com; Via Agatopisto 2, Comacchio; adult/reduced €6/3; ◷9.30am-1pm & 3-6.30pm Tue-Sun Mar-Aug, shorter hours Sep-Feb).

The Drive » From Comacchio, Ravenna is only an hour's drive away, 40km south on the SS309. The road spears down a narrow strip of land between

a lagoon and the Adriatic coast, but you won't see much water thanks to lengthy curtains of verdant trees and heavy foliage.

TRIP HIGHLIGHT

⑦ Ravenna

No tour of Emilia-Romagna would be complete without a stop at Ravenna to see its remarkable Unesco-protected mosaics. Relics of the city's golden age as capital of the Western Roman and Byzantine Empires, they are described by Dante in his *Divine Comedy,* much of which he wrote here.

The mosaics are spread over several **sites** (www.ravennamosaici.it; 5-site combo ticket €9.50, plus summer-only surcharge €2; ◷9am-7pm Mar-Oct, 10am-5pm Nov-Feb), five of which are covered by a single ticket – **Basilica di San Vitale** (Via San Vitale), **Mausoleo di Galla Placidia** (Via San Vitale), **Basilica di Sant'Apollinare Nuovo** (Via di Roma 52), **Museo Arcivescovile** (Piazza Arcivescovado 1), and **Battistero Neoniano** (Piazza del Duomo 1). Outside town you'll find more mosaics at the **Basilica di Sant'Apollinare in Classe** (Via Romea Sud 224; adult/reduced €5/2.50; ◷8.30am-7.30pm Mon-Sat, 1-7.30pm Sun).

🛏 p283

Eating & Sleeping

Parma ❶

✖ Ristorante Cocchi   Emilian €€

(📞0521 98 19 90; www.ristorantecocchi.it; Viale Antonio Gramsci 16a; meals €27-45; ⏱12.15-2.15pm & 7.30-10.15pm Sun-Fri; 🛜) You'll need to venture across the river to Oltretorrente for a traditional Parmigiano experience untainted by the city's influx of culinary tourism. Classy yet unpretentious, father and son duo Corrado and Daniele Cocchi woo you with tradition at this top restaurant.

🛏 B&B Pio   B&B €

(📞347 7769065; www.piorooms.it; Borgo XX Marzo 14; s/d from €70/80; 🛜) Location, comfort and hospitality all come together at this B&B run by a gregarious owner with a passion for local food and wine. Four lower-floor doubles and a kitchenette-equipped upper-floor suite share attractive features such as beamed ceilings, antique textiles and ultramodern fixtures.

Reggio Emilia ❷

✖ Caffè
Arti e Mestieri   Gastronomy €€€

(📞0522 43 22 02; www.giannidamato.it; Via Emilia San Pietro 14; meals €40-50, 5-course tasting menu €65; ⏱noon-2.30pm & 7.30-10.30pm Tue-Sat, to 2.30pm Sun; 🛜) Tucked back off the street around a lovely interior garden, this is Reggio's best spot for an elegant dinner. Chef Gianni d'Amato launched this new venture after his Michelin-starred Rigoletto was destroyed by the region's 2012 earthquake. In agreeable weather, the ivy-draped outdoor courtyard is absolutely wonderful.

Modena ❸

✖ Ristorante da Danilo   Italian €€

(📞059 21 66 91; www. ristorantedadanilomodena.it; Via Coltellini 31; meals €25-30; ⏱noon-3pm & 7pm-midnight Mon-Sat) Speedy waiters glide around juggling bread baskets and wine bottles in this deliciously traditional choice where first dates mingle with animated families and local characters. The impressive antipasti spread and perfect *gnocchi fritti* (fried dough; eat it with local prosciutto) are divine, but don't overdo it – the Vecchia Modena-style tortelloni (ricotta and spinach with bacon cream sauce) is nothing short of transcendent.

Bologna ❹

✖ Trattoria Da Me   Trattoria €€

(📞051 55 54 86; www.facebook.com/ trattoriadame; Via San Felice 50; meals €29-38; ⏱noon-2.30pm & 7.30-10.30pm) Bologna's most exciting reinvention is this formerly uneventful trattoria transformed by chef Elisa Rusconi, who triumphed on Italian television show *4 Ristoranti* and upgraded her grandfather's restaurant – at it since 1937 – into a daring, must-stop dining destination in the city's culinary landscape.

Ravenna ❼

🛏 Albergo Cappello   Boutique Hotel €€

(📞0544 21 98 13; www.albergocappello.it; Via IV Novembre 41; d €139-189; 🅿❄@🛜) Colour-themed rooms come in three categories at this finely coiffed seven-room boutique hotel smack in the town centre. Murano glass chandeliers, original 15th-century frescoes and coffered ceilings are set against modern fixtures and flat-screen TVs; some rooms has Venetian silk wallpaper and wood-panelled bathrooms. The ample breakfast features pastries from Ravenna's finest *pasticceria*.

STRETCH YOUR LEGS
ROME

Start/Finish: Largo di Torre Argentina

- -

Distance: 1.7km

- -

Duration: 2 hours

Rome's historic centre, much of which is closed to unauthorised traffic, is best explored on foot. Park near Stazione Termini, then hop on a bus to the *centro* where you'll discover picturesque cobbled lanes, showboating piazzas, basilicas and ancient ruins.

Take this walk on Trips

Largo di Torre Argentina

Start in **Largo di Torre Argentina**, a busy transport hub set around the remains of four temples dating to between the 4th and 2nd centuries BC. On the square's western flank, **Teatro Argentina**, Rome's premier theatre, stands near the spot where Julius Caesar was assassinated in 44 BC.

The Walk » From the square, head east along Corso Vittorio Emanuele II to Piazza del Gesù.

Chiesa del Gesù

The landmark **Chiesa del Gesù** (☎06 69 70 01; www.chiesadelgesu.org; Piazza del Gesù; ◷6.45am-12.45pm & 4-7.30pm, St Ignatius rooms 4-6pm Mon-Sat, 10am-noon Sun) is Rome's most important Jesuit church. Behind its imposing facade is an awe-inspiring baroque interior. Headline works include a swirling vault fresco by Il Baciccia and Andrea del Pozzo's opulent tomb for Ignatius Loyola, the Jesuits' founder.

The Walk » Cross Corso Vittorio Emanuele II and follow Via del Gesù north. Then turn left onto Via Santa Caterina da Siena.

Basilica di Santa Maria Sopra Minerva

Trumpeted by Bernini's much-loved **Elefantino** statue, this **basilica** (www.santamariasopraminerva.it; Piazza della Minerva 42; ◷6.55am-7pm Mon-Fri, 10am-12.30pm & 3.30-7pm Sat, 8.10am-12.30pm & 3.30-7pm Sun) is Rome's only Gothic church. Little remains of the original 13th-century structure and these days the main drawcard is a minor Michelangelo sculpture and its art-rich interior.

The Walk » From the basilica, it's an easy stroll up Via della Minerva to Piazza della Rotonda.

Pantheon

A 2000-year-old temple, now a church, the **Pantheon** (www.pantheonroma.com; Piazza della Rotonda; ◷8.30am-7.30pm Mon-Sat, 9am-6pm Sun; ▣Largo di Torre Argentina) is the best preserved of Rome's ancient monuments. Built by Hadrian over

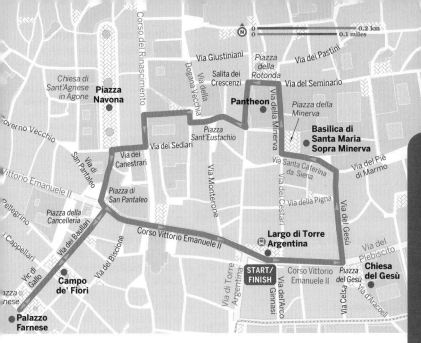

Marcus Agrippa's earlier 27 BC temple, it has stood since around AD 125, and it's an exhilarating experience to go in and gaze up at the largest unreinforced concrete dome ever built.

The Walk » Follow the signs to Piazza Navona, stopping en route for a quick coffee at Caffè Sant'Eustachio.

Piazza Navona

With its showy fountains, baroque *palazzi* (mansions) and colourful cast of street artists, hawkers and tourists, **Piazza Navona** is central Rome's elegant showcase square. Its grand centrepiece is Bernini's **Fontana dei Quattro Fiumi**, a flamboyant fountain featuring personifications of the Nile, Ganges, Danube and Plate rivers.

The Walk » Exit the piazza to the south, cross Corso Vittorio Emanuele II and continue up Via dei Baullari.

Campo de' Fiori

Colourful and always busy, **Il Campo** (🚇 Corso Vittorio Emanuele II) **is a major**

focus of Roman life: by day it hosts one of the city's best-known markets; by night it heaves with tourists and young drinkers. Amid the chaos look out for the sinister statue of philosopher Giordano Bruno who was burned for heresy here in 1600.

The Walk » Head up to Piazza Farnese, a matter of metres away.

Palazzo Farnese

Palazzo Farnese (www.inventerrome.com; Piazza Farnese; tours €9; ⊙ guided tours 3pm, 4pm & 5pm Mon, Wed & Fri) **is** one of Rome's finest Renaissance buildings. Home to the French Embassy, it can only be visited on a guided tour, but it's worth it to see Annibale Carracci's frescoes that are said by some to rival Michelangelo's in the Sistine Chapel.

The Walk » To get back to Largo di Torre Argentina, double back to Corso Vittorio Emanuele II and head right.

STRETCH YOUR LEGS
FLORENCE

Start/Finish: Galleria dell'Accademia

Distance: 2.5km

Duration: 1 day

To get the best out of Florence (Firenze) park your car at Piazza della Libertà, and head into the city's historic centre on foot. This tour provides a great introduction to the city, passing through its headlining piazzas, basilicas and galleries.

Take this walk on Trips

Galleria dell'Accademia

Before heading into the heart of the historic centre, take time to salute Florence's fabled poster boy. Michelangelo's *David* (1504) stands in all his naked glory in the **Galleria dell'Accademia** (☎055 238 86 09; www.galleriaaccademia firenze.beniculturali.it; Via Ricasoli 60; adult/reduced €12/6; ⊙8.15am-6.50pm Tue-Sun). He originally guarded Palazzo Vecchio but was moved here in 1873.

The Walk » From the gallery, head south along Via Ricasoli, past the Carabé gelateria, down to Via de' Pucci. Turn right, skirting past Palazzo Pucci, as you continue on to Piazza San Lorenzo.

Basilica di San Lorenzo

A fine example of Renaissance architecture, the **Basilica di San Lorenzo** (☎055 21 40 42; www.operamedicealaurenziana.org; Piazza San Lorenzo; €6, with Biblioteca Medicea Laurenziana €8.50; ⊙10am-5.30pm Mon-Sat) is best known for its Brunelleschi-designed **Sagrestia Vecchia** (Old Sacristy). Around the corner, at the rear of the basilica, the **Museo delle Cappelle Medicee** (Medici Chapels; ☎055 238 86 02; www.bargellomusei.beniculturali.it/musei/2/medicee; Piazza Madonna degli Aldobrandini 6; adult/reduced €8/4; ⊙8.15am-2pm, closed 2nd & 4th Sun, 1st, 3rd & 5th Mon of month) has some exquisite Michelangelo sculptures.

The Walk » From Piazza Madonna degli Aldobrandini, head down Via de' Conti and its continuation Via F Zanetti to Via de' Cerretani. Turn left and soon you'll see Piazza del Duomo ahead.

Duomo

Florence's 14th-century **Duomo** (Cattedrale di Santa Maria del Fiore; ☎055 230 28 85; www.museumflorence.com; Piazza del Duomo; ⊙10am-5pm Mon-Wed & Fri, to 4.30pm Thu & Sat, 1.30-4.45pm Sun) is the city's most iconic landmark with its pink, white and green marble facade and red-tiled **dome** (adult/reduced incl baptistry, campanile, crypt & museum €18/3; 8.30am-7pm Mon-Fri, to 5pm Sat, 1-4pm Sun). Nearby, you can climb the **campanile** (8.15am-7pm) and admire the bas-reliefs on the 11th-century **Battistero** (Baptistry; 8.15-10.15am

& 11.15am-7.30pm Mon-Fri, 8.15am-6.30pm Sat, 8.15am-1.30pm Sun).

The Walk » It's a straightforward 400m or so down Via dei Calzaiuoli to Piazza della Signoria.

Piazza della Signoria

This lovely cafe-lined piazza is over-looked by the **Torre d'Arnolfo**, the high point of **Palazzo Vecchio** (☏055 276 85 58; www.musefirenze.it; Piazza della Signoria; adult/reduced museum €12.50/10, tower €12.50/10, museum & tower €17.50/15, museum & archaeological tour €16/13.50, archaeological tour €4, combination ticket €19.50/17.50; ⏰ museum 9am-11pm Fri-Wed, to 2pm Thu Apr-Sep, 9am-7pm Fri-Wed, to 2pm Thu Oct-Mar, tower 9am-9pm Fri-Wed, to 2pm Thu Apr-Sep, 10am-5pm Fri-Wed, to 2pm Thu Oct-Mar), **Florence's medieval City Hall. It still houses the mayor's office but you can visit its lavish apartments.

The Walk » To get to the Galleria degli Uffizi takes a matter of seconds, although we can't vouch for how long it'll take to get inside. The gallery is just off the piazza's southeastern corner, in a grey porticoed *palazzo* (mansion).

Galleria degli Uffizi

The **Galleria degli Uffizi** (Uffizi Gallery; ☏055 29 48 83; www.uffizi.it; Piazzale degli Uffizi 6; adult/reduced Mar-Oct €20/10, Nov-Feb €12/6; ⏰8.15am-6.50pm Tue-Sun) has one of Italy's greatest art collections. The high-light is the Renaissance art, including Botticelli's *La nascita di Venere* (Birth of Venus) and Michelangelo's *Tondo doni* (Holy Family).

The Walk » Pick up Via Lambertesca, over the way from the gallery entrance, and follow it to Via Por Santa Maria. Go left and it's a short hop to the river.

Ponte Vecchio

Florence's celebrated bridge has twin-kled with the wares of jewellers since the 16th century. The bridge as it stands was built in 1345 and was the only one in Florence saved from destruction by the retreating Germans in 1944.

The Walk » To get back to the Galleria dell'Accademia, pick up bus C1 from Lungarno Generale Diaz and head up to Piazza San Marco.

Southern
Italy

**NATURE ITSELF SEEMS A LITTLE
WILDER IN SOUTHERN ITALY**, where a
single landscape might encompass smoking
volcanoes, fertile valleys, precipitous sea cliffs
and cobalt waters. Italy's greatest hits may lie
further north, but the south tugs hard at the
heartstrings with its magnificent food, wild
backcountry and exotic, palm-fringed cities.

Away from Naples' traffic-clogged roads, this is
also perfect driving country. Naples, Vesuvius
and the Amalfi Coast are Grand Tour musts,
but lesser-known routes reveal some wonderful
surprises, from Cilento's pristine coastline to
the conical-capped houses (*trulli*) of Puglia's
Valle d'Itria. Offshore, Sardinia has dreamy
beaches while Sicily thrills with bombastic
baroque architecture and sumptuous seafood.

Capri Boats off the coast
S-F/SHUTTERSTOCK ©

Southern Italy

Corsica
FRANCE

Viterbo
Tarquinia
ROME
Capo Linaro

Palau
Capo d'Orso
Stintino
Castelsardo
Sassari
Olbia
Monte Timidone (361m)
Alghero
Nuoro
Dorgali
Monte Oddeu (1063m)
Oristano
Punta La Marmora (1834m)
Laconi
SARDINIA
Sanluri
Iglesias
Muravera
SanPietro
Cagliari
Sant'Antioco
Capo Malfatano

Costa Verde

Tyrrhenian Sea

Trapa
Marettimo
Favignana
Marsala
Selir

MEDITERRANEAN SEA

Pantelleria

0 ——— 200 km
0 ——— 100 miles

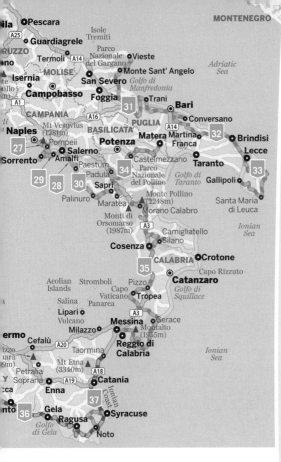

DON'T MISS

Vietri sul Mare

Bring back a piece of the Amalfi Coast from this seaside centre, renowned for its bright-hued ceramics.

Capo Palinuro

Hike this rocky promontory for gorgeous views of the Cilento coast, followed by a snorkel in its cobalt waters.

Matera

Visit Matera, where ancient cave dwellings have been transformed into cool wine bars and boutique sleeps.

Noto

Stroll one of Italy's most beautiful town centres, admiring golden baroque buildings in the southern Sicilian sun.

Isola della Maddalena

Crystalline waters lap onto weird, wind-whipped rock formations on this small Sardinian island.

Shadow of Vesuvius

Beginning in the tumult that is Naples, this trip winds around the Bay of Naples to magnificent Roman ruins and on to Sorrento – even daring the slopes of Vesuvius itself.

27

TRIP HIGHLIGHTS

...km

27 km

Naples
Incomparable city of magnificent art, architecture and street life

1 START

Mt Vesuvius
A silent time bomb with summit views worthy of fire god Vulcan

5

...km

3

Herculaneum
Superbly preserved ruins, from ancient advertisements to terror-struck skeletons

Oplontis

8

60 km

Castellammare di Stabia

Pompeii
An extraordinary, haunting portal to the 1st century AD

Sorrento
FINISH

**2–3 DAYS
90KM / 56 MILES**

GREAT FOR...

BEST TIME TO GO
Spring and autumn for best weather; December for stunning Christmas displays.

 ESSENTIAL PHOTO
Capture Vesuvius' brooding majesty from Naples' waterfront.

 BEST FOR HISTORY
Relive history amid Herculaneum's ruins.

27 Shadow of Vesuvius

This trip begins in Naples (Napoli), a city that rumbles with contradictions — grimy streets hit palm-fringed boulevards, crumbling facades mask golden baroque ballrooms. Rounding the Bay of Naples and the dense urban sprawl, you quickly reach some of the world's most spectacular Roman ruins including Pompeii and Herculaneum, as well as lesser-known jewels, from Portici's royal getaway to sprawling ancient villas. Above it all looms Vesuvius' dark beauty.

TRIP HIGHLIGHT

1 Naples

Italy's most misunderstood city is also one of its finest – an exhilarating mess of frescoed cupolas, mysterious shrines and catacombs, and boisterous, hyperactive street markets. Contradiction is the catchphrase here. It's a place where anarchy, pollution and poverty share the stage with lavish theatres, glorious museums and cafe-lounging artists and intellectuals.

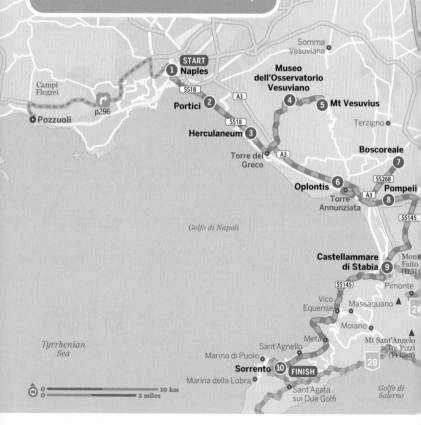

The Unesco-listed *centro storico* (historic centre) is an intoxicating warren of streets packed with ancient churches, citrus-filled cloisters and first-rate pizzerias. It's here, under the washing lines, that you'll find classic Neapolitan street life – overloaded Vespas hurtling through cobbled alleyways and clued-up *casalinghe* (housewives) bullying market vendors. Move towards the sea and the cityscape opens up. Imperious palaces flank show-off squares and seafront panoramas take in fabled Capri and mighty Vesuvius. This is Royal Naples, the Naples of the Bourbons that so impressed the 18th-century grand tourists.

LINK YOUR TRIP

Southern Larder
From Sorrento, you can embark on this culinary adventure along the Amalfi Coast and the Golfo di Salerno, where mozzarella rules the roost.

Amalfi Coast
Vico Equense kicks off this week-long adventure of hairpin turns and vertical landscapes amid the world's most glamorous stretch of coastline.

VESUVIAN WINES

Vesuvian wine has been relished since ancient times. The rare combination of rich volcanic soil and a favourable microclimate created by its slopes makes the territory one of Italy's most interesting viticultural areas. Lacryma Christi (literally 'tears of Christ') is the name of perhaps the most celebrated wine produced on the slopes of Mt Vesuvius.

Further afield, other top regional wines include Taurasi, Fiano di Avellino, Aglianico del Taburno and Greco di Tufo.

To prepare for Pompeii and Herculaneum, head to the **Museo Archeologico Nazionale** (☏848 800288; www.museoarcheologiconapoli.it; Piazza Museo Nazionale 19; adult/reduced €15/2; ☺9am-7.30pm Wed-Mon; Ⓜ Museo, Piazza Cavour). With one of the world's finest collections of Graeco-Roman artefacts, it stars a series of stunning sculptures, mosaics from Pompeii, and a room full of ancient erotica.

✖ 🍴 p47, p301

The Drive » A straight 8km drive along the SS18 provides a relatively easy journey from central Naples straight to the Palazzo Reale di Portici – if the other drivers behave, of course.

- - - - - - - - - - - - - - - -

❷ Portici

The town of Portici lies at the foot of Mt Vesuvius and had to be rebuilt in the wake of its ruin by the 1631 eruption. Charles III of Spain, king of Naples and Sicily, erected a stately royal palace here between 1738 and 1748. Known as the **Reggia di Portici** (☏081 253 20 16; www.centromusa.it; Via Università 100, Portici; adult/reduced €5/3; ☺3-6.30pm Thu, 9.30am-6.30pm Fri-Sun; Botanic Garden closes 1hr before sunset in winter), the palace today houses a couple of worthwhile museums, most notably the **Herculanense Museum** with artefacts from Pompeii and Herculaneum. Even if the museum is closed, the palace is worth a stop for its string of colourfully frescoed rooms. Outside, the exquisite **botanic gardens** are operated by the University of Naples Federico II.

The Drive » The entrance to the ruins of Herculaneum lie just down the street, a couple of kilometres down the SS18.

- - - - - - - - - - - - - - - -

❸ Herculaneum

The ruins of ancient **Herculaneum** (☏081 777 70 08; http://ercolano.beniculturali.it; Corso Resina 187, Ercolano;

adult/reduced €13/2;
⏱8.30am-7.30pm, last entry
6pm Apr-Oct, 8.30am-5pm, last
entry 3.30pm Nov-Mar; P)
are smaller, less daunting
and easier to navigate
than Pompeii. They also
include some of the area's
richest archaeological
finds, offering a rare,
intimate glimpse of daily
life as it was when the
Romans ruled the region.

Heavily damaged by
an earthquake in AD 63,
Herculaneum was com-
pletely submerged by the
AD 79 eruption of Mt Ve-
suvius. However, because
it was much closer to the
volcano than Pompeii, it
drowned in a sea of mud,
essentially fossilising the
town and ensuring that
even delicate items were
discovered remarkably
well preserved.

Seek out the **Casa
d'Argo** (Argus House) a
well-preserved example
of a Roman noble fam-
ily's house, complete with
porticoed garden and
triclinium (dining area).
Casa dei Cervi (House of
the Stags) is an impos-
ing example of a Roman
noble's villa, with two
storeys ranged around
a central courtyard and
animated with murals
and still-life paintings.
And don't miss the **Terme
del Foro** (Forum Baths),
with deep pools, stucco
friezes and, in the female
apodyterium (changing
room), a striking mosaic
of a naked Triton.

✕ p301

The Drive » The museum is
only 10km from Herculaneum.
Keep heading down the SS18

until you reach the centre of
Torre del Greco, where you will
turn left on Via Vittorio Veneto,
which will quickly turn into Via
Guglielmo Marconi. Follow the
signs as you wind your way
up the lower elevations of Mt
Vesuvius, and the Bay of Naples
comes into view.

- - - - - - - - - - - - - - - - - - -

❹ Museo dell'Osservatorio Vesuviano

Halfway up Mt Vesuvius,
this **museum** (Museum
of the Vesuvian Observatory;
☎081 610 85 60; www.ov.ingv.
it; Via dell'Osservatorio; ⏱by
reservation 9.30am-4pm
Mon-Sat, from 10am Sun)
contains an interesting
array of artefacts telling
the history of 2000 years
of Vesuvius-watching.
Founded in 1841 to moni-
tor Vesuvius' moods, it

DETOUR: CAMPI FLEGREI

Start: ❶ Naples

Stretching west of Posillipo Hill to the Tyrrhenian Sea, the oft-overlooked Campi
Flegrei (Phlegrean Fields) counterbalances its ugly urban sprawl with lush volcanic
hillsides and priceless ancient ruins without the crowds. While its Greek settlements
are Italy's oldest, its Monte Nuovo is Europe's youngest mountain. It's not every
week that a mountain just appears on the scene. At 8pm on 29 September 1538,
a crack appeared in the earth near the ancient Roman settlement of Tripergole,
spewing out a violent concoction of pumice, fire and smoke over six days. By the
end of the week, Pozzuoli had a new 134m-tall neighbour.

Today, Europe's newest mountain is a lush and peaceful nature reserve. Before
exploring the Campi Flegrei, stop at the **tourist office** (☎081 526 14 81; www.
infocampiflegrei.it; Largo Matteotti 1a; ⏱9am-8pm Mon-Fri, 9am-6pm Sat & Sun; Ⓜ Pozzuoli,
ⓇCumana to Pozzuoli) in Pozzuoli to get local information and purchase an €4
cumulative ticket (valid for two days) to four of the area's key sites: the **Anfiteatro
Flavio**, the **Parco Archeologico di Baia**, the **Museo Archeologico dei Campi
Flegrei** and the **Parco Archeologico di Cuma**.

SOUTHERN ITALY **27** SHADOW OF VESUVIUS

Pompeii Villa dei Misteri

is the oldest volcanic observatory in the world. To this day, scientists are still constantly monitoring the active volcanoes at Vesuvius, Campi Flegrei and Ischia.

The Drive >> It's many more hairpin turns as you make your way along the same road almost to Vesuvius' crater, about 7km away. Views across the Bay of Naples and Campania are magnificent.

- - - - - - - - - - - - - - - -

❺ Mt Vesuvius

Since exploding into history in AD 79, **Mt Vesuvius** (☎081 239 56 53; www.parconazionaledelvesuvio.it;

crater adult/reduced €10/8; ☺crater 9am-6pm Jul & Aug, to 5pm Apr-Jun & Sep, to 4pm Mar & Oct, to 3pm Nov-Feb, ticket office closes 1hr before crater) has blown its top more than 30 times. The most devastating of these was in 1631, and the most recent was in 1944. It is the only volcano on the European mainland to have erupted within the last 100 years. What redeems this lofty menace is the spectacular view from its **crater** – a breathtaking panorama that takes in Naples, its world-famous bay, and part of the Apennine mountains.

The end of the road is the summit car park, from where a shuttle bus reaches the ticket office and entry point further up the volcano. From here, a relatively easy 860m path leads up to the actual summit (allow 25 minutes), best tackled in comfy sneakers and with a jacket in tow (it can be chilly up top, even in summer). When the weather is bad the summit path is shut.

The Drive >> The first part of this 21km stretch heads back down Vesuvius the same way you came up. Head all the way down to the A3 motorway, turn left onto it and head southeast.

GREG ELMS/LONELY PLANET ©

The villas of Oplontis are just off the Torre Annunziata exit.

- - - - - - - - - - - - - - - - - -

⑥ Oplontis

Buried beneath the unappealing streets of modern-day Torre Annunziata, **Oplontis** (☏081 857 53 47; www. pompeiisites.org; Via dei Sepolcri, Torre Annunziata; adult/reduced incl Boscoreale €7/2; ☉8.30am-7.30pm, last entry 6pm Apr-Oct, 8.30am-5pm, last entry 3.30pm Nov-Mar; ☒Circumvesuviana to Torre Annunziata) was once a seafront suburb under the administrative control of Pompeii. First discovered in the 18th century, only two of its houses have been unearthed, and only one, **Villa Poppaea**, is open to the public. This villa is a magnificent example of an *otium* villa (a residential building used for rest and recreation), and may once have belonged to Emperor Nero's second wife.

The Drive ≫ This brief 5km jaunt has you once again heading south on the SS18 to SS268 (Via Settetermini), which leads through scruffy Neapolitan suburbs to Boscoreale.

Herculaneum Roman ruins

⑦ Boscoreale

Some 3km north of Pompeii, the archaeological site of **Boscoreale** (☎081 857 53 47; www.pompeiisites.org; Via Settetermini; adult/reduced incl Oplontis €7/2; ☺8.30am-7.30pm, last entry 6pm Apr-Oct, 8.30am-6.30pm, last entry 5pm Nov-Mar; ⓡ Circumvesuviana to Villa Regina–Antiquarium) consists of a rustic country villa dating back to the 1st century BC, and a fascinating antiquarium showcasing artefacts from Pompeii, Herculaneum and the surrounding region. Note that the villa was closed at the time of writing but the antiquarium was open to visitors.

The Drive ≫ Head straight back down the SS268 for 1.4km all the way back to the SS18, which will take you through about 2km of scruffy suburbs right up next to the ruins of Pompeii.

TRIP HIGHLIGHT

⑧ Pompeii

Nothing piques human curiosity like a mass catastrophe, and few beat the ruins of **Pompeii** (☎081 857 53 47; www.pompeiisites.org; entrances

PASS TO THE PAST

If you plan on blitzing the archaeological sites around Pompeii, consider purchasing a multi-attraction ticket (adult/reduced €18/2). Valid for three days, the pass includes entry to Pompeii, Boscoreale and Oplontis. The ticket is available at the ticket offices of all three sites.

at Porta Marina & Piazza Anfiteatro; adult/reduced €15/2; ⊙9am-7.30pm Mon-Fri, from 8.30am Sat & Sun, last entry 6pm Apr-Oct, 9am-5.30pm Mon-Fri, from 8.30am Sat & Sun, last entry 3.30pm Nov-Mar; ⊠Circumvesuviana to Pompei Scavi–Villa dei Misteri), a stark reminder of Vesuvius' malign forces.

Of Pompeii's original 66 hectares, 44 have now been excavated, with new discoveries unearthed regularly. Audio guides (€8) are a sensible investment, and a good guidebook will help – try *Pompeii* published by Electa Napoli. To do justice to the site, allow at least three hours.

Highlights include the 1st-century BC **Terme Suburbane**, famous for its risqué frescoes, and the **foro**, ancient Pompeii's main piazza. To the northeast of the *foro*, the **Lupanare** (brothel) harbours a series of erotic frescoes that originally served as a menu for clients. At the far east of the site, the **Anfiteatro** is the oldest known Roman amphitheatre in existence. Over on the

opposite side of town, the **Villa dei Misteri**, one of the site's most complete structures, contains the remarkable fresco *Dionysiac Frieze*. One of the world's largest ancient paintings, it depicts the initiation of a bride-to-be into the cult of Dionysus, the Greek god of wine.

🍴 p301

The Drive ≫ The 9km trip from Pompeii begins heading south along the SS145 (Corso Italia). It will take you through a mixture of suburbs and small farms. Ahead, you will see the mountains of the Amalfi Coast rear up. The ancient villas of Stabiae are just east of Corso Italia, off Via Giuseppe Cosenza.

❾ Castellammare di Stabia

South of Oplontis in modern-day Castellammare di Stabia, **Stabiae** (☎081 857 53 47; www.pompeiisites.org; Via Passeggiata Archeologica, Castellammare di Stabia; ⊙8.30am-7.30pm, last entry 6pm Apr-Oct, 8.30am-5pm, last entry 3.30pm Nov-Mar; ⊠Circumvesuviana to Via Nocera) was once a popular resort for wealthy

Romans. It stood on the slopes of the Varano hill overlooking the entire Bay of Naples, and according to ancient historian Pliny it was lined for miles with extravagant villas. You can visit two of these frescoed villas: the 1st-century-BC Villa Arianna and the larger Villa San Marco, said to measure more than 11,000 sq metres.

The Drive ≫ This trip is a bit longer, at 21km, than the last few. Head back to the SS145, which will soon head over to the coast. Enjoy beautiful views over the Bay of Naples as you wind your way past Vico Equense, Meta and Piano di Sorrento to Sorrento.

❿ Sorrento

For an unabashed tourist town, Sorrento still manages to preserve the feeling of a civilised coastal retreat. Even the souvenirs are a cut above the norm, with plenty of fine old shops selling ceramics, lacework and marquetry items. It is also the spiritual home of *limoncello,* a delicious lemon liqueur traditionally made from the zest of Femminello St Teresa lemons, also known as Sorrento lemons. Its tart sweetness makes the perfect nightcap, as well as a brilliant flavouring for both sweet and savoury dishes.

🛏 p301, p309, p319

Eating & Sleeping

Naples ❶

✖ Pizzeria Gino Sorbillo
Pizza €

(☎081 44 66 43; www.sorbillo.it; Via dei Tribunali 32; pizzas from €4; ☺noon-3.30pm & 7-11.30pm Mon-Sat; 🔊; MDante) Day in, day out, this cult-status pizzeria is besieged by hungry hordes. While debate may rage over whether Gino Sorbillo's pizzas are the best in town, there's no doubt that his giant, wood-fired discs – made using organic flour and tomatoes – will have you licking fingertips and whiskers. Head in superearly or prepare to wait.

✖ Da Ettore
Neapolitan €€

(☎081 764 35 78; Via Gennaro Serra 39; meals €25; ☺1-3pm & 8-10pm Tue-Sat, 1-3pm Sun; 🔊; 🚌R2 to Via San Carlo, MChiaia-Monte di Dio) This homey, eight-table trattoria has an epic reputation. Scan the walls for famous fans like comedy great Totò, and a framed passage from crime writer Massimo Siviero, who mentions Ettore in one of his tales. The draw is solid regional cooking, which includes one of the best *spaghetti alle vongole* (spaghetti with clams) in town. Book two days ahead for Sunday lunch.

🛏 Schiara
B&B €

(☎338 9264453, 081 033 09 77; www.maisonsdecharme.it; Vico Volpicelli 20; s €30-85, d €50-100, tr €65-110, q €80-125; ❄🔊; MDante) Schiara has five contemporary rooms, each with en-suite bathroom and playful details inspired by southern Italian themes. The 'Miti' room comes with its own soaking tub, while the upstairs 'Riti' room has a kitchenette and private rooftop terrace. All guests have access to a gorgeous outdoor terrace and communal rooftop garden with sunbeds and bewitching views.

🛏 La Ciliegina Lifestyle Hotel
Boutique Hotel €€€

(☎081 1971 8800; www.cilieginahotel.it; Via PE Imbriani 30; d from €200; ❄@🔊; MMunicipio) An easy walk from the hydrofoil terminal, this chic, contemporary slumber spot is a hit with fashion-conscious urbanites. Spacious white rooms are splashed with blue and red accents, each with top-of-the-range Hästens beds, flat-screen TVs and marble-clad bathrooms with a water-jet Jacuzzi shower.

Herculaneum ❸

✖ Viva Lo Re
Neapolitan €€

(☎081 739 02 07; www.vivalore.it; Corso Resina 261, Ercolano; meals €32; ☺noon-3.30pm & 7.30-11.30pm Tue-Sat, noon-3.30pm Sun; 🔊) Whether you're after an inspired meal or a simple glass of vino, this refined yet relaxed *osteria* (casual tavern) is a solid choice. The wine list is extensive and impressive, while the menu offers competent, produce-driven regional cooking with subtle modern twists. For an appetite-piquing overview, start with the multitaste *antipasto Viva Lo Re*.

Pompeii ❽

✖ President
Campanian €€€

(☎081 850 72 45; www.ristorantepresident.it; Piazza Schettini 12; meals €80, tasting menus €80-120; ☺noon-3.30pm & 7pm-late Tue-Sun; 🚉FS to Pompei, Circumvesuviana to Pompei Scavi–Villa dei Misteri) At the helm of this Michelin-starred standout is charming owner-chef Paolo Gramaglia, whose passion for local produce, history and culinary whimsy translates into bread made to ancient Roman recipes, yellowtail carpaccio with bitter orange and citrus zest, lemon emulsion and buffalo mozzarella, or impeccably glazed duck breast lifted by vinegar cherries, orange sauce and nasturtium.

Sorrento ❿

🛏 Hotel Cristina
Hotel €€

(☎081 878 35 62; www.hotelcristinasorrento.it; Via Privata Rubinacci 6, Sant'Agnello; d/tr/q from €150/220/240; ☺Mar-Oct; P❄🔊🏊) Located high above Sant'Agnello, this hotel has superb views, particularly from the swimming pool. The spacious rooms have sea-view balconies and combine inlaid wooden furniture with contemporary flourishes such as Philippe Starck chairs. There's an in-house restaurant and a free shuttle bus to/from Sorrento's Circumvesuviana train station.

Southern Larder

28

From the Amalfi Coast to Paestum, this trip packs in both jaw-dropping natural beauty and mouthwatering cuisine built on fresh fish, sun-kissed vegetables and the world's finest mozzarella.

TRIP HIGHLIGHTS

0 km

Sorrento
Civilised coastal resort and spiritual home of *limoncello* liqueur

118 km

Paestum
Glorious Greek ruins and the world's finest mozzarella

Pimonte

Cetara

START ① ⑥ ⑦

0 km

Conca dei Marini
Seaside birthplace of the scrumptious *sfogliatella* pastry

⑩

FINISH

55 km

Amalfi
A medieval naval power famous for its *scialatielli* pasta

3–4 DAYS
119KM / 73 MILES

GREAT FOR...

🍷 🌳

BEST TIME TO GO

Spring for sunny, clear weather; early autumn for abundant produce.

📷 ESSENTIAL PHOTO

Capture the hypnotically terraced cliffs of Agerola at sunset.

☑ BEST FOR FOODIES

Going to mozzarella's source in Paestum.

28 Southern Larder

Breathtaking natural beauty aside, this trip is a gourmand's Elysium. Food lovers flock to the Amalfi and Cilento coasts from across the globe for local specialities such as *limoncello* (lemon liqueur), ricotta-stuffed *sfogliatella* pastries, and wildly creamy mozzarella made from water-buffalo milk. Burn off the extra calories hiking the Amalfi's jaw-dropping coastal trails or clambering over Paestum's robust Greek ruins.

TRIP HIGHLIGHT

1 Sorrento

Most people come to seaside Sorrento as a pleasant stopover between Capri, Naples and the Amalfi Coast. And while it does offer dramatic views of the Bay of Naples and an upbeat holiday vibe, gluttons converge here for a very specific treat: *limoncello,* a simple lemon liqueur made from the zest of lemons (preferably the local Femminello St Teresa lemons), plus sugar

and grain alcohol. It's traditionally served after dinner in chilled ceramic cups, and its combination of sweetness and biting tartness makes for a satisfying culinary epilogue.

 p301, 309, 319

The Drive » Head north on the SS145, including a beautiful stretch along the Bay of Naples, for 12km to Vico Equense.

---

② Vico Equense

Known to the Romans as Aequa, Vico Equense is a small clifftop town east of Sorrento. Largely bypassed by international tourists, it's a laid-back, authentic place worth a quick stopover, if only to experience some of the famous pizza served by the metre at the justly celebrated **Ristorante & Pizzeria da Gigino** (☑081 879 83 09; www.pizzametro.it; Via Nicotera 15; pizza per metre €28-38; ⓧnoon-1.30am; 🔊🚹). Save room for some superb, made-from-scratch gelato at **Gabriele** (☑081 879 87 44; www.gabrieleitalia.com; Corso Umberto I 8; gelato from €2; ⓧ9am-2pm & 4pm-midnight Wed-Mon, daily Jul & Aug), another local institution.

The Drive » From Vico Equense to Pimonte is 18km. You'll again hug the beautiful Bay of Naples for a while, reaching the turnoff for the SR ex SS366 in Castellammare di Stabia. From here, head inland and uphill as you wind your way to Pimonte.

---

③ Pimonte

Tucked into the mountains in the easternmost end of the Amalfi peninsula, this small rural town is a far cry from the high-rolling coast, with tractors trundling through the narrow streets. Make a point of stopping at **Bar Pasticceria Palummo** (☑081 879 28 63; www.facebook.com/barpasticceriapalummo; Piazza Roma 27, Pimonte; pastries & cakes from €1.20; ⓧ6.30am-late, closed Tue winter; 🚹) for its cult-status *torta palummo*, a delicious concoction of *pan di spagna* (sponge cake) and almond cream. For a satisfying savoury snack, seek out the *taralli noci e provolone del monaco*, crunchy, savoury biscuits made with walnuts and a semi-hard local cheese.

The Drive » The 8km drive from Pimonte to Agerola takes you along a winding road through forested countryside along the SR ex SS366.

Acerno

Montecorvino

Eboli

Battipaglia

Sele

SP175

Capaccio Scalo

Paestum

FINISH ⑩

Parco Nazionale del Cilento e Vallo di Diano

LINK YOUR TRIP

27 Shadow of Vesuvius

From Sorrento, follow this itinerary in reverse, heading around the Bay of Naples to wander the ruins of Pompeii and Herculaneum, brave the slopes of Vesuvius, and conquer high-energy Naples.

29 Amalfi Coast

Vico Equense kicks off this week-long adventure of hairpin turns and vertical landscapes amid the world's most glamorous stretch of coastline.

④ Agerola

Agerola is located amid a wide green valley approximately 600m above sea level. It is surrounded by natural forests and offers amazing views of the nearby mountains and Mediterranean Sea. Be sure to make a stop here for the legendary *fior di latte* (cow's-milk mozzarella) and *cacio-cavallo* (gourd-shaped traditional curd cheese) produced on the fertile slopes around town.

The Drive » From Agerola, hop back on the SR ex SS366 for a quick 2km jaunt to Bomerano, enjoying a forest of beech trees and a backdrop of mountains thickly quilted with pines. You are now in the depths of the verdant Parco Regionale dei Monti Lattari.

⑤ Bomerano

Just a stone's throw from Agerola, you can easily follow your nose to tiny Bomerano for delicious buffalo-milk yogurt, an ultra-rich, mildly tangy and creamy treat. While in town, you can also feast your eyes on the ornate ceiling frieze in the 16th-century **Chiesa San Matteo Apostolo** (Piazza Paolo Capasso 56, Bomerano; ⊙7.30am-5pm summer, 7.30am-noon & 3-5pm winter).

The Drive » From Bomerano to Conca dei Marini, continue on the same road, SS366, for 9km as it winds dramatically down to the sea, with strategically placed lookouts along the way. From the SR ex SS366, you will do more switchbacking down to the town of Conca dei Marini itself.

TRIP HIGHLIGHT

⑥ Conca dei Marini

This charmingly picturesque fishing village has been beloved by everyone from Princess Margaret to Gianni Agnelli, Jacqueline Onassis and Carlo Ponti. Work up an appetite with an excursion to the **Grotta dello Smeraldo** (admission €5; ⊙9am-4pm), a seaside cavern where the waters glow an eerie emerald green. Then head back to the town for a *sfogliatella*, a scrumptious shell-shaped, ricotta-stuffed pastry that was probably invented here in the 18th century in the monastery of Santa Rosa. The local pastry is even honoured with its own holiday: the first Sunday in August.

The Drive » Head northeast on the SS163 to the town of Amalfi.

TRIP HIGHLIGHT

⑦ Amalfi

A picturesque ensemble of whitewashed buildings and narrow alleyways set around a sun-kissed central piazza, Amalfi is the main centre on the Amalfi Coast. To glean a sense of its medieval history, explore the hidden lanes that run parallel

DETOUR: CAPRI

Start: ① Sorrento

A mass of limestone rock that rises sheer through impossibly blue water, Capri (*ca*-pri) is the perfect microcosm of Mediterranean appeal – a smooth cocktail of chi-chi piazzas and cool cafes, Roman ruins and rugged seascapes. Need any more reason to go?

OK, here's one more: the *torta caprese*. Back in the 1920s, when an absent-minded baker forgot to add flour to the mix of a cake order, a great dessert was born. Now an Italian chocolate-and-almond (or chocolate-and-walnut) cake that is traditionally gluten-free, it is named for the island of Capri from which it originated. The cake has a thin hard shell covering a moist interior. It is usually covered with a light dusting of fine powdered sugar, and sometimes made with a small amount of Strega or other liqueur. **Alilauro** (☎081 807 18 12; www.alilauro.it) runs up to 12 daily hydrofoils from Sorrento to Capri (€20.70, 20 minutes).

ANTON_IVANOV/SHUTTERSTOCK ©

Sorrento

to the main street, with their steep stairways, covered porticos and historic shrine niches. And of course, gourmets shouldn't miss *scialatielli*. A fresh pasta resembling short, slightly widened strips of *tagliatelle*, it is a local speciality, most commonly accompanied by zucchini and mussels or clams, or a simple sauce of fresh cherry tomatoes and garlic.

🍴 🛏 p309

The Drive » It's about 15km on the SS163 from Amalfi to Cetara. Silver birches and buildings draped in bougainvillea add to the beauty of the drive.

8 Cetara

A picturesque tumbledown fishing village, Cetara is also a gastronomic highlight. Tuna and anchovies are the local specialities, especially the sauce from the latter. Known as *colatura di alici*, it flavours homemade pasta dishes like *scialatielli* with local yellow tomatoes and ravioli stuffed with buffalo mozzarella at Cetara Punto e Pasta (p309), a humble, affordable eatery a short walk up from the beach.

🍴 p309

The Drive » Head northeast on SS163 for Salerno. En route, colourful wildflowers spill over white stone walls as you travel the sometimes hair-raising 11km along the coast.

9 Salerno

Salerno may seem like a bland big city after the Amalfi Coast's glut of pretty towns, but the place has a charming, if gritty, individuality, especially around its vibrant *centro storico* (historic centre). Don't miss the **Duomo** (📞089 23 13 87; www.cattedraledisalerno.it; Piazza Alfano; ⏱8.30am-8pm Mon-Sat, 8.30am-1pm & 4-8pm Sun), built in the 11th

Amalfi Coast Amalfi

century and graced by a magnificent main entrance, the 12th-century **Porta dei Leoni**. And for *torta di ricotta e pera* (ricotta-and-pear tart), Salerno is the *ne plus ultra*. This dessert is an Amalfi Coast speciality, deriving its unique tang from the local sheep's-milk ricotta.

🛏 p309

The Drive » Head south on the SP175 and hug the coast all the way. Lush palm and lemon trees and the sparkling sea are your escorts for this 38km drive to Paestum.

TRIP HIGHLIGHT

⑩ Paestum

Work up an appetite amid Paestum's Unesco-listed Greek **temples** (Area Archeologica di Paestum; ☎0828 81 10 23; www.museopaestum.beniculturali.it; adult/reduced incl museum €12/2, ruins only €8/2; ◷8.30am-7.30pm daily, last entry 6.50pm, museum closed Mon), some of the best-preserved in the world. Then head to **Tenuta Vannulo** (☎0828 72 78 94; www.vannulo.it; Via G Galilei

101, Capaccio Scalo; 1hr group tour €5; ◷9.30am-5pm daily, tours 9am-noon Mon-Sat), a 10-minute drive from Paestum, for a superbly soft and creamy mozzarella made from the organic milk of water buffalo. Group tours are available (reservations are essential) but you can also stop just to buy the cheese. Be warned, though, it usually sells out by early afternoon.

🛏 p309

Eating & Sleeping

Sorrento ❶

✕ La Cantinaccia
del Popolo   Neapolitan €

(☎366 1015497; Vico Terzo Rota 3; meals €21; ⏱11am-3pm & 7-11pm Tue-Sun) Festooned with garlic and with cured hams hanging from the ceiling, this down-to-earth favourite proves that top-notch produce and simplicity are the keys to culinary success. A case in point is the *spaghetti al pomodoro*, a basic dish of pasta and tomato that bursts with flavour, vibrancy and balance. For extra authenticity, it's served directly to you in the pan.

Amalfi ❼

✕ Ristorante
La Caravella   Italian €€€

(☎089 87 10 29; www.ristorantelacaravella.it; Via Matteo Camera 12; meals €50-90, tasting menus €50-135; ⏱noon-2.30pm & 7-11pm Wed-Mon; 🅿) A restaurant of artists, art and artistry, Caravella once hosted Andy Warhol. No surprise that it doubles up as a de-facto gallery with frescoes, creative canvases and a ceramics collection. And then there's the food on the seven-course tasting menu, prepared by some of the finest culinary Caravaggios in Italy.

🛏 DieciSedici   B&B €€

(☎089 87 22 52; www.diecisedici.it; Piazza Municipio 10-16; d from €145; ⏱Mar-Oct; 🅿) DieciSedici (1016) dresses up an old medieval palace in the kind of style that only the Italians can muster. The half-dozen rooms dazzle with chandeliers, mezzanine floors, glass balconies and gorgeous linens. Two rooms (the Junior Suite and Family Classic) come complete with kitchenettes. All have satellite TV, air-con and Bose sound systems.

Cetara ❽

✕ Cetara Punto e Pasta   Campanian €€

(☎089 26 11 09; Corso Garibaldi 14; meals €25; ⏱noon-4pm & 7-11.30pm Mon, Wed, Thu & Sun, 11.30am-midnight Fri & Sat) This tiny eating joint in salt-of-the-earth Cetara is barely larger than a studio flat, with six tables and an open kitchen from which the industrious owner-chef performs minor miracles with local fish and homemade pasta. The menu is scrawled on a blackboard. Don't leave before tasting the fresh-off-the-boat *alici* (anchovies) ground deliciously into a fishy pesto.

Salerno ❾

🛏 Hotel Montestella   Hotel €€

(☎089 22 51 22; www.hotelmontestella.it; Corso Vittorio Emanuele II 156; d €90-125, tr €95-160; ❄ @ 🛜) Within walking distance of just about anywhere worth going to, the modern, if slightly bland, Montestella is on Salerno's main pedestrian thoroughfare, halfway between the *centro storico* and train station. Although some rooms are quite small, all are light and contemporary, with firm beds and patterned feature walls.

Paestum ❿

🛏 Casale Giancesare
Villa Agricola   B&B €

(☎0828 199 96 14; www.casalegiancesare. com/en; Via Giancesare 8, Capaccio Paestum; s €50-120, d €60-150, 4-person apt from €80-185; 🅿 ❄ @ 🛜 ❄) A 19th-century former farmhouse, this elegantly decorated, stone-clad B&B is run by the delightful Voza family, who will happily ply you with their homemade wine, *limoncello* and marmalades; they even make their own olive oil. The B&B is located 2.5km from Paestum and is surrounded by vineyards and olive and mulberry trees; views are marvellous, particularly from the swimming pool.

Classic Trip

Amalfi Coast

29

Not for the faint-hearted, this trip along the Amalfi Coast tests your driving skill on a 100km stretch, featuring dizzying hairpin turns and pastel-coloured towns draped over sea-cliff scenery.

TRIP HIGHLIGHTS

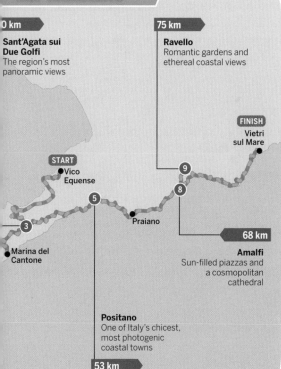

0 km

Sant'Agata sui Due Golfi
The region's most panoramic views

75 km

Ravello
Romantic gardens and ethereal coastal views

FINISH
Vietri sul Mare

9

START
Vico Equense

8

3

Praiano

Marina del Cantone

68 km

Amalfi
Sun-filled piazzas and a cosmopolitan cathedral

Positano
One of Italy's chicest, most photogenic coastal towns

53 km

7 DAYS
100KM / 62 MILES

GREAT FOR...

BEST TIME TO GO

June or September for beach weather without the peak summer crowds.

ESSENTIAL PHOTO

Positano's vertiginous stack of pastel-coloured houses cascading down to the sea.

☑ BEST FOR OUTDOORS

Hiking Ravello and its environs.

29 Amalfi Coast

This trip is all about dramatic landscapes, taking you where mountains plunge seaward in a stunning vertical landscape of precipitous crags, forests and fabled fishing towns. Stops include the celebrated coastal resorts of Positano and Amalfi, as well as serene, mountain-top Ravello, famed for its gardens and views. Cars are useful for inland exploration, as are the walking trails that provide a wonderful escape from the built-up coastal clamour.

1 Vico Equense

The Bay of Naples is justifiably famous for its pizza, invented here as a savoury way to highlight two local specialities: mozzarella and sun-kissed tomatoes. Besides its pretty little *centro storico* (historic centre), this little clifftop town overlooking the Bay of Naples claims some of the region's top pie, including a by-the-metre version at cult-status **Ristorante & Pizzeria da Gigino** (☎081 879 83 09; www.pizzametro.it; Via Nicotera 15; pizza per metre €28-38; ☻noon-1.30am; 🛜🍴).

The Drive ≫ From Vico Equense to Sorrento, your main route will be the SS145 roadway for 12km. Expect to hug the sparkling coastline after Marina di Equa before venturing inland around Meta.

2 Sorrento

On paper, cliff-straddling Sorrento is a place to avoid – a package-holiday centre with few sights, no beach to speak of, and a glut of brassy English-style pubs. In reality, it's strangely appealing, its laid-back southern Italian charm resisting all attempts to swamp it in souvenir tat and graceless development.

According to Greek legend, it was in Sorrento's waters that the mythical sirens once lived. Sailors of antiquity were powerless to resist the beautiful song of these charming maidens-cum-monsters, who would lure them to their doom.

🍴🛏 p301, p309, p319

The Drive ≫ Take the SS145 for 8km to Sant'Agata sui Due Golfi. Sun-dappled village streets give way to forest as you head further inland.

TRIP HIGHLIGHT

3 Sant'Agata sui Due Golfi

Perched high in the hills above Sorrento, sleepy Sant'Agata sui Due Golfi

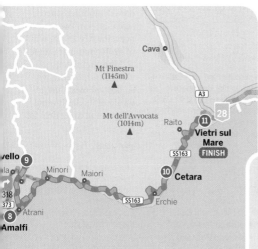

LINK YOUR TRIP

27 Shadow of Vesuvius

Follow the curve of the Bay of Naples, from simmering Vesuvius to loud, gregarious Naples.

28 Southern Larder

From Sorrento to Paestum, this trip savours the flavours of Campania's bountiful coast.

Classic Trip

commands spectacular views of the Bay of Naples on one side and the Bay of Salerno on the other (hence its name, Saint Agatha on the Two Gulfs). The best viewpoint is the **Convento del Deserto** (Monastero di San Paolo; ☎081 878 01 99; Via Deserto; ☺grounds 8am-7pm, viewpoint 10am-noon & 5-7pm summer, 10am-noon & 3-5pm winter), a Carmelite convent 1.5km uphill from the village centre. It's a knee-wearing hike, but make it to the top and you're rewarded with fabulous 360-degree vistas.

The Drive ≫ From Sant'Agata sui Due Golfi to Marina del Cantone it's a 9km drive, the last part involving some serious hairpin turns. Don't let the gorgeous sea views distract you.

❹ **Marina del Cantone**

From **Nerano**, where you'll park, a beautiful hiking trail leads down to the stunning Bay of Ieranto and one of the coast's top swimming spots, Marina del Cantone. This unassuming village with its small pebble beach is a lovely, tranquil place to stay as well as a popular diving destination. The village also has a reputation as a gastronomic hotspot and VIPs regularly catch a boat over from Capri to dine on superlative seafood at **Lo Scoglio** (☎081 808 10 26; www.hotelloscoglio.com; Piazza delle Sirene 15, Marina del Cantone; meals €60; ☺12.30-5pm & 7.30-11pm).

The Drive ≫ First, head back up that switchback to Sant'Agata sui Due Golfi. Catch the SS145 and then the SS163 as they weave their way along bluffs and cliff sides to Positano.

WALK OF THE GODS

Probably the best-known walk on the Amalfi Coast is the three-hour, 12km **Sentiero degli Dei**, which follows the high ridge linking Praiano to Positano. The walk commences in the heart of **Praiano**, where a thigh-challenging 1000-step start takes you up to the path itself. The route proper is not advised for vertigo sufferers: it's a spectacular, meandering trail along the top of the mountains, with caves and terraces set dramatically in the cliffs and deep valleys framed by the brilliant blue of the sea. You'll eventually emerge at Nocelle (p315), from where a series of steps will take you through the olive groves and deposit you on the road just east of **Positano**.

Most of the 24km offer stunning sea views.

TRIP HIGHLIGHT

❺ **Positano**

The pearl in the pack, Positano is the coast's most photogenic and expensive town. Its steeply stacked houses are a medley of peaches, pinks and terracottas, and its near-vertical streets (many of which are, in fact, staircases) are lined with voguish shop displays, elegant hotels and smart restaurants. Look closely, though, and you'll find reassuring signs of everyday reality – crumbling stucco, streaked paintwork and occasionally a faint whiff of problematic drainage.

John Steinbeck visited in 1953 and was so bowled over that he wrote of its dream-like qualities in an article for *Harper's Bazaar*.

🛏 p319

The Drive ≫ From Positano to Praiano it's a quick 6km spin on the SS163, passing Il San Pietro di Positano at the halfway point, then heading southeast along the peninsula's edge.

❻ **Praiano**

An ancient fishing village, a low-key summer resort and, increasingly, a popular centre for the arts, Praiano is a delight. With no centre as such, its whitewashed houses pepper the verdant ridge of Monte Sant'Angelo as it slopes towards Capo Sottile. Exploring involves lots of steps and there are several trails that start from town, including the legendary **Sentiero degli Dei**.

For those who'd rather venture below sea level, **La Boa** (🖉 089 81 30 34; www.laboa.com; Marina di Praia; one dive €70) runs dives that explore the area's coral, marine life and grottoes.

The Drive » From Praiano, Marina di Furore is just 3km further on, past beautiful coves that cut into the shoreline.

---

❼ Marina di Furore

A few kilometres further on, Marina di Furore sits at the bottom of what's known as the fjord of Furore, a giant cleft that cuts through the Lattari mountains. The main village, however, stands 300m above, in the upper Vallone del Furore. A one-horse place that sees few tourists, it breathes a distinctly rural air despite the presence of colourful murals and unlikely modern sculpture.

The Drive » From Marina di Furore to Amalfi, the sparkling Mediterranean Sea will be your escort as you drive eastward along the SS163 coastal road for 6km. Look for Vettica Minore and Conca dei Marini along the way, along with fluffy bunches of fragrant cypress trees.

TRIP HIGHLIGHT

❽ Amalfi

It is hard to grasp that pretty little Amalfi, with its sun-filled piazzas and small beach, was once a maritime superpower with a population of more than 70,000. For one thing, it's not a big place – you can easily walk from one end to the other in about 20 minutes. For another, there are very few historical buildings of note. The explanation is chilling – most of the old city, along with its populace, simply slid into the sea during an earthquake in 1343.

One happy exception is the striking **Cattedrale di Sant'Andrea** (🖉 089 87 35 58; Piazza del Duomo; adult/reduced €3/1 between 10am-5pm; ☉7.30am-8.30pm, closed Nov-Mar), parts of which date from the early 10th century.

DETOUR: NOCELLE

Start: ❺ Positano

A tiny, still relatively isolated mountain village above Positano, Nocelle (450m) commands some of the most memorable views on the entire coast. A world apart from touristy Positano, it's a sleepy, silent place where not much ever happens, nor would its few residents ever want it to. If you want to stay, consider delightful **Villa della Quercia** (🖉 089 812 34 97; http://villalaquercia.com; Via Nocelle 5; d €75-85; ☉Apr–mid-Oct; 🛜), a former monastery with spectacular vistas. Nocelle lies eight very winding kilometres northeast of Positano.

THE BLUE RIBBON DRIVE

Stretching from Vietri sul Mare to Sant'Agata sui Due Golfi near Sorrento, the SS163 – nicknamed the Nastro Azzurro (Blue Ribbon) – remains one of Italy's most breathtaking roadways. Commissioned by Bourbon king Ferdinand II and completed in 1853, it wends its way along the Amalfi Coast's entire length, snaking round impossibly tight curves, over deep ravines and through tunnels gouged out of sheer rock. It's a magnificent feat of civil engineering – although it can be challenging to drive – and in certain places it's not wide enough for two cars to pass, a fact John Steinbeck alluded to in a 1953 essay.

Classic Trip

SVARIOPHOTO/GETTY IMAGES ©

WHY THIS IS A CLASSIC TRIP
CRISTIAN BONETTO, WRITER

From Richard Wagner to Gore Vidal, the Amalfi Coast has bewitched some of the world's most illustrious figures. This is Italy's most arresting coastline, with a natural beauty that borders on the ethereal. While this trip takes in the fabled, sun-drenched towns the Amalfi Coast is famous for, it also sees you hitting the sleepy, hike-friendly hills above, where the views demand a symphony.

Above: Positano
Left: Buffalo mozarella
Right: Ravello

Between 10am and 5pm entrance to the cathedral is through the adjacent **Chiostro del Paradiso** (☏089 87 13 24; Piazza del Duomo; adult/reduced €3/1; ☺9am-7.45pm Jul & Aug, reduced hours Sep-early Jan & Mar-Jun, closed early Jan-Feb), a 13th-century Moorish-style cloister.

Be sure to take the short walk around the headland to neighbouring **Atrani**, a picturesque tangle of whitewashed alleys and arches centred on a lively, lived-in piazza and popular beach.

🍴 🛏 p309, p319

The Drive » Start the 7km trip to Ravello by heading along the coast to Atrani. Here turn inland and follow the SR373 as it climbs the steep hillside in a series of second-gear hairpin turns up to Ravello.

TRIP HIGHLIGHT

9 Ravello

Sitting high in the hills above Amalfi, polished Ravello is a town almost entirely dedicated to tourism. With impeccable artistic credentials – Richard Wagner, DH Lawrence and Virginia Woolf all lounged here – it's known today for its ravishing gardens and stupendous views, the best in the world according to former resident the late Gore Vidal.

To enjoy these views, head south of Ravello's cathedral to the 14th-century tower that

marks the entrance to **Villa Rufolo** (089 85 76 21; www.villarufolo.it; Piazza Duomo; adult/reduced €7/5; 9am-9pm summer, reduced hours winter, tower museum 10am-7pm summer, reduced hours winter). Created by Scotsman Scott Neville Reid in 1853, these gardens combine celestial panoramic views, exotic colours, artistically crumbling towers and luxurious blooms.

Also worth seeking out is the wonderful **Camo** (089 85 74 61; www.museo delcorallo.com; Piazza Duomo 9, Ravello; 10am-noon & 3-4pm Mon-Sat). Squeezed between tourist-driven shops, this very special place is, on the face of it,

a cameo shop. And exquisite they are too, crafted primarily out of coral and shell. But don't stop here; ask to see the treasure trove of a museum beyond the showroom.

 p319

The Drive » Head back down to the SS163 for a 19km journey that twists and turns challengingly along the coast to Cetara. Pine trees and a variety of flowering shrubs line the way.

🔟 Cetara

Cetara is a picturesque, tumbledown fishing village with a reputation as a gastronomic delight. Since medieval times it has been an important fishing centre, and today its deep-sea tuna fleet is considered one of the Mediterranean's most important. At night, fishermen set out in small

boats armed with powerful lamps to fish for anchovies. No surprise then that tuna and anchovies dominate local menus, including at Cetara Punto e Pasta, a sterling seafood restaurant near the small harbour.

p309

The Drive » From Cetara to Vietri sul Mare, head northeast for 6km on the SS163 for more twisting, turning and stupendous views across the Golfo di Salerno.

🔟 Vietri sul Mare

Marking the end of the coastal road, Vietri sul Mare is the ceramics capital of Campania. Although production dates back to Roman times, it didn't take off as an industry until the 16th and 17th centuries. Today, ceramics shopaholics can get their fix at the **Ceramica Artistica Solimene** (089 21 02 43; www.ceramicasolimene. it; Via Madonna degli Angeli 7; 9am-8pm Mon-Fri, 9am-1.30pm & 4-8pm Sat, 9am-1.30pm & 4-7pm Sun), a vast factory outlet with an extraordinary glass and ceramic facade.

For a primer on the history of the area's ceramics, seek out the **Museo della Ceramica** (089 21 18 35; Villa Guariglia, Via Nuova Raito; 9am-3pm Tue-Sat, 9.30am-1pm Sun) in the nearby village of Raito.

DETOUR: RAVELLO WALKS

Start: 9️⃣ **Ravello**

Ravello is the starting point for numerous walks that follow ancient paths through the surrounding Lattari mountains. If you've got the legs for it, you can walk down to **Minori** via an attractive route of steps, hidden alleys and olive groves, passing the picturesque hamlet of **Torello** en route. Alternatively, you can head the other way, to Amalfi, via the ancient village of **Scala**. Once a flourishing religious centre with more than 100 churches and the oldest settlement on the Amalfi Coast, Scala is now a pocket-sized, sleepy place where the wind whistles through empty streets, and gnarled locals go patiently about their daily chores.

Eating & Sleeping

Sorrento ②

✖ Soul & Fish — Seafood €€

(📞081 878 21 70; Marina Grande; meals
€38-46; 🕐noon-2.30pm & 7-10.30pm, closed
Nov-Easter; 🛜) Soul & Fish has a hipper vibe
than Marina Grande's no-nonsense seafood
restaurants. Your bread comes in a bag, your
dessert might come in a Kilner jar and your
freshly grilled fish with a waiter ready to slice
it up before your eyes. The decor is more
chic beach shack than sea-shanty dive bar,
with wooden decks, director chairs and puffy
cushions.

🛏 Palazzo Marziale — Boutique Hotel €€€

(📞081 807 44 06; www.palazzomarziale.com;
Largo San Francesco 2; d/ste from €220/455;
❄🛜) From cascading vines, Chinese porcelain
urns and Persian rugs in the lobby lounge,
to antique furniture, *objets* and artworks in
the hallways, and inlaid wood in the lift, this
sophisticated, 11-room hideaway is big on
details. The family's elegant tastes extend
to the rooms, resplendent with high ceilings,
chaises longues and classy mattresses and
linens.

Positano ⑤

🛏 Albergo California — Hotel €€

(📞089 87 53 82; www.hotelcaliforniapositano.it;
Via Cristoforo Colombo 141; d €150-190; 🕐Mar–
mid-Oct; 🅿❄🛜) If you were to choose the
best place to take a quintessential Positano
photo, it might be from the balcony of this
hotel. But the view isn't all you get. The rooms
in the older part of this grand 18th-century
palace are magnificent, with original ceiling
friezes and decorative doors. New rooms are
simply decorated but tasteful, spacious and
minimalist.

Amalfi ⑧

✖ Le Arcate — Italian €€

(📞089 87 13 67; Largo Orlando Buonocore,
Atrani; pizzas from €6, meals €30; 🕐12.30-
3.30pm & 7.30-11.30pm daily Jul & Aug, closed
Mon Sep-Jun; 🛜) If you've had it with the tourist
tumult of Amalfi, try temporarily relocating to
its quieter cousin Atrani to eat al fresco at one
of its traditional restaurants. Arcate is right
on the seafront with huge parasols shading
its sprawl of tables, and a dining room in a
stone-walled natural cave. Fresh fish and decent
pizzas (including gluten-free options) feature
on the menu.

🛏 Hotel Luna Convento — Hotel €€€

(📞089 87 10 02; www.lunahotel.it; Via
Pantaleone Comite 33; d from €320; 🕐mid-
Mar–Dec; 🅿❄@🛜🛝) This former convent
was founded by St Francis in 1222 and has
been a hotel for some 200 years. Rooms in the
original building are in the former monks' cells,
but there's nothing poky about the bright tiles,
balconies and seamless sea views. The newer
wing is equally beguiling, with religious frescoes
over the beds. The cloistered courtyard is
magnificent.

Ravello ⑨

✖ Da Salvatore — Italian €€

(📞089 85 72 27; Via della Repubblica 2; meals
€38-45, pizzas from €5; 🕐12.30-3pm & 7.30-
10pm Tue-Sun Easter-Nov) Located just before
the bus stop, Da Salvatore doesn't merely rest
on the laurels of its spectacular terrace views.
This is one of the coast's best restaurants,
serving arresting dishes that showcase local
produce with creativity, flair and whimsy; your
premeal *benvenuto* (welcome) may include
an *aperitivo* of Negroni encased in a white-
chocolate ball.

Cilento Coastal Trail

30

Following the wild and rugged coastline of the Cilento peninsula, this trip takes in atmospheric fishing villages, fascinating hilltop towns and glorious ruins hailing from the region's ancient Greek past.

TRIP HIGHLIGHTS

0 km

Paestum
Three of the world's best-preserved Greek temples

74 km

Velia
A sprawl of Greek, Roman and medieval ruins

TART

cciaroli ●

7

8

San Giovanni a Piro ●

● Sapri
FINISH

9

km

isciotta
abyrinthine village treets and dizzying iews

95 km

Palinuro
A laid-back resort with a long, inviting beach

4–5 DAYS
143KM / 89 MILES

GREAT FOR...

BEST TIME TO GO
Spring and autumn for hikers; high summer for beach types.

ESSENTIAL PHOTO
Capture rugged coast and royal-blue sea from hilltop Pisciotta.

BEST FOR HISTORY
Paestum's magnificent ancient Greek temples.

30 | Cilento Coastal Trail

Barely accessible by road until the 20th century, the jagged cliff-bound Cilento peninsula is one of Italy's least-explored stretches of coastline. After flourishing under the Greeks and Romans, the Cilento was abandoned for centuries to the vagaries of Mediterranean pirates. Today, its fishing villages and pretty hill towns remain largely free of mass development, despite long, sandy beaches, pristine blue waters, and superb local seafood.

TRIP HIGHLIGHT

❶ Paestum

The three stately, honey-coloured temples (p308) at Paestum are among the best preserved in Magna Graecia – the Greek colonies that once held sway over much of southern Italy. The Greeks capitulated to the Romans in 273 BC, and Poseidonia, as it was known, remained a thriving trading port until the fall of the Roman Empire.

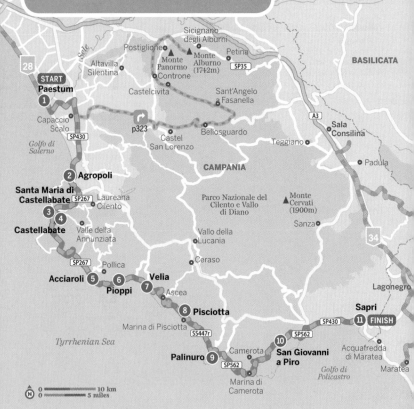

Buy tickets to the temples at the **museum**, itself a fascinating repository of frescoes, statues and archaeological artefacts, before entering the site's main entrance.

The first structure you encounter is the 6th-century-BC **Tempio di Cerere** (Temple of Ceres), the smallest of the three temples, which later served as a Christian church. As you head south, you can pick out the remnants of the Roman city, including an amphitheatre, housing complexes and the **foro** (forum). Beyond lies the **Tempio di Nettuno** (Temple of Neptune), the largest and best preserved of the three temples.

Almost next door, the equally beautiful **basilica**

DETOUR: PARCO NAZIONALE DEL CILENTO E VALLO DI DIANO

Start: ① Paestum

Italy's second-largest national park, the **Parco Nazionale del Cilento e Vallo di Diano** (www.cilentoediano.it) occupies the lion's share of the Cilento peninsula. Some of the most interesting and accessible parts lie within an hour's drive northeast of Paestum, in the park's northwest corner. Near the town of **Castelcivita**, you can explore the **Grotte di Castelcivita** (📞0828 77 23 97; www.grottedicastelcivita.com; Piazzale N Zonzi, Castelcivita; adult/reduced €10/8; ⏱standard tours 10.30am, noon, 1.30pm, 3pm, 4.30pm & 6pm Apr-Sep, 10.30am, noon, 1.30pm & 3pm Mar & Oct; 🅿🚻), a complex of otherworldly prehistoric caves. For hikers, the town of **Sicignano degli Alburni**, capped by a medieval castle, makes a good base for the tough trek up 1742m-high **Monte Panormo**. Finally, the medieval centre of **Postiglione**, crowned by an 11th-century Norman castle, makes for a lovely stroll.

(in reality, a temple to the goddess Hera) is Paestum's oldest surviving monument, dating from the middle of the 6th century BC.

🛏 p309

The Drive » Heading 10km south down the SP430 from Paestum, you quickly start winding into the foothills of the Cilento. Agropoli's historic centre will loom up on the right. Follow signs to the 'Centro Storico'.

- - - - - - - - - - - - - - - - -

② Agropoli

Guarding the northern flank of the Cilento peninsula, the ancient town of Agropoli proffers stunning views across the Gulf of Salerno to the Amalfi Coast. The outskirts are made up of

a rather faceless grid of shop-lined streets, but the historic kernel, occupying a rocky promontory, is a charming tangle of cobbled streets with ancient churches, the remains of a **castle** and superlative views up and down the coast.

The Drive » South of Agropoli, the 13km stretch of the SR ex SS267 turns inland, giving a taste of Cilento's rugged interior, but you'll quickly head west and to the sea.

- - - - - - - - - - - - - - - - -

③ Santa Maria di Castellabate

Because of the danger of sudden pirate attacks, all the coastal towns on the Cilento once consisted of a low-lying coastal

LINK YOUR TRIP

Southern Larder

28 Join this culinary adventure through Campania where this trip begins – amid the ancient ruins of Paestum.

Across the Lucanian Apennines

34 A stunning 20km from Sapri along Basilicata's coastline, Maratea kicks off this journey over the gorgeous Lucanian Apennines to otherworldly Matera.

fishing community and a nearby highly defended hilltop town where the peasants and fishing families could find quick refuge.

These days, the fishing district of Castellabate – known as Santa Maria di Castellabate – has outgrown its hilltop protector, thanks to the town's 4km beach of golden sand. Despite the development, the town's historic centre preserves a palpable southern Italian feel, with dusky-pink and ochre houses blinkered by traditional green shutters. The little harbour is especially charming, with its 19th-century *palazzi* (mansions) and the remnants of a much older castle. Note that these charms can diminish quickly when summer crowds overwhelm the scant parking.

✗ 🏠 p327

The Drive » Just past Santa Maria di Castellabate along the SR ex SS267 is the turnoff to Castellabate. The road then winds through orchards and olive groves for 8km.

----

④ Castellabate

One of the most endearing towns on the Cilento coast, medieval Castellabate clings to the side of a steep hill 280m above sea level. Its summit is marked by the broad **Belvedere di San Costabile**, from where there are sweeping coastal

views, and the shell of a 12th-century castle. The surrounding labyrinth of narrow streets is punctuated by ancient archways, small piazzas and the occasional *palazzo*.

The Drive » Head back down to the SR ex SS267 and follow for 21km. The road leads inland, but you'll see the sea soon enough as you twist down to Acciaroli.

----

⑤ Acciaroli

Despite a growing number of concrete resorts on its outskirts, the tastefully restored historic centre of this fishing village makes it worth a stop, especially for Hemingway lovers. The author spent time here in the early 1950s, and some say he based

Acciaroli

The Old Man and the Sea on a local fisherman.

The Drive >> After Acciaroli, the coastal highway climbs quickly for 8km to Pioppi, proffering stunning views down the Cilento coast to Capo Palinuro.

- - - - - - - - - - - - - - -

6 Pioppi

A tiny, seaside hamlet, Pioppi enjoys culinary fame as the spiritual home of the Mediterranean diet. For more than 30 years, the American medical researcher Dr Ancel Keys lived here, observing the vigorous residents and studying the health benefits of their diet. Join the latest generation of locals on lovely Piazza del Millenario, before heading to the pristine, pale pebble beach a few steps away for a picnic.

The Drive >> By Cilento standards, it's practically a straight shot for 8km along the coastal highway to the archaeological site of Velia. Some 6km further southeast is Ascea, where coastal mountains make way for the small but rich plains that once fed ancient Velia.

❼ Velia

Founded by the Greeks in the mid-6th century BC, and subsequently a popular resort for wealthy Romans, Velia (formerly Elea) was once home to philosophers Parmenides and Zeno. Today, you can wander around the town's evocative ruins at the **Parco Archeologico di Elea Velia** (0974 97 23 96; Contrada Piana di Velia; adult/reduced €3/1.50; ☾9am-90min before sunset, Wed-Mon), and explore intact portions of the original city walls, plus remnants of thermal baths, an Ionic temple, a Roman theatre and even a medieval castle.

The Drive » You are now headed into the most hair-raising stretch of the Cilento's coastal highway, but spectacular views are your reward. Olive trees start multiplying as you near Pisciotta. The total distance is about 10km.

❽ Pisciotta

The liveliest town in the Cilento and also its most dramatic, hilltop Pisciotta consists of a steeply pitched maze of medieval streets. Life centres on the lively main square, Piazza Raffaele Pinto, where the town's largely elderly residents rule the roost. The hills surrounding the town are terraced into rich olive groves and produce particularly prized oil, while local fishermen specialise in anchovies. When their catch is marinated in the local oil, the result is mouthwateringly good.

🍴 🛏 p327

The Drive » The 11km trip begins with a steep descent from Pisciotta, and a straight road to Palinuro. Before reaching town, you'll see its beautiful, miles-long beach.

❾ Palinuro

The Cilento's main resort, Palinuro remains remarkably low-key (and low rise), with a tangible fishing-village feel, though its beaches become crowded in August. Extending past its postcard-pretty harbour, the remarkable 2km-long promontory known as **Capo Palinuro** affords wonderful walking trails and views up and down the coast. Better yet, you can visit its sea cliffs and hidden caves, including Palinuro's own version of Capri's famous Grotta Azzurra, with a similarly spectacular display of water, colour and light. To arrange an excursion, **Da Alessandro** (347 6540931; www.costieradel cilento.it; Spiaggia del Porto di Palinuro; trips from €15; ☾mid-Mar–mid-Nov) runs two-hour trips to the grotto and other local caves.

🍴 p327

The Drive » Begin the 27km drive with a beautiful jaunt along the water before heading inland at Marina di Camerota. Get ready for plenty of sharp turns as you wind up the stunning SR ex SS562.

❿ San Giovanni a Piro

With its tight-knit historic centre and jaw-dropping views across the Gulf of Policastro to the mountains of Basilicata and Calabria, this little agricultural town makes a worthy stop as you wind your way around the wild, southern tip of the Cilento peninsula.

The Drive » The final 21km of this trip begins with a winding descent from San Giovanni a Piro to the pretty port town of Scario; the road flattens out as you make your way around the picturesque Golfo di Policastro.

⓫ Sapri

Set on an almost perfectly round natural harbour, Sapri is the ideal place to wave goodbye to the Cilento. The peninsula's dramatic interior mountains rear up across the beautiful Golfo di Policastro. Admire the views from the town's seafront promenade or from one of its nearby beaches.

Eating & Sleeping

Agropoli ②

✘ Pecora Nera   Pizza €

(☎320 6115112; Piazza della Mercanzia; pizzas €5-12; ⏰7:30pm-1am) Agropoli's self-proclaimed 'black sheep', Pecora Nera has emerged as a new challenger for the title of the town's 'best pizza' and they might just be on to something. The small but slickly furnished pizzeria in a piazza by the port is run by a hip team of *ragazzi* (guys) whose uncluttered pizzas use a light chewy dough and carefully sourced DOP ingredients.

Santa Maria di Castellabate ③

✘ Arlecchino   Seafood €€

(☎0974 96 18 89; Via Guglielmini, Santa Maria di Castellabate; meals €22-40, pizzas from €4; ⏰noon-2.30pm & 7-11pm Mar-Nov; 🚗) Located across from the beach in the pretty southernmost part of Santa Maria, popular Arlecchino has picture windows overlooking the small sweep of sand. Packed to the gills at weekends, the restaurant primarily offers seafood, although the *ravioli salsa di noci* (ravioli in walnut sauce) gives the tuna and sea urchins a run for their money.

✘ Perbacco   Campanian €€

(☎0974 96 18 32; Via Andrea Guglielmini 19, Santa Maria di Castellabate; meals €35-40; ⏰6pm-midnight Wed-Mon, closed Nov) Set opposite the charming town beach, epicure favourite Perbacco offers an expertly curated wine list and unconventional takes on local seafood specialities, like *tortino di alici* (anchovies with smoked cheese, creamed potatoes and eggplant) and ravioli stuffed with sea urchin. Reservations recommended.

⌂ Residenza d'Epoca 1861   Guesthouse €€

(☎0974 96 14 54; www.residenzadepoca1861. it; Lungomare Perrotti, Santa Maria di Castellabate; d €130-160, ste €170; ❇🛜) Occupying an 18th-century mansion on Santa Maria di Castellabate's historic waterfront, this small, impeccably run guesthouse offers sea views from every room, plus creamy white interiors with discreet splashes of modernist colour. There's an affiliated restaurant called Osteria 1861.

Pisciotta ⑧

✘ Osteria del Borgo   Campanian €€

(☎0974 97 01 13; Via Roma 17, Pisciotta; meals €20-35; ⏰noon-3pm & 7-11pm) From your perch on the stone terrace, you'll hear your order loudly repeated to the chef (ie Mamma), followed by the requisite banging of pots and pans. In a land of simple food, this *osteria* is an expert in making things uncomplicated, from the rustic bread to the scalding espresso via stalwart *primi* (first courses) where the prices rarely stray north of €10.

⌂ Marulivo Hotel   Boutique Hotel €€

(☎0974 97 37 92; www.marulivohotel.it; Via Castello, Pisciotta; d €70-140, ste €130-220; ⏰Easter-Oct; ❇🛜) *The* hotel in tiny Pisciotta is a sublime place; a beautifully restored 14th-century monastery daubed with elegant antique touches and crowned with a wisteria-flecked terrace. Great for romance, the 11 handsome rooms feature earthy colours, carefully chosen furnishings, crisp white linen and exposed stone walls. The owners love their village and their enthusiasm is contagious.

Palinuro ⑨

✘ Ristorante Core a Core   Italian €€

(☎0974 93 16 91; www.coreacorepalinuro.it; Via Piano Faracchio 13; meals €30-40; ⏰12.45-2.45pm & 8pm-midnight; 🚗) Ignore the cheesy heart-shaped sign: with its glorious garden setting and great reputation for seafood, Core a Core is your best bet in Palinuro. The *antipasti al mare* (€19.50) is superb, and there's a menu of proper kids' food. Book in advance – it's popular. The restaurant is a 15-minute uphill walk from the centre of Palinuro.

Puglia's Pilgrim Trail

31

From basilicas in Bari to pilgrimage sites on the wild Promontorio del Gargano, this trip spotlights the medieval castles and churches that Puglia's Norman and German conquerors bequeathed the region.

TRIP HIGHLIGHTS

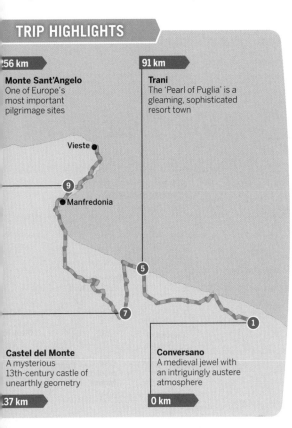

56 km

Monte Sant'Angelo
One of Europe's most important pilgrimage sites

91 km

Trani
The 'Pearl of Puglia' is a gleaming, sophisticated resort town

Vieste

9

Manfredonia

5

7

Castel del Monte
A mysterious 13th-century castle of unearthly geometry

137 km

1

Conversano
A medieval jewel with an intriguingly austere atmosphere

0 km

4 DAYS
312KM / 194 MILES

GREAT FOR...

BEST TIME TO GO

April to June for hiking amid wildflowers. Autumn for mushrooms and mild weather.

ESSENTIAL PHOTO

Capture the isolated mountaintop splendour of the Monte Sant'Angelo.

BEST FOR HISTORY

Conversano's restrained medieval splendour.

31 Puglia's Pilgrim Trail

Both pilgrims and princes have long been partial to this stretch of the Adriatic coast, and you'll understand why as you weave your way from the sun-kissed seaside to fertile inland plains, which together form the basis for Puglia's extraordinary cuisine. All the way to the dramatic Promontorio del Gargano, you'll see evidence of Puglia's medieval golden age, when Norman and Swabian overlords built bristling castles and distinctive Romanesque churches.

TRIP HIGHLIGHT

① Conversano

Conversano's historic centre is a medieval jewel that generates its own austerely intriguing atmosphere. The main attraction is the Norman-Swabian **Castello di Conversano**, which commands views over the coastal plains all the way to Bari. And don't miss the beautiful Romanesque **cathedral** (Largo Cattedrale). Built between the 9th and the 14th centuries, it has a

typical graven portal, large rose window and pointy gabled roof.

The Drive » Head northwest through Puglia's rich agricultural flatlands along the SP240 for the 31km to Bari.

- - - - - - - - - - - - - - - - -

❷ Bari

A lively university town and regional transport hub, Bari is often overlooked by time-poor travellers. But Puglia's capital, and southern Italy's second-largest city, deserves more than a cursory glance. The most interesting area is

0 ━━━━━━━━━━ 30 km
0 ━━━━━━━━━━ 15 miles

Bari Vecchia (Old Bari), an atmospheric warren of tight alleyways, unfussy trattorias and graceful piazzas. In the heart of the district, the 12th-century **Basilica di San Nicola** (☎080 573 71 11; www.basilicasan nicola.it; Piazza San Nicola; ☺7am-8.30pm Mon-Sat, to 10pm Sun) was one of the first Norman churches built in southern Italy. A splendid example of Puglian-Romanesque architecture, it's best known for housing the bones of St Nicholas (aka Santa Claus).

✕ 🛏 p335

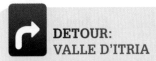

DETOUR: VALLE D'ITRIA

Start: ❶ Conversano

Just south of Conversano rises the great limestone plateau of the Murgia (473m), a strange landscape riddled with holes and ravines through which small streams and rivers gurgle. At the heart of the Murgia lies the idyllic Valle d'Itria, famous for its *trulli*. Unique to Puglia, these Unesco-protected circular stone-built houses have curious conical roofs. The Murgia is also famous for its *masserie*. Modelled on the classical Roman villa, these fortified farmhouses – equipped with oil mills, storehouses, chapels and accommodation for workers and livestock – functioned as self-sufficient communities. These days, many offer stylish country accommodation, including lovely **Biomasseria Lama di Luna** (☎0883 56 95 05, 328 0117375; www.lamadiluna.com; Contrada Lama Di Luna, Montegrosso; s/d from €130/160; ᴾ❄🛜), a working farm redesigned according to principles of green architecture.

LINK YOUR TRIP

33 Salento Surprises
From Bari, head 153km along coastal highways SS16, SS379 and SS613 until you reach jewel-like Lecce, then along the fascinating, beach-lined high heel of the Italian boot.

34 Across the Lucanian Apennines
About 67km south of Bari via the SS96 and SS99 lies Matera, the culmination of this trip over the gorgeous and little-explored Lucanian Apennines.

giano
SS16
240 **Conversano**
❶ START   90km to
SP101 Castellana   33
Grotte
tignano ⊙
Valle d'Itria
p331
Locorotondo

The Drive » A not-very-interesting 19km drive leads to Bitonto. From Bari, follow the SS96 through the city's flat, industrial suburbs to the town of Modugno, where you should connect with the SP231 to Bitonto.

❸ Bitonto

Surrounded as it is by olive groves, it's no surprise Bitonto produces a celebrated extra-virgin oil. However, it is the town's medieval core that makes it worth seeking out. Its magnificent 12th-century **cathedral** is romantically dedicated to St Valentine. There's also an impressive 14th-century **tower**, and smaller medieval churches to refresh the spirit.

The Drive » Heading along the SP231, the flat Puglia landscape becomes increasingly rural, until you reach the outskirts of Ruvo di Puglia, 19km to the west.

❹ Ruvo di Puglia

Situated on the eastern slopes of the Murgia plateau and surrounded by olive and almond orchards, Ruvo is an attractive country town. Its historic core is dominated by a famous 13th-century **cathedral**, a gorgeous example of Puglia's distinctive version of Romanesque architecture. A short walk away, the **Museo Nazionale Jatta** (📞080 361 28 48; http://musei.puglia. beniculturali.it; Piazza Bovio 35, Ruvo; ⏰8.30am-1.30pm Mon-Wed & Fri, to 7.30pm Thu & Sat) showcases an interesting collection of ancient Greek ceramics. And don't leave town without trying the exquisite cakes and pastries made with Ruvo's prized local almonds.

The Drive » Head through fields and olive orchards along the SP2 for 8km to Corato, where you'll catch the SP238 – a

straight shot north for 14km through dozens of olive groves to seaside Trani.

TRIP HIGHLIGHT

❺ Trani

Known as the 'Pearl of Puglia', Trani has a sophisticated feel, particularly in summer when well-heeled visitors pack the bars on the marina. The marina is the place to promenade and watch the boats, while the historic centre, with its medieval churches, glossy limestone streets and faded yet charming *palazzi* (mansions), is enchanting. The most

---

↱ DETOUR: LUCERA

Start: ❽ Canosa di Puglia

About 85km north of Canosa di Puglia, Lucera has one of Puglia's most impressive castles and a handsome old town centre of mellow sand-coloured brick and stone, with chic shops lining wide, shiny stone streets. Frederick II's enormous **castle** (📞800 76 76 06; adult/reduced €3/1; ⏰9am-1pm & 3.30-7.30pm Tue-Sun), built in 1233, lies 14km northwest of the town on a rocky hillock surrounded by a perfect 1km-long pentagonal wall, guarded by 24 towers.

Puglia Vieste

arresting sight is the austere, 12th-century **cathedral** (www.cattedrale trani.it; Piazza del Duomo; campanile €5; ◷8.30am-12.30pm & 3.30-7pm Mon-Sat, 9am-12.30pm & 4-8.30pm Sun Apr-Oct, shorter hours Nov-Mar), white against the deep-blue sea.

🍴 🛏 p335

The Drive » Following the coastline, the SS16 heads quickly into agricultural land until you reach Barletta's suburbs after 15km.

❻ Barletta

Barletta's crusading history is a lot more exotic than the modern-day town, although the historic centre is pretty enough with its **cathedral, colossus**, and fine **castle**. However, the history of the town is closely linked with the nearby archaeological site of **Canne della Battaglia** (☎0883 51 09 92; €2; ◷8.30am-7.30pm Tue-Sun), where Carthaginian Hannibal whipped the Romans. Barletta also has some of the nicest beaches along this stretch of coast.

The Drive » From Barletta it's a straight drive south to Andria along the SS170dir. Continue on the same road and follow as the land begins to rise near Castel del Monte. In all, it's approximately 31km.

TRIP HIGHLIGHT

❼ Castel del Monte

With its unearthly geometry and hilltop location, this 13th-century, Unesco-protected **castle** (☎0883 56 99 97; www.casteldelmonte.beniculturali.it; adult/reduced €10/3.50; ◷10.30am-7.30pm Apr-Sep, 9am-6.30pm Oct-Mar) is visible for miles around. No one knows why Frederick II built this mysterious structure – there's no nearby town or strategic crossroads, and it lacks typical defensive features like a moat or arrow slits. Some theories claim that, in accordance with mid-13th-century beliefs, the octagon represented the union between the circle (representing the sky and the infinite) and square (the Earth and the temporal).

The Drive » From Castel del Monte this leg is 34km, heading northeast along the SS170dir, then picking up the SP234 and SP149 at Montegrosso. The road winds through a hilly and rather barren stretch until you reach the SP231 and the flatter lands around Canosa di Puglia.

- - - - - - - - - - - - - - - - -

8 Canosa di Puglia

Predating the arrival of the Romans by many centuries, this rather drab provincial town was once rich and powerful Canusium, Roman capital of the region. Today you can see remnants of this prosperity in the massive **Arco Traiano**, the **Roman Bridge**,

and the **Basilica di San Leucio**. Once a huge Roman temple, it was converted into a massive Christian basilica in the 4th and 5th centuries. Today only tantalising fragments remain at the **Parco Archeologico di San Leucio**.

The Drive » From Canosa head towards Cerignola on the A14 autostrada. Exit at Cerignola Est and follow the SP77 past olive groves to Manfredonia at the southern end of the Promontorio del Gargano. Join the SS89 and then the SP55 for the climb to hilltop Monte Sant'Angelo. Allow two hours for the 85km drive.

- - - - - - - - - - - - - - - - -

 TRIP HIGHLIGHT

9 Monte Sant'Angelo

One of Europe's most important pilgrimage sites; it was here in AD 490 that St Michael the Archangel is said to have appeared in a grotto. During the Middle Ages, the **Santuario di San**

Michele (☎0884 56 11 50; www.santuariosanmichele.it; Via Reale Basilica; ☉7.30am-7.30pm Jul-Sep, shorter hours rest of year) marked the end of the Route of the Angel, which began in Mont St-Michel in Normandy and passed through Roma (Rome). Today the sanctuary is a remarkable conglomeration of Romanesque, Gothic and baroque elements. Etched bronze and silver doors, cast in Constantinople in 1076, open into the grotto itself. Inside, a 16th-century statue of the archangel covers a sacred spot: the site of St Michael's footprint.

✕ p335

The Drive » From Monte Sant'Angelo, you head back towards the sea, eventually reaching SS89 and then the fiercely winding SP53 as you head to the tip of the peninsula. This 56km drive is the most scenic of the trip.

- - - - - - - - - - - - - - - - -

10 Vieste

Jutting off the Gargano's easternmost promontory into the Adriatic, Vieste is an attractive white-washed town overlooking a lovely sandy beach – a gleaming wide strip flanked by sheer white cliffs and overshadowed by the towering rock monolith, **Scoglio di Pizzomunno**. It's packed in summer and ghostly quiet in winter.

✕ 🛏 p335

DETOUR: ISOLE TREMITI

Start: 10 Vieste

This three-island archipelago is a picturesque vision of rugged cliffs, medieval structures, lonesome caves, sandy coves and thick pine woods – all surrounded by a glittering, dark-blue sea. It's packed to the gills in July and August, but makes a wonderful off-season getaway. Ferries depart in summer from Vieste and Peschici, and year-round from Termoli, about a three-hour drive up the Adriatic coast.

Eating & Sleeping

Bari ❷

✗ Terranima — Puglian €€

(☎0805 21 97 25, 334 6608618; www.
terranima.com; Via Putignani 213; meals €30-35;
⊙noon-3pm daily, 7-11pm Mon-Sat) Peep
through the lace curtains into the cool interior
of this rustic trattoria, where worn flagstone
floors and period furnishings make you feel
like you're dining in someone's front room.
The menu features fabulous regional offerings
such as veal, lemon and caper meatballs, and
sporcamuss, a sweet flaky pastry.

⊨ B&B Casa Pimpolini — B&B €

(☎333 9580740, 0805 21 99 38; www.
casapimpolini.com; Via Calefati 249; s €50-65,
d €75-90; ❄ 🕸) This lovely B&B in Bari's new
town is within easy walking distance to shops,
restaurants and Bari Vecchia (the old town).
The two rooms are warm and welcoming, and
the superb homemade breakfast is an absolute
treat. Great value and great hospitality from the
friendly, well-travelled owner, Dyria.

Trani ❺

✗ Corteinfiore — Seafood €€

(☎0883 50 84 02; www.corteinfiore.it; Via
Ognissanti 18; meals €40-45; ⊙1-2.15pm
Tue-Sun, 8-10.15pm Tue-Sat) The decking, stiff
tablecloths and marquee setting of this famed
Trani seafood restaurant set hopes racing,
and the food, wine and service deliver in full.
Expect lots of seafood, and expect it to be
excellent: try the *frutti di mari antipasti,* or the
Gallipoli prawns with candied lemon. Also rents
delightful rooms (double €120) decked out in
pale colours.

⊨ Palazzo Filisio — Hotel €€

(☎0883 50 09 31; www.palazzofilisio.it; Piazza
Addazi 2; d/ste €145/190; P ❄ 🕸) A lovely
building facing the cathedral and the Adriatic,
the 18th-century Palazzo Filisio houses this
charmingly understated grand hotel. Stylish
rooms were renovated in 2018 with colours
referencing the cobalt Adriatic and the location
is superb. The in-house Regia restaurant (meals

€60) maintains the upmarket vibe with dishes
such as risotto with prawns, asparagus and
black truffle.

Monte Sant'Angelo ❾

✗ Casa li Jalantuúmene — Trattoria €€

(☎0884 56 54 84; www.li-jalantuumene.it;
Piazza de Galganis 5; meals €45; ⊙noon-3pm
& 7.30-10.30pm Wed-Mon; 🍴) This renowned
restaurant owned by well-known chef Gegè
Mangano serves excellent fare amid an intimate
setting. The seasonal menu always features
good vegetarian options, there's a select wine
list and, in summer, tables spill onto the piazza.
There are also four suites on-site (from €100),
decorated in traditional Pugliese style. Chef
Gegè has also opened an informal **wine bar**
(☎087 97 63 21; Via Gambadoro 27; ⊙7.30pm-
late) nearby.

Vieste ❿

✗ Osteria degli Archi — Italian €€

(☎0884 70 51 99; www.osteriadegliarchivieste.
it; Via Ripe 2; meals €35-40; ⊙noon-2.30pm
& 7-11pm) A classy cut above other Vieste
restaurants, Osteria degli Archi offers
innovative spins on established flavours and
recipes. Standout dishes include tartare of
red tuna and gossamer-light ravioli stuffed
with smoked cheese, mint and fennel. Wine
bottles lining the stone walls hint at the
restaurant's excellent wine list with many
Puglian and Salento labels available. Bookings
recommended on summer weekends.

⊨ Relais Parallelo 41 — B&B €€

(☎0884 35 50 09; www.bbparallelo41.it; Via
Forno de Angelis 3; r €120; ⊙Mar-Oct; ❄ 🕸)
This small B&B in an updated *palazzo* in the
midst of the old town has five renovated rooms
decorated with hand-painted ceilings, luxurious
beds and super modern bathrooms. Breakfasts
consist of a buffet, and the reception area acts
as a mini information centre for local activities.
Note that there are minimum stays in July and
August.

Valle d'Itria

With its grey drystone walls, endless oceans of olive trees, and Hobbit-like trulli homes, Puglia's rural heartland sets the backdrop to this tour of the Valle d'Itria.

32

TRIP HIGHLIGHTS

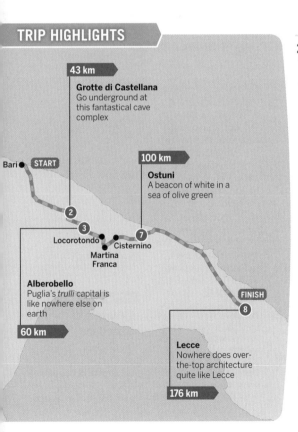

43 km

Grotte di Castellana
Go underground at this fantastical cave complex

Bari ● START

100 km

Ostuni
A beacon of white in a sea of olive green

② ③
Locorotondo ● ⑦ Cisternino
Martina Franca

Alberobello
Puglia's *trulli* capital is like nowhere else on earth

FINISH

⑧

60 km

Lecce
Nowhere does over-the-top architecture quite like Lecce

176 km

2–3 DAYS
176KM / 109 MILES

GREAT FOR...

BEST TIME TO GO

May and June when the weather's warm and the spring flowers are out.

📷 ESSENTIAL PHOTO

Alberobello's *trulli* from the Belvedere Trulli.

☑ BEST FOR FOODIES

A grilled *bombetta* (a ball of local *capocollo* meat) in Cisternino.

32 | Valle d'Itria

It might only be an hour's drive from big-city Bari but the Valle d'Itria is another world. This is farming country, where quiet back roads run past orderly fruit orchards and gnarled, centuries-old olive trees writhe out of the rusty red soil. Attractive hilltop towns harbour whitewashed historic centres and strange *trulli* (circular stone-built houses) litter the rock-strewn landscape. Marking the end of the road is Lecce, Puglia's great baroque city.

---

1 Bari

Start your trip with a blast of urban grit in Bari. Pugila's regional capital and main transport hub is a city of busy, shop-lined boulevards and grand municipal buildings, its large student population ensuring there's always plenty of life in its piazzas, bars and cafes.

Much of the city's grid-patterned centre dates to the 19th century but it's in the tightly-packed Old Town, known as **Bari Vecchia**, that you'll find the city's greatest treasures. Chief among these is the mighty **Basilica di San Nicola** (⏹080 573 71 11; www.basilicasan

nicola.it; Piazza San Nicola; ⏰7am-8.30pm Mon-Sat, to 10pm Sun), a towering Puglian-Romanesque cathedral that houses the miraculous bones of St Nicholas (aka Santa Claus). Nearby, the hulking **Castello Svevo** (Swabian Castle; ⏹080 521 37 04; Piazza Federico II di Svevia; adult/reduced €9/3.50; ⏰8.30am-7.30pm Wed-Mon) harks back to Puglia's golden age under the Swabian king Frederick II.

The Drive » From Bari pick up the SS100, following signs for Taranto. Exit at Casamassima and push on to Turi on the SS172. The road traverses typical Pugliese countryside, drystone walls and orchards of fruit and olive trees. After Turi,

head left on the SP32 for the Grotte, some 43km from Bari.

TRIP HIGHLIGHT

2 Grotte di Castellana

On the northwestern edge of the Valle d'Itria, the **Grotte di Castellana** (⏹080 499 82 21; www.grottedicastellana.it; Piazzale

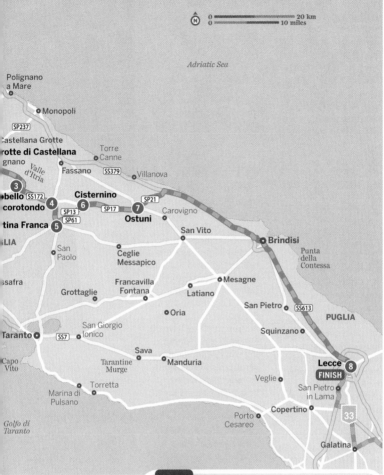

Anelli; short/full tour €12/16; ⏱9am-6pm Aug, shorter hours other months, by appointment Jan & Feb) are a series of spectacular limestone caves that link to form Italy's longest natural subterranean network. The galleries, first discovered in 1938, contain an incredible range of underground landscapes,

LINK YOUR TRIP

31 Puglia's Pilgrim Trail

Instead of turning south at Bari, head north to join this tour of Puglia's architectural splendours and medieval castles.

33 Salento Surprises

Lecce is the starting point for this trip through the fashionable summer hotspots of Puglia's deep south.

with extraordinary stalactite and stalagmite formations – look out for the jellyfish, the bacon and the stocking. The highlight is the **Grotta Bianca** (White Grotto), visitable on the full tour only, an eerie white alabaster cavern hung with stiletto-thin stalactites.

The Drive » On this short 17km drive up to Alberobello via the SP237 to Putignano and then the SS172, you'll catch sight of the Valle d'Itria's unique *trulli* houses dotted amid the roadside fields and olive groves.

TRIP HIGHLIGHT

❸ Alberobello

The Unesco-listed town of Alberobello is Puglia's *trulli* capital. There are more than 1000 of these gnomic conical-capped houses spread across town, many huddled together on the hillside in the **Rione Monti** district southwest of the central strip, Via Indipendenza.

Alberobello, which was named after a primitive oak forest, Arboris Belli (beautiful trees), that once covered the area, is an amazing sight, but it does get very touristy – from May to October busloads of tourists pile into *trullo* homes, drink in *trullo* bars and shop in *trullo* shops.

To get the best views of the whole higgledy-piggledy scene, park in Largo Martellotta and follow the steps up to Piazza del Popolo and the **Belvedere Trulli** lookout.

🗡🛏 p343

The Drive » It's a straightforward 9km drive up along the SS172 to Locorotondo. Once arrived, don't attempt to take your car into the *centro storico* (historic centre) but park on the road downhill from the centre.

❹ Locorotondo

Perched on a ridge overlooking the valley, Locorotondo has one of Puglia's most beautiful historic centres. There are few 'sights' as such; rather, the town is a sight in itself with its circular *centro storico* – the name Locorotondo is a derivation of the Italian for 'round place' – where everything is a shimmering white, and blood-red geraniums tumble down from pretty window boxes. The streets are paved with smooth ivory-coloured stones, with the church of **Santa Maria della Greca** as their sun-baked centrepiece.

You can enjoy inspiring views of the surrounding valley from the **Villa Comunale**, while for inspiration of another kind, make sure to try some of the town's celebrated white wine.

🗡 p343

The Drive » Yet another short drive. Follow the southbound SS172 as it undulates to Martina Franca, passing more *trulli*, rock

walls, and giant *fichi d'India* (prickly pears).

❺ Martina Franca

The main town in the Valle d'Itria, Martina Franca is known for its graceful baroque buildings and lovely old quarter, a picturesque ensemble of winding alleys, blinding white houses and curlicue wrought-iron balconies.

Passing under the **Arco di Sant'Antonio** at the western end of pedestrianised Piazza XX Settembre, you emerge into Piazza Roma, dominated by the 17th-century

rococo **Palazzo Ducale**
(☎080 480 57 02; Piazza
Roma 28; ⏰9am-8pm Mon-Fri,
from 10am Sat & Sun mid-Jun–
Sep, shorter hours rest of year),
whose upper rooms have
semi-restored frescoed
walls and host temporary
art exhibitions.

From the piazza, Corso
Vittorio Emanuele leads
to Piazza Plebiscito, the
centre's baroque heart.
The square is overlooked
by the 18th-century
Basilica di San Martino
and at its centre a statue
of city patron, St Martin,
swings a sword and
shares his cloak with a
beggar.

The Drive » This quick 9km
leg takes you off the main roads
onto the quiet backcountry
SP61 and its continuation the
SP13. All around you extends
bucolic farmland littered with
rocks and the unbiquitous olive
trees.

- - - - - - - - - - - - - - - - - -

❻ Cisternino

An appealing, white-
washed hilltop town,
slow-paced Cisternino
has been designated
as one of Italy's *borghi
più belli* (most beauti-
ful towns). Beyond its
bland modern outskirts
it harbours a charming
casbah-like *centro storico*. Highlights include

the 13th-century **Chiesa
Matrice** and the **Torre
Civica**, a defensive tower
dating to the Norman-
Swabian period (11th to
12th centuries). There's
also a pretty communal
garden with rural views.
If you take Via Basilioni
next to the tower you
can amble along an
elegant route right to the
central piazza, **Vittorio
Emanuele**.

Cisternino is also
famous for its *fornelli
pronti* (literally 'ready
ovens') and in many
butchers' shops and
trattorias you can select
a cut of meat and have

TRULLI

Unique to this part of Puglia, the white-grey, conical-capped *trulli* (circular stone-built houses) are a characteristic part of the Valle d'Itria's landscape. They first appeared in the late-15th century when they were built without mortar, making them easy to dismantle and allowing their wily owners to avoid local taxes. But while their design looks simple, it is well suited to the local climate – they are made out of whitewashed limestone and have thick walls that keep them cool in the baking summers.

it grilled to eat straight away.

 p343

The Drive » From Cisternino, the SP17 makes for an attractive drive as it passes through yet more typically Puglian countryside as it heads to Ostuni, 15km away.

- - - - - - - - - - - - - - - - - - -

TRIP HIGHLIGHT

⑦ Ostuni

Surrounded by an ocean of olive trees, chic Ostuni shines like a pearly white tiara, extending across three hills. The town, which marks the end of the *trulli* region and the beginning of the hot, dry Salento, heaves in summer as crowds flock to its excellent restaurants and stylish bars.

The historic centre is a great place to hang out, but if you're in the mood for exploring there are a couple of worthy sights. First up, there's the dramatic 15th-century

cathedral (Piazza Beato Giovanni Paolo II; by donation; ⊘9am-noon & 3.30-7pm) with an unusual Gothic-Romanesque facade. Then there's the **Museo di Civiltà Preclassiche della Murgia** (✆0831 33 63 83; www.ostunimuseo. it; Via Cattedrale 15; adult/reduced €5/3; ⊘10am-7pm), a small museum showcasing finds from a nearby Palaeolithic burial ground, including the skeleton of a 25,000-year-old woman nicknamed Delia.

🛏 p343

The Drive » This last 76km leg takes you south of the Valle d'Itria to the sun-scorched Salento district and the handsome city of Lecce. From Ostuni head seawards on the SP21 to join up with the SS379, which parallels the coast down to Brindisi. Continue south, following signs to Lecce and hook up with the fast-flowing SS613 for the final push.

- - - - - - - - - - - - - - - - - - -

TRIP HIGHLIGHT

⑧ Lecce

Lecce, the so-called Florence of the South, is a lively, laid-back university city celebrated for its extraordinary 17th-century baroque architecture. Known as *barocco leccese* (Lecce baroque), this local style is an expressive and hugely decorative incarnation of the genre replete with gargoyles, asparagus columns and cavorting gremlins. Swooning 18th-century traveller Thomas Ashe thought Lecce was Italy's most beautiful city, but the less-impressed Marchese Grimaldi said the facade of the **Basilica di Santa Croce** (✆0832 24 19 57; Via Umberto I; full ticket incl admission to 4 other churches €9, incl admission to 1 other church €3; ⊘9am-9pm) made him think a lunatic was having a nightmare.

For a taste head to **Piazza del Duomo**, the city's prized focal square overlooked by a 12th-century **cathedral** (✆0832 30 85 57; Piazza del Duomo; full ticket incl admission to 4 other churches €9, incl admission to 1 other church €3; ⊘9am-9pm) and 15th-century **Palazzo Vescovile** (Episcopal Palace; Piazza del Duomo) with an arched arcade loggia.

🍴 🛏 p343, p351

Eating & Sleeping

Alberobello ❸

✖ Trattoria Terra Madre   Vegetarian €€
(☎080 432 38 29; www.trattoriaterramadre.it; Piazza Sacramento 17; meals €26-57; ⊙12.15-2.45pm & 7.15-9.45pm Tue-Sat, 12.15-2.45pm Sun; ♪) Vegetables take pride of place in Italian kitchens, especially at this enthusiastic vegetarian-ish (some meat is served) restaurant. The farm-to-table ethos rules – most of what you eat comes from the organic garden outside. Start with the huge vegetable antipasti and save room for *primi* like *capunti* 'Terra Madre' (pasta with eggplant, zucchini and peppers) and the perfect house-baked desserts.

▸ Trullidea   Rental House €€
(☎080 432 38 60; www.trullidea.it; Via Monte Sabotino 24; trulli from €140; ☎) Based on the *albergo diffuso* concept, Trullidea has numerous renovated, quaint, cosy and atmospheric *trulli* in Alberobello's historic centre available on a self-catering, B&B, or half- or full-board basis. Half board is €30 person, and a buffet breakfast is included in the price.

Locorotondo ❹

✖ La Taverna del Duca   Trattoria €€
(☎080 431 30 07; www.tavernadelducascatigna. it; Via Papatodero 3; meals €38; ⊙noon-3pm & 7.30pm-midnight Tue-Sat, noon-3pm Sun & Mon) In a narrow side street off Piazza Vittorio Emanuele, this well-regarded trattoria serves robust Itrian fare such as pork cheek in a *primitivo* reduction and donkey stew. If they sound daunting, there's always Puglia's favourite pasta (*orecchiette* 'little ears' pasta), thick vegetable soup and other more familiar foods.

Cisternino ❻

✖ Rosticceria L'Antico Borgo   Barbecue €€
(☎080 444 64 00; www.rosticceria-lanticoborgo.it; Via Tarantini 9; meals €30-35; ⊙6.30-11pm daily summer, Mon-Sat winter) A classic *fornello pronto* (half butcher's shop, half trattoria), this is the place for a cheerful, no-frills meat fest. The menu is brief, listing a few simple pastas and various meat options (priced per kilo), including Cisternino's celebrated *bombette* (skewered pork wrapped around a piece of cheese). Choose your roast meat and eat it with red wine, chips and salad.

Ostuni ❼

▸ Il Frantoio   Agriturismo €€€
(☎0831 33 02 76; www.masseriailfrantoio.it; SS16 km 874, Ostuni; d €220; P ✳ @ ☎ ☎) Stay at this charming, whitewashed farmhouse and estate where the owners still live and work producing high quality olive oil. Even if you're not staying here, book in for one of the marathon eight-course lunches – the food is local, organic and superb. Il Frantoio's new swimming pool is a welcome addition for warmer Puglian days.

Lecce ❽

✖ La Cucina di Mamma Elvira   Puglian €€
(☎331 5795127; www.mammaelvira.com; Via Maremonti 33; meals €30-35; ⊙12.30pm-midnight) An offshoot of the stylish Enoteca Mamma Elvira, 'The Kitchen' makes use of a bigger space than that available to its older sibling to deliver more ambitious and substantial food. There's a focus on Pugliese wine, simply augmented by a seasonal menu that offers seafood antipasti, lovely vegetarian options, robust Pugliese pastas and more. Booking ahead is recommended.

Salento Surprises

33

This journey into Italy's heel takes you to a land of crickets and cacti. You'll find Greek, Roman and much older relics, but also gorgeous beaches lined by a new generation of sun worshippers.

TRIP HIGHLIGHTS

...km

Lecce
Sophisticated town serving up an extravagant baroque feast

1 START

Galatina

FINISH

9

Castro

Gallipoli
This once-rich city now has an intriguingly faded beauty

...7 km

60 km

Otranto
A pocket-sized seaside port guarded by a 15th-century castle

3

Santa Maria di Leuca

**5–7 DAYS
177KM / 110 MILES**

GREAT FOR...

BEST TIME TO GO

Summers are scorching and crowded, but good for beach lovers.

ESSENTIAL PHOTO

Lecce's Basilica di Santa Croce illuminated at night.

✓ **BEST FOR HISTORY**

Gape at Lecce's hypnotic baroque treasures.

Basilica di Santa Croce

345

33 Salento Surprises

Until quite recently the Salento was a poor, isolated region littered with the relics of a better past, from crumbling Greek ports to Bronze Age dolmens. Nowadays, it's a fashionable summer destination, attracting crowds of sun-seeking Italians and VIP holidaymakers such as Meryl Streep and Helen Mirren. This trip highlights the area's great cultural and natural treasures, taking you from Lecce's baroque splendours to some of Italy's finest beaches.

TRIP HIGHLIGHT

❶ Lecce

As you stare open-mouthed at Lecce's madcap baroque architecture, it's almost hard not to laugh. It's so joyously extravagant that it can be considered either grotesquely ugly or splendidly beautiful. The 18th-century traveller Thomas Ashe called it the most beautiful city in Italy, while the Marchese Grimaldi called the facade of Santa Croce the nightmare of a lunatic.

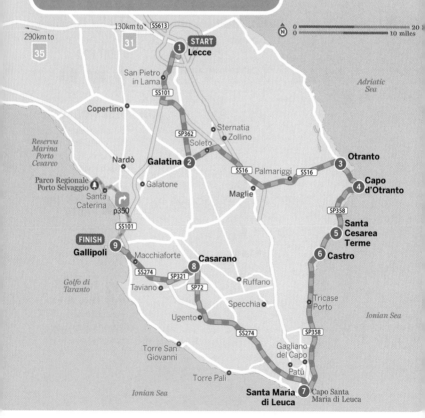

What is certain is that, with more than 40 churches and at least as many *palazzi* (mansions) from the 17th and 18th centuries, the city has an extraordinary cohesion.

A baroque feast, **Piazza del Duomo** is the city's focal point and a sudden open space amid the surrounding enclosed lanes. However, the most hallucinatory spectacle has to be the **Basilica di Santa Croce** (📞0832 24 19 57; Via Umberto I; full ticket incl admission to 4 other churches €9, incl admission to 1 other church €3; 🕐9am-9pm), a swirling allegorical feast of sheep, dodos, cherubs and unidentified beasties. A short walk away, the

LINK YOUR TRIP

31 **Puglia's Pilgrim Trail**

From Lecce, head about 130km north along the SS613, SS379 and SS16 to Conversano, which kicks off this exploration of northern Puglia's great castles and churches.

35 **The Calabrian Wilderness**

From the wild snow-capped peaks of the Pollino to Tropea's violet-coloured seas, get lost in Italy's least-explored region – about 290km from Lecce along the SS106, SP653 and SP4.

LOCAL KNOWLEDGE: PUGLIA ON YOUR PLATE

Puglia's bold, brawny cuisine adheres very closely to its roots in *cucina povera* – literally, 'cooking of the poor'. Yet that cuisine is built on an incredibly rich set of raw ingredients: seafood from the long coastline; durum wheat, olives and extraordinary produce from its rich plains; abundant grapes that are being turned into rapidly improving wines; and some of the world's best almonds. For pasta, Puglians tend to favour broccoli or *ragù* (meat sauce) topped with the pungent local *ricotta forte*. Like their Greek forbears, they're also partial to lamb and kid. Also, raw fish (such as anchovies or baby squid) are marinated to perfection in olive oil and lemon juice.

Museo Faggiano (📞0832 30 05 28; www.museofaggiano.it; Via Grandi 56/58; €5; 🕐9.30am-8pm) is an archaeological treasure trove revealing layers of local history dating back to the 5th century BC.

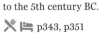 p343, p351

The Drive » Head south for 26km, first on the SS101, then on the SS367 and SP362 through fertile plains to Galatina.

- - - - - - - - - - - - - - - - - -

② Galatina

With a charming historic centre, Galatina is the capital of the Salento's Greek-inflected culture. It is almost the only place where the ritual of tarantism – a folk cure for the bite of a tarantula – is still remembered. The *taranta* folk dance evolved from it, and each year the ritual is performed on the feast

day of Sts Peter and Paul (29 June). However, most people come to Galatina to see the incredible 14th-century **Basilica di Santa Caterina d'Alessandria** (Piazzetta Orsini; 🕐4-6.30pm daily, 8.30am-12.30pm Mon-Sat Apr-Sep, shorter hours rest of year), its interior a kaleidoscope of Gothic frescoes set off by the serenity of a pure-white altarpiece.

📍 p351

The Drive » Head back to the SS16 and strike east for a total of 34km, mostly through flat agricultural fields and olive orchards.

- - - - - - - - - - - - - - - - - -

TRIP HIGHLIGHT

③ Otranto

Overlooking a pretty harbour on the blue Adriatic, whitewashed Otranto is today a pocket-sized resort town, but for 1000 years it was Italy's main port to the

East. The small historic centre is watched over by a beautiful 15th-century **castle** (☏0836 21 00 94; www.castelloaragoneseotranto. com; Piazza Castello; adult/ reduced €6/4; ☉10am-8pm). Long a target of jealous neighbours, Otranto was besieged by Turks, in league with Venezia (Venice), in 1480. They brutally murdered 800 of Otranto's faithful who refused to convert to Islam. Their bones are preserved in a chapel of the 11th-century Norman **cathedral** (☏0836 80 27 20; Piazza Basilica; ☉7am-noon & 3-8pm, shorter hours in winter). The cathedral also features a vast 12th-century mosaic of a stupendous tree of life balanced on the back of two elephants. The town itself has a pretty beach, though there are much longer strands just outside of town.

✗ ⌂ p351

The Drive » It is a fairly straight shot for 7km through the farmland south of Otranto to Capo d'Otranto. As you get close, you'll see the white lighthouse against the blue Adriatic.

DAVIDE TORNESE/500PX ©

❹ Capo d'Otranto

As you head down Salento's dreamy coast, take a pit stop on this small peninsula, which serves as the official division between the Ionian and Adriatic Seas. Its restored 19th-century **lighthouse** sits picturesquely at its tip. On clear days you can see the mountains of Albania across a sparkling blue Adriatic Sea.

The Drive » Heading south for 13km, the coastal road (the SP87 and its continuation the SP358) suddenly starts twisting and turning as the coastline turns more rugged, with broad rocky flatlands.

❺ Santa Cesarea Terme

Santa Cesarea Terme has a number of Liberty-style (art nouveau) villas, reminiscent of the days when spa-going was all the rage. There are still hotels that cater to the summer crowds of Italians who come to bathe in the thermal spas. But

Capo d'Otranto Waterfront

don't have visions of stylish hammams and soothing massages; here spa-going is a serious medical business, and the Terme di Santa Cesarea feels like a fusty old hospital with a lingering smell of sulphur about it. Still, this makes a great stop to ease the aches and pains of life on the road.

The Drive >> From Santa Cesarea Terme to Castro, it is a quick 7km drive along the coastal SP358.

6 Castro

Almost midway between Santa Maria and Otranto lies the town of Castro, which is dominated by an austere, Romanesque **cathedral** and forbidding **castle**. Just downhill, its marina serves as a popular boating and diving hub for the rocky coastline, which is riddled with fascinating sea caves. Most famous is the **Grotta Zinzulusa**, which is filled with stalactites that hang like sharp daggers from the ceiling. It can only be visited on a guided tour. Note that in summer it

DETOUR: PARCO REGIONALE PORTO SELVAGGIO

Start: 9 Gallipoli

The Ionian coast can be holiday hell in July and August, but head about 25km north from Gallipoli and you'll soon find the real belle of the region, the **Parco Regionale Porto Selvaggio**, a protected area of rocky coastline covered with umbrella pines, eucalyptus trees and olives. Right in the middle of the park is elegant **Santa Caterina**, a summer seaside centre.

gets maniacally busy. Get details at www.castropro mozione.it.

The Drive » Keep hugging the coastline south along SP358 for 31km as you pass pine and eucalyptus groves, farmland and a series of small resort towns until you reach the southernmost point of the peninsula.

---

7 Santa Maria di Leuca

At the very tip of Italy's high heel, the resort town of Santa Maria di Leuca occupies what Romans called *finibus terrae,* the end of the earth. The spot is marked by the **Basilica Santuario di Santa Maria di Leuca**, an important place of pilgrimage built over an older Roman temple dedicated to Minerva. These days, with its Gothic- and Liberty-style villas, this

is a holiday resort, pure and simple. Many people come here to take one of the boat trips to visit sea grottoes like the **Grotta del Diavolo**, the **Grotta della Stalla** and the **Grotta Grande di Ciolo**. Trips depart from the little *porto* between June and September.

The Drive » Head 29km inland on the SS274 through seemingly endless olive groves and sunburnt farms to around Ugento, then 10km along the SP72 to Casarano.

---

8 Casarano

Sitting amid the Salento's rich olive groves, laid-back Casarano is home of **Chiesa di Santa Maria della Croce**. One of the oldest sites in Christendom, it holds mosaics that date to the 5th century as well as frescoes from the Byzantine period.

The Drive » From Casarano to Gallipoli, head west on the SP321 and SS274 roadways. You'll drive 20km through olive trees and ochre-coloured fields, passing Taviano and Macchiaforte en route.

TRIP HIGHLIGHT

9 Gallipoli

Kallipolis, the 'beautiful city' of the Greeks, may be a faded beauty now, but it still retains its island charm. The Salentines see it as a kind of southern Portofino, and its weathered white *borgo* (historic centre) has a certain grungy chic: part fishing village, part fashion model. In the 16th and 17th centuries, Gallipoli was one of the richest towns in the Salento, exporting its famous olive oil to Napoli (Naples), Paris and London to illuminate their street lamps. That explains the rather elegant air of the old town, which is divided into two distinct halves: the patrician quarter, which housed the wealthy merchant class, to the north of Via Antonietta de Pace; and the popular quarter, with its rabbit-warren of streets to the south.

✕ ⌂ p351

Eating & Sleeping

Lecce ❶

✕ L'Arzilla Furcina   Italian €€
(☎391 3320419; www.larzillafurcina.it; Via
Bacile 25; meals €30-35; ☺7.30-11.30pm
Tue-Sun, 12.30-2.30pm Tue, Thu & Sun) Tucked
away down a shopping street in Lecce's New
Town, L'Arzilla Furcina features a compact and
stylish space showcasing seasonal and local
ingredients and Salento wines. Traditional
Puglian recipes are given a modern spin and
could feature local seafood such as *cozze*
(mussels). Thoroughly unpretentious and
friendly service also makes L'Arzilla Furcina
worth the short detour from Lecce's historic
centre.

🛏 Palazzo Rollo   B&B €
(☎0832 30 71 52; www.palazzorollo.it;
Corso Vittorio Emanuele II 14; s/d/ste from
€75/90/100; P ✳ @) This tastefully restored
17th-century *palazzo* – the Rollo family seat for
more than 200 years – makes a delightful base
from which to explore Lecce. The grand B&B
suites (with kitchenettes) have high curved
ceilings and chandeliers while, downstairs,
contemporary-chic studios open onto an ivy-
hung courtyard. There are also self-catering
apartments (from €120) and a rooftop garden
with wonderful views.

Galatina ❷

🛏 Samadhi   Agriturismo €€
(☎0836 60 02 84; www.agricolasamadhi.it;
Via Stazione 116, Zollino; d €149; P ✳ 🤖 ✪)
Soothe the soul with a stay at Samadhi, located
around 7km east of Galatina in tiny Zollino.
It's on a 10-hectare organic farm and the
owners are multilingual. As well as Ayurvedic
treatments, shiatsu and yoga courses, there's
a vegan restaurant offering organic meals.
Check the website for upcoming retreats and
courses.

Otranto ❸

✕ L'Altro Baffo   Seafood €€
(☎0836 80 16 36; www.laltrobaffo.com; Via
Cenobio Basiliano 23; meals €40-45; ☺noon-
2.30pm & 7.30pm-midnight Tue-Sun) This elegant
modern restaurant near the castle stays in
touch with basic Pugliese and Italian principles,
but ratchets things up several notches: the
'carbonara' made with sea-urchin roe is a daring
instant classic. The menu is mainly seafood,
but there are a few vegetarian dishes that are
anything but afterthoughts.

🛏 Palazzo Papaleo   Hotel €€€
(☎0836 80 21 08; www.hotelpalazzopapaleo.
com; Via Rondachi 1; r from €230; P ✳ @ 🤖)
Located next to the cathedral, this sumptuous
hotel, the first to earn the EU Eco-label in Puglia,
has magnificent rooms with original frescoes,
exquisitely carved antique furniture and walls
washed in soft greys, ochres and yellows.
Soak in the panoramic views while enjoying
the rooftop spa, or steam yourself pure in the
hammam. The staff are exceptionally friendly.

Gallipoli ❾

✕ La Puritate   Seafood €€€
(☎0833 26 42 05; Via Sant'Elia 18; meals €50;
☺12.30-3pm & 7.30-10.30pm, closed Wed
winter) Book ahead to ensure your table at *the*
place for fish in this seafood-loving town. Follow
the practically obligatory seafood *antipasti* with
delicious *primi* (first courses). Anything fishy
is good (especially the prawns, swordfish and
tuna) and the picture windows allow splendid
views of the waters whence it came.

🛏 Insula   B&B €
(☎329 8070056, 0833 20 14 13; www.
bbinsulagallipoli.it; Via Antonietta de Pace
56; d €80; ☺Apr-Oct; ✳ @) A magnificent
16th-century building houses this memorable
B&B. The five rooms are all different but share
the same princely atmosphere with exquisite
antiques, vaulted high ceilings and cool pastel
paintwork. Directly adjacent to the cathedral, it
couldn't be any more central.

Across the Lucanian Apennines

From seaside Maratea to otherworldly Matera, this trip crosses the hinterlands of Basilicata, a gorgeous region of hilltop towns, purple peaks, fertile valleys and possibly the world's best cheese.

34

TRIP HIGHLIGHTS

km

Padula
Wander through this sprawling, splendid and impossibly grand monastery

288 km

Matera
Haunting cave dwellings overlay a ruggedly unforgiving landscape

FINISH
9

Tricàrico

6 Pietrapertosa

185 km

Castelmezzano
This otherwordly town clings for dear life to rocky spires

3
Viggiano

Grumentum

0 km

Maratea
Basilicata's only bijou resort town has an enchanting medieval centre

Rivello

START **1**

5–7 DAYS
288KM / 179 MILES

GREAT FOR...

BEST TIME TO GO

Spring and autumn for sunny weather without summer heat and crowds.

 ESSENTIAL PHOTO

Capture Matera's ancient cave dwellings at sunset.

 BEST FOR FOODIES

Try the heavenly local cheeses in Castelmezzano's Al Becco della Civetta.

34

Across the Lucanian Apennines

This trip begins on Basilicata's Tyrrhenian coast, which may be diminutive but rivals Amalfi for sheer drama. The trip ends in a completely different world – the chalky, sunburnt landscape around Matera, a strange and remarkable city with timeless troglodyte dwellings that are Unesco-protected. In between, you'll cross the dramatic peaks of the Lucanian Apennines, a gorgeous land of alpine forests, green valleys and bristling hilltop towns.

TRIP HIGHLIGHT

❶ Maratea

Sitting in stately fashion above the cliffs and pocket-sized beaches of the Golfo di Policastro, Maratea is Basilicata's only bijou resort town. Uphill, the enchanting medieval centre has elegant hotels, pint-sized piazzas, wriggling alleys and startling coastal views. Still further up, a 22m-high statue of **Christ the Redeemer** lords it over the rugged

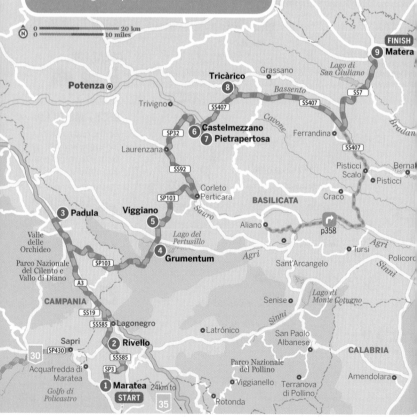

landscape. Down at sea level, the town's **harbour** shelters sleek yachts and bright-blue fishing boats. The deep green hillsides that encircle this tumbling conurbation offer excellent walking trails, while the surrounding coastline hides dozens of tiny beaches.

 p359

The Drive » The 23km to Rivello takes you into the heights of the coastal range. From Maratea, follow signs north to Trecchina. Expect great sea views along the way. At Trecchina, head down to a short but blessedly straight stretch of highway SS585. Rivello will appear quickly on your left.

---

❷ Rivello

Perched on a high ridge and framed by the southern Apennines, Rivello is not just another picture-

LINK YOUR TRIP

30 Cilento Coastal Trail

From Maratea, take the coastal SS18 north to Sapri to explore this wild coastline.

35 The Calabrian Wilderness

From Rivello take the A3 south to Mormanno to get lost in Italy's least-explored region.

pretty medieval village. Due to its strategic position, it was contested for centuries by both Lombards and Byzantines. Eventually, they reached an unlikely compromise – the Lombards settled in the lower part of town, the Byzantines in the upper. This resulted in two separate centres with two diverse cultures developing in a single town. Today, Rivello's charm lies in its narrow alleys, where homes both grand and humble are graced with wrought-iron balconies.

The Drive » For the 40km to Padula, return to the SS585 and head to the northbound A3 autostrada. Rugged mountains will suddenly open out into the wide, fertile Vallo di Diano. Take the Padula exit and follow signs to the abbey.

TRIP HIGHLIGHT

❸ Padula

In the plains just below hilltop Padula lies one of southern Italy's most extraordinary sites. The **Certosa di San Lorenzo** (📞0975 7 77 45; www.polomu sealecampania.beniculturali.it; Viale Certosa, Padula; adult/reduced €6/3; ⊙9am-7pm Wed-Mon) is among the largest monasteries in southern Europe, with 320 rooms and halls, 13 courtyards, 100 fireplaces, 52 stairways, 41 fountains and the world's largest cloisters. Founded in 1306, its

buildings represent more than four centuries of construction, though primarily it is a 17th- and 18th-century baroque creation.

The Drive » From Padula, double back along the SS19. Just past Montesano Scalo, follow signs to Sarconi along the SP ex SS103. Here begins a beautiful, winding ascent into the Lucanian Apennines, then a descent towards the verdant Val d'Agri. Reckon on just over an hour for the 44km journey.

---

❹ Grumentum

Set amid the fertile Val d'Agri, Grumentum was once an important enough Roman city that the invading Hannibal made it his headquarters. Eventually it was abandoned for hilltop Grumento Nova in the 9th century. Today, its **ruins** (📞0975 6 50 74; Contrada Spineta, Grumento Nova; incl museum €2.50; ⊙9am-1hr before sunset Tue-Sun, from 2pm Mon; 🅿) sit humbly amid agricultural fields and leave much to the imagination. Still, they make for a fascinating and atmospheric ramble, especially the miniature version of the Colosseum.

The Drive » Head back to the SP ex SS103 for a 15km drive along the pastoral valley floor following signs to Viggiano. The last few kilometres are pure switchback.

5 Viggiano

Hilltop Viggiano stands guard above the beautiful Val d'Agri. Aside from its fine views, the town has an illustrious music history. Since the 18th century, it has been celebrated for its harp makers and players, and has a long tradition of producing lively street musicians.

Viggiano is also a historic pilgrimage destination thanks to its ancient statue of the Black Madonna, the *Madonna Nera del Sacro Monte*.

The Drive ⟫ The 63km ride to Castelmezzano is breathtaking. Head back down the switchback and look for the SP ex SS103 and signs to the town Corleto Perticara. At Corleto Perticara, pick up the SS92 and wind past Laurenzana with its beautiful Romanesque church and castle. Then catch the SP32 and head north. After passing a pretty reservoir signs will lead to Castelmezzano.

MAUDANROS/SHUTTERSTOCK ©

TRIP HIGHLIGHT

6 Castelmezzano

Clinging to a series of impossibly narrow ledges, the houses of tiny Castelmezzano look like something out of a fairy tale, bounded on one side by rocky spires and on the other by the vertigo-inducing gorges of the Caperrino river. When the mist swirls in (as it often does) the effect is otherworldly.

For an adrenaline rush, fly across the gorge to neighbouring Pietrapertosa at 120km/h attached to a steel cable via **Il Volo dell'Angelo**. (Angel's Flight; ☑Castelmezzano 0971 98 60 20, Pietrapertosa 0971 98 31 10; www.volodellangelo.com; s €35-42, couples €63-75; ☺9.30am-6.30pm May-Oct)

This region is also know for its incomparable goat's and sheep's milk cheese, the best of which is on the menu at Al Becco della Civetta (p359).

✕ ⤵ p359

The Drive ⟫ Though you could practically throw a stone across the gorge separating Castelmezzano from

Pietrapertosa, the 10km drive requires dozens of hairpin turns and a strong stomach. But views of the gorges are gorgeous indeed. The way is well marked.

---

7 Pietrapertosa

As the highest town in Basilicata, Pietrapertosa is possibly even more dramatically situated than neighbouring Castelmezzano. Pietrap-

ertosa literally translates as 'perforated stone' and, indeed, the village sits in the midst of bizarrely shaped rocky towers. Literally carved into the mountainside, its 10th-century **Saracen fortress** is difficult to spot, but once you've located it you won't regret the long climb up. The views are breathtaking.

The Drive » After the winding descent from Pietrapertosa, take SS407 to the Tricàrico exit, 29km from Pietrapertosa. You'll notice the peaks of the Dolomiti Lucani disappear in favour of the chalky plains and gorges that define the landscape around Matera.

---

8 Tricàrico

Perched on a ridge above the Basento river valley, Tricàrico may

DETOUR: CARLO LEVI COUNTRY

Start: ⑨ Matera

Aliano, a tiny and remote village about 80km south of Matera, would still languish unknown had not writer, painter and political activist Carlo Levi been exiled here in the 1930s during Mussolini's regime. In his extraordinary book *Christ Stopped at Eboli*, Levi graphically describes the aching hardship of peasant life in 'Gagliano' (in reality, Aliano) where 'there is no definite boundary between the world of human beings and that of animals and even monsters'. Today, Aliano is a sleepy town that only seems to come alive late in the afternoon when old men congregate on the park benches in the pleasant tree-lined Via Roma, and black-shrouded women exchange news on the streets.

not be as dazzlingly odd as Castelmezzano and Pietrapertosa, but it does have one of the best-preserved medieval cores in Basilicata, with Gothic and Romanesque religious buildings capped by a picturesque Norman **tower**. Its ramparts also proffer lovely views over the surrounding countryside.

The Drive » Head back to the SS407 and continue east along the snaking Bassento river valley, until you see the castle of Migliònico far off on your left. Shortly after, exit the main road onto the SS7 and follow the signs to Matera.

TRIP HIGHLIGHT

⑨ Matera

Haunting and beautiful, Matera's unique *sassi* (districts of cave houses and churches) sprawl below the rim of the steep-sided Gravina gorge like a giant nativity scene. The houses' rock-grey facades once hid grimy, filthy abodes, but in recent years many have been converted into restaurants and swish cave-hotels. Overlooking the *sassi* – divided into the **Sasso Barisano** and **Sasso Caveoso** – the new town is a lively place, with its elegant baroque

churches, exquisite Romanesque **cathedral**, and elegant *palazzi* (mansions).

Matera is said to be one of the world's oldest towns, dating back to the Palaeolithic Age and continuously inhabited for around 7000 years. The simple natural grottoes that dotted the gorge were adapted to become homes, and an ingenious system of canals regulated the flow of water and sewage. In his great book, *Christ Stopped at Eboli,* Carlo Levi describes the appalling poverty he saw in the city in the 1930s and how children would beg passers-by for quinine to stave off the deadly malaria. Such publicity finally galvanised the authorities into action and in the late 1950s about 15,000 inhabitants were forcibly relocated to new government housing schemes. For a fascinating glimpse into Matera's past, search out the **Casa Noha** (☎0835 33 54 52; www.fondoambiente. it/casa-noha-eng; Recinto Cavone 9; adult/reduced €6/2; ☺9am-7pm Apr-Oct, shorter hours rest of year) in the Sasso Caveoso.

✕ ⌷ p359

Eating & Sleeping

Maratea ①

✖ Lanterna Rossa — Seafood €€

(📞0973 87 63 52; www.facebook.com/lantern arossamarateaporto; Via Arenile, Maratea Porto; meals €35-40; ⏱11am-3pm & 7-11.30pm) This terrace restaurant, above the Bar del Porto overlooking the marina, has been knocking out delightful Lucanian seafood for over 20 years. Sit in the art-strewn interior or on the terrace to enjoy dishes such as *zuppa di pesce* (fish soup) and octopus with wild beans and fennel. Bookings advised, especially in July and August.

✖ Il Sacello — Italian €€

(📞0973 87 61 39; www.facebook.com/ ristoranteilsacellomaratea; Via Mazzei 4, Maratea Borgo; meals €40-45; ⏱12.30-2.30pm & 7.30-10pm; 🛜) The in-house *ristorante* of the Locanda delle Donne Monache hotel, Il Sacello serves wonderful Lucanian fare and seafood, overlooking the red rooftops of Maratea *borgo* (medieval hamlet). Try the pasta with local sausage, the beef tartare or delicately wrought desserts such as the buffalo-ricotta souffle. Il Sacello sometimes closes on Monday or Tuesday night in June.

▟ Locanda delle Donne Monache — Hotel €€

(📞0973 87 61 39; www.locandamonache.com; Via Mazzei 4, Maratea Borgo; d/ste €180/300; ⏱Apr-Oct; 🅿 ❄ @ 🛜 🛝) Overlooking the *borgo*, this exclusive hotel is in a converted 18th-century convent with a lofty setting. It's a hotchpotch of vaulted corridors, terraces and gardens fringed with bougainvillea and lemon trees. The rooms are elegantly decorated and there's a fitness centre, Jacuzzi and a stunning panoramic outdoor pool.

Castelmezzano ⑥

✖ Al Becco della Civetta — Ristorante €€

(📞0971 98 62 49; www.beccodellacivetta.it; Vico I Maglietta 7, Castelmezzano; meals €35-40; ⏱1-3pm & 8-10pm) Don't miss this authentic Lucano restaurant in Castelmezzano, which serves excellent regional cuisine based on seasonal local ingredients. It also offers 22

traditionally furnished, simple whitewashed rooms (doubles €80), some with lots of dark wood, others with vivid murals, and many with fabulous views. Booking recommended.

▟ La Casa di Penelope e Cirene — B&B €

(📞338 3132196; Via Garibaldi 32, Pietrapertosa; d €75) This delightful B&B, the 'House of Penelope and Cirene', offers just two handsomely furnished rooms in the heart of Pietrapertosa. There's a sitting room, kitchenette, and great views over the Lucanian Dolomites.

Matera ⑨

✖ I Vizi degli Angeli — Gelato €

(📞0835 31 06 37; www.ivizidegliangeli.it; Via Ridola 36; medium cone €23; ⏱noon-11pm Thu-Tue) 'The Angels' Vices', an artisanal gelato 'laboratory' on the busy promenade of Via Domenico Ridola, is Matera's best. Alongside classics such as pistachio, you'll find experimental flavours such as grapefruit with pink pepper and thyme and mallow, which taste even better than they read.

✖ Osteria La Pignata — Osteria €€

(📞366 3187292; www.osterialapignata.com; Via Duni 20; meals €30-35; ⏱12.30-3pm & 8-10.30pm) Pasta is highly recommended at this popular *sassi osteria*, perhaps *cavatellini ceci e vongole* (little handmade pasta curls with chickpeas and clams) or *paccheri alla murgiana* (little tubes with *cardoncelli* mushrooms, rocket and fennel sausage). *Secondi* tend towards the meaty, as epitomised by the house stew of lamb, pork sausage and mushrooms.

▟ Hotel Il Belvedere — Hotel €€

(📞0835 31 17 02; www.hotelbelvedere.matera. it; Via Casalnuovo 133; d from €135; ❄ 🛜) This cave boutique looks unremarkable from its street-side perch on the edge of the Sasso Caveoso, but you'll feel your jaw start to drop as you enter its luxurious entrails and spy the spectacle of Old Matera sprawling below a jutting terrace. Cavernous rooms sport mosaics, mood lighting and curtained four-poster beds. Two-night minimums apply in August.

The Calabrian Wilderness

35

From the peaks of the Pollino to the crystalline waters of the Tropea peninsula, this trip immerses you in the natural beauty of Calabria, one of Italy's wildest and least explored regions.

TRIP HIGHLIGHTS

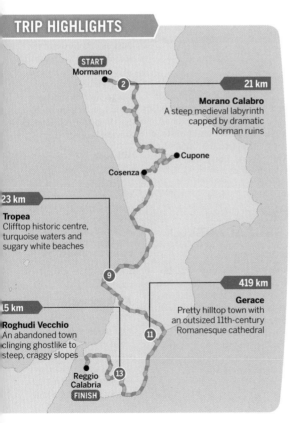

START
Mormanno

2

21 km

Morano Calabro
A steep medieval labyrinth capped by dramatic Norman ruins

●**Cupone**

Cosenza ●

23 km

Tropea
Clifftop historic centre, turquoise waters and sugary white beaches

9

419 km

Gerace
Pretty hilltop town with an outsized 11th-century Romanesque cathedral

15 km

Roghudi Vecchio
An abandoned town clinging ghostlike to steep, craggy slopes

11

13

Reggio Calabria
FINISH

**8–10 DAYS
606KM / 376 MILES**

GREAT FOR...

BEST TIME TO GO

Spring and autumn for sunny weather without summer heat and crowds.

ESSENTIAL PHOTO

Sweeping views of mountains and sea from Capo Vaticano.

✔ BEST FOR OUTDOORS

From Cupone, strike out into the wilds of Calabria's Sila mountain range.

35 The Calabrian Wilderness

From the alpine Pollino to the thickly forested slopes of the Aspromonte, Calabria possesses some of Italy's wildest landscapes. Avoid the overbuilt coast and you'll often feel you have the place to yourself. Plagued by earthquakes, poverty and organised crime, its artistic heritage is limited, yet its rough beauties are gripping. Besides three sprawling national parks, ancient towns seem to grow out of craggy hilltops, while amethyst waters wash Tropea's beaches.

❶ Mormanno

In the heart of the **Parco Nazionale del Pollino** (www.parcopollino.gov.it), this bristling hilltop town of 3000 souls stands guard over the narrow Lao river valley. Mormanno makes a convenient base from which to explore the peaks and forests of the surrounding national park. Don't miss its prized local lentils, best served in a deliciously simple soup loaded with oregano.

✗ p368

The Drive ›› Instead of the A3 autostrada, take the pleasant SP241, which winds its way for 21km through forested hills and green valleys as you sneak up on the back side of Morano Calabro.

TRIP HIGHLIGHT

❷ Morano Calabro

One of the most dramatic hill towns in southern Italy, Morano Calabro is a dense, steeply rising medieval labyrinth capped by the dramatic ruins of a **Norman castle**. Just as extraordinary is its setting at the foothills of a dramatic stretch of the Pollino mountain range. Morano makes a good jumping-off point for the beautiful Gole del Raganello canyon.

🛏 p368

The Drive ›› Head down the A3, dramatically framed by the Pollino mountain range, until you reach the exit for Altomonte, which is about 30km from Morano Calabro. The town itself sits at the end of a series of well-marked country roads, a further 10km away.

-----

❸ Altomonte

The views from this well-preserved hilltop town encompass the snowy heights of the Pollino range, the rich patchwork of farms that covers its foothills and

DETOUR: GOLE DEL RAGANELLO

Start: ❷ Morano Calabro

Located just outside the town of Civita, about 20km east of Morano Calabro, the dramatic gorges carved by the Raganello river are well worth seeking out. In addition to the majesty of their sheer limestone walls, the gorges are also home to rich flora and fauna, from foxes and martens to soaring golden eagles. Note also that the towns in this region still preserve traces of Albanian culture more than five centuries after their ancestors fled to Calabria when Turks invaded Albania.

even a glimpse of the blue Mediterranean off to the east. Don't miss the 14th-century **Chiesa di Santa Maria della Consolazione**, one of the finest examples of Gothic architecture in Calabria.

The Drive ≫ For this 51km leg, head back to the A3, then south to the Montalto exit, where you'll then twist and turn along SS559 as you head for Santa Maria Assunta in Sambucina.

④ Santa Maria Assunta in Sambucina

Tucked in the foothills of the Sila mountains, this once-vast **abbey** has, over the centuries, been reduced to just a few atmospheric remnants,

LINK YOUR TRIP

34 **Across the Lucanian Apennines**

From Mormanno, head north 66km to seaside Maratea to begin your adventure into the beautiful interior of Basilicata.

36 **Wonders of Ancient Sicily**

From Reggio Calabria, it's a 30-minute ferry ride to Messina in Sicily. Continue 50km south to Taormina to begin this trip taking in the island's Greek, Norman and Arab heritage.

thanks to a devastating combination of earthquakes and landslides. Today, all that is left is a transept of the original church, which incorporates both Romanesque and Gothic elements.

The Drive >> Back on the SS559, you will soon wind your way up to the SP247, then along a high plain, where pastureland alternates with pine and oak forests offering a distinct alpine flavour. Signs lead you the 38km to Camigliatello Silano.

- - - - - - - - - - - - - - - -

⑤ Camigliatello Silano

A popular ski-resort town with 6km of trails, Camigliatello Silano looks much better under snow – think Swiss chalets in poured concrete. However, even in the summer it makes a comfortable base from which to explore the Sila mountains, with their upland meadows, pine and oak forests and well-marked hiking trails.

✖️ 🛏️ p368

The Drive >> As you gently wind your way along the 10km jaunt on the SP250 to Cupone, you will soon see the blue waters of Lago Cecita appear through the trees.

- - - - - - - - - - - - - - - -

⑥ Cupone

Home to the headquarters of the **Parco Nazionale della Sila** (www.parcosila.it), Cupone sits on the edge of pretty, meandering Lago Cecita. Well-marked hikes

into the surrounding heights radiate out from here, and there is a helpful **visitors centre** and small **museum** devoted to the local ecology and geology.

The Drive >> Head back to Camigliatello Silano then catch the SS107, which winds its way down to Cosenza, for a total distance of 43km. The last part of the drive is particularly beautiful.

- - - - - - - - - - - - - - - -

⑦ Cosenza

Though surrounded by uninspiring sprawl, Cosenza's medieval core is one of the best-preserved historic centres in Calabria, one of the few areas to have survived the constant earthquakes that have ravaged the region over the centuries. Its narrow, winding lanes have a gritty feel with their antiquated shopfronts and fading, once-elegant *palazzi* (mansions). Follow **Corso Telesio** and you eventually reach **Piazza XV Marzo**, an appealing square fronted by the Renaissance-style **Palazzo del Governo** and the neoclassical **Teatro Rendano**. Behind the piazza, the lovely **Villa Vecchia** park provides some welcome shade.

✖️ 🛏️ p368

The Drive >> Head south on the A3 until you reach sweeping views of the Golfo di Sant'Eufemia. Pizzo sits at its southern end, 90km away.

THOMAS ROCHE/GETTY IMAGES ©

- - - - - - - - - - - - - - - -

⑧ Pizzo

Stacked high on a sea cliff with sweeping views down to the Tropean peninsula, Pizzo has a distinct ramshackle charm. On its main square, cafes compete to offer the town's best *tartufo,* a death-by-chocolate ice-cream ball. A kilometre north of town, the **Chiesa di Piedigrotta** (📞0963 53 25 23; Via Riviera Prangi; adult/reduced €3/2.50; ⏰9am-1pm & 3-7.30pm Jul & Aug, shorter hours rest of year) is a rock church that was first carved into the tufa rock by Neapolitan shipwreck

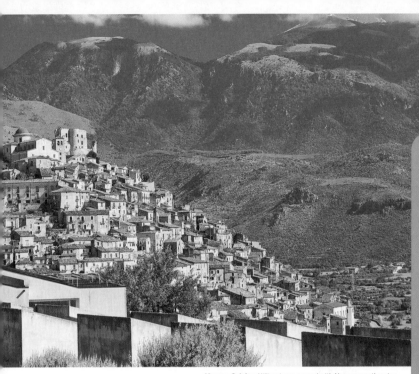
Morano Calabro Hilltop town capped with Norman castle ruins

survivors in the 17th century. It has since been filled with tufa saints as well as less godly figures like Fidel Castro and JFK.

✗ 🛏 p368

The Drive ≫ Head 30km south along coastal route SS522, which winds its way through uninspired beach resorts that alternate with farmland prized for its sweet red onions.

TRIP HIGHLIGHT

⑨ Tropea

Much of the Calabrian coast has been decimated by poorly planned mass development. Tropea is a jewel-like exception. Set on a rocky promontory, the town's small but well-preserved historic centre sits above a sugary, white-sand beach. At sunset, the clear turquoise waters are known to turn garish shades of purple. And don't miss the sweet fire of the region's prized red onions, which come from the surrounding peninsula.

Note that the town's attractions are compromised in high summer by teeming crowds, when parking can become a blood sport.

✗ 🛏 p369

The Drive ≫ It is a lovely drive to Capo Vaticano for 13km along SP22, mostly following the coastline. When you reach the little town of San Nicoló, follow signs to Faro Capo Vaticano.

⑩ Capo Vaticano

Even if you don't have time to explore its beaches, ravines and limestone sea cliffs, stop at this cape on the southwestern corner of the Promontorio di Tropea for its jaw-dropping views. On a clear day, you can see past the Aeolian Islands all the way to Sicily.

The Drive ≫ For this 83km drive, wind your way along the

coastal SP23, skirting Rosarno until you reach the SS682. Take this and head across the pretty northern reaches of the Aspromonte to the Ionian coast. Push on south to Locri, from where hilltop Gerace is a short inland hop – follow signs from Via Garibaldi and follow the tortuously winding SP1.

TRIP HIGHLIGHT

⓫ Gerace

A spectacular medieval hill town, Gerace is worth a detour for the views alone. On one side lies the Ionian Sea, and on the other the dark, dramatic heights of the Aspromonte mountains. It also has Calabria's largest Romanesque **cathedral** (Via Duomo 28; adult/reduced €3/2; ☺9.30am-12.30pm & 3-6.30pm), a majestically simple structure that dates to 1045 and incorporates columns pilfered from nearby Roman ruins.

 p369

The Drive ≫ After heading back down the SP1, turn south on the SS106, which parallels the blue Ionic coast. At the town of Bova Marina, follow signs inland along the sharply twisting road to hilltop Bova. The total distance is 77km.

⓬ Bova

Perched at 900m above sea level, this mountain eyrie possesses a photogenic ruined **castle**, plus stupendous surf-and-turf views that rival Gerace's. Don't miss the bilingual signage – the townspeople are among the few surviving speakers of Griko, a Greek dialect that dates at least to the Byzantine period and possibly to the times when ancient Greeks ruled here.

The Drive ≫ The 19km road from Bova to Roghudi Vecchio features the most stunning stretch of driving on this trip – though it's also the most tortuous – and has some pretty

rough patches. Note that it's important to ask about road conditions before setting out as roads can be washed out. It may be advisable to skip Roghudi and head straight to Gambarie.

TRIP HIGHLIGHT

⓭ Roghudi Vecchio

The wild, winding ride to Roghudi Vecchio takes you through a stunning stretch of the Aspromonte mountains. This ghostly town clings limpet-like to a steep, craggy slope above an eerily white bed of the Amendolea river, which is formed by limestone washed down from the surrounding peaks. The river is barely a trickle most of the year, but two terrible floods in the 1970s caused the town itself to be abandoned.

Note that the town is still uninhabited and unpoliced, so wandering off the main road is not recommended.

The Drive ≫ On the 59km drive to Gambarie, it's more dramatic switchbacks down to the Amendolea river and back up, past the very poor town of Roccaforte del Greco and eventually back to the SS183, which climbs quickly from the olive trees and cacti of the lower altitudes to pines, oaks and chestnut trees along the flat peaks of the Aspromonte.

⓮ Gambarie

Headquarters of the **Parco Nazionale dell'Aspromonte** (www.parcoaspromonte.gov.it)

DREADED 'NDRANGHETA

While the Sicilian mafia, known as Cosa Nostra, and Naples' Camorra get more press, Calabria's 'ndrangheta is one of the world's most feared organised crime networks. EURISPES, an independent Italian think tank, estimated its annual income reached more than €40 billion in 2007, much of it coming from drug trafficking, usury, construction and skimming off public-works contracts. Estimates of its strength vary but the *Guardian* has reported that the loosely organised group, which is cemented by actual family bonds, has up to 7000 members worldwide. The Aspromonte mountains have long served as the group's traditional refuge.

Bova Rooftops and mountains

and the park's largest town, faux-Swiss Gambarie is more convenient than charming. It does make a great base to explore the pine-covered heights that surround it. This is wonderful walking country, and the park has several colour-coded trails. There is also skiing in winter, with a lift right from the town centre.

🛏 p369

The Drive » It's now time to return to sea level. This 32km leg begins on the SP7 as it winds its way down through the towns of San Stefano and Sant'Alessio in Aspromonte, all the way to the A3. On the way down, gape at the views across the Strait of Messina to Sicily, weather permitting.

- - - - - - - - - - - - - - -

⑮ Reggio Calabria

Reggio is the main launching point for ferries to Sicily, which sparkles temptingly across the Strait of Messina. Though the city's grid of dusty streets has the slightly dissolute feel shared by most port cities, Reggio's wide, sea-front promenade, lined

with art-deco palaces, is delightful.

The city is also home to what are, probably, the world's finest examples of ancient Greek sculpture: the spectacular **Bronzi di Riace**. Dating from around 450 BC, these two full-sized Greek bronze nudes now reside at the **Museo Nazionale di Reggio Calabria** (☎0965 81 22 55; www.museoarcheologi coreggiocalabria.it; Piazza de Nava 26; adult/reduced €8/5; ⏰9am-8pm Tue-Sun; ♿).

🍴 🛏 p369

367

Eating & Sleeping

Mormanno ❶

✗ Osteria del Vicolo — Calabrian €€

(📞0981 8 04 75; www.osteriadelvicolo.it; Vico Primo San Francesco 5, Mormanno; meals €28-30; ⊘noon-3pm & 7.30-11.30pm Thu-Tue) Follow signs from Mormanno's church to this humble but much-lauded eatery. The menu stars the region's highly prized lentils, which accompany local grilled meats, form the base for pasta sauce, or come infused with oregano in a divinely simple soup. There's also wood-fired pizza in the evenings. The family runs a B&B nearby, too.

Morano Calabro ❷

🛏 Albergo Villa San Domenico — Hotel €€

(📞0981 39 98 81; www. albergovillasandomenico.it; Via Sotto gli Olmi, Morana Calabro; s/d/tr/q €80/110/135/160; 🅿 ❄ 🛜) This handsome four-star hotel occupies an 18th-century palace that sits picturesquely next to Santa Magdalena church at the foot of Morana Calabro old town. The antique-strewn rooms are fitted out with all the modern comforts and have balconies looking towards the wooded hills of the Parco Nazionale del Pollino. Half and full board is available, for €15 per meal.

Camigliatello Silano ❺

✗ La Tavernetta — Calabrian €€€

(📞0984 57 90 26; www.sanlorenzosialberga.it; Campo San Lorenzo, near Camigliatello Silano; meals €50-55; ⊘12.30-3pm & 7.30-11pm Tue-Sun) Among Calabria's best eats, La Tavernetta marries rough country charm with citified elegance in warmly colourful dining rooms. The food is first-rate and based on the best local ingredients, from wild anise seed and mushrooms to mountain-raised lamb and kid. Reserve ahead on Sundays and holidays.

🛏 Albergo San Lorenzo — Hotel €

(📞0984 57 08 09; www.sanlorenzosialberga. it; Campo San Lorenzo; d/tr/q/ste €90/105/120/135; 🅿 ❄ 🛜) Above their famous restaurant, the owners of La Tavernetta have opened the area's most stylish sleep, with 21 large, well-equipped rooms done up in colourful, modernist style.

Cosenza ❼

✗ Ristorante Calabria Bella — Calabrian €€

(📞0984 79 35 31; www.ristorantecalabriabella. it; Piazza del Duomo 20; meals €30; ⊘noon-3pm & 7pm-midnight) Traditional Calabrian cuisine, such as *cavatelli con cozze e fagioli* (pasta with mussels and beans) and *grigliata mista di carne* (mixed grilled meats), is dished up with aplomb at this cosy restaurant in the old town.

🛏 B&B Via dell'Astrologo — B&B €

(📞338 9205394; www.viadellastrologo.com; Via Benincasa 16; s/d from €41/71; 🛜) A gem in the historic centre, this small B&B is tastefully decorated with polished wooden floors, white bedspreads and good-quality artwork. Host Marco is a mine of information on Cosenza and Calabria in general.

Pizzo ❽

✗ Pepe Nero — Seafood €€

(📞348 8124618; www.facebook.com/pg/pepeneropizzo; Via Marconi; meals €30-35) This family-owned restaurant just off Pizzo's main square has a stylish outdoor deck, the ideal spot to enjoy local seafood like *spada* (swordfish), prawn and lobster. We can also recommend the *calamaretti ripieni* (stuffed baby squid) and tuna tartare. Wine selections of local Calabrian varietals are also excellent. An essential stop for seafood fans.

Piccolo Grand Hotel
Boutique Hotel €€

(☎0963 53 32 93; www.piccolograndhotel.com; Via Chiaravalloti 32; s/d €110/130; ❋ 🛜) This pleasant four-star boutique hotel is hidden on an unlikely and rather dingy side street. But its exuberant blue-and-white design, upscale comforts and panoramic rooftop breakfasts make it one of Pizzo's top sleeps. There's also a small fitness area and e-bikes to rent.

Tropea 9

Genus Loci
Italian €€

(☎345 5896475; Largo Vaccari; €35-40; ⏱noon-2.30pm & 6.30-10.30pm) Dining options include a slender and modern dining room or an outside terrace with excellent views, both great locations to enjoy Genus Loci's light and innovative approach to the freshest of local seafood. Try the eggplant layered with shrimps and basil before a *secondi* course of baked grouper with anchovies. A concise wine list features mainly Calabrian varietals.

Donnaciccina
B&B €€

(☎0963 6 21 80; www.donnaciccina.com; Via Pelliccia 9; s/d/ste €75/150/200; ❋ 🛜) Look for the sign of a bounteous hostess bearing fruit and cake to find this delightful B&B, overlooking the main *corso*. The 17th-century *palazzo* retains a tangible sense of history with carefully selected antiques, canopy beds and terracotta tiled floors. There are nine restful rooms, a nearby suite (itself dating to the 15th century) and a chatty parrot at reception.

Gerace 11

Ristorante A Squella
Calabrian €

(☎0964 35 60 86; Via Ferruccio 21; meals €20-25; ⏱12.30-2.30pm daily & 7.30-10.30pm Mon-Sat) For a taste of traditional Calabrian cooking, modest, welcoming Ristorante a Squella makes for a great lunchtime stop. It serves reliably good dishes, specialising in seafood and Calabrian pasta dishes. The views from just outside are spectacular and the service from the friendly family that owns the restaurant is warm and heartfelt. Try the delicious deep-fried doughnuts for dessert.

L'Antico Borgo
B&B €

(☎327 2330095; https://lanticoborgogerace.it; Via IV Novembre 38; d €70; 🛜) L'Antico Borgo's five rooms are tucked away in Gerace's medieval labyrinth adjacent to the restaurant and pizzeria of the same name. Decor is relatively simple, but rooms are kept spotless and are a good option to enjoy the hill town's shadowed streets and laneways after the day trippers have departed.

Gambarie 14

Hotel Miramonti
Hotel €

(☎0965 74 31 90; www.hotelmiramontigambarie.it; Via degli Sci 10, Gambarie; s/d €60/90; ❋ 🛜 ⛷) A few hundred metres uphill from Gambarie's main square, the Miramonti provides all the necessary comforts (including a bar and spa), all steps from the ski lifts. Rooms are modest and basically furnished, and the restaurant serves hearty mountain fare, including soups and stews, mountain-grown meats, and first-rate local cheeses.

Reggio Calabria 15

La Cantina del Macellaio
Trattoria €€

(☎0965 2 39 32; www.lacantinadelmacellaio.com; Via Arcovito 26/28; meals €35; ⏱12.30-3pm & 7.30-11.30pm Wed-Mon) One of the best restaurants in Reggio, serving *maccheroni al ragù di maiale* (handmade pasta with pork sauce) and *involtini di vitello* (veal rolls) in an open, tiled dining room with exposed stonework and green flasks on the walls. The mostly Calabrian wines are equally impressive, as is the service. Aficionados of excellent meat dishes should order the mixed grill.

B&B Kalavria
B&B €

(☎347 5637038; ww.kalavriabb.com; Via Pellicano 21F; s/d €70/80; 🛜) Owner Domenico is a brilliant host at this modern and elegant B&B a few blocks from Reggio's waterfront *lungomare*. Bathrooms are particularly stylish, and in warmer months the rooftop terrace is a great place to relax. Breakfast features the best of local baked goods and Domenico can offer well-researched recommendations on where to eat and drink in his interesting hometown.

Classic Trip

Wonders of Ancient Sicily

36

More than a trip around la bella Sicilia, this is also a journey through time, from spare Greek temples to Norman churches decked out with Arab and Byzantine finery.

TRIP HIGHLIGHTS

82 km

Segesta
A huge 5th-century-BC Greek temple amid desolate mountains

664 km

Taormina
Marvel at the ancient Greek theatre suspended between sea and sky

START
● Palermo

rapani
②

FINISH ⑭

●Catania

⑧

18 km

Agrigento
Pay homage to this mesmerising complex of five Doric temples

Ragusa ●

⑫

545 km

Syracuse
Extraordinary tapestry of Graeco-Roman ruins, baroque piazzas and medieval streets

**12–14 DAYS
664KM / 412 MILES**

GREAT FOR...

BEST TIME TO GO

Spring and autumn are best. Avoid the heat and crowds of high summer.

ESSENTIAL PHOTO

Mt Etna from Taormina's Greek theatre.

BEST FOR HISTORY

Exploring layers of Sicily's past in Syracuse.

Classic Trip

36 Wonders of Ancient Sicily

A Mediterranean crossroads for 25 centuries, Sicily is heir to an unparalleled cultural legacy, from the temples of Magna Graecia to Norman churches made kaleidoscopic by Byzantine and Arab artisans. This trip takes you from exotic, palm-fanned Palermo to the baroque splendours of Syracuse and Catania. On the way, you'll also experience Sicily's startlingly diverse landscape, including bucolic farmland, smouldering volcanoes and long stretches of aquamarine coastline.

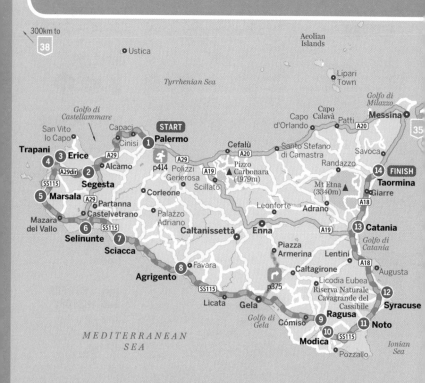

① Palermo

Palermo is a fascinating conglomeration of splendour and decay. Unlike Florence or Rome, many of its treasures are hidden rather than scrubbed up for endless streams of tourists. The city's cross-cultural history infuses its daily life, lending its dusty backstreet markets a distinct Middle Eastern feel and its architecture a unique East-meets-West look.

A trading port since Phoenician times, the city, which is best explored on foot (p414), first came to prominence as the capital of Arab Sicily in the 9th century AD. When the Normans rode into town in the 11th century, they

 LINK YOUR TRIP

35 The Calabrian Wilderness

To experience the wild peaks of the Pollino, head over to Reggio Calabria on the mainland via Messina.

 38 Sardinia's South Coast

From Palermo, car ferries sail to Cagliari, the starting point for a journey through some of Sardinia's most beautiful, less-trodden landscapes.

used Arab know-how to turn it into Christendom's richest and most sophisticated city. The **Cappella Palatina** (Palatine Chapel; 091 705 56 11; www.federicosecondo.org; Piazza del Parlamento; adult/reduced incl exhibition Fri-Mon €12/10, Tue-Thu €10/8; 8.15am-5.40pm Mon-Sat, to 1pm Sun) is the perfect expression of this marriage, with its gold-inflected Byzantine mosaics crowned by a honeycomb *muqarnas* ceiling – a masterpiece of Arab craftsmanship.

For an insight into Sicily's long and turbulent past, the **Museo Archeologico Regionale Antonio Salinas** (091 611 68 07; www.regione.sicilia.it/bbccaa/salinas; Piazza Olivella 24; adult/reduced €6/3; 9am-6pm Tue-Sat, to 1.30pm Sun) houses some of the island's most valuable Greek and Roman artefacts.

 p380

The Drive » From Palermo the 82km trip to Segesta starts along the fast-moving A29 as it skirts the mountains west of Palermo, then runs along agricultural plains until you reach the hills of Segesta. The Greek ruins lie just off the A29dir.

TRIP HIGHLIGHT

② Segesta

Set on the edge of a deep canyon in the midst of desolate mountains, the 5th-century-BC ruins of **Segesta** (0924 95 23 56; adult/child €6/free;

9am-7.30pm Apr-Sep, to 6.30pm Mar & Oct, to 5pm Nov-Feb) are a magical sight. The city, founded by the ancient Elymians, was in constant conflict with Selinunte, whose destruction it sought with dogged determination and singular success. Time, however, has done to Segesta what violence inflicted on Selinunte; little remains now, save the theatre and the never-completed Doric temple. The latter dates from around 430 BC and is remarkably well preserved. On windy days its 36 giant columns are said to act like an organ, producing mysterious notes.

The Drive » Keep heading along A29dir through a patchwork of green and ochre fields and follow signs for the 40km to Trapani. As you reach its outskirts, you'll head up the very windy SP31 to Erice, with great views of countryside and sea.

---

③ Erice

A spectacular hill town, Erice combines medieval charm with astounding 360-degree views from atop the legendary **Mt Eryx** (750m) – on a clear day, you can see as far as Cape Bon in Tunisia. Wander the medieval streets interspersed with churches, forts and tiny cobbled piazzas. Little remains from its ancient past, though as a centre for the cult of Venus, it has a seductive history.

The best views can be had from the **Giardino del Balio**, which overlooks the rugged turrets and wooded hillsides down to the saltpans of Trapani and the sea. Adjacent to the gardens is the Norman **Castello di Venere** (Castle of Venus; 320 8672957; www.fondazioneericearte. org/castellodivenere.php; Via Castello di Venere; adult/ reduced €4/2; 10am-8pm Aug, to 7pm Jul & Sep, to 6pm Apr-Jun & Oct, 10am-1pm Sat & Sun Nov-Mar), built in the 12th and 13th centuries over the ancient Temple of Venus. And while Venus may be the goddess of love, Erice's goddess of all things sweet is Maria Grammatico, whose eponymous **pasticceria** (0923 86 93 90; www. mariagrammatico.it; Via Vittorio Emanuele 14; pastries from €2; 9am-10pm May, Jun & Sep, to 1am Jul & Aug, to 7pm Oct-Apr) is revered around the globe. Don't leave town without savouring one of her cannoli or lemon-flavoured *cuscinetti* (small fried pastries).

The Drive >> For the 12km to Trapani, it's back down the switchbacks of the SP31.

④ Trapani

Once a key link in a powerful trading network that stretched from Carthage to Venice, Trapani occupies a sickle-shaped spit of land that hugs its ancient harbour. Although Trapani's industrial outskirts are rather bleak, its historic centre is filled with atmospheric pedestrian streets and some lovely churches and baroque buildings. The narrow network of streets remains a Moorish labyrinth, although it takes much of its character from the fabulous 18th-century baroque of the Spanish period. Make time for the **Chiesa Anime Sante del Purgatorio** (0923 56 28 82; Via San Francesco d'Assisi; by donation; 7.30am-noon & 4-7pm Mon-Sat, 10am-noon & 4-7pm Sun), home to the 18th-century *Misteri*, 20 life-sized effigies depicting the Passion of Christ.

p380

The Drive >> For the 33km trip from Trapani to Marsala, head south on the SS115. Small towns alternate with farmland until you reach Marsala on Sicily's west coast.

⑤ Marsala

Best known for its eponymous sweet dessert wines, Marsala is an elegant town of stately baroque buildings within a perfect square of city walls. Founded by Phoenicians escaping Roman attacks, the city still has remnants of the 7m-thick ramparts they built,

ensuring that it was the last Punic settlement to fall to the Romans.

Marsala's finest treasure is the partially reconstructed remains of a Carthaginian *liburna* (warship) – the only remaining physical evidence of the Phoenicians' seafaring superiority in the 3rd century BC. You can visit it at the **Museo Archeologico Baglio Anselmi** (0923 95 25 35; Via Lungomare Boeo 30; adult/reduced €4/2; 9am-6.30pm Wed-Sat, to 1.30pm Tue & Sun).

p380

The Drive >> For this 52km leg, once again head down the SS115, passing through farmland and scattered towns until you reach the A29. Continue on the autostrada to Castelvetrano, then follow the SS115 and SS115dir for the last leg through orchards and fields to seaside Selinunte.

⑥ Selinunte

Built on a promontory overlooking the sea, the Greek ruins of **Selinunte** (Selinunte Archaeological Park; 334 6040459, 0924 4 62 77; www.selinunte.gov. it; Via Selinunte, Castelve-trano; adult/reduced €6/3; 9am-6pm Mar-Oct, to 5pm Nov-Feb) are among the most impressive in Sicily, dating to around the 7th century BC. There are few historical records of the city, which was once one of the world's most powerful, and even the names of the various temples have been forgotten and are now identified by letters. The most impressive, **Temple E**, has been partially re-built, its columns pieced together from their fragments with part of its tympanum. Many of the carvings, which are on a par with the Parthenon marbles, particularly those from **Temple C**, are now in Palermo's archaeological museum.

The Drive » Head back up to the SS115 and past a series of hills and plains for the 37km trip to Sciacca.

7 Sciacca

Seaside Sciacca was founded in the 5th century BC as a thermal resort for nearby Seli-nunte. Until 2015, when financial woes forced the spa to shut down indefi-nitely, Sciacca's healing waters continued to be the big drawcard, attract-ing coachloads of Italian tourists who came to wallow in its sulphurous vapours and mineral-rich mud. Spas and thermal cures apart, it remains a laid-back town with an attractive medieval core and some excellent seafood restaurants.

The Drive » Continue eastwards on the SS115 as it follows the southern coast onto Porto Empedocle and then, 10km inland, Agrigento's hilltop centre. In all, it's about 62km.

TRIP HIGHLIGHT

8 Agrigento

Seen from a distance, Agrigento's unsightly apartment blocks loom incongruously on the hillside, distracting attention from the splen-did Valley of Temples below. In the valley, the mesmerising **ruins** (Valle dei Templi; ☎0922 62 16 11; www.parcovalledeitempli. it; adult/reduced €10/5, incl Museo Archeologico €13.50/7, incl Museo Archeologico & Gi-ardino della Kolymbetra €15/10; ⏱8.30am-8pm, to 11pm mid-Jul–mid-Sep) of ancient Akragas claim the best-preserved Doric temples outside of Greece.

The ruins are spread over a 13-sq-km site that is divided into eastern and western halves.

Head first to the eastern zone, where you'll find the three best temples: the **Tempio di Hera**, the **Tempio di Ercole**, and, most spectacularly, the **Tempio della Concordia** (Temple of Concord). This, the only temple to survive relatively intact, was built around 440 BC and was converted into a Christian church in the 6th century.

Uphill from the ruins, Agrigento's **medi-eval centre** also has its charms, with a 14th-century cathedral and a number of medieval and baroque buildings.

 p380

The Drive » For this 133km leg head back to the SS115, which veers from inland farmland to brief encounters with the sea. Past the town of Gela, you will head into more

DETOUR: VILLA ROMANA DEL CASALE

Start: 8 Agrigento

Near the town of Piazza Armerina in central Sicily, the stunning 3rd-century Roman **Villa Romana del Casale** (☎0935 68 00 36; www.villaromanadelcasale.it; adult/reduced €10/5, combined ticket including Morgantina and Museo Archeologico di Aidone €14/7; ⏱9am-7pm Apr-Oct, to 5pm Nov-Mar, open to 11pm Fri-Sun Jul & Aug) is thought to have been the country retreat of Diocletian's co-emperor Marcus Aurelius Maximianus. Buried under mud in a 12th-century flood, the villa remained hidden for 700 years before its floor mosaics – considered some of the finest in existence – were discovered in the 1950s. Covering almost the entire villa floor, they are considered unique for their range of hues and natural, narrative style.

WHY THIS IS A CLASSIC TRIP
DUNCAN GARWOOD, WRITER

Sicily claims some of the most spectacular artistic and archaeological treasures you've never heard of. The great Greek ruins of Agrigento and Syracuse might be on many travellers' radars but what about Palermo's Cappella Palatina or Noto's flamboyant baroque streets? These masterpieces are all the more rewarding for being so unexpected, and make this round-island trip an unforgettable experience.

Above: Syracuse
Left: Mosaic, Villa Romana del Casale
Right: Cappella Palatina, Palermo

hilly country, including a steep climb past Comiso, followed by a straight shot along the SP52 to Ragusa.

----

9 Ragusa

Set amid the rocky peaks northwest of Modica, Ragusa has two faces. Atop the hill sits **Ragusa Superiore**, a busy town with all the trappings of a modern provincial capital, while etched into the hillside is **Ragusa Ibla**. This sloping area of tangled alleyways, grey stone houses and baroque *palazzi* (mansions) is Ragusa's magnificent historic centre.

Like other towns in the region, Ragusa Ibla collapsed after the 1693 earthquake. But the aristocracy, ever impractical, rebuilt their homes on exactly the same spot. Grand baroque churches and *palazzi* line the twisting, narrow lanes, which then open suddenly onto sun-drenched piazzas. Piazza del Duomo, the centre of town, is dominated by the 18th-century baroque **Duomo di San Giorgio** (Piazza Duomo, Ragusa Ibla; ⊙10am-1pm & 3-6.30pm Apr-Oct & Dec, reduced hours rest of year), with its magnificent neoclassical dome and stained-glass windows.

The Drive >> Follow the SS115 for this winding, up-and-down 15km drive through rock-littered hilltops to Modica.

377

Classic Trip

---

⑩ Modica

Atmospheric Modica recalls a *presepe* (traditional nativity crib), its medieval buildings climbing steeply up either side of a deep gorge. But unlike some of the other Unesco-listed cities in the area, it doesn't package its treasures into a single easy-to-see street or central piazza: rather, they are spread around the town and take some discovering. Its star attraction is the baroque **Duomo di San Giorgio** (☎0932 94 12 79; Corso San Giorgio, Modica Alta; ⏱8am-12.30pm & 3.30-7pm), which stands in isolated splendour atop a majestic 250-step staircase.

The city's nerve centre is Corso Umberto. A wide avenue flanked by graceful palaces, churches, restaurants and bars, the thoroughfare is where the locals take their evening *passeggiata* (stroll). Originally a raging river flowed through town, but after major flood damage in 1902 it was dammed and Corso Umberto was built over it.

🛏 p381

The Drive » Head back onto the SS115, which becomes quite curvy as you close in on Noto, 40km away.

---

⑪ Noto

Flattened in 1693 by an earthquake, Noto was rebuilt quickly and grandly, and its golden-hued sandstone buildings make it the finest baroque town in Sicily, especially impressive at night when illuminations accentuate its intricately carved facades. The pièce de résistance is **Corso Vittorio Emanuele**, an elegantly manicured walkway flanked by thrilling baroque *palazzi* and churches.

Just off Corso Vittorio Emanuele, the **Palazzo Castelluccio** (☎0931 83 88 81; http://palazzocastelluccio.it; Via Cavour 10; adult/child €12/free; ⏱11am-7pm) reveals the luxury to which the local nobility were accustomed. Recently restored, its suite of lavish rooms is awash with murals, evocative paintings, gilded settees, and worn glazed floors revealing the paths of long-gone servants.

The Drive » The 39km drive to Syracuse from Noto takes you down the SP59 and then northeast on the A18/E45, past the majestic Riserva Naturale Cavagrande del Cassibile as you parallel Sicily's eastern coast.

TRIP HIGHLIGHT

⑫ Syracuse

Syracuse is a dense tapestry of overlapping cultures and civilisations. Ancient Greek ruins rise out of lush citrus orchards, cafe tables spill out onto baroque piazzas, and medieval lanes meander to the sea. Your visit, like the city itself, can be split into two easy parts: one dedicated to the archaeological site, the other to Ortygia, the ancient island neighbourhood connected to the modern town by bridge.

It's difficult to imagine now but in its heyday

THE 1693 EARTHQUAKE

On 11 January, 1693, a devastating 7.4-magnitude earthquake hit southeastern Sicily, destroying buildings from Catania to Ragusa. The destruction was terrible, but it also created a blank palette for architects to rebuild the region's cities and towns out of whole cloth, in the latest style and according to rational urban planning – a phenomenon practically unheard of since ancient times. In fact, the earthquake ushered in an entirely new architectural style known as Sicilian baroque, defined by its seductive curves and elaborate detail, which you can see on display in Ragusa, Modica, Catania and many other cities in the region.

Syracuse was the largest city in the ancient world, bigger even than Athens and Corinth. The **Parco Archeologico della Neapolis** (0931 6 62 06; Viale Paradiso 14; adult/reduced €10/5, incl Museo Archeologico €13.50/7; 8.30am-1hr before sunset) is home to well-preserved Greek (and Roman) remains, with the remarkably intact **Teatro Greco** – constructed in the 5th century BC and rebuilt two centuries later – as the main attraction. In the grounds of Villa Landolina, about 500m east of the archaeological park, is the exceptional **Museo Archeologico Paolo Orsi** (0931 48 95 11; www.regione.sicilia.it/beni culturali/museopaoloorsi; Viale Teocrito 66; adult/reduced €8/4, incl Parco Archeologico €13.50/7; 9am-6pm Tue-Sat, to 1pm Sun).

Compact, labyrinthine **Ortygia** encompass 25 centuries of history. At its heart, the city's 7th-century **Duomo** (Piazza del Duomo; adult/reduced €2/1; 9am-6.30pm Mon-Sat Apr-Oct, to 5.30pm Nov-Mar) lords it over Piazza del Duomo, one of Italy's most magnificent squares. The cathedral was built over a pre-existing 5th-century-BC Greek temple, incorporating most of the original Doric columns in its three-aisled structure. The sumptuous baroque

facade was added in the 18th century.

 p381, p389

The Drive » From Syracuse to Catania, it is a 66km drive north along the A18/E45. This is orange-growing country and you will see many orchards, which can be gorgeously fragrant when in bloom.

----

⑬ Catania

Gritty, vibrant Catania is a true city of the volcano, much of it constructed from the lava that poured down on it during Mt Etna's 1669 eruption. The baroque centre is lava-black in colour, as if a fine dusting of soot permanently covers its elegant buildings, most of which are the work of Giovanni Battista Vaccarini. The 18th-century architect almost single-handedly rebuilt the civic centre into an elegant, modern city of spacious boulevards and set-piece piazzas.

Long buried under lava, the **Graeco-Roman Theatre & Odeon** (095 715 05 08; Via Vittorio Emanuele II 262; adult/reduced incl Casa Liberti €6/3; 9am-7pm) remind you that Catania's history goes back much further. Picturesquely sited in a crumbling residential area, the ruins are occasionally brightened by laundry flapping on the rooftops of vine-covered

buildings that appear to have sprouted organically from the half-submerged stage.

 p381, p389

The Drive » The 53km drive to Taormina along the A18/E45 is a coast-hugging northern run, taking in more orange groves as well as glimpses of the sparkling Ionian Sea.

TRIP HIGHLIGHT

⑭ Taormina

Over the centuries, Taormina has seduced an exhaustive line of writers and artists, from Goethe to DH Lawrence. The main reason for their infatuation? The perfect horseshoe-shaped **Teatro Greco** (0942 2 32 20; Via Teatro Greco; adult/reduced €10/5; 9am-1hr before sunset), a lofty ancient marvel looking out towards mighty Mt Etna and the Ionian Sea. Built in the 3rd century BC, the *teatro* is the most dramatically situated Greek theatre in the world and the second largest in Sicily (after Syracuse).

The 9th-century capital of Byzantine Sicily, Taormina also has a well-preserved, if touristy, **medieval town**, its chi-chi streets dotted with fashionable cafes and bars made for a glamorous wrap-up toast to your journey.

 p381

Eating & Sleeping

Palermo ❶

🍴 Aja Mola   Seafood €€

(📞091 611 91 59, 334 1508335; www.
ajamolapalermo.it; Via Cassari 39; meals €35-40;
🕐12.30-3pm & 7.30-11pm Tue-Sun; 🛜) On-
point Aja Mola is among Palermo's top seafood
eateries. The interior's smart, subtle take on a
nautical theme is reflected in the open kitchen,
which eschews stock-standard cliches for
modern, creative dishes. The result: appetite-
piquing options like teriyaki-style tartare with
caperberries, or surf-turf *tagliolini* pasta with
succulent shrimps and pork jowl. Bar seating
available; ideal for solo diners. Book ahead.

🛏 Butera 28   Apartment €€

(📞333 3165432; www.butera28.it; Via Butera
28; apt per day €80-240, per week €520-1600;
❄️🛜) Delightful multilingual owner Nicoletta
rents 12 apartments in the 18th-century Palazzo
Lanzi Tomasi, the last home of Giuseppe Tomasi
di Lampedusa, author of *The Leopard*. Graced
with family antiques, the units range from 30
to 180 sq metres, most sleeping a family of
four or more. Five apartments face the sea and
all feature laundry facilities, well-equipped
kitchens and sound-proofed windows.

Trapani ❹

🍴 La Bettolaccia   Sicilian €€

(📞0923 2 59 32; www.labettolaccia.it; Via Enrico
Fardella 25; meals €35-45; 🕐12.45-3pm &
7.45-11pm Mon-Fri, 7.45-11pm Sat) Unwaveringly
authentic, this on-trend Slow Food favourite,
squirrelled away down a sleepy side street, is
the hotspot to feast on spicy couscous with
fried fish or mixed seafood, *caponata* (eggplant
and sun-dried tomatoes with capers in a
sweet-and-sour sauce), the catch of the day, and
other traditional Trapanese dishes in a sharp,
minimalist white space. Reservations essential.

🛏 La Gancia Residence   Hotel €€

(📞0923 43 80 60; www.lagancia.com; Piazza
Mercato del Pesce; d €110-170, tr €200, q €189-
280; 🕐reception 7am-midnight; ❄️🛜) Spoon
yourself a jelly sweet out of the huge sweetie jar
at reception, admire the soaring centuries-old
ceiling and chic Moorish-styled lounge, and
congratulate yourself on landing a room at one
of the most beautiful spots in town, practically
on the water. Sea views from many rooms
could not be bolder or more romantic, and the
breakfast terrace is a dream.

Marsala ❺

🍴 Quimera   Sandwiches €

(📞349 0765524; www.facebook.com/
quimerapub; Via Sarzana 34-36; sandwiches &
salads from €5; 🕐noon-3pm & 6.30pm-2am
Mon-Sat, 6.30pm-2am Sun) Smack in the heart
of Marsala's pedestrianised centre, this buzzy
eating-drinking hybrid is the local hotspot for
artisanal craft beers, gourmet sandwiches
and meal-sized salads – all served with a big
smile and bags of charm by the friendly young
owners. Linger over a shared cutting board of
cheeses or salami, or agonise over the choice of
creatively filled *panini* and *piadine* (wraps).

Agrigento ❽

🍴 Kalòs   Sicilian €€

(📞0922 2 63 89; www.ristorantekalos.it; Piazzetta San Calogero; meals €35-45; 🕐12.30-3pm
& 7-11pm Tue-Sun) For fine dining, head to this
restaurant just outside the historic centre.
Tables on little balconies offer a delightful setting
to enjoy homemade *pasta all'agrigentina* (with
fresh tomatoes, basil and almonds), grilled
lamb chops or *spada gratinata* (baked swordfish
in breadcrumbs). Superb desserts include
homemade *cannoli* (pastry shells with a sweet
filling) and almond *semifreddi*.

PortAtenea
B&B €

(📱349 0937492; www.portatenea.com; Via Atenea, cnr Via Cesare Battisti; s/d/ tr €50/75/95; 🌸🛜) This five-room B&B wins plaudits for its panoramic roof terrace overlooking the Valley of the Temples, and its superconvenient location at the entrance to the old town, five minutes' walk from the train and bus stations. Best of all is the generous advice about Agrigento offered by hosts Sandra and Filippo (witness Filippo's amazing Google Earth tour of nearby beaches!).

Modica ⑩

Masseria Quartarella
Agriturismo €

(📱360 654829; www.quartarella.com; Contrada Quartarella Passo Cane 1; s €40, d €75-80, tr €85-100, q €90-120; 🅿🌸🛜🏊) Spacious rooms, welcoming hosts and ample breakfasts make this converted farmhouse in the countryside south of Modica an appealing choice for anyone travelling by car. Owners Francesco and Francesca are generous in sharing their love and encyclopaedic knowledge of local history, flora and fauna and can suggest a multitude of driving itineraries in the surrounding area.

Syracuse ⑫

Il Pesce Azzurro
Seafood €€

(📱366 2445056; Via Cavour 53; meals €30-35; 🕐noon-3.30pm & 7-11pm) Seafood-loving locals swear by this easy-to-miss *osteria*, with its white-and-blue interior somewhat reminiscent of a Greek-island taverna. The menu favours simplicity and top-notch produce, whether it's sweet, succulent Mazara shrimps drizzled in lime juice, plump *vongole* (clams) paired with spaghetti and garlic, or tender *polpo* (octopus) served *alla luciana* (in a rich tomato and onion sauce). Honest, flavour-packed goodness.

Catania ⑬

Pescheria Fratelli Vittorio
Seafood €€

(📱339 7733890; Via Dusmet 1; meals €25-40; 🕐11.30am-3.30pm & 7pm-midnight Tue-Sun, closed Sun dinner Nov–mid-May) Cats would kill for a table at Fratelli Vittorio, a cult-status eatery whose counter glistens with Catania's freshest fish and seafood. It's not surprising given that co-owner Giovanni is a fishmonger, handpicking the best ingredients from the nearby market. For an overview, order the *degustazione di antipasti del giorno,* or feel the love in the generous *zuppa di pesce* (seafood soup).

Taormina ⑭

Osteria Nero D'Avola
Sicilian €€

(📱0942 62 88 74; Piazza San Domenico 2b; meals €40-50; 🕐7-11pm daily mid-Jun–mid-Sep, noon-2.30pm & 7-11pm Tue-Sun rest of year; 🛜) Owner Turi Siligato fishes, hunts and forages for his smart *osteria,* and if he's in, he'll probably share anecdotes about the day's bounty and play a few tunes on the piano. This is one of Taormina's top eateries, where seasonality, local producers and passion underpin outstanding dishes, such as grilled meatballs in lemon leaves, and fresh fish with Sicilian pesto.

Hotel Villa Belvedere
Hotel €€€

(📱0942 2 37 91; www.villabelvedere.it; Via Bagnoli Croce 79; d €120-690, ste €190-890; 🕐Mar-late Nov; 🌸@🛜🏊) Built in 1902, the distinguished, supremely comfortable Villa Belvedere was one of Taormina's original grand hotels. Well positioned with fabulous views, luxuriant gardens and wonderful service, its highlights include plush, communal lounge areas and a swimming pool complete with a century-old palm. Neutral hues and understated style typify the hotel's 57 rooms, with parking costing an extra €16 per day.

Sicilian Baroque

37

Stretching from the sparkling blue of the Ionian Sea to the green hills and gorges of the interior, this trip showcases Sicily's most spectacular, Unesco-listed baroque towns.

TRIP HIGHLIGHTS

Catania ● START

66 km

Syracuse
Graeco-Roman ruins aside, Syracuse features masterly baroque town planning

7 km

Modica
Ancient buildings climb up either side of a deep gorge

FINISH
8

6

● **Scicli**   **Ispica**

Ragusa
Labyrinthine streets, rock-grey palazzi and sun-drenched piazzas

3 km

Noto
Sicily's finest baroque town, carved from golden sandstone

138 km

5 DAYS
213KM / 132 MILES

GREAT FOR...

BEST TIME TO GO
Spring and autumn bring fewer crowds and better weather for hiking in the hillsides of the Monti Iblei.

ESSENTIAL PHOTO
A nighttime shot of Noto's Corso Vittorio Emanuele.

BEST FOR HISTORY
Wander the labyrinthine lanes of Ragusa Ibla.

37 Sicilian Baroque

Shattered by a devastating earthquake in 1693 (p378), the towns of the Val di Noto rose collectively as reinvented beauties, becoming 18th-century poster kids for Sicily's own exuberant brand of baroque. The result is a rare example of aesthetic cohesion, a vision of honey-coloured towns sitting delightfully in a landscape of citrus and olive groves, and checkerboard fields shot through with limestone cliffs and rocky gorges.

❶ Catania

Though surrounded by ugly urban sprawl, Sicily's second-largest city is a thriving metropolis with a large university and a beautiful, Unesco-listed centre. Brooding on the horizon, snow-capped Mt Etna is a powerful presence.

The volcano is deeply set in Catania's DNA. Much of the city's historic core was built from lava that poured down Etna's slopes during a massive eruption in 1669. From its exuberant baroque *palazzi* (mansions) to grand set-piece squares, this is a city dressed in shades of charcoal

and ashen grey. At its heart is elegant **Piazza del Duomo**, the city's collective living room. It's also where you'll find Catania's majestic **Cattedrale di Sant'Agata** (☎095 32 00 44; Piazza del Duomo; ⏱7am-noon & 4-7pm Mon-Sat, 7.30am-12.30pm & 4.30-7.30pm Sun), final resting place of homegrown composer Vincenzo Bellini. Just off the square is famous fish market **La Pescheria** (Via Pardo; ⏱7am-2pm Mon-Sat), serving up more colour, noise and theatrics than any Bellini opera.

✕ ⊨ p381, p389

The Drive ≫ From Catania to Syracuse, it is a 66km drive down the A18/E45 autostrada. This is orange-growing country

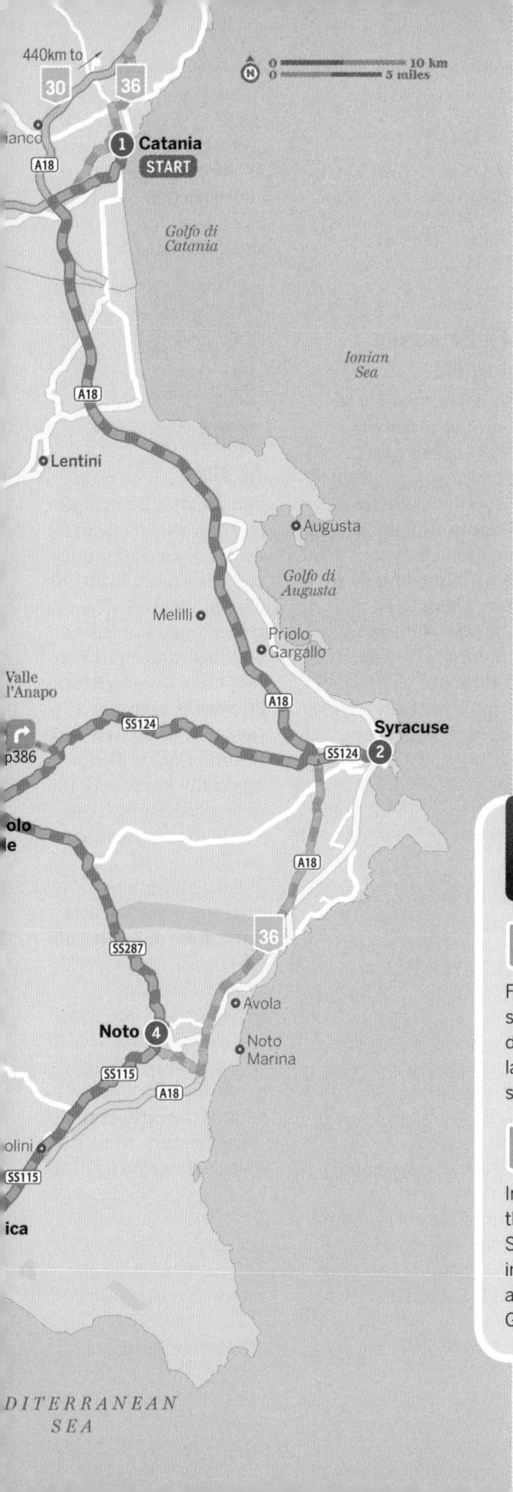

and you'll see many orchards, which are gorgeously fragrant when in bloom. Exit onto the SS124 for the last 4km into central Syracuse.

TRIP HIGHLIGHT

2 Syracuse

Settled by colonists from Corinth in 734 BC, Syracuse was considered the most beautiful city of the ancient world, rivalling Athens in power and prestige. You can still explore the city's ancient heart at the extraordinary **Parco Archeologico della Neapolis** (☎0931 6 62 06; Viale Paradiso 14; adult/reduced €10/5, incl Museo Archeologico €13.50/7; ⏲8.30am-1hr before sunset), the star attraction of which is the huge 5th-century BC Greek theatre.

LINK YOUR TRIP

30 Cilento Coastal Trail

From Catania, car ferries sail to Salerno, a short drive from Paestum, the launching pad for this spectacular coastal jaunt.

36 Wonders of Ancient Sicily

In Catania, you can join the grand tour of Ancient Sicily, which begins in Arab-inflected Palermo and ends at Taormina's spectacular Greek theatre.

In the wake of the 1693 earthquake, Syracuse, like most cities in the region, underwent a baroque facelift. While you'll find a number of baroque paintings at the **Galleria Regionale di Palazzo Bellomo** (📞0931 6 95 11; www.regione.sicilia.it/beniculturali/palazzobellomo; Via Capodieci 16; adult/reduced €8/4; ⏰9am-7pm Tue-Sat, to 1.30pm Sun), the city's true period masterpiece is **Piazza del Duomo**, home of numerous architectural masterpieces. Top billing goes to the **Duomo** (Piazza del Duomo; adult/reduced €2/1; ⏰9am-6.30pm Mon-Sat Apr-Oct, to 5.30pm Nov-Mar), its 18th-century facade considered a masterpiece of high Sicilian baroque. Look beneath the baroque veneer, though, and you can still see traces of the city's Greek origins, including 5th-century-BC temple columns embedded in the Duomo's exterior.

 p381, p389

The Drive ≫ From Syracuse, head through rolling and unspoilt countryside along the SS124 for 42km to Palazzolo Acreide.

---

❸ Palazzolo Acreide

A charming town of baroque architecture and ancient ruins, Palazzolo Acreide's focal point is **Piazza del Popolo**, a striking square dominated by the ornate bulk of the **Chiesa di San Sebastiano** and **Palazzo Municipale**, an impressive town hall. A 20-minute uphill walk from Piazza del Popolo leads to the archaeological park of **Akrai** (📞0931 87 66 02; Colle dell'Acromonte; adult/reduced €4/2; ⏰8am-6pm Jun-Sep summer, to 4pm Oct-May), once a thriving Greek colony and one of the area's best-kept secrets. You'll discover an ancient Greek theatre and Christian burial chambers with exquisitely carved reliefs.

The Drive ≫ Head southeast along the SS287 for a 30km drive through more beautiful countryside. The road becomes curvier as you head into Noto.

TRIP HIGHLIGHT

❹ Noto

Rebuilt after being flattened by the 1693 earthquake, Noto claims one of Sicily's most beautiful baroque centres. The golden-hued sandstone buildings and churches that flank **Corso Vittorio Emanuele**, many designed by local architect Rosario Gagliardi, are especially impressive in the early evening light and at night when they are illuminated.

Particularly eye-catching is the **Basilica Cattedrale di San Nicolò** (📞327 0162589; www.oqdany.it; Piazza Municipio; ⏰10am-2pm & 4.30-9pm Jul & Aug, 10am-6pm Sep-Jun), crowned by a distinctive dome. For an elevated view of the cathedral, hit the panoramic terrace at **Palazzo Ducezio** (📞0931 83 64 62; www.comune.noto.sr.it/la-cultura/la-sala-degli-specchi; Piazza Municipio; Sala degli Specchi €2, panoramic terrace €2; ⏰10am-6pm).

To see how the local aristocracy lived in

 DETOUR: VALLE DELL'ANAPO

Start: ❷ Syracuse

For some beautifully wild and unspoilt countryside, turn off the SS124 between Syracuse and Palazzolo Acreide and head down into the beautiful Valle dell'Anapo – a deep limestone gorge. Follow signs to **Ferla**, with its small but lovely baroque centre. Another 11km past Ferla, you'll find the **Necropoli di Pantalica** an important Iron and Bronze Age necropolis. Dating from the 13th to the 8th century BC, it is an extensive area of limestone rocks honeycombed by more than 5000 tombs. There's no ticket office – just a car park at the end of the long, winding road down from Ferla.

Noto Basilica Cattedrale di San Nicolò

baroque times, wander through nearby **Palazzo Nicolaci di Villado-rata** (☎338 7427022; www.comune.noto.sr.it/palazzo-nicolaci; Via Corrado Nicolaci; admission €4; ⏲10am-6pm mid-Mar–mid-Oct, 10am-1pm & 3-5pm rest of year) or take a guided tour of Palazzo Castelluccio (p378).

✖ p389

The Drive ⟫ Head southwest 22km along SS115 through more fields and orchards, passing through the town of Rosolini. Hilltop Ispica will rise up in front of you. Catch the sharply winding SP47 to the town centre.

- - - - - - - - - - - - - - - - -

⑤ Ispica

Between Noto and Modica, this hilltop town claims a number of fine baroque build-ings. However, the real reason to stop is to peer into the **Cava d'Ispica** (☎0932 95 26 08; www.

cavadispica.org; Crocevia Cava Ispica; adult/reduced €4/2; ⏲9am-6.30pm May-Oct, to 1.15pm Mon-Sat Nov & Dec), a verdant, 13km-long gorge studded with thousands of natural caves and grot-toes. Evidence of human habitation here dates to about 2000 BC, and over the millennia the caves have served as Neolithic tombs, early Christian catacombs and medieval dwellings.

The Drive ⟫ Start this 17km leg on the SS115 through relatively flat agricultural land. As you reach the suburbs of Modica, follow signs to Modica Centro and then to Corso Umberto I, the town's main thoroughfare.

- - - - - - - - - - - - - - - - -

TRIP HIGHLIGHT

⑥ Modica

With its steeply stacked medieval centre and lively central strip (Corso Umberto I), Modica is

one of southern Sicily's most atmospheric towns. The highlight is the **Chiesa di San Giorgio** (Corso San Giorgio, Modica Alta; ⏲8am-12.30pm, 3.30-6.30pm), a spectacular baroque church con-sidered to be architect Rosario Gagliardi's great masterpiece. It stands in isolated splendour atop a majestic 250-step staircase in Modica Alta, the high part of town.

Modica is also famous for its distinctly grainy chocolate, worked at low temperature using an ancient method. To stock up on it, hit **Antica Dol-ceria Bonajuto** (☎0932 94 12 25; www.bonajuto.it; Corso Umberto I 159, Modica Bassa; ⏲9am-8.30pm Sep-Jul, to midnight Aug), Sicily's oldest chocolate factory, or visit award-winning **Caffè Adamo** (☎0932 197 25 46; www.caffeadamo.it; Via Maresa Tedeschi 15-17,

Modica Bassa; cup/cone from €2/2.50; ⏰6am-1am summer, to 11pm rest of year, closed Mon Sep-Mar; 📶).

The Drive ≫ From Modica to Scicli, wind your way southwest along the SP54 for 10km through rugged, rocky countryside.

❼ Scicli

Compact Scicli is the most authentic of the Val di Noto towns, with an easy, salubrious vibe favoured by a growing number of VIP residents.

Its wealth of baroque churches includes the **Chiesa di Santa Teresa** (☎333 2613428; www.face book.com/agirescicli; Via Santa Teresa 16; admission incl guided tour €3; ⏰10am-10pm summer, 10am-2pm & 3-6.30pm winter), home to

a 16th-century fresco featuring a rare inscription in Sicilianised Latin. Pedestrianised Via Francesco Mormino Penna claims a number of interesting sights, including **Palazzo Bonelli Patanè** (☎340 4756053; Via Francesco Mormino Penna; adult/reduced €9/5; ⏰10am-1pm & 4-7.30pm daily mid-Mar–early Nov), charming apothecary **Antica Farmacia Cartia** (La Farmacia di Montalbano; ☎338 8614973; www.tanitscicli.wix. com; Via Francesco Mormina Penna 24; adult/reduced €2/1; ⏰10am-1pm & 5-8pm Jul-Sep, 10am-1pm & 4-7pm Apr-Jun & Oct–mid-Nov, 10am-1pm & 3-6pm Mar & Dec, closed rest of year) and **Palazzo Municipio** (Palazzo Iacono; ☎333 2613428; www.facebook. com/agirescicli; Via Francesco

Mormino Penna; admission incl guided tour €3; ⏰10am-10pm summer, 10am-2pm & 3-6.30pm winter), home to sets from TV series *Inspector Montalbano*.

The Drive ≫ The first half of this 26km stretch winds north on SP94, passing along the rim of a pretty canyon typical of the region. Then catch the winding SS115 as it heads up to Ragusa. Across a small canyon, you will see the old, hillside historic centre of Ragusa rising grandly.

❽ Ragusa

Set amid rocky peaks, **Ragusa Ibla** – Ragusa's historic centre – is a joy to wander, with its labyrinthine lanes weaving through rock-grey *palazzi,* then opening suddenly onto beautiful, sun-drenched piazzas. It's easy to get lost but sooner or later you'll end up at **Piazza Duomo**, Ragusa's sublime central space. At the top end of the sloping square is the 1744 **Duomo di San Giorgio** (Piazza Duomo, Ragusa Ibla; ⏰10am-1pm & 3-6.30pm Apr-Oct & Dec, reduced hours rest of year), one of Rosario Gagliardi's finest accomplishments.

Up the hill from Ragusa Ibla is **Ragusa Superiore**, the town's modern and less attractive half.

 p389

LOCAL KNOWLEDGE: HITTING THE HIGH NOTE

Catania's most famous native son, Vincenzo Bellini (1801–35), was the quintessential composer of *bel canto* opera. Hugely successful in his lifetime, he was known for his inimitable ability to combine sensuality with melodic clarity and his works still woo audiences today. The **Museo Belliniano** (☎095 715 05 35; Piazza San Francesco 3; adult/reduced €5/2; ⏰9am-7pm Mon-Sat, to 1pm Sun), in the composer's former Catania home, has an interesting collection of his memorabilia. Catania's lavish, 19th-century **Teatro Massimo Bellini** (☎095 730 61 11; www.teatromassimobellini.it; Via Perrotta 12) is the place to hear *I Puritani, Norma* and his other masterworks.

Eating & Sleeping

Catania ❶

✗ Mè Cumpari Turiddu   Sicilian €€

(☎095 715 01 42; www.mecumparituriddu.
it; Piazza Turi Ferro 36-38; meals €26-40;
🕑11.30am-12.30am; 🛜) Old chandeliers,
recycled furniture and vintage mirrors exude
a nostalgic air at this quirky bistro-restaurant-
providore, where tradition and modernity meet
to impressive effect. Small producers and Slow
Food sensibilities underline sophisticated,
classically inspired dishes like ricotta-and-
marjoram ravioli in a pork sauce, soothing
Ustica lentil stew or a playful 'deconstructed'
cannolo. There's a fabulous selection of Sicilian
cheeses, lighter bistro grub and cakes.

🛏 B&B Crociferi   B&B €

(☎095 715 22 66; www.bbcrociferi.it; Via
Crociferi 81; d €75-85, tr €100-110, apt €98-110,
ste €120-140; 🅿🛜) Perfectly positioned
on pedestrianised Via Crociferi, this B&B in
a beautifully decorated family home affords
easy access to Catania's historic centre.
Three palatial rooms (each with a private,
refurbished bathroom across the hall) feature
high ceilings, antique tiles, frescoes and artistic
accoutrements from the owners' travels. The
B&B also houses two apartments; the largest
(called Lilla) has a spectacular, leafy panoramic
terrace. Book ahead.

Syracuse ❷

✗ Don Camillo   Sicilian €€€

(☎0931 6 71 33; www.ristorantedoncamillo.it;
Via della Maestranza 96; meals €45-75; 🕑12.30-
2.30pm & 8-10.30pm Mon-Sat; 🛜🍴) One of
Ortygia's most elegant restaurants, Don Camillo
specialises in sterling service and innovative
Sicilian cuisine. Pique the appetite with a *crudo*
of crustaceans paired with sweet-and-sour
celery gelato, swoon over decadent braised-
beef ravioli with butter, sage and *ragusano*
cheese, or (discreetly) lick your whiskers over
an outstanding *tagliata di tonno* (tuna steak)
with red-pepper 'marmalade'. A must for Slow
Food gourmands.

🛏 Hotel Gutkowski   Hotel €€

(☎0931 46 58 61; www.guthotel.it; Lungomare
Vittorini 26; d €90-150, tr €150, q €160; 🅿🛜)
Book well in advance for one of the sea-view
rooms at this stylish, eclectic hotel on the
Ortygia waterfront, at the edge of the Giudecca
neighbourhood. Divided between two buildings,
its rooms are simple yet chic, with pretty tiled
floors, walls in teals, greys, blues and browns,
and a sharply curated mix of vintage and
industrial details.

Noto ❹

✗ Manna   Sicilian €€

(☎0931 83 60 51; www.mannanoto.it; Via
Rocco Pirri 15; meals €35-47; 🕑noon-2.30pm
& 7-10.30pm Wed-Mon Easter-Jul & Sep-Dec,
7-10.30pm daily Aug; 🛜) Divided into a hip front
bar and sultry back dining rooms, Manna wows
with its competent, contemporary creations.
Premium produce dictates the menu, which
might see *tagliatelle* pasta paired with duck *ragù*
and Parmesan crisps, or mackerel fillet served
with aromatic herbs, seaweed and a salted
lemon *gelo* (Sicilian jelly). Staff are competent
and friendly, and the wine list is focused on
worthy drops.

Ragusa ❽

✗ Ristorante Duomo   Sicilian €€€€

(☎0932 65 12 65; www.cicciosultano.it; Via
Capitano Bocchieri 31, Ragusa Ibla; tasting
menus €135-150; 🕑12.30-2pm Mon, 12.30-2pm
& 7.30-10.30pm Tue-Sat) Widely regarded
as one of Sicily's finest restaurants, Duomo
comprises a cluster of small rooms outfitted
like private parlours behind its stained-glass
door, ensuring a suitably romantic ambience
for chef Ciccio Sultano's refined creations. The
menu abounds in classic Sicilian ingredients
such as pistachios, fennel, almonds and Nero
d'Avola wine, combined in imaginative and
unconventional ways. Reservations essential.

Sardinia's South Coast

38

Sardinia's less-trodden southern coast reveals itself in all its glory on this trip from Cagliari to Iglesias. En route, you'll encounter spectacular scenery, dreamy beaches and intriguing archaeological finds.

TRIP HIGHLIGHTS

33 km

Isola di San Pietro
A classic Mediterranean island with bobbing boats and a ravishing coastline

0 km

Cagliari
Explore Sardinia's cultured and cosmopolitan capital

FINISH
● Iglesias

START
①

⑥

● Tratalias

Sant'Antioco

● Pula

③

53 km

Chia
Enjoy exhilarating driving and sublime sea views

4–5 DAYS
168KM / 104 MILES

GREAT FOR...

BEST TIME TO GO
June and September mean perfect beach weather without the August crowds.

ESSENTIAL PHOTO
Isola di San Pietro's coastline from Capo Sandalo.

✔ BEST FOR FAMILIES
Splashing about on the beaches at Chia.

38 Sardinia's South Coast

From Cagliari's cultural gems to ancient ruins and stunning stretches of coastline, this trip is a real eye-opener. Outside the peak months of July and August, the roads are quiet and you'll be able to concentrate on the natural spectacle as it unfurls before you: spectacular coastal vistas on the Costa del Sud; searing Mediterranean colours on the Isola di San Pietro; melancholy woods and *macchia*-clad hills around Iglesias.

TRIP HIGHLIGHT

❶ Cagliari

Rising from the sea in a helter-skelter of golden-hued *palazzi,* domes and facades, Cagliari is Sardinia's regional capital and most cosmopolitan city. As a working port it exudes an infectious energy, particularly down by the waterfront where Vespas buzz down wide boulevards, locals stop by busy cafes and diners crowd into popular trattorias.

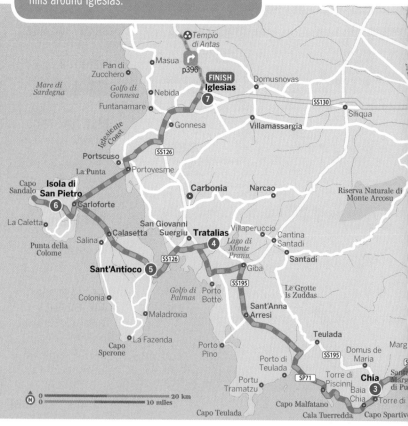

The big trophy sights are huddled in the **Castello** district, where the hilltop citadel rises above the city's sturdy battlements. Up here you'll find the graceful 13th-century **Cattedrale di Santa Maria** (☏070 864 93 88; www.duomodicagliari.it; Piazza Palazzo 4; ☺8am-noon & 4-8pm Mon-Sat, to 1pm & 4.30-8.30pm Sun), and Cagliari's premier museum, the **Museo Archeologico Nazionale** (☏070 6051 8245; http://museoarcheocagliari. beniculturali.it; Piazza Arsenale 1; adult/reduced €7/3, incl Pinacoteca Nazionale €9/4.50;

☺9am-8pm Tue-Sun), whose collection casts light on Sardinia's ancient and mysterious nuraghic culture. For stunning views, head down to the **Bastione di Saint Remy**, a monumental viewing platform.

A short hop east of the city, **Poetto beach** is the hub of summer life with its limpid waters and upbeat party scene.

✖ 🍴 p397

The Drive » Once you've cleared central Cagliari, it's a straightforward 32km drive along the SS195 to Pula. From Pula, the archaeological site of Nora is signposted, 4km away to the southwest. As you approach it, look out for pink flamingos in the nearby lagoon.

----

❷ Pula

The village of Pula makes a good base for exploring the southern beaches and the nearby archaeological site of Nora. There's little to see in the village itself, but in summer visitors throng its vibrant cafes and various restaurants

lending it a bubbly holiday atmosphere.

A short drive out of Pula, the ruins of **Nora** (☏070 920 91 38; http://nora. beniculturali.unipd.it; adult/ reduced €6/3.50, incl Torre di Coltellazzo €8/5, tower only €2.50/1.50; ☺10am-8pm mid-May–Sep, to 5.30pm Nov–mid-Feb, to 6pm mid-Feb–mid-May & Oct) are all that remain of what was once one of Sardinia's most powerful cities. Highlights include a beautifully preserved Roman theatre and an ancient baths complex, the **Terme al Mare**.

Just before you get to the site, keep an eye out for the beachside **Chiesa di Sant'Efisio** (☏340 485 18 60; ☺4-7pm Sat, 10am-noon & 4-7pm Sun), a 12th-century Romanesque church that plays a starring role in Cagliari's big May festival, the **Festa di Sant'Efisio** (www.festadisantefisio.com; ☺1-4 May).

The Drive » From Pula, push on along the SS195 for the 18km drive to Chia, which is signposted off to the left

SOUTHERN ITALY **38** SARDINIA'S SOUTH COAST

LINK YOUR TRIP

39 Emerald Coast
From Cagliari take the SS131 up to Alghero, 250km away, to join up with this tour of Sardinia's gorgeous, wind-whipped north coast.

40 Historic Sardinia
About 100km along the SS131 from Cagliari, Oristano is the start point for this compelling drive through Sardinia's wild and mysterious hinterland.

shortly after the village of Santa Margherita di Pula. For much of the way the sea view is blocked by trees and foliage, but don't worry as there are plenty of vistas to be had on the next leg.

`TRIP HIGHLIGHT`

❸ Chia

Extending from Chia to Porto di Teulada, the **Costa del Sud** is one of southern Sardinia's most beautiful coastal stretches.

At its eastern end, Chia is a hugely popular summer hang-out. More a collection of hotels, holiday homes and campsites than a traditional village, it has two ravishing beaches – to the west, the **Spiaggia Sa Colonia**, and to the east, the smaller **Spiaggia Su Portu**.

Running the length of the Costa, the **Strada Panoramica della Costa del Sud** is a stunning drive, with dreamy views at every turn and a succession of bays capped by Spanish-era watchtowers.

The Drive ≫ This 56km drive is the most spectacular leg of the trip. From Chia, the SP71, aka the Strada Panoramica della Costa del Sud, snakes along the coast, offering ever more beautiful views as it winds on to Porto di Teulada. Shortly before Porto, turn inland towards Teulada and pick up the northbound SS195 to Tratalias.

❹ Tratalias

Now a sleepy backwater, Tratalias was

once a major religious centre. When the town of Sant'Antioco was abandoned in the 13th century, the local Sulcis archdiocese was transferred to Tratalias and the impressive **Chiesa di Santa Maria** (www.chiesaiglesias.org; Via degli Angeli 18, Piazza Chiesa; incl Museo del Territorio Trataliese €2.50; ☉9am-1pm & 3-5pm Wed-Sun winter, longer hours summer) was built. A prime example of Sardinia's Romanesque-Pisan architecture, the church today presides over the town's lovingly renovated **borgo antico**, a medieval quarter that was abandoned in the 1950s after water from the nearby Lago di Monte Pranu started seeping into the subsoil.

The Drive ≫ From Tratalias, it's a short 14km haul over to the Isola di Sant'Antioco via the SS126, which runs over a causeway to the island's main settlement, Sant'Antioco.

❺ Sant'Antioco

The **Isola di Sant'Antioco** is the larger and more developed of the two islands off Sardinia's southwestern coast. Unlike many Mediterranean islands, it's not dramatically beautiful – although it's by no means ugly. Instead it feels very much part of Sardinia, both in character and look, with a happy, casual vibe.

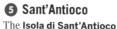

The animated main town, Sant'Antioco, was established by the Phoenicians in the 8th century BC. Evidence of its early history lies all around, and the town's small centre is riddled with Phoenician necropolises and fascinating archaeological litter. Just outside the centre, the **Museo Archeologico** (MAB; ☎0781 8 21 05; www.

Pula Mosaic in the ruins of Nora

mabsantantioco.it; Via Sabatino Moscati; €6, ; ☺9am-7pm) is one of the best museums in this part of southern Sardinia. It has a fascinating collection of local archaeological finds, as well as models of nuraghic houses and Sant'Antioco as it would have looked in the 4th century BC.

✖ p397

The Drive ≫ To get to the neighbouring island of San Pietro requires a ferry crossing (up to 16 daily, 45 minutes, per adult/car €4.50/8.50) from Calasetta, 10km northwest of Sant'Antioco on the island's north coast. There are not many roads to choose from, so just head north and follow the signs through the green, rugged interior.

TRIP HIGHLIGHT

❻ Isola di San Pietro

With an elegant main town and some magnificent coastal scenery, the Isola di San Pietro is a hugely popular summer destination.

The island's principal port of call is **Carloforte**,

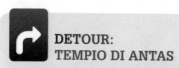

TEMPIO DI ANTAS

Start: ❼ Iglesias

From Iglesias the SS126 twists and turns for 17km through wooded hills up to the **Tempio di Antas** (☏0781 58 09 90; www.startuno.it; adult/reduced €4/3; ⊙9.30am-7.30pm summer, to 5.30pm spring & autumn, to 4.30pm Tue-Sun winter), an impressive 3rd-century Roman temple set in lush bucolic greenery.

Built by the emperor Caracalla, the temple was constructed over a 6th-century BC Punic sanctuary, which was itself set over an earlier nuraghic settlement. It lay abandoned for centuries until it was discovered in 1836 and extensively restored in 1967. Most impressively, the original Ionic columns were excavated and re-erected. From the site several paths branch off into the surrounding countryside. One of them, the **Strada Romana**, leads from near the ticket office to what little remains of the original nuraghic settlement and on to the **Grotta di Su Mannau** (☏0781 58 04 11; www.sumannau.it; Località Su Mannau, off SS 126; adult/reduced €10/6; ⊙9.30am-5pm Easter-Jun & mid-Sep–Oct, to 6.30pm Jul–mid-Sep, by appointment Nov-Easter), 2.5km away.

SOUTHERN ITALY 38 SARDINIA'S SOUTH COAST

a refined town with an elegant waterfront, graceful *palazzi* and a reputation for excellent seafood – tuna is a local speciality. There are no must-see sights as such, but a slow wander through the quaint, cobbled streets makes for a pleasant prelude to an *aperitivo* and a fine restaurant meal.

Over on the island's west coast, **Capo Sandalo** is well worth searching out. A superb vantage point, it commands breathtaking coastal views and offers some relaxed walking. From the car park near the lighthouse, marked trails head through the rocky, red scrubland that carpets the cliffs.

✖ ╞═ p397

The Drive ❯❯ Once the ferry (up to 17 daily, one hour; adult/car €4.90/12) from Carloforte has docked at Portovesme, head northeast towards Gonnesa to pick up the SS126 for the final run in to Iglesias. The 35km route is not the most scenic, but there is something atmospheric about the dark, macchia-cloaked hills of Sardinia's traditional mining heartland south of Iglesias.

- - - - - - - - - - - - - - - - - -

❼ Iglesias

Surrounded by the skeletons of Sardinia's once-thriving mining industry, Iglesias is a historic town that bubbles in the summer and slumbers in the colder months. Its historic centre, an appealing ensemble of lived-in piazzas, sun-bleached buildings and Aragonese-style wrought-iron balconies, creates an atmosphere that's as much Iberian as Sardinian – a vestige of its time as a Spanish colony.

In the heart of the *centro storico* (historic centre), the 13th-century **Cattedrale di Santa Chiara** (Duomo; Piazza del Municipio; ⊙9am-12.30pm & 3-8pm) is the most impressive of the city's many churches with its Pisan-flavoured facade and chequerboard stone bell tower.

╞═ p397

Eating & Sleeping

Cagliari ❶

✕ Martinelli's   Italian €€

(📞070 65 42 20; www.martinellis.it; Via Principe
Amedeo 18; meals from €35; ⏱8.30-11.30pm
Tue-Sat) Simplicity is the ethos underpinning
this intimate, subtly lit bistro in the Marina
district. Service is friendly without being
overbearing, and the menu plays up seasonal,
winningly fresh seafood along the lines of
tagliolini (flat spaghetti) with octopus ink and
sea bass cooked in Vernaccia wine.

✕ L'Imperfetto   Sardinian €€

(📞070 461 99 09; www.facebook.com/
imperfettoristorante; Via dei Genovesi 111;
meals €30-40; ⏱8-11pm Tue-Sat, plus 12.45-
2.45pm Sat, 12.45-3.15pm Sun) If you have
only one swank meal out in Sardinia, make
it at L'Imperfetto. Tucked into a quiet lane in
the Castello, this arched-stone dining room is
both elegant and welcoming, with fantastic,
fresh Sardinian fare. It's a chance to try the
specialties of the island executed with flair and
integrity. Reserve ahead.

⊨ Il Cagliarese   B&B €

(📞339 6544083; www.ilcagliarese.com;
Via Vittorio Porcile 19; s €45-60, d €60-75;
❄ @ 🛜) Bang in the heart of the Marina
district, this snug B&B is a real find. It has three
immaculate rooms, each with homey touches
such as embroidered fabrics and carved
wooden furnishings. Breakfast is scrumptious,
and Mauro, your welcoming host, bends over
backwards to please.

Sant'Antioco ❺

✕ Rubiu   Pizza €

(📞346 7234605; www.rubiubirra.it; Via Bologna
25; pizzas €5-11.50; ⏱7pm-1am) Craft beer,
creative pizzas and a laid-back warehouse vibe
await at this contemporary microbrewery.
Housed in an industrial-grey building, complete
with bar and shiny aluminium brewing tanks, it

has a terrific selection of home-brewed beers
and does a nice line in original pizzas, salads
and small plates.

Isola di San Pietro ❻

✕ Osteria Della
Tonnara da Andrea   Seafood €€

(📞0781 85 57 34; www.ristorantedaandrea.it;
Corso Battellieri 36; meals €40; ⏱12.30-2.30pm
& 8-10.30pm Thu-Tue, closed mid-Jan–early Mar)
Located at the waterfront's southern end, this
charming restaurant is one of the best places to
taste the local tuna (though it's only available
fresh in the tuna-fishing season: May to mid-
June). Signature dishes include *lasagnetta
di tonno con gocce di pesto* (tuna and pesto
lasagne) and *ventresca di tonno* (succulent red
tuna steaks grilled and served with aromatic
olive oil).

⊨ Nichotel   Hotel €€

(📞0781 85 56 74; http://nichotel.it; Via
Garibaldi 7; d €80-255, ste €120-300; ❄ 🛜)
Style, comfort and a warm welcome await at
this great little hotel. Located just off the main
seafront strip, it has lovely, spacious rooms with
quietly elegant modern decor and gleaming
designer bathrooms; some also have balconies
and rooftop views over to the port. Capping
everything is the excellent, abundant breakfast.

Iglesias ❼

⊨ B&B Mare Monti Miniere   B&B €

(📞0781 4 17 65, 348 3310585; www.
maremontiminiere-bb.it; Via Trento 10; s €35-45,
d €45-55, tr €65-80; ❄ 🛜) A warm welcome
awaits at this cracking B&B. Situated in a quiet
side street near the historic centre, it has two
cheery and immaculately kept rooms in the
main house and an independent studio with its
own kitchen facilities. Thoughtful extras include
beach towels and a regular supply of home-
baked cakes and biscuits.

Emerald Coast

39

This journey takes you around Sardinia's extraordinary northern coast, a land of wind-carved rocks, pearly white beaches and emerald-green seas that entertain divers and dolphins alike.

TRIP HIGHLIGHTS

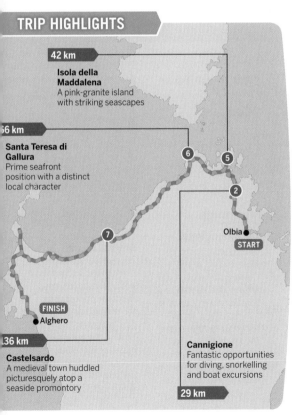

42 km

Isola della Maddalena
A pink-granite island with striking seascapes

56 km

Santa Teresa di Gallura
Prime seafront position with a distinct local character

FINISH
● Alghero

136 km

Castelsardo
A medieval town huddled picturesquely atop a seaside promontory

Olbia ●
START

Cannigione
Fantastic opportunities for diving, snorkelling and boat excursions

29 km

5–7 DAYS
253KM / 157 MILES

GREAT FOR...

BEST TIME TO GO

May, June, September and October, for beach weather without huge crowds.

ESSENTIAL PHOTO

The bizarre shapes of Capo Testa's natural sculpture garden.

BEST FOR OUTDOORS

Dive into the crystalline waters of the Maddalena Archipelago.

From unassuming Olbia, this trip rockets you into the dazzling coastline that the Aga Khan turned into a playground for oligarchs and their bikini-clad admirers. Head further north, however, and the coast grows wilder, with rocky coves washed by the startlingly blue waters of La Maddalena marine reserve. Rounding Sardinia's northwest corner, popular resorts alternate with timelessly silent stretches of coast, until finally you arrive at lovely, Spanish-inflected Alghero.

❶ Olbia

Scratch Olbia's industrial outskirts and find a fetching city with a *centro storico* (historic centre) crammed with boutiques, wine bars and cafe-rimmed piazzas. Olbia is also a refreshingly authentic and affordable alternative to the purpose-built resorts stretching to the north and south.

To get a feeling for old Olbia, head south of Corso Umberto to the tightly packed warren of streets that represents the original fishing village. You'll find it has a special charm, particularly in the evening when the cafes and trattorias fill with hungry locals.

✖ ⊨ p405

The Drive » Heading north on the SS125 and then the SP13 for this 29km leg, you'll pass through a rocky, sun-bleached landscape that alternates with patchwork farmland.

TRIP HIGHLIGHT

❷ Cannigione

Cannigione sits on the western side of the Golfo di Arzachena, the largest *ria* (inlet) along this coast. Originally a fishing village established in 1800 to supply the Maddalena islands with food, it is now a prosperous, and reasonably priced, tourist town.

Down at the port, various operators offer excursions to the Arcipelago di La Maddalena, plus fantastic opportunities for diving, snorkelling and boat trips that nose around the gorgeous and complex shoreline.

The operators here include **Consorzio del Golfo** (📞0789 8 84 18, 335

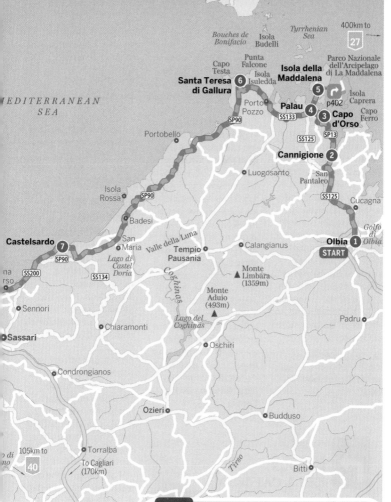

7742392; www.consorzio
delgolfo.it; adult/child incl
lunch €45/25; ⊙ticket office
8-10am & 5-7pm) and **An-
thias** (☏345 4512689; www.
anthias-diving.com; Villaggio
Camping Golfo di Arzachena;
⊙9am-7.30pm).

The Drive » Hugging the
coast as you head north along
the SP13 and SP121, this
beautiful 8km drive is defined

LINK
YOUR
TRIP

 **Shadow of
Vesuvius**

Regular ferries sail
from Cagliari to Naples
where you can join this
journey around the Bay
of Naples.

 **Historic
Sardinia**

This trip into the
Sardinian heartland
starts in Oristano, 110km
south of Alghero on the
SS292.

by the famously beautiful blue-green waters of the Costa Smeralda. Near the village of Le Saline, you'll see the inlet on which the Capo d'Orso sits.

❸ Capo d'Orso

Watching over the strait that separates Sardinia from the Isola della Maddalena, Capo d'Orso (Cape Bear) owes its name to a giant granite rock that resembles a rather ferocious-looking bear. The ursine lookout commands a dramatic view that, in a single sweep of the eye, takes in Sardinia's rugged northern coast, the Arcipelago di La Maddalena and, to the north, the mountains of Corsica.

The Drive » From Capo d'Orso, head northwest along the SP121 to Palau, just 5km away.

❹ Palau

Palau is a lively summer resort and also the main gateway to the granite islands and jewel-coloured waters of the Arcipelago di La Maddalena. Three kilometres west of town, you can tour the **Fortezza di Monte Altura** (adult/reduced €5/2.50; ⊙ guided tours 10.15am-12.15pm & 3.15-5.15pm daily, last tour 3.15pm Apr, May & Sep–mid-Oct), a 19th-century sentinel standing guard over the rocky crag. **Dea del Mare** (📞 334 7882993, 349 4909260; www.deadelmare. com; Via Fonte Vecchia 76; day trips €100-130; ⊙ office 10.30am-1pm & 3.30-7pm) offers sailing excursions around the Maddalena islands. If diving is your thing, there's excellent diving in the marine park. **Nautilus Diving Centre** (📞0789 70 90 58, 340 6339006; www.dive

sardegna.com; Via Roma 14; ⊙9am-5.30pm) runs dives to up to 40 sites.

 p405

The Drive » Actually, it's a boat trip. From Palau, there are at least hourly passenger and car ferry services to Isola della Maddalena. The journey takes 15 minutes.

TRIP HIGHLIGHT

❺ Isola della Maddalena

Just over the water from Palau, the pink-granite island of La Maddalena lies at the heart of the Arcipelago di La Maddalena. From the moment you dock at **Cala Gavetta** (La Maddalena's main port), you'll be in the thrall of its cobbled piazzas and infectious holiday atmosphere.

Beyond the harbour, the island offers startlingly lovely seascapes. A 20km panoramic road circles the island, allowing easy access to several attractive bays.

The ravishing **Parco Nazionale dell'Arcipelago di La Maddalena** (www. lamaddalenapark.it) consists of seven main islands, including La Maddalena, and 40 granite islets, plus several small islands to the south. They form the high points of a (now underwater) mountain range that once joined Sardinia and Corsica. Over the centuries, the *maestrale* (northwesterly wind) has moulded the

DETOUR: ISOLA CAPRERA

Start: ❺ Isola della Maddalena

Just over a causeway from the Isola della Maddalena, Isola Caprera was once Giuseppe Garibaldi's 'Eden' – a wild, wonderfully serene island, covered in green pines, which look stunning against the ever-present seascape and ragged granite cliffs. The green, shady Caprera is ideal for walking, and there are plenty of trails weaving through the pines. The island's rugged coast is indented with several tempting coves. You can also tour the **Compendio Garibaldino** (www. compendiogaribaldino.it; adult/reduced €7/3.50; ⊙9am-8pm Tue-Sun), the serene compound the Italian revolutionary built for himself here.

Castelsardo Old fort overlooking the town

granite into bizarre natural sculptures. But the great delight lies in its crystalline waters, which are rich in marine life and also assume priceless shades of emerald, aquamarine and sapphire.

To explore the archipelago and some of the smaller, lesser-known islands, **Elena Tour Navigazioni** (☑380 3032664; www.elenatournavigazioni.com; Lungomare Via Amendola; ☺office 10am-5.30pm) is one of various outfits offering boat cruises.

The Drive » Hop on the ferry back to Palau, then head northwest on the SS133, which will veer off as the SS133bis. Along the 24km, mostly inland, journey you'll pass Mediterranean scrub and granite boulders, with a brief seaside encounter at Porto Pozzo.

- - - - - - - - - - - - - - - -

TRIP HIGHLIGHT

⑥ Santa Teresa di Gallura

Bright, breezy and relaxed, Santa Teresa di Gallura bags a prime seafront position on Gallura's north coast. The resort gets extremely busy in high season, yet somehow retains a distinct local character. When not on the beach, most people hang out at cafe-lined **Piazza Vittorio Emanuele**. Otherwise, you can wander up to the 16th-century **Torre di Longonsardo** (€2; ☺10am-1pm & 4-8pm Apr-Sep, 10am-1pm & 3-5pm Oct), a defensive tower near the entrance to **Spiaggia Rena Bianca**, the town's idyllic (but crowded) beach.

Well worth the 4km hike west of Santa Teresa, the small peninsula known as **Capo Testa** resembles a bizarre sculpture garden. Giant boulders lay strewn about the grassy slopes, their weird and wonderful forms the result of centuries of wind

LOCAL KNOWLEDGE: MUST-TRY SARDINIAN DISHES

Zuppa gallurese Layers of bread and cheese drenched in broth and baked to a crispy crust.

Porceddu Suckling pig, often spit roasted.

Aragosta alla catalana Alghero's lobster speciality, with tomato and onion.

Fregola con cozze e vongole Sardinian semolina pasta (similar to couscous) with mussels and clams.

Seadas Light pastry turnovers filled with *pecorino* and lemon zest and drizzled with honey.

erosion. The walk itself is also stunning, passing through boulder-strewn scrub and affording magnificent views of rocky coves and the cobalt Mediterranean. Stop en route for a swim and to admire the views of not-so-distant Corsica.

 p405

The Drive >> It's rugged, hilly terrain on this 70km southwestern route along the SP90, with a brief stint along the winding SS134 to Castelsardo and the sea.

TRIP HIGHLIGHT

7 Castelsardo

Medieval Castelsardo huddles atop a high, cone-shaped promontory that juts picturesquely into the Mediterranean. Originally designed as a defensive fort by a 12th-century Genoese family, the dramatic, hilltop *centro storico* is an ensemble of dark alleyways and medieval buildings

seemingly melded into the rocky grey peak.

The Drive >> Hug Sardinia's rugged northern coastline as you head west to Porto Torres along the SS200 and SP81. Then turn inland into desolately beautiful country to reach Stintino, 63km from Castelsardo, on the SP34.

----

8 Stintino

With its saltpans and hard-scrabble landscape, the northwest corner of Sardinia has a particularly desolate feel, especially when the *maestrale* wind blows in, whipping the *macchia* (Mediterranean scrub) and bleak rocks. But it also shelters the welcoming and laid-back resort town of Stintino, gateway to the **Isola dell'Asinara**, formerly home to one of Italy's toughest prisons. Nearby, the fabulous **Spiaggia della Pelosa** is one of Sardinia's most celebrated beaches.

The Drive >> For this 54km drive, head back down south along the SP34 to the coastal SP57, followed by the SP69. Soon you will reach the flat agricultural plain just north of Alghero, then it's a straight shot on the SS291 into Alghero itself.

----

9 Alghero

For many people a trip to Sardinia means a trip to Alghero, the main resort in the northwest and an easy flight from a host of European cities. Although largely given over to tourism, the town has managed to avoid many of its worst excesses, and it retains a proud and independent spirit.

The main focus is the spectacular *centro storico,* one of the best preserved in Sardinia. Enclosed by robust, honey-coloured seawalls, this is a tightly knit enclave of shady cobbled lanes, Spanish Gothic *palazzi* (mansions) and cafe-lined squares. Below, yachts crowd the marina and long, sandy beaches curve away to the north. Hanging over everything is a palpably Spanish atmosphere, a leftover of the city's past as a Catalan colony. Even today, more than three centuries after the Iberians left, the Catalan tongue is still spoken and street signs and menus are often in both languages.

 p405

Eating & Sleeping

Olbia ❶

✖ Agriturismo Agrisole   Sardinian €€
(📞349 0848163; www.agriturismo-agrisole.
com; Via Sole Ruiu 7, Località Casagliana;
menu incl drinks €40; ⏰ dinner by reservation
Thu-Sun Apr-Sep) Tucked serenely away in the
countryside around 10km north of Olbia, this
Gallurese *stazzo* (farmhouse) dishes up a feast
of home cooking. Monica, your charming host,
brings dish after marvellous dish to the table
– antipasti, *fregola* (granular pasta), *porceddu*
(roast suckling pig) and ricotta sweets. From
Olbia, take the SS125 towards Arzachena/
Palau, turning left at the signs about 11km north
of the city.

🛏 Porto Romano   B&B €
(📞349 1927996; www.
bedandbreakfastportoromano.it; Via A Nanni 2;
d €65-90; ❄🛜) We love the chilled vibe and
the heartfelt *benvenuto* at this welcoming B&B
in an old family home near the train station.
Light, spacious and well kept, the rooms have
tiled floors and wood furnishings, and some
come with balconies. Homey touches include
the shared kitchen and barbecue area, and the
friendly reception from owner Simonetta and
her lovable dog, Lilly.

Palau ❹

✖ Del Porticciolo   Sardinian €
(📞0789 70 70 51; Via Omero; pizzas €4-9, meals
€25-35; ⏰12.15-2pm & 7.15-10.30pm Sat-Thu)
Locals swear by the authentic antipasti, pasta
and fresh fish at this no-frills restaurant just
south of the harbour. Stop by for a good-value
lunch, or for pizza in the evening when chefs fire
up the ovens.

Santa Teresa di Gallura ❻

✖ Agriturismo Saltara   Sardinian €€€
(📞0789 75 55 97; www.agriturismosaltara.it;
Località Saltara; meals €40-60; ⏰7-11pm; 👶)
Natalia and Gian Mario welcome you warmly

at this *agriturismo*, 10km south of town off
the SP90 (follow signs up a dirt track). Tables
are scenically positioned under the trees for
a home-cooked feast. Wood-fired bread and
garden-vegetable antipasti are a delicious lead
to dishes such as *pulilgioni* (ricotta-filled ravioli
with orange zest) and roast suckling pig or wild
boar.

🛏 B&B Domus de Janas   B&B €€
(📞338 4990221; www.bbdomusdejanas.it; Via
Carlo Felice 20a; s €70-100, d €80-160, q €130-
170; ❄🛜) Daria and Simone are your affable
hosts at this sumptuous six-room B&B smack in
the centre of town (as photos on the wall attest,
the rambling home has belonged to Daria's
family since her great-great-grandmother's
days). The colourfully decorated rooms are
spacious and regally comfortable, the rooftop
terrace enjoys cracking sea views, and guests
rave about the varied, abundant self-service
breakfast.

Alghero ❾

✖ La Botteghina   Sardinian €€
(📞079 973 83 75; www.labotteghina.biz; Via
Principe Umberto 63; meals €35; ⏰7-11.30pm
Wed-Sun plus noon-3pm Sat & Sun) Cool, casual
dining in a stylish *centro storico* setting – with
blond-wood decor and low sandstone arches
– is what La Botteghina is all about. In keeping
with the upbeat, youthful vibe, the food is
simple, seasonal and local, so expect steaks
of *bue rosso* beef, cured meats and Sardinian
cheeses, alongside inventive pizzas and
Sardinian wines and craft beers.

🛏 Angedras Hotel   Hotel €€
(📞079 973 50 34; www.angedras.it; Via
Frank 2; s €75-110, d €90-200; 🅿❄🛜) A
15-minute walk from the historic centre, the
Angedras – Sardegna backwards – is a model of
whitewashed Mediterranean simplicity. Rooms,
which come with their own small balcony, are
decorated in an understated Sardinian style
with cool white tiles and aquamarine-blue
touches. There's also an airy terrace, good for
iced drinks on hot summer evenings.

Historic Sardinia

40

Head straight into the wild heart of Sardinia, a strange and hauntingly beautiful landscape littered with Bronze Age nuraghic ruins and isolated mountain towns legendary for feuding and banditry.

TRIP HIGHLIGHTS

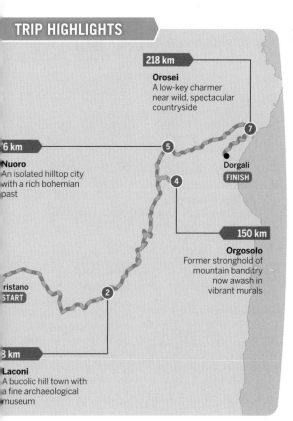

218 km

Orosei
A low-key charmer near wild, spectacular countryside

7

'6 km

Nuoro
An isolated hilltop city with a rich bohemian past

5

Dorgali
FINISH

4

150 km

Orgosolo
Former stronghold of mountain banditry now awash in vibrant murals

ristano
START

2

3 km

Laconi
A bucolic hill town with a fine archaeological museum

7 DAYS
239KM / 148 MILES

GREAT FOR...

BEST TIME TO GO

March to May for wildflowers and green hillsides.

ESSENTIAL PHOTO

The spectacular coastal scenery on the Golfo di Orosei.

BEST FOR OUTDOORS

Great hikes abound around Dorgali.

Sindia

Macomer

Cuglieri San Leonardo
de Siete Fuen

Abbasa

Narbolia

Santa
Cristina Fordong

START *Tirso*
Oristano Simaxis SP3
①
Santa
Giusta Villaurbana

Arborea

SS4

Terralba 71km to
Uras **38**

40 | Historic Sardinia

This trip immerses you in Sardinia's strange and captivating hinterlands. You'll discover remnants of the prehistoric *nuraghi* (Bronze Age fortified settlements) and the lonesome villages of the Barbagia, which are still steeped in bandit legend. And you'll end up in the wilds of the eastern coast, where limestone mountains and deep canyons roll down to the aquamarine waves of the Golfo di Orosei.

❶ Oristano

One of Sardinia's most important medieval cities, Oristano has a historic centre that retains traces of its former greatness, most notably the 13th-century **Torre di Mariano II** (Piazza Roma). The centre is a pleasant place to wander, with its elegant shopping streets, ornate central square – **Piazza Eleonora d'Arborea**– and crowded cafes.

The region around Oristano was an important centre of the Bronze Age nuraghic people, and the **Museo Archeologico Antiquarium Arborense** (☎0783 79 12 62; www.

antiquariumarborense.it; Piazza Corrias; adult/reduced €5/2.50; ☺9am-8pm Mon-Fri, to 2pm & 3-8pm Sat & Sun) is home to one of Sardinia's major archaeological collections.

Located 3km south of town, the 12th-century **Basilica di Santa Giusta** (☺7.30am-6.30pm) – one of Sardinia's finest Tuscan-style Romanesque churches – is worth seeking out.

🍴 🛏 p413

The Drive » Your main routes on the 58km drive to Laconi will be the meandering SP35 and SS442. You'll traverse a widely varied land of patchwork farms, small towns, rocky crags and wooded slopes.

❷ Laconi

Laconi is a charismatic mountain town with a blissfully slow pace of life and bucolic views of rolling green countryside. Its cobbled lanes hide some genuine attractions,

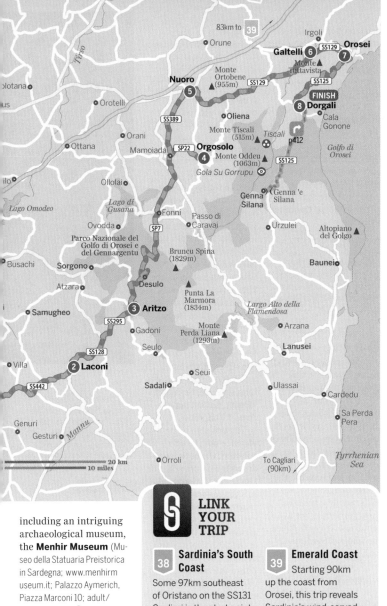

including an intriguing
archaeological museum,
the **Menhir Museum** (Museo della Statuaria Preistorica
in Sardegna; www.menhirm
useum.it; Palazzo Aymerich,
Piazza Marconi 10; adult/
reduced €5/3; ☺10am-1pm &
3.30-7pm Tue-Sun Apr-Sep, to
6pm Oct-Mar). Occupying
an elegant 19th-century
palazzo (mansion), this

LINK YOUR TRIP

38 Sardinia's South Coast

Some 97km southeast
of Oristano on the SS131
Cagliari is the start point
for this visually stunning
tour of the island's south
coast.

39 Emerald Coast

Starting 90km
up the coast from
Orosei, this trip reveals
Sardinia's wind-carved
northern coast.

museum beautifully exhibits a collection of 40 menhirs – stark anthropomorphic slabs probably connected with prehistoric funerary rites.

Just outside town, the **Parco Aymerich** (☉8am-6pm Mon-Sat, to 8pm Sun summer, to 4pm winter) is a gorgeous 22-hectare park with exotic trees, lakes, grottoes, great views and the remains of 11th-century **Castello Aymerich**.

The Drive » For this 27km leg, you'll head northeast along the SS128 and then the SS295 as you enter a wilder, more barren landscape, eventually reaching the pine-covered slopes around Aritzo.

---

❸ Aritzo

With its cool climate and Alpine character, this vivacious mountain resort (elevation 796m) has been attracting visitors since the 19th century, when it caught the imagination of boar-hunting Piedmontese nobility. But long before tourism took off, the village flourished thanks to its lucrative trade in snow gathering. For five centuries, Aritzo supplied the whole of Sardinia with ice, and snow farmers, known as *niargios,* collected the white stuff from the slopes of **Punta di Funtana Cungiada** (1458m) and stored it in straw-lined wooden chests before sending it off to the high tables of Cagliari.

The Drive » Heading northeast along Via Marginigola, turn onto the sharply curving SP7 for the 65km to Orgosolo through the deserted mountains and valleys of central Sardinia. At the town of Mamoiada, take the winding SP22 for the last 10km up to Orgosolo.

TRIP HIGHLIGHT

❹ Orgosolo

High in the brooding mountains, Orgosolo is Sardinia's most notorious town, its name long a byword for the banditry and bloody feuds that once blighted this region. Between 1901 and 1950, the village was averaging a murder every two months as rival families feuded over disputed inheritances. In the 1950s and '60s, feuding gave way to more lucrative kidnapping, led by the village's most infamous son, Graziano Mesina, nicknamed the Scarlet Pimpernel.

The problem of violence now largely resolved, Orgosolo is drawing visitors with the vibrant graffiti-style murals that adorn its town centre. Like satirical caricatures, they depict all the big political events of the 20th century and are often very moving. But in the evening, the villagers reclaim their streets – the old boys staring at anyone they don't recognise and the lads with crew cuts racing up and down in their mud-splattered cars.

IVAN HLOBEJ/SHUTTERSTOCK ©

The Drive » For the 26km to Nuoro, head back down the SP22 to Mamoiada, and take the SS389 northeast through a particularly sun-bleached landscape of cacti and macchia.

TRIP HIGHLIGHT

❺ Nuoro

Once an isolated hilltop village synonymous with banditry, Nuoro had its cultural renaissance in the 19th and early 20th centuries, attracting a hotbed of artistic talent, from author Grazia Deledda to sculptor Francesco Ciusa. This legacy is reflected in the fine **Museo MAN** (☏0784

25 21 10; www.museoman.it; Via Sebastiano Satta 27; adult/reduced €5/3; ⏱10am-7pm Tue-Sun). The only serious contemporary-art gallery in Sardinia, it displays more than 400 works by the island's top 20th-century painters. Nuoro is also home to the **Museo Etnografico Sardo** (Museo del Costume; ☎0784 25 70 35; www.isresardegna.it; Via Antonio Mereu 56; adult/reduced €5/3; ⏱10am-1pm & 3-8pm Tue-Sun mid-Mar–Sep, to 7pm Oct–mid-Mar), a peerless collection of Sardinian arts and crafts, including filigree jewellery, rich embroidery, weapons and masks.

The city's spectacular backdrop is the granite peak of **Monte Ortobene** (955m). Capped by a 7m-high bronze statue of the *Redentore* (Christ the Redeemer), it makes for good hiking.

🍴 🛏 p413

The Drive » Head 33km east along SS129 as mountains give way to a green-and-ochre checkerboard of farmland.

- - - - - - - - - - - - - - - -

6 Galtelli

Crouched at the foot of **Monte Tuttavista** and hemmed in by olive groves, vineyards and sheep-nibbled pastures,

Galtelli is quite the village idyll. Its tiny medieval centre is a joy to wander, with narrow lanes twisting to old stone houses and sun-dappled piazzas. If you fancy tiptoeing off the map for a while, this is the place.

The Drive » It's a quick and relatively straight 9km jaunt along SS129 to Orosei, as rugged limestone peaks rear up again on your right.

- - - - - - - - - - - - - - - -

TRIP HIGHLIGHT

7 Orosei

Scenically positioned at the northernmost point of the Golfo di

Orosei and surrounded by marble quarries and fruit orchards, Orosei is an unsung treasure. Over the centuries the silting of the Cedrino river – plus malaria, pirate raids and Spanish neglect – took their toll on the town, once an important Pisan port. However, its demise left behind an atmospheric historic centre laced with cobbled lanes, pretty stone houses, medieval churches and leafy piazzas.

The Drive » From the plains around Orosei, head southwest on the SS125 for 21km. Expect glimpses of both mountains and sea as you wind your way to Dorgali.

8 Dorgali

Nestled at the foot of **Monte Bardia** and framed by vineyards and olive groves, Dorgali is a down-to-earth town with a grandiose backdrop. Limestone peaks loom above the centre's pastel-coloured houses and steep, narrow streets, luring hikers and climbers to their summits. For more outdoor escapades, the dramatic **Golfo di Orosei** and spectacularly rugged **Supramonte** mountain range are within easy striking distance.

Just south of town lies one of Sardinia's most dramatically sited *nuraghe*. Follow signs along the Dorgali–Cala Gonone road to the **Nuraghe Mannu** (adult/reduced €3/2; 9am-noon & 5-8pm Jul & Aug, 9am-noon & 4-7pm May, Jun & Sep, 10am-1pm & 3-6pm Apr & Oct). First inhabited around 1600 BC, the tower is a modest ruin, but it more than makes up for this by offering spectacular views of the gulf. The site captured ancient Roman imaginations, too, and you can see the rectilinear remnants of their constructions alongside the elliptical shapes of earlier buildings.

 p413

DETOUR: GOLA SU GORROPU & TISCALI

Start: 8 Dorgali

Dubbed the 'Grand Canyon of Europe', the **Gola Su Gorropu** (328 8976563, Chintula Company 389 4208595; www.gorropu.info; adult/reduced €5/3.50; 10.30am-5.30pm) is a spectacular gorge flanked by vertical 400m rock walls that, at their narrowest point, stand just 4m apart. The hike down to and through the canyon floor takes you into a strangely silent world of gnarled holm oaks, sheer limestone slopes and pockmarked cliffs. There are two main approach routes. The shorter and more dramatic begins from the car park opposite Hotel Silana at the **Genna 'e Silana** pass on the SS125 at Km 183. The easier, but longer, route is via the **Sa Barva bridge** over the Rio Flumineddu, about 15km from Dorgali.

Also at the Sa Barva bridge is the trailhead for the walk to one of Sardinia's archaeological highlights. Hidden in a mountaintop cave deep in the Valle Lanaittu is the nuraghic village of **Tiscali** (338 8341618; www.museoarcheologicodorgali.it; adult/reduced €5/2; 9am-7pm daily May-Sep, to 5pm Oct-Apr, closed in rainy weather). The hike up to the village is part of the pleasure, as you strike into the heart of the limestone Supramonte highlands. You'll need sturdy footwear for some rock hopping, but most of the path is easy going, and canopies of juniper and cork oaks afford shady respite. Allow five hours for the return hike, including breaks and time for visiting Tiscali. Note: the bridge on the SP46 between Dorgali and Oliena was closed for years but is due to reopen in 2019. Plan accordingly as you map your route to the trailheads.

Eating & Sleeping

Oristano ❶

🍴 Trattoria Gino   Trattoria €€

(📞0783 7 14 28; Via Tirso 13; meals €25-33; 🕐12.30-3pm & 8-11pm Mon-Sat) For excellent food and a bustling, authentic vibe, head to this old-school trattoria. Since the 1930s, locals and visitors alike have been squeezing into Gino's simple dining room to feast on tasty seafood and classic pastas. Don't miss the seafood antipasto, the butter-soft roast *seppie* (cuttlefish) and the scrumptious *seadas* (fried dough pockets with fresh *pecorino*, lemon and honey) for dessert.

🛏 Eleonora B&B   B&B €

(📞0783 7 04 35, 347 4817976; www.eleonora-bed-and-breakfast.com; Piazza Eleonora d'Arborea 12; s €40-60, d €65-90, tr €80-110; ❄🖥) This charming B&B scores on all counts: location – it's in a medieval *palazzo* on Oristano's central piazza; decor – rooms are tastefully decorated with a mix of antique furniture, exposed-brick walls and gorgeous old tiles; and hospitality – owners Andrea and Paola are helpful and hospitable hosts. All this and it's excellent value for money.

Nuoro ❺

🍴 Il Portico   Sardinian €€

(📞0784 21 76 41; www.ilporticonuoro.it; Via Monsignor Bua 13; meals €35-45; 🕐12.30-2.30pm & 8-10.30pm Tue-Sat, 12.30-2.30pm Sun) You'll receive a warm welcome at this restaurant, where abstract paintings grace the walls and jazzy music plays. Behind the scenes, the talented Graziano and Vania rustle up a feast of local fare such as *spaghetti ai ricci* (spaghetti with sea urchins) and fresh gnocchi with lamb *ragù*. Save room for the delectable caramel-nougat semifreddo.

🍴 Agriturismo Testone   Sardinian €€

(📞329 4115168, 328 3150592; www.agriturismotestone.com; Via Verdi 49, Testone;

meals €30; 🚗) You'll feel immediately part of *la famiglia* at this *agriturismo*, which rests in peaceful solitude in the countryside, 20km northwest of Nuoro. The welcome is heartfelt, mealtimes are cheerful and communal affairs, and the mostly homegrown food is terrific. The farm rears lamb and produces its own *formaggi, salumi*, honey, sweets, olive oil and wine.

🛏 Casa Solotti   B&B €

(📞0784 3 39 54, 328 6028975; www.casasolotti.it; Località Monte Ortobene; per person €26-35; 🅿❄🖥) This B&B reclines in a rambling garden amid woods and walking trails near the top of Monte Ortobene, 5km from central Nuoro. Decorated with stone and beams, the elegantly rustic rooms have tremendous views of the surrounding valley and the Golfo di Orosei in the distance. Staying here is a delight.

Dorgali ❽

🍴 Ristorante Ispinigoli   Sardinian €€

(📞0784 9 52 68; www.hotelispinigoli.com; off SS125; meals €30-36; 🕐12.30-2.30pm & 7.30-9.30pm) Linger for dinner and panoramic sunset views at the Ristorante Ispinigoli, just below the entrance to the Grotta di Ispingoli. Located in Hotel Ispinigoli, the well-known restaurant rolls out local delights such as stone-bass-stuffed black ravioli with mullet roe, herb-infused roast kid and a waistline-expanding selection of *formaggi*.

🍴 Ristorante Colibrì   Sardinian €€

(📞340 7211564; www.ristorantecolibridorgali.it; Via Floris 7; meals €30-35; 🕐12.30-2.30pm & 7-10.30pm, closed Sun Sep-Jun) Hidden away in an incongruous residential area (follow the numerous signs), this lemon-walled restaurant is the real McCoy for meat eaters. Stars of the menu include *cinghiale al rosmarino* (wild boar with rosemary), *capra alla selvatiza* (goat with thyme) and *porcetto* (suckling pig).

STRETCH YOUR LEGS
PALERMO

Start/Finish: Quattro Canti

Distance: 2.8km

Duration: 3 hours

Take in the complex weave of Sicily's capital, from medieval Arab-Norman mosaics and a Renaissance fountain to mouthwatering market stalls. Leave your car at Piazzale Ungheria and walk 800m south along Via Ruggero Settimo (which becomes Via Maqueda) to the start point at Quattro Canti.

Take this walk on Trip

36

Quattro Canti

The **intersection** (Piazza Vigliena) of Corso Vittorio Emanuele and Via Maqueda forms the civic heart of Palermo. Built in the early 17th century, the crossroads is adorned with four elaborate facades.

The Walk >> Head west on Corso Vittorio Emanuele and admire the decaying splendour of its baroque and neoclassical facades.

Cattedrale di Palermo

A feast of geometric patterns, crenulations and majolica cupolas, Palermo's **cathedral** (☏329 3977513; www.cattedrale. palermo.it; Corso Vittorio Emanuele; cathedral free, royal tombs €1.50, treasury & crypt €3, roof €5, all-inclusive ticket adult/reduced €8/4; ⊙7am-7pm Mon-Sat, 8am-1pm & 4-7pm Sun; royal tombs, treasury, crypt & roof 9am-1.30pm Mon-Sat, royal tombs & roof also 9am-12.30pm Sun) is an extraordinary example of Sicily's unique Arab-Norman architecture.

The Walk >> Continue west down Corso Vittorio Emanuele. The archway in the distance is the baroque Porta Nuova, once Palermo's main gate.

Palazzo dei Normanni

This austere palace, once the seat of a magnificent court, houses Sicily's parliament and greatest treasure, the **Cappella Palatina** (Palatine Chapel; ☏091 705 56 11; www.federicosecondo.org; Piazza del Parlamento; adult/reduced incl exhibition Fri-Mon €12/10, Tue-Thu €10/8; ⊙8.15am-5.40pm Mon-Sat, to 1pm Sun). Designed by Norman King Roger II in 1130, the mosaic-clad chapel swarms with figures in glittering gold.

The Walk >> Head down the steps at the southern end of Piazza della Vittoria and continue along Via Generale Cadorna Luigi, turning left into Via Porta di Castro.

Mercato di Ballarò

Snaking for several city blocks east of Palazzo dei Normanni is Palermo's busiest **street market** (Via Ballaro 1; ⊙7.30am-8.30pm), which throbs with activity well into the early evening.

The Walk >> Head east along Via Casa Professa (which becomes Via del Ponticello) to Via Maqueda. Turn left into Via Maqueda and continue one block north to Piazza Bellini.

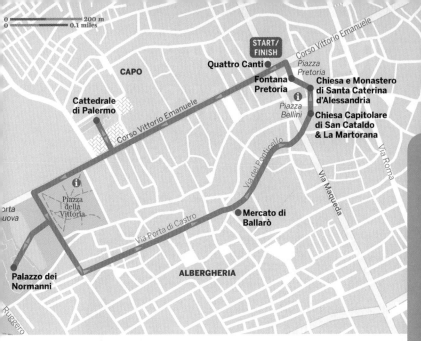

Chiesa Capitolare di San Cataldo & La Martorana

With its Arabic domes and delicate tracery, the 12th-century **Chiesa Capitolare di San Cataldo** (Piazza Bellini 3; adult/reduced €2.50/1.50; ⏱9am-6.30pm summer, to 5.30pm winter) echoes the city's rich Islamic influence. It's almost bare inside, in sharp contrast to the adjacent **La Martorana** (Chiesa di Santa Maria dell'Ammiraglio; ☎345 8288231; Piazza Bellini 3; adult/reduced €2/1; ⏱9.30am-1pm & 3.30-5.30pm Mon-Sat, 9-10.30am Sun), a luminously beautiful 12th-century church adorned with magnificent Byzantine mosaics.

The Walk » It's only a few steps across Piazza Bellini to reach one of Palermo's most fascinating monastic complexes, home to architectural riches and lofty city views.

Chiesa e Monastero di Santa Caterina d'Alessandria

The baroque Chiesa di Santa Caterina d'Alessandria belongs to the **Chiesa e Monastero di Santa Caterina**

d'Alessandria (☎091 271 38 37; Piazza Bellini; church, convent & rooftop adult/reduced €10/9, church only adult/reduced €3/2; ⏱church 9am-7pm, convent & rooftop 10am-7pm), a labyrinthine former convent with a colourful, majolica-tiled cloister and heavenly views from its rooftop. It's also home to one of the city's best pastry makers, **I Segreti del Chiostro** (☎327 5882302; www.isegretidelchiostro. com; Monastero di Santa Caterina d'Alessandria, Piazza Bellini; sweets from €1; ⏱10am-7pm summer, to 6pm winter; ✈ 🎒).

The Walk » Follow the pedestrian thoroughfare flanking the side of the convent's church. It links Piazza Bellini to Piazza Pretoria, the latter claiming Palermo's most celebrated fountain.

Fontana Pretoria

This huge and ornate **fountain** (Piazza Pretoria) originally graced a garden in Florence, but was bought by Palermo in 1573.

The Walk » Stairs lead down from Piazza Pretoria to Via Maqueda, from where the Quattro Canti is a few short steps to the north.

ROAD TRIP ESSENTIALS

Italy Driving Guide

Italy's stunning natural scenery, comprehensive road network and passion for cars makes it a wonderful road-trip destination.

DRIVING LICENCE & DOCUMENTS

➡ All EU driving licences are recognised in Italy.

➡ Travellers from other countries should obtain an International Driving Permit (IDP) through their national automobile association. This should be carried with your licence; it is not a substitute for it.

When driving in Italy you are required to carry with you:

➡ The vehicle registration document

➡ Your driving licence

➡ Proof of third-party liability insurance

INSURANCE

➡ Third-party liability insurance is mandatory for all vehicles in Italy, including cars brought in from abroad.

➡ If driving an EU-registered vehicle, your home country insurance is sufficient. Ask your insurer for a European Accident Statement (EAS) form, which can simplify matters in the event of an accident.

➡ Residents of non-EU countries should contact their insurance company to see if they need a green card international insurance certificate.

➡ Hire agencies provide the minimum legal insurance, but you can supplement it if you choose.

HIRING A CAR

Car-hire agencies are widespread in Italy but prebooking costs less than hiring a car once you arrive in Italy. Online booking agency Rentalcars.com (www.rentalcars.com) compares the rates of numerous car-rental companies.

Considerations before renting:

➡ Bear in mind that a car is generally more hassle than it's worth in cities, so only hire one for the time you'll be on the open road.

➡ Consider vehicle size carefully. High fuel prices, extremely narrow streets and tight parking conditions mean that smaller is often better.

➡ Road signs can be iffy in remote areas, so consider booking and paying for satnav.

Standard regulations:

➡ Many agencies have a minimum rental age of 25 and a maximum of 79. You can sometimes

---

Driving Fast Facts

Right or left? Drive on the right

Manual or automatic? Mostly manual

Legal driving age 18

Top speed limit 130km/h (on autostradas)

Signature car Flaming red Ferrari or Fiat 500

Driving Tips

A representative of the Automobile Club d'Italia (ACI) offers these pearls to ease your way on Italian roads:

➡ Pay particular attention to the weather. In summer it gets very hot, but, in winter, watch out for ice, snow and fog.

➡ On the extra-urban roads and autostradas, cars must have their headlights on even during the day.

➡ Watch out for signs at the autostrada toll booths – the lanes marked 'Telepass' are for cars that pay through an automatic electronic system without stopping.

➡ Watch out in the cities – big and small – for the Limited Traffic Zones (ZTL) and pay parking. There is no universal system for indicating these or their hours.

hire if you're over 21 but supplements will apply.

➡ To rent you'll need a credit card, valid driver's licence (with IDP if necessary) and passport or photo ID. Note that some companies require that you've had your licence for at least a year.

➡ Hire cars come with the minimum legal insurance, which you can supplement by purchasing additional coverage.

➡ Check with your credit-card company to see if it offers a Collision Damage Waiver, which covers you for additional damage if you use that card to pay for the car.

The following companies have pickup locations throughout Italy:

Auto Europe (www.autoeurope.it)
Avis (www.avisautonoleggio.it)
Budget (www.budgetinternational.com)
Europcar (www.europcar.it)
Hertz (www.hertz.it)
Italy by Car (www.italybycar.it)
Maggiore (www.maggiore.it)
Sixt (www.sixt.it)

Motorcycles

Agencies throughout Italy rent motorbikes, ranging from small Vespas to large touring bikes. Prices start at around €35/150 per day/week for a 50cc scooter; upwards of €80/400 per day/week for a 650cc motorcycle.

BRINGING YOUR OWN VEHICLE

➡ All foreign vehicles entering Italy should display the nationality plate of its country of registration.

➡ If you're driving a left-hand-drive UK vehicle you'll have to adjust its headlights to avoid dazzling oncoming traffic.

➡ You'll need to carry snow chains in your car if travelling in mountainous areas between 15 October and 15 April.

MAPS

We recommend you purchase a good road map for your trip. The best driving maps are produced by the Touring Club Italiano (www.touringclub.com), Italy's largest map publisher. They are available at bookstores across Italy or online at the following:

Stanfords (www.stanfords.co.uk) Excellent UK-based shop that stocks many useful maps.
Omni Resources (www.omnimap.com) US-based online retailer with an impressive selection of Italian maps.

ROAD CONDITIONS

Italy's extensive road network covers the entire peninsula and with enough patience you'll be able to get just about anywhere. Most roads are in good condition but a lack of maintenance in some areas means that you should be prepared for potholes and bumpy surfaces, particularly on smaller, secondary roads.

Traffic in and around the main cities is bad during morning and evening rush hours. Coastal roads get very busy on summer weekends. As a rule, traffic is quietest between 2pm and 4pm.

Road Categories

Autostradas Italy's toll-charging motorways. On road signs they're marked by a white 'A' and number on a green background. The main north–south artery is the A1, aka the Autostrada del Sole (the 'Motorway of the Sun'), which runs from Milan to Naples via Bologna, Florence and Rome. The main road south from Naples to Reggio di Calabria is the A3. To drive on an autostrada pick up a ticket at the entry barrier and pay (by cash or credit card) as you exit.

Strade statali (state highways) Represented on maps by 'S' or 'SS'. Vary from four-lane highways to two-lane roads. The latter can be extremely slow, especially in mountainous regions.

Strade regionali (regional highways) Like SS roads but administered by regional authorities rather than the state. Coded 'SR' or 'R'.

Strade provinciali (provincial highways) Smaller and slower roads. Coded 'SP' or 'P'.

Along with their A or SS number, some Italian roads are labelled with an E number – for example, the A4 autostrada is also shown as the E64 on maps and signs. This E number refers to the road's designation on the Europe-wide E-road network. E routes, which often cross national boundaries, are generally made up of major national roads strung together.

Limited Traffic Zones

Many Italian cities, including Rome and Florence, have designated their historic centres as Limited Traffic Zones (ZTL). These areas are off-limits to unauthorised

Coins

Always try to keep some coins to hand. They come in very useful for parking meters.

Road Trip Websites

AUTOMOBILE ASSOCIATIONS

Automobile Club d'Italia (www.aci.it) Has a comprehensive online guide to motoring in Italy. Provides 24-hour roadside assistance.

CONDITIONS & TRAFFIC

Autostrade (www.autostrade.it) Comprehensive site with real time traffic info on Italy's motorways. Also lists service stations, petrol prices and toll costs.

CCISS (www.cciss.it) Italian-language site with updates on road works and real time traffic flows.

MAPS & ROUTE PLANNING

Michelin (www.viamichelin.it) Online road-trip planner.

Tutto Città (www.tuttocitta.it) Good for detailed town and city maps.

Mappy (https://en.mappy.com) Online mapping tool.

vehicles and entry points are covered by street cameras. If you're caught entering one without the necessary permission you risk a fine. Being in a hire car will not exempt you from this rule.

Contact your hotel or accommodation supplier if you think you'll need to access a ZTL.

ROAD RULES

➡ Drive on the right; overtake on the left.

➡ It's obligatory to wear seat belts (front and rear), to drive with your headlights on outside built-up areas, and to carry a warning triangle and fluorescent waistcoat in case of breakdown.

➡ Wearing a helmet is compulsory on all two-wheeled vehicles.

➡ Motorbikes can enter most restricted traffic areas in Italian cities, and traffic police generally turn a blind eye to motorcycles or scooters parked on footpaths.

→ The blood alcohol limit is 0.05%; it's zero for drivers under 21 and for those who have had their licence for less than three years.
Unless otherwise indicated, speed limits are as follows.

→ 130km/h on autostradas

→ 110km/h on main roads outside built-up areas

→ 90km/h on secondary roads outside built-up areas

→ 50km/h in built-up areas

Road Etiquette

→ Italian drivers are fast, aggressive and skilful. Lane hopping and late braking are the norm and it's not uncommon to see cars tailgating at 130km/h. Don't expect cars to slow down for you or let you out. As soon as you see a gap, go for it. Italians expect the unexpected and react swiftly, but they're not used to ditherers, so be decisive.

→ Headlight flashing is common on the roads and has several meanings. If a car behind you flashes it means: 'Get out of the way' or 'Don't pull out, I'm not stopping'. But if an approaching car flashes you, it's warning you that there's a police check ahead.

→ Use of the car horn is widespread. It might be a warning but it might equally be an expression of frustration at slow-moving traffic or celebration that the traffic light's just turned green.

Driving Problem Buster

I can't speak Italian, will that be a problem? When at a petrol station you might have to ask the attendant for your fill-up. Ask for the amount you want, so *venti euro* for €20 or *pieno* for full. Always specify *benzina senza piombo* for unleaded petrol or *gasolio* for diesel.

What should I do if my car breaks down? Call the service number of your car-hire company. The Automobile Club d'Italia (ACI) provides 24-hour roadside assistance – call 803 116 from an Italian landline or mobile, or 800 116800 from a foreign mobile phone. Foreigners do not have to join but instead pay a per-incident fee. Note that in the event of a breakdown, a warning triangle is compulsory, as is use of an approved yellow or orange safety vest if you leave your vehicle.

What if I have an accident? For minor accidents there's no need to call the police. Fill in an accident report – *Constatazione Amichevole di Incidente* (CAI; Agreed Motor Accident Statement) – through your car-hire firm or insurance company.

What should I do if I get stopped by the police? The police will want to see your passport (or photo ID), licence, car registration papers and proof of insurance.

Will I need to pay tolls in advance? No. When you join an autostrada you have to pick up a ticket at the barrier. When you exit you pay based on the distance you've covered. Pay by cash or credit card.

Are the road signs easy to understand? Most signs are fairly obvious but it helps to know that town/city centres are indicated by the word *centro* and a kind of black-and-white bullseye sign; *divieto fermata* means 'no stopping'; and *tutte le direzione* means 'all directions'. See the inside back cover of this book for some of the most common road signs.

Will I be able to find ATMs along the road? Some autostrada service stations have ATMs (known as *bancomat* in Italian). Otherwise they are widely available in towns and cities.

PARKING

➡ Parking can be a major headache. Space is at a premium in towns and cities and Italy's traffic wardens are annoyingly efficient.

➡ Parking spaces outlined in blue are designated for paid parking – get a ticket from the nearest meter (coins only) or *tabaccaio* (tobacconist) and display it on your dashboard. Note that charges often don't apply overnight, typically between 8pm and 8am.

➡ White or yellow lines almost always indicate that residential permits are needed.

FUEL

➡ Staffed filling stations (*benzinai*, *stazioni di servizio*) are widespread. Smaller stations tend to close between about 1pm and 3.30pm and sometimes also on Sunday afternoons.

➡ Many stations have self-service (*fai da te*) pumps that you can use 24 hours a day. To use one insert a banknote into the payment machine and press the number of the pump you want.

➡ Unleaded petrol is marked as *benzina senza piombo*; diesel as *gasolio*.

➡ Italy's petrol prices are among the highest in Europe and vary from one station to another. At the time of writing, unleaded petrol was averaging €1.46 per litre; diesel €1.29 per litre.

➡ At petrol stations, it costs slightly less to fill up yourself rather than have an assistant do it for you.

➡ Fuel costs most at austostrada service stations.

Road Distances (KM)

Note

Distances between Palermo and mainland towns do not take into account the ferry from Reggio di Calabria to Messina. Add an extra hour to your journey time to allow for this crossing.

	Bari	Bologna	Florence	Genoa	Milan	Naples	Palermo	Perugia	Reggio di Calabria	Rome	Siena	Trento	Trieste	Turin	Venice
Bologna	681														
Florence	784	106													
Genoa	996	285	268												
Milan	899	218	324	156											
Naples	322	640	534	758	858										
Palermo	734	1415	1345	1569	1633	811									
Perugia	612	270	164	432	488	408	1219								
Reggio di Calabria	490	1171	1101	1325	1389	567	272	816							
Rome	482	408	302	526	626	232	1043	170	664						
Siena	714	176	70	296	394	464	1275	103	867	232					
Trento	892	233	339	341	218	874	1626	459	1222	641	375				
Trieste	995	308	414	336	420	948	1689	543	1445	715	484	279			
Turin	1019	338	442	174	139	932	1743	545	1307	702	460	349	551		
Venice	806	269	265	387	284	899	799	394	1296	567	335	167	165	415	
Verona	808	141	247	282	164	781	1534	377	1139	549	293	97	250	295	120

SAFETY

➡ The main safety threat to motorists is theft. Hire cars and foreign vehicles are a target for robbers and although you're unlikely to have a problem, thefts do occur.

➡ As a general rule, always lock your car and never leave anything showing, particularly valuables, and certainly not overnight. If at all possible, avoid leaving luggage in an unattended car.

➡ It's a good idea to pay extra to leave your car in supervised car parks.

RADIO

➡ RAI, Italy's state broadcaster, operates three national radio stations (Radiouno, Radiodue, Radiotre) offering news, current affairs, classical and commercial music.

➡ Isoradio, another RAI station, provides regular news and traffic bulletins.

➡ There are also thousands of commercial radio stations, many broadcasting locally. Major ones include Radio Capital, good for modern hits; Radio Deejay, aimed at a younger audience; and Radio 24, which airs news and talk shows.

Italy Travel Guide

GETTING THERE & AWAY

AIR

The following are Italy's main international airports. Car hire is available at all these airports.

Rome Fiumicino (www.adr.it/fiumicino) Officially known as Leonardo da Vinci International Airport.

Rome Ciampino (www.adr.it/ciampino) Hub for Ryanair flights to Rome.

Milan Malpensa (www.milanomalpensa-airport.com)

Milan Linate (www.milanolinate-airport.com) Milan's second airport.

Venice Marco Polo (www.veniceairport.it)

Pisa International (www.pisa-airport.com) Main international gateway for Tuscany.

Naples International (www.aeroportodinapoli.it) Also known as Capodichino.

Catania Fontanarossa (www.aeroporto.catania.it) Sicily's busiest airport.

Bergamo Orio al Serio (www.orioaeroporto.it) Used by European low-cost carriers.

Turin Caselle (www.aeroportoditorino.it)

Bologna Guglielmo Marconi (www.bologna-airport.it)

Bari Karol Wojtyła (www.aeroportidipuglia.it)

Palermo Falcone-Borsellino (www.gesap.it)

Cagliari Elmas (www.cagliariairport.it) Main gateway for Sardinia.

CAR & MOTORCYCLE

Driving into Italy is fairly straightforward – thanks to the Schengen Agreement, there are no customs checks when driving in from neighbours France, Switzerland, Austria and Slovenia.

Aside from the coastal roads linking Italy with France and Slovenia, border crossings into Italy mostly involve tunnels through the Alps (open year-round) or mountain passes (seasonally closed and requiring snow chains).

The list below outlines the major points of entry.

Austria From Innsbruck to Bolzano via A22/E45 (Brenner Pass); Villach to Tarvisio via A23/E55.

France From Nice to Ventimiglia via A10/E80; Modane to Turin via A32/E70 (Fréjus Tunnel); Chamonix to Courmayeur via A5/E25 (Mont Blanc Tunnel).

Slovenia From Sežana to Trieste via SR58/E70.

Switzerland From Martigny to Aosta via SS27/E27 (Grand St Bernard Tunnel); Lugano to Como via A9/E35.

SEA

International car ferries sail to Italy from Albania, Croatia, France (Corsica), Greece, Malta, Montenegro, Morocco, Slovenia, Spain and Tunisia. Some routes only operate in summer, when ticket prices rise. Prices for vehicles vary according to their size. Car hire is not always available at ports, so check beforehand.

The helpful website www.directferries.co.uk allows you to search routes and compare prices between international ferry companies.

Principal operators include the following:

Adria Ferries (www.adriaferries.com) Albania to Bari (nine hours), Ancona (20 hours), Trieste (37 hours).

Anek Lines (www.anekitalia.com) Greece to Bari (eight to 18½ hours), Ancona (eight to 22 hours), Venice (25 to 32 hours).

GNV (Grandi Navi Veloci; www.gnv.it) Spain to Genoa (20 hours).

Grimaldi Lines (www.grimaldi-lines.com) Spain to Civitavecchia (20 hours), Savona (17 to 20 hours).

Jadrolinija (www.jadrolinija.hr) Croatia to Ancona (from nine hours), Bari (10 hours).

Minoan Lines (www.minoan.it) Greece to Ancona (17 to 23 hours).

Montenegro Lines (www.montenegrolines. net) Bar to Bari (10 hours).

Superfast (www.superfast.com) Greece to Bari (nine to 16 hours), Ancona (eight to 22 hours), Venice (14 to 33 hours).

TRAIN

Regular trains on two western lines connect Italy with France (one along the coast and the other from Turin into the French Alps). Trains from Milan head north into Switzerland and on towards the Benelux countries. Further east, two lines connect with Central and Eastern Europe.

Car hire is generally available at principal city stations.

Practicalities

Smoking Banned in enclosed public spaces, which includes restaurants, bars, shops and public transport.

Time Italy uses the 24-hour clock and is on Central European Time, one hour ahead of GMT/UTC.

TV The main terrestrial channels are Rai 1, 2 and 3 run by Rai (www. rai.it), Italy's state-owned national broadcaster, and Canale 5, Italia 1 and Rete 4 run by Mediaset (www. mediaset.it).

Weights & Measures Italy uses the metric system, so kilometres not miles, litres not gallons.

DIRECTORY A–Z

ACCESSIBLE TRAVEL

Italy is not an easy country for travellers with disabilities. Cobblestone streets and pavements blocked by parked cars and scooters make getting around difficult for wheelchair users. And while many buildings have lifts, they are not always wide enough for wheelchairs. Not a lot has been done to make life easier for hearing- or vision-impaired travellers either. However, awareness of accessibility issues and a culture of inclusion are steadily growing.

➡ The Italian National Tourist Office in your country may be able to provide advice on Italian associations for travellers with disabilities and information on what help is available.

➡ Airline companies will arrange assistance at airports if you notify them of your needs in advance. For help at Rome's Fiumicino or Ciampino airports contact ADR Assistance (www. adrassistance.it).

➡ Some taxis are equipped to carry passengers in wheelchairs; ask for a taxi for a *sedia a rotelle* (wheelchair).

➡ If you are driving, EU disabled parking permits are recognised in Italy, giving you the same parking rights that local drivers with disabilities have.

➡ If you have an obvious disability and/or appropriate ID, many museums and galleries offer free admission for yourself and a companion.

Resources include the following:

Village for All (www.villageforall.net/en) Performs on-site audits of tourist facilities in Italy and San Marino. Most of the 67 facilities are accommodation providers, ranging from camping grounds to high-class hotels.

Tourism without Barriers (www.turismosenzabarriere.it) Has a searchable database of accessible accommodation and tourist attractions in Tuscany, with a scattering of options in other regions.

Fondazione Cesare Serono (www. fondazioneserono.org/disabilita/spiagge-accessibili/spiagge-accessibili) A list (in Italian) of accessible beaches.

Download Lonely Planet's free Accessible Travel guide from http://shop.lonelyplanet.com/accessible-travel.

Accommodation Tax

➡ Italy's *tassa di soggiorno* (accommodation tax) sees visitors charged an extra €1 to €7 per night as a 'room occupancy tax'.

➡ Exactly how much you're charged depends on the type of accommodation (campground, guesthouse, hotel), a hotel's star rating, and the number of people under your booking.

➡ Our listings do not include the hotel tax, although it's always a good idea to confirm whether taxes are included when booking.

ACCOMMODATION

From dreamy villas to chic boutique hotels, historic hideaways and ravishing farm stays (*agriturismi*), Italy offers accommodation to suit every taste and budget.

Seasons & Rates

➡ Accommodation rates fluctuate enormously from high to low season, and even from day to day depending on demand, season and booking method (online, through an agency etc).

➡ As a rule, peak rates apply at Easter, in summer (July and August) and over the Christmas/New Year period. But there are exceptions – in the mountains, high season means the ski season (December to late March). Also, August is high season on the coast but low season in many cities where hotels offer discounts.

➡ Southern Italy is generally cheaper than the north.

Reservations

➡ Always book ahead in peak season, even if it's only for the first night or two.

➡ Reserving a room is essential during key festivals and events when demand is very high.

➡ In the off-season, it always pays to call ahead to check that a hotel is open. Many coastal hotels close for winter, typically opening from late March or Easter to late October.

➡ Hotels usually require that reservations be confirmed with a credit-card number. No-shows will be docked one night's accommodation.

B&Bs

B&Bs are a burgeoning sector of the Italian accommodation market and can be found throughout the country in both urban and rural settings. Options include everything from restored farmhouses, city *palazzi* (mansions) and seaside bungalows to rooms in family houses. In some cases, a B&B can also refer to a self-contained apartment with basic breakfast provisions provided. Tariffs for a double room cover a wide range, from around €60 to €140.

Hotels & Pensioni

While the difference between an *albergo* (hotel) and a *pensione* is often minimal, a *pensione* will generally be of one- to three-star quality while an *albergo* can be awarded up to five stars. *Locande* (inns) long fell into much the same category as *pensioni*, but the term has become a trendy one in some parts and reveals little about the quality of a place. *Affittacamere* are simple rooms for rent in private houses.

All hotels are rated from one to five stars:

➡ One-star hotels and *pensioni* tend to be basic and often do not offer private bathrooms.

➡ Two-star places are similar but rooms will generally have a private bathroom.

➡ Three-star hotel rooms will come with a hairdryer, minibar (or fridge), safe and air-con.

➡ Four- and five-star hotels offer facilities such as room service, laundry and dry-cleaning.

Tourist offices usually have booklets with local accommodation listings. Many hotels are also signing up with online accommodation-booking services.

Sleeping Price Ranges

The following price ranges refer to a double room with private bathroom (breakfast included) in high season.

€ less than €110

€€ €110–€200

€€€ more than €200

Agriturismi

From rustic country houses to luxurious estates and fully functioning farms, Italian farm stays, known as *agriturismi* (singular – *agriturismo*) are hugely popular. Comfort levels, facilities and prices vary but the best will offer swimming pools and top-class accommodation. Many also operate restaurants specialising in traditional local cuisine.

For listings and further details, check the following:

Agriturismo.it (www.agriturismo.it)

Agriturismo.net (www.agriturismo.net)

Agriturismo.com (www.agriturismo.com)

Agriturismo-Italia.net (www.agriturismo-italia.net)

Other Options

Camping A popular summer option. Most campsites are big, summer-only complexes with swimming pools, restaurants and supermarkets. Many have space for RVs and offer bungalows or simple, self-contained flats. Minimum stays sometimes apply in high season. Check out www.campeggi.com and www.camping.it.

Hostels Official HI hostels and a growing contingent of independent hostels offer dorm beds and private rooms. Breakfast is usually included in rates and dinner is sometimes available for about €10 to €15. For listings and further details, see www.aighostels.com or www.hostelworld.com.

Convents & Monasteries Some convents and monasteries provide basic accommodation. Expect curfews, few frills and value for money. Useful resources include www.stpatricksamericanrome.org and www.initaly.com/agri/convents.htm.

Refuges Mountain huts (*rifugi*) with rooms sleeping anything from two to a dozen or more people. Many also offer hot meals and/or communal cooking facilities. Generally open from June to late September.

Villas Villas and *fattorie* (farmhouses) can be rented in their entirety or sometimes by the room. Many have swimming pools.

ELECTRICITY

230V/50Hz

230V/50Hz

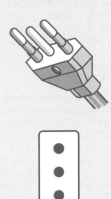

230V/50Hz

and *crostini* (little toasts) to accompany your tipple.

Agriturismo A farmhouse offering food made with farm-grown produce. Booking generally required.

Pizzeria Alongside pizza, many pizzerias also offer antipasti, pastas, meat and vegetable dishes. They're often only open in the evening. The best have a wood-oven (*forno a legna*).

Bar & Cafe Italians often breakfast on a *cornetto* (Italian croissant) and cappuccino at a bar or cafe. Many places sell *panini* (bread rolls with simple fillers) at lunchtime and serve a buffet of hot and cold dishes during the early evening *aperitivo* (aperitif) hour.

Market Most towns and cities have morning produce markets where you can stock up on picnic provisions.

FOOD

A full Italian meal consists of an antipasto (appetiser), *primo* (first course, usually a pasta, risotto or polenta), *secondo* (second course, meat or fish) with *contorno* (vegetable side dish) or *insalata* (salad), and *dolce* (dessert) and/or fruit. When eating out it's perfectly OK to mix and match and order, say, a *primo* followed by an *insalata* or *contorno*.

Where to Eat

Italy has no shortage of eating options, and reserving a table on the day of your meal is usually fine. Top-end restaurants may need to be booked a month or more in advance, while popular eateries in tourist areas should be booked at least a few days ahead in peak season.

Ristorante (Restaurant) Formal dining, often with comprehensive wine lists and more sophisticated local or national fare.

Trattoria Informal, family-run restaurant cooking up traditional regional dishes. Generally cheap to mid-range.

Osteria Similar to a trattoria, with a focus on traditional cooking.

Enoteca Wine bars invariably double as a casual place to graze or dine, typically serving snacks such as cheese, cold meats, bruschette

HEALTH

➡ Italy has a public health system (*Servizio Sanitario Nazionale, SSN*) that is legally bound to provide emergency care to everyone.

➡ EU nationals are entitled to reduced-cost, sometimes free, medical care with a European Health Insurance Card (EHIC), available from your home health authority.

➡ Non-EU citizens should take out medical insurance.

➡ For emergency treatment, go to the *pronto soccorso* (casualty department) of an *ospedale* (public hospital), though be prepared for a long wait.

Eating Price Ranges

The following price ranges refer to a two-course meal with a glass of house wine and *coperto* (cover charge).

€ less than €25

€€ €25–€45

€€€ more than €45

Note that most eating establishments add a *coperto* of around €2 to €3. Some also include a service charge (*servizio*) of 10% to 15%.

➡ Pharmacists can give advice and sell over-the-counter medication for minor illnesses.

➡ Pharmacies typically open from 8.30am to 7.30pm Monday to Friday and on Saturday mornings. Outside these hours, they open on a rotational basis. When closed, a pharmacy is legally required to post a list of places open in the vicinity.

➡ In larger cities, English-speaking doctors are often available for house calls or appointments through private clinics.

➡ Italian tap water is fine to drink.

➡ No vaccinations are required for travel to Italy.

LGBT+ TRAVELLERS

➡ Homosexuality is legal in Italy and even widely accepted in the major cities. However, discretion is still wise and overt displays of affection by LGBT+ couples can attract a negative response, especially in smaller towns.

➡ There are gay venues in Rome, Milan and Bologna, and a handful in places such as Florence and Naples. Some coastal towns and resorts (such as the Tuscan town of Viareggio or Taormina in Sicily) have much more action in summer.

Resources include the following:

Arcigay (www.arcigay.it) Bologna-based national organisation for the LGBT+ community.

Tipping Guide

Italians are not big tippers. The following is a rough guide.

Taxis Optional, but most round up to the nearest euro.

Hotels Tip porters about €5 at high-end hotels.

Restaurants Service (servizio) is generally included – otherwise, a euro or two is fine in pizzerias and trattorias, and 5% to 10% in smart restaurants.

Bars Not necessary, although many leave small change if drinking coffee at the bar, usually €0.10 or €0.20.

Gay.it (www.gay.it) Website featuring LGBT+ news, features and gossip.

Pride (www.prideonline.it) Culture, politics, travel and health with an LGBT+ focus.

INTERNET ACCESS

➡ Free wi-fi is widely available in hotels, hostels, B&Bs and agriturismi (farm stays), though signal quality varies. Some places also provide laptops/computers.

➡ Many bars and cafes offer free wi-fi.

➡ Numerous Italian cities and towns offer public wi-fi hotspots, including Rome, Milan, Bologna, Florence and Venice. To use them, you'll need to register online using a credit card or an Italian mobile number.

➡ A free smartphone app, wifi.italia.it, allows you to connect to participating networks through a single login. Released in summer 2017, it gets mixed reports.

MONEY

Italy uses the euro. Euro notes come in denominations of €500, €200, €100, €50, €20, €10 and €5; coins come in denominations of €2 and €1, and 50, 20, 10, five, two and one cents.

For the latest exchange rates, check out www.xe.com.

Admission Prices

➡ State museums and sites offer free admission to under-18s and discounted entry to 18-to-25-year-olds.

➡ You'll need photo ID to claim reduced entry.

➡ State-run museums are free on the first Sunday of the month between October and March.

ATMs & Credit Cards

➡ ATMs (known as bancomat) are widely available throughout Italy and most will accept cards tied into the Visa, MasterCard, Cirrus and Maestro systems.

➡ Credit cards such as Visa, MasterCard, Eurocard, Cirrus and Eurocheques are widely accepted. Amex is also recognised, though less common.

➡ Virtually all midrange and top-end hotels accept credit cards, as do most restaurants and large shops. Some cheaper *pensioni* (pensions), trattorias and pizzerias only accept cash. Don't rely on credit cards at smaller museums or galleries.

➡ Always inform your bank of your travel plans to avoid your card being blocked for payments made in unusual locations.

➡ Check any charges with your bank. Most banks charge a foreign exchange fee as well as a transaction charge of around 1% to 3%.

➡ If your card is lost, stolen or swallowed by an ATM, call to have it blocked:

Amex ☏06 7290 0347
Diners Club ☏800 393939
MasterCard ☏800 870866
Visa ☏800 819014

Moneychangers

➡ You can change money at a *cambio* (exchange office) or post office. Some banks might change money, though many now only do this for account holders. Post offices and banks offer the best rates; exchange offices keep longer hours, but watch for high commissions and inferior rates.

➡ Take your passport or photo ID when exchanging money.

OPENING HOURS

Opening hours vary throughout the year. We've provided high-season hours, which are generally in use over summer. Summer refers to the period between April and September (or October); winter is October (or November) to March.

Banks 8.30am–1.30pm and 2.45pm–4.30pm Monday to Friday

Bars & cafes 7.30am–8pm, sometimes to 1am or 2am

Clubs 10pm–4am or 5am

Restaurants noon–3pm and 7.30pm–11pm (later in summer)

Shops 9am–1pm and 3.30pm–7.30pm (or 4pm to 8pm) Monday to Saturday. In main cities some shops stay open at lunchtime and on Sunday mornings. Some shops close Monday mornings.

Italian Wine Classifications

Italian wines are classified according to strict quality-control standards and carry one of four denominations:

DOCG (*Denominazione di Origine Controllata e Garantita*) Italy's best wines; made in specific areas according to stringent production rules.

DOC (*Denominazione di Origine Controllata*) Quality wines produced in defined regional areas.

IGT (*Indicazione di Geografica Tipica*) Wines typical of a certain region.

Vino da Tavola Wines for everyday drinking; often served as house wine in trattorias.

PUBLIC HOLIDAYS

Most Italians take their annual holiday in August. Many businesses and shops close for at least part of the month, particularly around *Ferragosto* (Feast of the Assumption) on 15 August.

Individual towns have public holidays to celebrate the feasts of their patron saints. National public holidays include the following:

Capodanno (New Year's Day) 1 January

Epifania (Epiphany) 6 January

Pasquetta (Easter Monday) March/April

Giorno della Liberazione (Liberation Day) 25 April

Festa del Lavoro (Labour Day) 1 May

Festa della Repubblica (Republic Day) 2 June

Ferragosto (Feast of the Assumption) 15 August

Festa di Ognisanti (All Saints' Day) 1 November

Festa dell'Immacolata Concezione (Feast of the Immaculate Conception) 8 December

Natale (Christmas Day) 25 December

Festa di Santo Stefano (Boxing Day) 26 December

Important Numbers

Italy country code (☏39)

International access code (☏00)

Police (☏112, 113)

Ambulance (☏118)

Fire (☏115)

Roadside assistance (☏803 116 from an Italian landline or mobile phone; ☏800 116800 from a foreign mobile phone)

SAFE TRAVEL

Italy is a safe country but petty theft can be a problem. There's no need for paranoia but be aware that thieves and pickpockets operate in touristy areas, so watch out when exploring the sights in Rome, Florence, Venice and Naples.

Cars, particularly those with foreign number plates or rental-company stickers, provide rich pickings for thieves.

In case of theft or loss, report the incident to the police within 24 hours and ask for a statement.

Some tips:

➡ Wear your bag/camera strap across your body and away from the road – thieves on mopeds can swipe a bag and be gone in seconds.

➡ Never drape your bag over an empty chair at a street-side cafe or put it where you can't see it. Also, never leave valuables in coat pockets in restaurants or other places with communal coat hooks.

➡ Always check your change to see you haven't been short changed.

TELEPHONE

Domestic Calls

➡ Italian area codes begin with 0 and consist of up to four digits. They are an integral part of all phone numbers and must be dialled even when calling locally.

➡ Mobile-phone numbers begin with a three-digit prefix starting with a 3.

➡ Toll-free numbers are known as *numeri verdi* and usually start with 800.

➡ Some six-digit national rate numbers are also in use (such as those for Alitalia and Trenitalia).

International Calls

➡ To call Italy from abroad, dial your country's international access code, then Italy's country code (39) followed by the area code of the location you want (including the first zero) and the rest of the number.

➡ To call abroad from Italy dial 00, then the country code, followed by the full number.

➡ Avoid making international calls from hotels, as rates are high.

➡ The cheapest way to call is to use an app such as Skype or Viber, connecting through the wi-fi at your hotel/B&B etc.

Mobile Phones

➡ Italian mobile phones operate on the GSM 900/1800 network, which is compatible with the rest of Europe and Australia but not always with the North American GSM or CDMA systems – check with your service provider.

➡ The cheapest way of using your mobile is to buy a prepaid (*prepagato*) Italian SIM card. TIM (*Telecom Italia Mobile*; www.tim.it), Wind (www.wind.it), Vodafone (www.vodafone.it) and Tre (www.tre.it) all offer SIM cards and have retail outlets across the country. You can then top up as you go, either online or at one of your provider's shops.

➡ Note that by Italian law all SIM cards must be registered in Italy, so make sure you have your passport or ID card when you buy one.

TOILETS

Besides in museums, galleries, train stations and autostrada service stations, there are few public toilets in Italy. If you're caught short, the best thing to do is to nip into a cafe or bar. The polite thing to do is to order something at the bar.

You may need to pay to use some public toilets (usually €0.50 to €1.50).

TOURIST INFORMATION

➡ Italy's national tourist board, ENIT – Agenzia Nazionale del Turismo – has offices across the world. Its website, www.italia.it, provides both practical information and inspirational travel ideas.

➡ Most cities and towns in Italy have a tourist office that can provide maps, lists of local accommodation, and information on sights in the area.

➡ In larger towns and major tourist areas, English is generally spoken, along with other languages, depending on the region (for example, German in Alto Adige, French in Valle d'Aosta).

➡ Most tourist offices will respond to written or telephone requests for information.

➡ Office hours vary: in major tourist destinations, offices generally open daily, especially in the summer high season. In smaller centres, they generally observe regular office hours and open Monday through to Friday, perhaps also on Saturday mornings.

➡ Affiliated information booths (at train stations and airports, for example) may keep slightly different hours.

➡ Tourist offices in Italy go under a variety of names, depending on who they're administered by (the local municipality, province, or region), but most perform similar functions. On the ground, look for signs to the *Ufficio Turistico*.

Regional Tourist Authorities

Regional offices are generally more concerned with marketing and promotion than offering a public information service. However, they have useful websites.

Abruzzo (www.abruzzoturismo.it)
Basilicata (www.basilicataturistica.it)
Calabria (www.turiscalabria.it)
Campania (www.incampania.com)

Emilia-Romagna (www.emiliaromagna turismo.it)
Friuli Venezia Giulia (www.turismo.fvg.it)
Lazio (www.visitlazio.com)
Le Marche (www.turismo.marche.it)
Liguria (www.lamialiguria.it)
Lombardy (www.in-lombardia.it)
Molise (www.visitmolise.eu)
Piedmont (www.piemonteitalia.eu)
Puglia (www.viaggiareinpuglia.it)
Sardinia (www.sardegnaturismo.it)
Sicily (www.visitsicily.info)
Trentino-Alto Adige (www.visittrentino.it)
Tuscany (www.visittuscany.com)
Umbria (www.umbriatourism.it)
Valle d'Aosta (www.lovevda.it)
Veneto (www.veneto.eu)

VISAS

➡ Italy is one of the 26 European countries making up the Schengen area. There are no customs controls when travelling between Schengen countries, so the visa rules that apply to Italy apply to all Schengen countries.

➡ EU citizens do not need a visa to enter Italy.

➡ Nationals of some other countries, including Australia, Canada, Israel, Japan, New Zealand, Switzerland and the USA, do not need a visa for stays of up to 90 days.

➡ Nationals of other countries will need a Schengen tourist visa – to check requirements see www.schengenvisainfo.com/tourist-schengen-visa.

➡ All non-EU and non-Schengen nationals entering Italy for more than 90 days or for any reason other than tourism (such as study or work) may need a specific visa. Check http://vistoperitalia.esteri.it for details.

➡ Ensure your passport is valid for at least six months beyond your departure date from Italy.

Language

Italian sounds can all be found in English. If you read our coloured pronunciation guides as if they were English, you'll be understood. Note that ai is pronounced as in 'aisle', ay as in 'say', ow as in 'how', dz as the 'ds' in 'lids', and that r is strong and rolled. If the consonant is written as a double letter, it's pronounced a little stronger, eg *sonno son*·no (sleep) versus *sono so*·no (I am). The stressed syllables are indicated with italics.

BASICS

Hello.	*Buongiorno.*	bwon·*jor*·no
Goodbye.	*Arrivederci.*	a·ree·ve·*der*·chee
Yes./No.	*Sì./No.*	see/no
Excuse me.	*Mi scusi.*	mee *skoo*·zee
Sorry.	*Mi dispiace.*	mee dees·*pya*·che
Please.	*Per favore.*	per fa·*vo*·re
Thank you.	*Grazie.*	*gra*·tsye

You're welcome.
Prego. pre·go

Do you speak English?
Parli inglese? *par*·lee een·*gle*·ze

I don't understand.
Non capisco. non ka·*pee*·sko

How much is this?
Quanto costa questo? *kwan*·to *kos*·ta *kwe*·sto

ACCOMMODATION

Do you have a room?
Avete una camera? a·*ve*·te *oo*·na *ka*·me·ra

How much is it per night/person?
Quanto costa per *kwan*·to *kos*·ta per
una notte/persona? *oo*·na *no*·te/per·*so*·na

DIRECTIONS

Where's ...?
Dov'è ...? do·*ve* ...

Can you show me (on the map)?
Può mostrarmi pwo mos·*trar*·mee
(sulla pianta)? (*soo*·la *pyan*·ta)

EATING & DRINKING

What would you recommend?
Cosa mi consiglia? *ko*·za mee kon·*see*·lya

I'd like ..., please.
Vorrei ..., per favore. vo·*ray* ... per fa·*vo*·re

I don't eat (meat).
Non mangio (carne). non *man*·jo (*kar*·ne)

Please bring the bill.
Mi porta il conto, mee *por*·ta eel *kon*·to
per favore? per fa·*vo*·re

EMERGENCIES

Help!
Aiuto! a·*yoo*·to

I'm lost.
Mi sono perso/a. (m/f) mee *so*·no *per*·so/a

I'm ill.
Mi sento male. mee *sen*·to *ma*·le

Call the police!
Chiami la polizia! *kya*·mee la po·lee·*tsee*·a

Call a doctor!
Chiami un medico! *kya*·mee oon *me*·dee·ko

Want More?

For in-depth language information and handy phrases, check out Lonely Planet's *Italian Phrasebook*. You'll find it at **shop.lonelyplanet.com**, or you can buy Lonely Planet's iPhone phrasebooks at the Apple App Store.

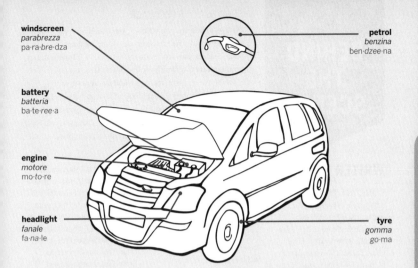

windscreen
parabrezza
pa·ra·bre·dza

petrol
benzina
ben·dzee·na

battery
batteria
ba·te·ree·a

engine
motore
mo·to·re

headlight
fanale
fa·na·le

tyre
gomma
go·ma

ON THE ROAD

I'd like to hire a/an ...	*Vorrei noleggiare ...*	vo·ray no·le·ja·re ...
4WD	*un fuoristrada*	oon fwo·ree·stra·da
automatic/ manual	*una macchina automatica/ manuale*	oo·na ma·kee·na ow·to·ma·tee·ka/ ma·noo·a·le
motorbike	*una moto*	oo·na mo·to

How much is it ...?	*Quanto costa ...?*	kwan·to kos·ta ...
daily	*al giorno*	al jor·no
weekly	*alla settimana*	a·la se·tee·ma·na

Does that include insurance?
E' compresa l'assicurazione?
e kom·pre·sa la·see·koo·ra·tsyo·ne

Does that include mileage?
E' compreso il chilometraggio?
e kom·pre·so eel kee·lo·me·tra·jo

What's the city/country speed limit?
Qual'è il limite di velocità in città/campagna?
kwa·le eel lee·mee·te dee ve·lo·chee·ta een chee·ta/kam·pa·nya

Is this the road to (Venice)?
Questa strada porta a (Venezia)?
kwe·sta stra·da por·ta a (ve·ne·tsya)

(How long) Can I park here?
(Per quanto tempo) Posso parcheggiare qui?
(per kwan·to tem·po) po·so par·ke·ja·re kwee

Please fill it up.
Il pieno, per favore.
eel pye·no per fa·vo·re

Where's a service station?
Dov'è una stazione di servizio?
do·ve oo·na sta·tsyo·ne dee ser·vee·tsyo

I'd like (30) litres.
Vorrei (trenta) litri.
vo·ray (tren·ta) lee·tree

Please check the oil/water.
Può controllare l'olio/ l'acqua, per favore?
pwo kon·tro·la·re lo·lyo/ la·kwa per fa·vo·re

I need a mechanic.
Ho bisogno di un meccanico.
o bee·zo·nyo dee oon me·ka·nee·ko

The car/motorbike has broken down.
La macchina/moto si è guastata.
la ma·kee·na/mo·to see e gwas·ta·ta

I had an accident.
Ho avuto un incidente.
o a·voo·to oon een·chee·den·te

Signs	
Alt	Stop
Dare la Precedenza	Give Way
Deviazione	Detour
Divieto di Accesso	No Entry
Entrata	Entrance
Pedaggio	Toll
Senso Unico	One Way
Uscita	Exit

433

BEHIND THE SCENES

SEND US YOUR FEEDBACK

We love to hear from travellers – your comments help make our books better. We read every word, and we guarantee that your feedback goes straight to the authors. Visit **lonelyplanet. com/contact** to submit your updates and suggestions.

Note: We may edit, reproduce and incorporate your comments in Lonely Planet products such as guidebooks, websites and digital products, so let us know if you don't want your comments reproduced or your name acknowledged. For a copy of our privacy policy visit lonelyplanet.com/privacy.

WRITER THANKS

DUNCAN GARWOOD

A big *grazie* to all the locals and tourist office staff who helped and offered advice: Sara Cappelli, Roberta Magi, Elisa Fabri, Barbara Ravaglia, Cinzia at Narni, Silvia in Perugia, Nicola Santarelli, Luana Fringuelli, Carolina Grisanti, Vania Di Cicco, Ilaria Lucentini and Giulia in Tarquinia. Thanks also to Anna Tyler at Lonely Planet for all her support. Finally, a huge hug to Lidia and the boys, Ben and Nick.

BRETT ATKINSON

Exploring southern Italy and Sicily with my LP hat on was a great experience thanks to Anna Rita in Bari, Luisa in Lecce and Domenico in Reggio Calabria. Thanks also to Amy in Matera for helping me negotiate the town's storied laneways, and to Tony in Vieste for securing me a slow boat to the Isole Tremiti. Special thanks to Anna Tyler for the commission, and to Carol on our gelato- and *aperitivi*-fuelled reconnaissance trip 12 months earlier.

ALEXIS AVERBUCK

Ahhh, Sardinia. My thanks go to this ever-fascinating and gorgeous island, and its warm and welcoming people. It has been a lifelong dream to get to know Sardinia and reality exceeded all fantasies. Huge thanks to my road-warrior sister and Zodiac-skipper, Rachel Averbuck, for dropping everything and joining me in our zippy Fiat cabriolet when I told her how grand it is! Many thanks to Anna Tyler who helmed the project with superb attention to detail, guidance and grace.

CRISTIAN BONETTO

Grazie infinite to all those who shared their love and intimate knowledge of the Mezzogiorno. In Sicily, special thanks to Ornella Tuzzolino, Giorgio Ferravioli and Carla Bellavista, Pierfrancesco Palazzotto, Lorenzo Chiaramonte, Rosario Fillari, Giorgio Puglisi, Gennaro Mattiucci, Ernesto Magri, Giovanni Gurrieri, Joe Brizzi, Giuseppe Savà, Luigi Nifosì, Antonio Adamo, Cesare Setmani, Norma Gritti and Cristina Delli Fiori. In Campania, *grazie di cuore* to my *Re e Regina di Napoli*, Federica Rispoli and Ivan Palmieri, as well as to Igor Milanese.

GREGOR CLARK

Grazie mille to the many dozens of people who shared their love and knowledge of Sicily, Trentino and South Tyrol with me, especially Fausto Ceschi, Fabiana Mariotti, Micol Beittel, Stefano Musaico, Mark, Giovanna, Angela, Francesco, Marcello, Paola, Carmelina, Marian, Diego

THIS BOOK

This 3rd edition of Lonely Planet's *Italy's Best Trips* guidebook was researched and written by Duncan Garwood, Brett Atkinson, Alexis Averbuck, Cristian Bonetto, Gregor Clark, Peter Dragicevich, Paula Hardy, Virginia Maxwell, Stephanie Ong, Kevin Raub, Brendan Sainsbury, Regis St Louis and Nicola Williams. The previous edition was written by Duncan Garwood

and Paula Hardy. This guidebook was produced by the following:

Destination Editor Anna Tyler

Regional Senior Cartographer Anthony Phelan

Senior Product Editor Elizabeth Jones

Product Editor Kate James

Book Designer Jessica Rose

Assisting Editors Judith Bamber, Michelle Coxall, Andrea Dobbin, Emma Gibbs, Jennifer Hattam, Gabrielle Innes, Anita Isalska, Kellie Langdon, Jodie Martire, Kate Morgan, Lauren O'Connell, Susan Paterson, Saralinda Turner, Fionnuala Twomey, Simon Williamson

Assisting Cartographer Mick Garrett

Cover Researcher Meri Blazevski

Thanks to Andrea Aiolfi, Alexandra Bruzzese, Melanie Dankel, Gemma Graham, Martin Heng, Joe Revill, Sophia Seymour, Ross Taylor, Jo-Ann Titmarsh, Brana Vladisavljevic and Patrizia. Back in Vermont, big hugs to Gaen, Meigan and Chloe, who always make coming home the best part of the trip.

PETER DRAGICEVICH

I still pinch myself that my work continues to allow me to spend time in such a magical city as Venice, and for that I have editor extraordinaire Anna Tyler to thank. Many thanks to Lonely Planet Local Jo-Ann Titmarsh for your good company and excellent advice on this assignment, and for the wealth of new listings that you had already uncovered. My eternal gratitude goes to my dear friend Bain Duigan, who accompanied me in spirit at least.

PAULA HARDY

Mille grazie to all the creative and passionate people who shared their insights. In Venice: Luisella Romeo, Gioele and Heiby Romanelli, Emanuele dal Carlo, Valeria Duflot, Sebastian Fagarazzi, Fabio Carrera, Jo-Ann Titmarsh, Alice Braveri and Anat at the Comunità Ebraica di Venezia. In Friuli: Tatjana Familio, Laura Fiorino, Maja de'Simoni, Roberto Mezzina, Cristiana Fiandra, Susanna Guerrato, Chiara Pigni, Fabio Tarlao, Francesca Boscarol, Alessia Drigo, Elisa Nervi, Anna Cleva, Monica Bertarelli, Raffaella Grasselli, Sonia Macor, and Fabio Stulin for his incredible patience on the road. And thank you Rob for sharing my love of the *bel paese*.

VIRGINIA MAXWELL

As always, many locals assisted me in my research for this project. Many thanks to Ilaria Crescioli, Elisa Grisolaghi, Serena Nocciolini, Sean Lawson, Valentina de Pamphilis, Rodolfo Ademollo, Sonia Corsi, Elena Giovenco, Eleonora Sandrelli, Valentina Pierguidi, Maria Guarriello and the staff at Strada Vino Nobile Montepulciano e

Sapori Valdichiana Senese, Maja Malbasa, Lucrezia Lorini, Vanessa Brezzi, Roberta Benini, Gerardo Giorgi, Caterina Mori and Silvia Fiorentini. Thanks to Anna Tyler for giving me this and many past Italy gigs, and thanks and much love to my favourite travelling companion, Peter Handsaker, who loves Italy as much as I do.

STEPHANIE ONG

A big heartfelt thanks to Anna Tyler for trusting me with this update, Duncan Garwood for his sage writerly advice and the LP team for their great work. I'd also like to thank all the Milan locals, especially DJ Uabos for his nightlife tips and Jackie DeGiorgio for her foodie insight. Last but not least, I'd like to thank my partner in crime and life, Alessandro Sorci, for always being close to me and keeping me sane with regular post-work gelato.

KEVIN RAUB

Thanks to Anna Tyler and all my fellow partners in crime at LP. On the road, Alice Brignani, who puts out cultural fires, uncovers hidden gems, even leaps buildings in a single bound (all well beyond her Bologna borders!) and still wants to share an Italian IPA with me after it's all said and done. Claudia Valentini, Francesca Soffici, Franca Rastelli, Sara Laghi, Fabrizio Raggi, Errica Dall'Ara, Maria Grazia Martini and Giovanni Pellegrini, too!

BRENDAN SAINSBURY

Many thanks to all the skilled bus drivers, helpful tourist information staff, generous hotel owners, expert cappuccino makers, dogs that didn't growl at me, and numerous passers-by who helped me, unwittingly or otherwise, during my research trip. Special thanks to my wife, Liz, and my son, Kieran, for keeping the home fires burning while I was away.

REGIS ST LOUIS

I'm grateful to countless Italians and expats who provided tips and insight into Liguria, Valle d'Aosta and Piemonte while on the road. Special thanks to Catherina Unger, Eugenio Bordoni and Arbaspàa staff in Cinque Terre, Erika Carpaneto and Gloria Faccio in Turin, and Alberto and Fulvio Peluffo in Noli. Hugs to Cassandra and our daughters Magdalena and Genevieve, who joined for the great Ligurian adventure.

NICOLA WILLIAMS

Heartfelt thanks to those who shared their love and insider knowledge with me: family tour guide and art historian extraordinaire Molly McIlwrath; Ambra Nepi and Avila Fernandez (Duomo); Doreen and Carmello (Hotel Scoti); Betti Soldi; Coral Sisk (@curiousappetite); Nardia Plumridge (@lostinflorence); Katja Meier, Ilaria and Stella (Mus.e); Mary Gray; Anne Davis; Georgette Jupe (@girlinflorence); and Paolo Bresci (Pistoia tourist office). Finally, kudos to my very own expert, trilingual, family-travel research team: Niko, Mischa and Kaya.

ACKNOWLEDGEMENTS

Climate map data adapted from Peel MC, Finlayson BL & McMahon TA (2007) 'Updated World Map of the Köppen-Geiger Climate Classification', *Hydrology and Earth System Sciences*, 11, 1633–44.

Front cover photographs (clockwise from top): Montepulciano, Tuscany, Francesco Iacobelli/AWL Images©; Leaning Tower, Pisa, Marco Simoni/AWL Images ©; Fiat rally, Camogli, Liguria, PavloBaliukh/Getty Images ©

Back cover photograph: Emerald Coast near Santa Teresa di Gallura, Sardinia, Daniele Macis/AWL Images ©

INDEX

BRENDAN SAINSBURY

Born and raised in the UK in a town that never merits
a mention in any guidebook (Andover, Hampshire),
Brendan spent the holidays of his youth caravanning
in the English Lake District and didn't leave Blighty
until he was 19. Making up for lost time, he's since
squeezed 70 countries into a sometimes precarious
existence as a writer and professional vagabond. In
the last 12 years, he has written over 40 books for
Lonely Planet from Castro's Cuba to the canyons of
Peru.

https://auth.lonelyplanet.com/profiles/
brendansainsbury

REGIS ST LOUIS

Regis grew up in a small town in the American
Midwest – the kind of place that fuels big dreams
of travel – and he developed an early fascination
with foreign dialects and world cultures. He spent
his formative years learning Russian and a handful
of Romance languages, which served him well
on journeys across much of the globe. Regis has
contributed to more than 50 Lonely Planet titles,
covering destinations across six continents. His
travels have taken him from the mountains of
Kamchatka to remote island villages in Melanesia,
and to many grand urban landscapes. When not on
the road, he lives in New Orleans. Follow him on www.
instagram.com/regisstlouis.

https://auth.lonelyplanet.com/profiles/
regisstlouis

NICOLA WILLIAMS

Border-hopping is a way of life for British writer,
runner, foodie, art aficionado and mum-of-three
Nicola, who has lived in a French village on the
southern side of Lake Geneva for more than a decade.
Nicola has authored more than 50 guidebooks on
Paris, Provence, Rome, Tuscany, France, Italy and
Switzerland for Lonely Planet and covers France
as a destination expert for the *Telegraph*. She also
writes for the *Independent, Guardian,* lonelyplanet.
com, *Lonely Planet Magazine, French Magazine, Cool
Camping France* and others. Catch her on the road on
Twitter and Instagram at @tripalong.

https://auth.lonelyplanet.com/profiles/
NicolaWilliams

PAULA HARDY

Paula is an independent travel writer and editorial consultant, whose work for Lonely Planet and other flagship publications has taken her from nomadic camps in the Danakil Depression to Seychellois beach huts and the jewel-like bar at the Gritti Palace on the Grand Canal. Over two decades, she has authored more than 30 Lonely Planet guidebooks and spent five years as commissioning editor of Lonely Planet's bestselling Italian list. These days you'll find her hunting down new hotels, hip bars and up-and-coming artisans primarily in Milan, Venice and Marrakesh. Get in touch at www.paulahardy.com.

VIRGINIA MAXWELL

Although based in Australia, Virginia spends at least half of her year updating Lonely Planet destination coverage across the globe. The Mediterranean is her major area of interest – she has covered Spain, Italy, Turkey, Syria, Lebanon, Israel, Egypt, Morocco and Tunisia for Lonely Planet – but she also covers Finland, Bali, Armenia, the Netherlands, the US and Australia. Follow her @maxwellvirginia on Instagram and Twitter.

STEPHANIE ONG

Stephanie is a writer/editor who's lived in Melbourne, Barcelona, London and now finds herself based in Milan, Italy. She's written travel pieces for various publications, including coffee-table books and guidebooks for Lonely Planet and Le Cool Publishing. When she's not immersed in the world of writing and travel, she's eating well and complaining about tax – like every good Italian.

KEVIN RAUB

Atlanta native Kevin started his career as a music journalist in New York, working for *Men's Journal* and *Rolling Stone* magazines. He ditched the rock 'n' roll lifestyle for travel writing and has written over 95 Lonely Planet guides, focused mainly on Brazil, Chile, Colombia, USA, India, the Caribbean and Portugal. Kevin also contributes to a variety of travel magazines in both the USA and UK. Along the way, the self-confessed hophead is in constant search of wildly high IBUs in local beers. Follow him on Twitter and Instagram (@RaubOnTheRoad).

← MORE WRITERS

ALEXIS AVERBUCK

Alexis has travelled and lived all over the world, from Sri Lanka to Ecuador, Zanzibar and Antarctica. In recent years she's lived on the Greek island of Hydra, in the wilds of NYC and on the California coast. A travel writer for over two decades, Alexis has lived in Antarctica for a year, crossed the Pacific by sailboat and written books on her journeys through Asia, Europe and the Americas. She's also a painter – visit www.alexisaverbuck.com – and promotes travel and adventure on video and television.

CRISTIAN BONETTO

Cristian has contributed to over 30 Lonely Planet guides to date, including *New York City*, *Italy*, *Venice & the Veneto*, *Naples & the Amalfi Coast*, *Denmark*, *Copenhagen*, *Sweden* and *Singapore*. Lonely Planet work aside, his musings on travel, food, culture and design appear in numerous publications around the world, including the *Telegraph* (UK) and *Corriere del Mezzogiorno* (Italy). When not on the road, you'll find the reformed playwright and TV scriptwriter slurping espresso in his beloved hometown, Melbourne. Instagram: rexcat75.

GREGOR CLARK

Gregor is a US-based writer whose love of foreign languages and curiosity about what's around the next bend have taken him to dozens of countries on five continents. Chronic wanderlust has also led him to visit all 50 states and most Canadian provinces on countless road trips through his native North America.Since 2000, Gregor has regularly contributed to Lonely Planet guides, with a focus on Europe and the Americas. He has lived in California, France, Spain and Italy prior to settling with his wife and two daughters in his current home state of Vermont.

PETER DRAGICEVICH

After a successful career in niche newspaper and magazine publishing, both in his native New Zealand and in Australia, Peter finally gave into Kiwi wanderlust, giving up staff jobs to chase his diverse roots around much of Europe. Over the last decade he's written literally dozens of guidebooks for Lonely Planet on an oddly disparate collection of countries, all of which he's come to love. He once again calls Auckland, New Zealand, his home – although his current nomadic existence means he's often elsewhere.

OUR WRITERS

OUR STORY

A beat-up old car, a few dollars in the pocket and a sense of adventure. In 1972 that's all Tony and Maureen Wheeler needed for the trip of a lifetime – across Europe and Asia overland to Australia. It took several months, and at the end – broke but inspired – they sat at their kitchen table writing and stapling together their first travel guide, *Across Asia on the Cheap*. Within a week they'd sold 1500 copies. Lonely Planet was born.

Today, Lonely Planet has offices in Franklin, London, Melbourne, Oakland, Dublin, Beijing and Delhi, with more than 600 staff and writers. We share Tony's belief that 'a great guidebook should do three things: inform, educate and amuse'.

DUNCAN GARWOOD

From facing fast bowlers in Barbados to sidestepping hungry pigs in Goa, Duncan's travels have thrown up many unique experiences. These days he largely dedicates himself to the Mediterranean and Italy, his adopted homeland where he's been living since 1997. He's worked on around 50 Lonely Planet titles, including guidebooks to Italy, Rome, Sardinia, Sicily, Spain and Portugal, and has contributed to books on world food and epic drives. He's also written on Italy for newspapers, websites and magazines.

BRETT ATKINSON

Brett is based in Auckland, New Zealand, but is frequently on the road for Lonely Planet. He's a full-time travel and food writer specialising in adventure travel, unusual destinations, and surprising angles on more well-known destinations. Craft beer and street food are Brett's favourite reasons to explore places, and he is featured regularly on the Lonely Planet website, and in newspapers, magazines and websites across New Zealand and Australia. Since becoming a Lonely Planet author in 2005, Brett has covered areas as diverse as Vietnam, Sri Lanka, the Czech Republic, New Zealand, Morocco, California and the South Pacific.

https://auth.lonelyplanet.com/profiles/duncangarwood

https://auth.lonelyplanet.com/profiles/BrettAtkinson

 MORE WRITERS

Published by Lonely Planet Global Limited
CRN 554153
3rd edition – Mar 2020
ISBN 978 1 78657 626 2
© Lonely Planet 2020   Photographs © as indicated 2020
10 9 8 7 6 5 4 3 2 1
Printed in Singapore